Women in Horror Films, 1940s

Also by Gregory William Mank

Women in Horror Films, 1930s
(McFarland, 1999)

Hollywood Cauldron: Thirteen Horror Films from the Genre's Golden Age
(McFarland, 1994)

Karloff and Lugosi: The Story of a Haunting Collaboration, with a Complete Filmography of Their Films Together
(McFarland, 1990)

Women in Horror Films, 1940s

by Gregory William Mank

McFarland & Company, Inc., Publishers
Jefferson, North Carolina, and London

This book is published with the author's
Women in Horror Films, 1930s (McFarland, 1999)

Cover: Elizabeth Russell (left) and Julia Dean in The Curse of the Cat People *(1944).*

Frontispiece: Evelyn Ankers, queen of 1940s horror cinema, strikes a publicity pose for Hold That Ghost *(1941).*

British Library Cataloguing-in-Publication data are available

Library of Congress Cataloguing-in-Publication Data

Mank, Gregory W.
Women in horror films, 1940s / by Gregory William Mank.
p. cm.
Includes filmographies and index.
ISBN 0-7864-0464-7 (case binding : 50# alkaline paper) ♾
1. Women in motion pictures. 2. Horror films. 3. Motion picture actors and actresses—United States—Biography. I. Title.
PN1995.9.W6M355 1999 98-21544
791.43'6164'082—dc21 CIP
[b]

Manufactured in the United States of America

McFarland & Company, Inc., Publishers
Box 611, Jefferson, North Carolina 28640

For my beloved Mom,
Frances Mank
Always know how much
you are loved.

Acknowledgments

First of all, my very sincere thanks to the ladies in this book who gave me interviews, and their time, patience and trust: Louise Currie, Peggy Moran, Elizabeth Russell, Simone Simon, Jane Randolph, Acquanetta, Susanna Foster, Elena Verdugo, the late Virginia Christine, Jane Adams and Anna Lee.

Also, many thanks to the late Richard Denning, who for 43 years was married to Evelyn Ankers, the 1940s' beloved "Queen of the Horrors," and who so graciously shared his happy memories with me for this book; thanks, too, to their daughter, Dee Denning Dwyer. (Aloha, and God's blessing, to you both!) And much gratitude to the late Gloria White and her daughter Cecilia Maskell, the cousins of actress Jean Brooks; Gloria and Cecilia dynamically solved the puzzle of whatever happened to the decades-lost leading lady of Val Lewton's *The Leopard Man* and *The Seventh Victim*.

Special thanks to Ned Comstock, curator of the Film and Television Archive at the University of Southern California, who was unfailingly pleasant, polite and courteous. The kind and very helpful Kristine Krueger of National Film Information Service of the Margaret Herrick Library of the Academy of Motion Picture Arts and Sciences in Los Angeles also deserves special appreciation, as does the staff of the Lincoln Center Library of the Performing Arts in New York.

To those colleagues and friends who provide such generosity and humor and fun on these projects, I must salute Roger Hurlburt, Tom Johnson, Doug McClelland, Gary Don Rhodes, Gary and Sue Svehla (MidMar Press) and, of course, Tom Weaver. Critic Lawrence Tucker in *Sci-Fi Entertainment* magazine recently hailed Weaver as "a consummate pro in a field of doofuses," and I hate to imagine how much more "doofusey" I'd appear in my work if not for Tom's leads, assistance and incredible knowledge.

Thanks, too, to John Antosiewicz, Ed Bansak, Buddy Barnett (Cinema Collectors, Hollywood), the late Charles T. Barton, the late Charles Bennett, the late DeWitt Bodeen, Richard Bojarski, John Brunas, Michael Brunas, Robert Clarke, Jim Clatterbaugh, Kevin Clement, Dr. Jim Coughlin, Kirk Crivello, the late William K. Everson, the late Fritz Feld, *Film Favorites*, Michael Fitzgerald, Roy Frumkes (editor, *Films in Review*), Eve Golden, Dean Goodman, Richard Gordon, Charles Heard, David J. Hogan, Don Leifert, the late Ruth Lewton, Val Lewton, Jr., Jessie Lilley, Bob Madison, Ron and Howard Mandelbaum (Photofest), Dick and Julie May, Mark Miller, Bryan Moore, Jerry Ohlinger's Memorabilia Shop, Ted Newsom, Doug Norwine, Paul Parla, John Parnum, Simone Peterson, Frances Rafferty, Philip J. Riley, Curt Siodmak, David J. Skal, Sally Stark, Michael Stein, Tony Timpone (*Fangoria*), Major General Tom Turnage (Ret.), Marie Wilson, Scott Wilson, Robert Wise, Nathalie and Steven Yafet and Stella Zucco. Thanks, too, to all who participated in the survey in the back of the book.

As always, the final paragraph must be devoted to my wonderful wife, Barbara, and terrific children, Jessica and Christopher. This book is finally done—let's all go buy ourselves a present!

—GWM

Contents

INTRODUCTION

The great fog swirls, all around the satanic, twisted trees of that Stygian forest under a full moon. As the Frank Skinner–Charles Previn–Hans J. Salter score roars away, a lovely heroine comes a-loping through the woods, her blonde tresses bouncing on her shoulders, gracefully running in her high heels through that foggy, misty hell of a forest.

She is, of course, Evelyn Ankers, Universal's "Queen of the Horrors." As Gwen Conliffe, she is seeking Lon Chaney—the Wolf Man.

The Wolf Man sees her, leers horribly—and attacks. Evelyn's heroine unleashes one of her magnificent classic screams, as the werewolf fondles her with his paws, growling in her face.

Claude Rains, as Sir John Talbot, the werewolf's father, arrives on the scene and clubs the beast to death with the silver-headed cane. Maria Ouspenskaya, as the old gypsy Maleva, arrives to recite the prayer over the dead lycanthrope:

> The way you walked was thorny,
> through no fault of your own...

The beast turns back into Larry Talbot. Rains' Sir John looks heartbroken. The music becomes mournful, and audience members get lumps in their throats from this Greek tragedy in wolf's clothing.

And Evelyn Ankers regards the final, tragic tableau. She is already in the arms of her fiancé (Patric Knowles). She has survived the attack of the Wolf Man without losing a false eyelash, without getting a run in her stockings—triumphantly undefiled. And, with Chaney dead on the forest floor, *The Wolf Man* gives Evelyn Ankers the curtain line of the movie.

"Larry!" she gasps.

THE END.

As with Hollywood's Golden Age of horror of the 1930s, movie horror of the 1940s took a sly, twisty route to the libido and subconscious of its audience. Yes, women were still the playthings, the objects of the sometimes sinister fantasies of the makers of Hollywood horror. Universal's *Mummy* series alone featured enough starlets in negligees (all swooning in the arms of that moldy old Mummy) to fill a section of a *Victoria's Secret* catalogue.

Yet once again, in the romantic tradition of 1930s horror, women were victorious—alive, well and unspoiled in the final reel while their menace faced a spectacle of destruction. As before, women of the 1940s fit into three basic categories: monsters, femmes fatales, and misfits.

Monsters. As in the 1930s, the true show-stealing ladies of the 1940s melodramas were actual monsters themselves. Val Lewton's *Cat People* gives us Irena

Dubrovna (Simone Simon)—a cat-woman at worst, a frigid bride at best, mauled to death by a panther she looses upon herself. The Southern belle vampire of *Son of Dracula* is a sensation: Louise Allbritton, a towering beauty, sporting a raven-black wig, flashing dazzling, sexy eyes, is so diabolic a vamp (in every sense of the word) that she completely steals the thunder (what there is of it) from Lon Chaney's Count. Acquanetta's *Captive Wild Woman* was one of the most outrageous male fantasies of all; a lady who, whenever sexually jealous, suffers acute embarrassment: Those female hormones rage, and she turns into a gorilla. And come the climax of that movie, Paula the Ape Woman (now full-blown in the form of Ray "Crash" Corrigan in his famous gorilla suit) is shot while rescuing the man she loves ... and trying to carry him away from Evelyn Ankers.

Of course, a psychologist or sociologist can have grand fun with these old movies. The undercurrent here can't be missed: These monstrous gals had rejected, tried to exploit, or disappointed a man. The threat seems to be: Woman, swing both ways sexually, or be frigid, or shaft your lover, or have hormone trouble—and you die. Males concocted the stories and screenplays for these films. *Captive Wild Woman*, in fact, provided paychecks for no fewer than five male writers, and while one is tempted to theorize about the boys' delight in writing a story about a glamourpuss who turns into a gorilla, it's more likely that each hack was just eyeing the dollar signs.

Yet, for whatever reasons, the old ritual prevailed.

Femmes Fatales. In the wake of Miriam Hopkins' Ivy in the Fredric March 1931 *Dr. Jekyll and Mr. Hyde*, the sexually promiscuous continued to suffer horribly for their sins. Evelyn Ankers, as the evil "other woman" of *Weird Woman*, receives a lulu of a death scene: Fleeing Chaney, Anne Gwynne and the rest of the "good guys," she climbs out a window, falls through an arbor and hangs herself on a vine. One of the most horrific demises of '40s cinema is that of Linda Darnell in *Hangover Square*, who pays dearly for that painted mouth, those fishnet stockings and her vampy seductions: Laird Cregar strangles her, dresses up her body as a masked dummy and cremates her corpse atop the Guy Fawkes bonfire.

Presumably the producers of some of these movies felt they were providing a moral social service, much like the men who produced the army's films on venereal disease.

Misfits. These were the ladies who fit no "acceptable" social category (at least by Hollywood standards) while their films played the theaters of the Depression and the war years. Ramsay Ames and Virginia Christine, respectively of *The Mummy's Ghost* and *The Mummy's Curse*, weren't monsters per se, but reincarnated Egyptian princesses—hardly to be accommodated in the age of Betty Grable, and thus doomed along with Lon Chaney's pudgy old Kharis. Hollywood believed Jean Brooks' character deserved to hang herself in Lewton's *The Seventh Victim*; she was a morbid, self-pitying devil worshipper, when she should have been jitterbugging with soldiers at the USO. Elena Verdugo is delightful as the dancing Ilonka of *House of Frankenstein*, yet she must die in the claws of the Wolf Man. After all, not only did she flirt outrageously, but she was a gypsy—in 1994 presumably a sufficiently unsavory combination to rate Hollywood's cinematic death penalty.

One of the oddest fates was that of the hunchbacked nurse Nina, played by Jane Adams, in *House of Dracula*. She is totally sympathetic, self-sacrificing, very touching, and certainly deserving of a break from the writers. However, Universal decided that the mad Dr. Edlemann (Onslow Stevens), whom Nina has served (and no doubt loved) so faithfully, should grab her in a climactic Jekyll/Hyde fit, strangle her, and throw her onto the laboratory floor—where she performs an acrobatic (and very unfeminine) backward somersault and falls into a hole. Her only crime apparently, is her physical imperfection—crime enough, in 1945 Hollywood.

The overall attitude of Hollywood toward women in the old horror films makes a movie like 20th Century–Fox's *The Lodger* (1944) all the more impressive—and disturbing. This greatest of all Jack the Ripper movies features such a mad hatred of women, as conveyed by the Ripper (brilliantly played by Laird Cregar), that it becomes truly frightening. That Cregar slyly plays the role with homosexual frills adds to the film's misogynist strength—as does the famous episode, superbly staged by director John Brahm, in which the camera (and audience) *become* the Ripper, jerking and twitching toward a Whitechapel hag (Doris Lloyd) so horribly afraid of "our" knife that she can't even scream. The sadism and ferocity are so sharp that *The Lodger* almost seems not to have been made in '40s Hollywood at all. Only the finale, as an immaculately lacquered Merle Oberon walks safely by the river where the Ripper (who almost butchered her) has drowned, suggests the style we expect from a horror show of *The Lodger*'s era.

As in the 1930s, Hollywood horror heroes were a rather drab lot. Only a few actors in the genre—e.g., Patric Knowles—ever tackled a male horror hero with a winning combination of intelligence, restraint and attractiveness.

In truth, there was an erratic evolution in the style, courage and tenacity of women in horror films from the 1930s through the end of the war years. Heroines became increasingly feisty; often, they fought back, with the success of Fay Wray in *Mystery of the Wax Museum*. Hence, we have some memorable (if sometimes kinky) vignettes, ranging from Evelyn Ankers' unleashing gorilla/Acquanetta on John Carradine in *Captive Wild Woman*, to Louise Currie's notorious whipping of hairy Bela Lugosi in *The Ape Man*. Columbia's *The Return of the Vampire* presented Frieda Inescort in the Van Helsing–type role, combatting Bela's vampire (although the finale allows his male werewolf crony Matt Willis to actually destroy the bloodsucker). PRC's *Strangler of the Swamp* even let former Miss America Rosemary La Planche rescue the leading man.

It was Val Lewton, Hollywood horror's most daring and novel producer, who provided a poetically proper finale for women in the Golden Age of horror. RKO's *Bedlam* (1946), arguably the last great horror movie of the era (some would call it a "costume melodrama"), pits Karloff's splendidly evil Master Sims, apothecary of the Bedlam madhouse, against Anna Lee's spirited actress and crusader, Nell Bowen. When Karloff commits her to the horrors of the asylum, she uses her charm, intelligence, bravery and feminine wiles to win the help of the tragic inmates and escape the horror house. There's something very significant about the scene: Karloff, the great horror star of *Frankenstein*, *The Mummy*, *The Black Cat*, *The Body Snatcher*, here in the clutches of the inmates; Miss Lee's Nell, free, liberated, turns to take a final look at her old bogeyman—and laughs at him, escaping victoriously into the new Age of Enlightenment.

And as our leading lady escapes, Karloff is stripped of wig, dignity and fright power, looking little and gray and helpless, doomed to be sealed up behind a wall and forgotten...

Just as the old horror films appeared to be, come the late 1940s.

As has been the case with every book I've written, the interviews became the most memorable and valuable aspect of this project. It was a very different world when these ladies hacked their way through the Hollywood jungle, and listening to their sagas was a great adventure.

There were delights like Louise Currie, who warmly remembered the breakneck speed with which Monogram films like *The Ape Man* were shot; she enjoyed that camaraderie and brisk pace more than she liked Orson Welles' painstaking genius on *Citizen Kane*. There were inspirations like Anna Lee, blonde and breathtakingly lovely in her West Hollywood home, glowing as she remembered *Bedlam*, Val Lewton and Karloff, and delighted to have signed a new contract at age 80 to continue as Lila Quartermaine on *General Hospital*.

Yet, in many cases, the pain of exploitation came back. It was there in the words of Susanna Foster, who, almost 40 years after the giant success of *Phantom of the Opera*, was found living in a car in Hollywood. It was there in the words of veteran actress Virginia Christine, even though she laughed as she remembered how Universal buried her alive in a back lot swamp in full female Mummy makeup for that famous resurrection scene in *The Mummy's Curse*—and why that scene wasn't shot until the final day. Just as Universal had waited until the end of *The Mummy* to throw Zita Johann to the lions, so had the studio waited to the end of *The Mummy's Curse* to bury Virginia in the swamp—in case the leading lady expired.

There were others I regret never meeting, yet who came alive for me in the research. There was Ilona Massey, temporarily blackballed by MGM in the wake of a studio sex scandal; Anne Nagel, agonized by the suicide of her bridegroom of four months, actor Ross Alexander; Gale Sondergaard, a victim of the Hollywood witch-hunt; and Jean Brooks, the satanic Jacqueline of *The Seventh Victim*, whose real-life cousins told me the story of her alcoholism, post–Hollywood obscurity and stranger-than-fiction funeral.

And Evelyn Ankers—victim of too many pictures with Lon Chaney. Chaney's crass practical jokes helped persuade her to accept an early retirement, which fortunately brought her a true happy ending with husband Richard Denning (who graciously consented to speak to me about his beloved "Evie," who died in 1985).

It had been a colorful era, with the curtain rung down by *Abbott and Costello Meet Frankenstein* in the summer of 1948. And the research for this book made it very clear that for the women of 1940s horror there had been far fewer happily-ever-after endings in real life than there had been in their movies.

Perhaps it's absurdly romantic to imagine that any of today's "mega-star" ladies who have appeared in the horror films in the last 25 years—Sissy Spacek (*Carrie,*

1976), Jamie Lee Curtis (*Halloween,* 1978), Linda Blair (*The Exorcist,* 1973), Jodie Foster (*The Silence of the Lambs,* 1991)—with high-powered agents and movie colony clout, would want to take a time machine back to 1941 and clock in at Universal like Anne Gwynne and Evelyn Ankers.

Yet the Golden Age of horror, 1930s *and* 1940s, still holds its own power, poetry and wonderful folklore.

So do its ladies.

—Gregory William Mank
Delta, Pennsylvania
Fall 1998

Anne Nagel

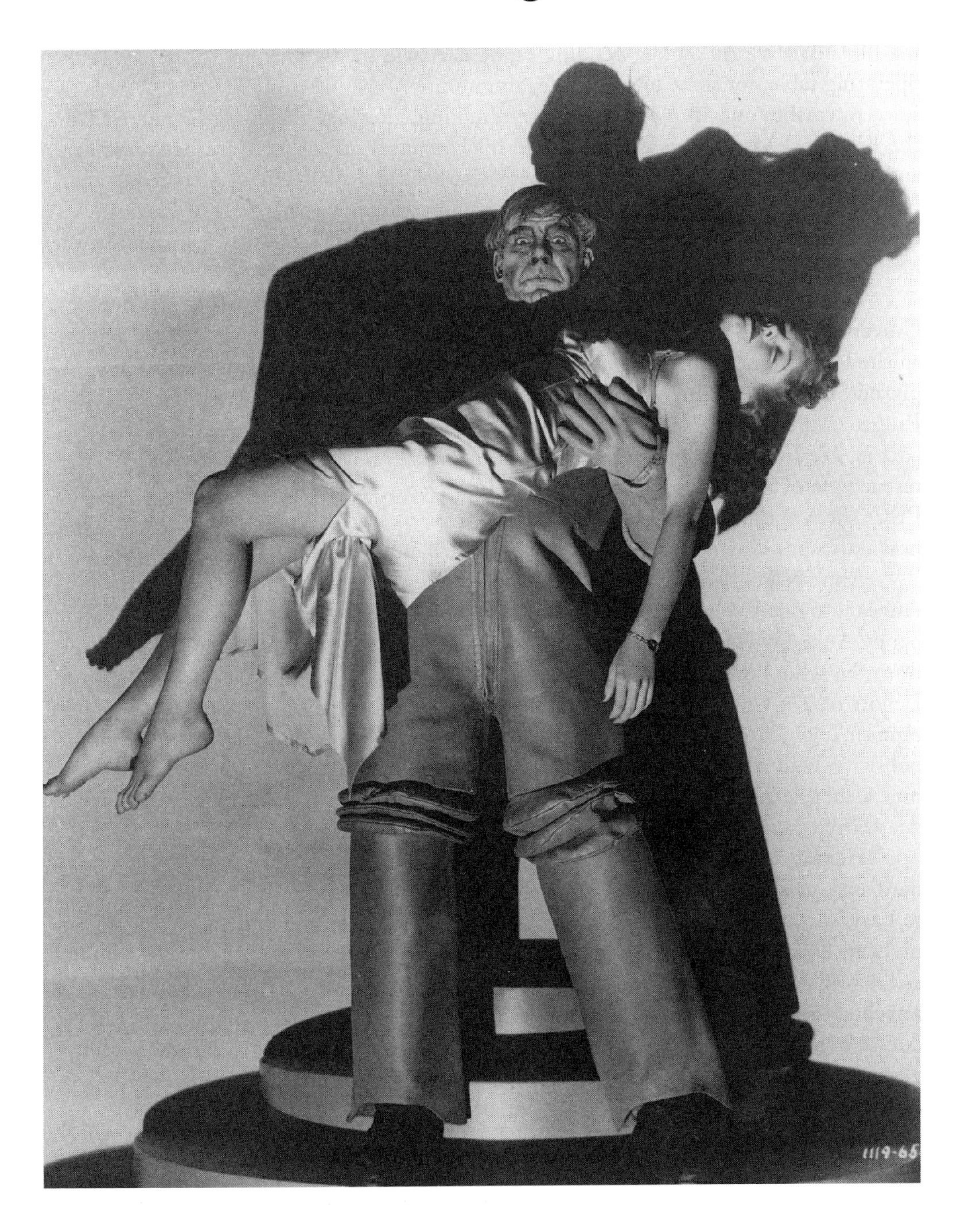

The famous cat eyes of Lionel Atwill are wild, depraved—perhaps understandably so. The heroine he's menacing is lovely; a shapely, wide-eyed redhead who looks like a tragic Lucille Ball. And she's wearing a breathtaking Vera West negligee, looking like a 1941 virgin on her wedding night as Atwill madly pins her to the laboratory operating table, for some unspeakable "impulse."

In crashes our *Man Made Monster*—hulking, glowing, glowering Dynamo Dan, the Electrical Man—Lon Chaney, Jr., in his Universal star debut. Saturday matinee audiences cheered as the electrical dynamo barbecued Atwill—then screamed as the monster grabbed our heroine, escaping the laboratory to the rhapsody of Hans J. Salter's thrilling musical score, Electric Man carrying Girl across the countryside, the hero, police and pet dog in traditional "villager" pursuit.

It runs only 59 minutes; it cost only $86,000. Yet *Man Made Monster* is one of Universal's most briskly entertaining horror shows, with Anne Nagel one of the most spirited of heroines. Of course, this was not Anne's only Universal shocker. She played Sunny, the nightclub chanteuse/gangster's moll, killed by Jekyll/Hyde Stanley Ridges in the Karloff/Lugosi *Black Friday* (1940); had a humble, one-of-the-models part in *The Invisible Woman* (1941); played a virtual bit as the crying, too-late-to-the-rescue wife of Atwill's first victim of *The Mad Doctor of Market Street* (1942). And at PRC, she was the daughter of a wonderfully over-the-top George Zucco, whose madness unleashes Glenn Strange's hairy werewolf/handyman *The Mad Monster* (1942).

Anne Nagel had a curvy, slender figure; indeed, one could have squeezed two Annes into one Evelyn Ankers girdle. And she had even more sass and charm than peppy Anne Gwynne. From 1939 through 1941, Anne played everything at Universal from the school marm of the Mae West/W. C. Fields *My Little Chickadee* to heroine Lenore of *The Green Hornet* serial (and its sequel cliffhanger, *The Green Hornet Strikes Again*). Then, after two and-a-half years, 19 features, four serials, cheesecake and publicity, Universal dumped Anne. It was a quick, trapdoor drop to Poverty Row, bits, alcoholic anonymity, and, in 1966—over 16 years after her last movie—an early death from cancer.

Her legacy, for those who even remembered her, was one of Hollywood's true hard-luck gals. For the curse on Anne Nagel was unique and pitifully tragic: Her cross to bear was the ghost of a suicide husband, actor Ross Alexander, who, on a January night in 1937, went into his Van Nuys barn and reportedly fired a rifle into his mouth as his bride of four months sat quietly knitting in the house. A stigma of suffering attached itself to this starlet, and in later years—be she accusing a prominent L.A. doctor of sterilizing her, or claiming her second husband had broken her radio and given away her dog—she was always that sad girl who was hysterical that cold 1937 night as authorities took away her suicide bridegroom.

"The least you could have let me done," she sobbed that night, "was to let me see Ross again."

She would see him again, in her nightmares, for the rest of her career and her life.

***Chapter opener:* Anne Nagel, with Lon Chaney, Jr., shows much more leg in this publicity shot than she does in the movie *Man Made Monster*, 1941.**

"Her earliest ambition was to be a nun," read a July 1940 Universal publicity release on Anne Nagel—born Anne Dolan in Boston, Massachusetts, September 29 or 30 (sources vary), 1915 (some sources say 1912). Anne attended Notre Dame Academy, where, according to Universal, "she began her preparation to enter the church."

However, other inspirations entered the girl's life. Her stepfather, Curtis F. Nagel, was an expert on Technicolor who had a Tiffany-Stahl director's contract; she worked during school as a commercial photographer. Leaving Notre Dame, Anne joined a Boston stock company, playing "time-tried character roles" at the Shubert.

Anne's entry into Hollywood is vague. A Fox press release of 1935 reported, "She came to Hollywood at the age of 16," working as an extra. Universal later claimed she was "a dancer in silent pictures," also breaking into the business in Technicolor short subjects directed by her stepfather. Anne's first documented feature credit: World Wide's *Hypnotized*, starring the comedy team of Charlie Mack and George Moran, directed by Mack Sennett and released in December of 1932. Anne became a Fox Studios showgirl, festooning such films as 1933's *I Loved You Wednesday*, 1934's *Stand Up and Cheer* and the Alice Faye/James Dunn/Eleanor Powell *George White's 1935 Scandals*.

Anne won her first flurry of publicity in the spring of 1935, as Fox announced of the red-haired, blue-eyed, 5'4", 108 lb. starlet:

> Anne Nagel, a native of Boston, has been chosen for a featured role in *Redheads on Parade*, Jesse L. Lasky's musical extravaganza for Fox... She was one of the 48 titian-topped beauties assembled from various sections of the country to appear in the big musical. In addition to representing her home state of Massachusetts in the picture, she was judged most beautiful of the 48 selections, and awarded the role, "Queen of the Redheads"...

Redheads on Parade starred John Boles, Dixie Lee and Jack Haley. By the time it was released in September 1935, Fox had merged with 20th Century, under the reign of Darryl F. Zanuck. The "Queen of the Redheads" was at liberty—and signed a stock contract with Warner Bros./First National, starting at $75 per week.

Anne was decorative in such 1936 Warner Bros. films as the Edward G. Robinson/Joan Blondell/Humphrey Bogart *Bullets or Ballots*. Talented, hard-working and very likable, she progressed in her first year there to the top female spot in the 57-minute *King of Hockey*, co-starring Dick (*Captain America*) Purcell—and landed the crooning second female lead (Glenda Farrell had the first) in *Here Comes Carter*.

Her leading man was Ross Alexander, born A. Ross Smith in New York City, July 27, 1907; a tall, lean dark-haired player who looked like a baby-faced David Manners. He had come to Warner Bros. via Broadway, where (rumor insisted) he had been "kept" by a series of rich homosexuals. Alexander scored in such major 1935 Warner Bros. product as *A Midsummer Night's Dream*, as Demetrius, and *Captain Blood*, as Errol Flynn's pirate pal Jeremy Pitt—lashed half-naked at a post by Lionel Atwill.

Alexander "clicked," especially in light comedy. He and his actress girlfriend from the stage, Aleta Friele, had married, and now enjoyed a house at 7357 Woodrow Wilson Drive in the Hollywood Hills. His star was rising.

Then tragedy came. The official version claimed wife Aleta was despondent because she could land no film roles. However, the gossip (later validated in the autobiography of Henry Fonda, one of Alexander's friends from the stage) insisted that Ross was enjoying the company of "easy women." Anita Louise, who had been so beautiful a Titania in *A Midsummer Night's Dream*, was reputed to be one of Ross' affairs. Aleta's heart was broken.

Friday night, December 6, 1935. Alexander later testified at the coroner's inquiry that they had dined at home about 9:15 that night; that Aleta had made tests at nearly every studio and had failed; that she was talking about returning to New York, hoping a stage success would win her a Hollywood offer; that as they went upstairs to bed and he undressed, Aleta reiterated plans to go to New York. "Well, for God's sake go home," said Alexander:

> She turned on her heel—she was still dressed—and without a word walked away. I heard her walk downstairs. I was still sitting on the bed when I heard a shot outside the house. Before I could move, I heard another. Calling for William Bolden, my colored valet, I ran outside. As I came to the corner of the house, I fell headlong, tripping on her body. The rifle lay beside her.

Aleta Alexander had shot herself in the head with a .22 caliber rifle. She died at Cedars of Lebanon Hospital two hours later.

Ross Alexander nearly collapsed with horror and guilt. He accompanied his wife's body to New Jersey for burial; returning to Hollywood, he broke down totally. "Ross gave up women for port," remembered Henry Fonda, who took the despondent widower into his own home after the tragedy. Warner Bros. loyally kept Alexander working: He starred in such films as *Hot Money* and *China Clipper*, both of which featured Anne Nagel in small roles. And then they co-starred on *Here Comes Carter*.

"They heard the fluttering of Cupid's wings," rhapsodized the *Los Angeles Examiner* as Alexander and Anne wed Wednesday, September 16, 1936, eloping by plane to Yuma. They seemed happy. When Anne underwent an appendectomy at Hollywood Hospital October 14, four weeks after the wedding, Alexander took the room adjoining hers "to spend as much time as possible with his bride." The newlyweds settled on a ranch at 17221 Ventura Boulevard in the San Fernando Valley, and all wished the shaken widower and his starlet wife the best.

In fact, Anne had married a violently disturbed man. Lawrence Quirk's book *Fasten Your Seat Belts: The Passionate Life of Bette Davis* reports Ross Alexander lore: that he had an obsession with Ms. Davis, who "cast aspersions on his manhood"; that Davis' husband of the time once beat up Alexander in a Warner Bros. men's room; that this obsession caused Anne to leave Alexander "several times" during their brief marriage; that the neurotic actor also had "picked up a male hobo on the highway, and had sex with him"; that the hobo promptly blackmailed the star; and that Warners lawyers had their hands full trying to cover the scandal.

Opposite: **Anne Nagel and Ross Alexander croon together in Warner Bros.'** ***Here Comes Carter!*** **(1936). They fell in love during the shooting.**

KLA
210

Of course, haunting Ross Alexander most agonizingly was the suicide of his first wife. Cornelius Stevenson, his black chauffeur and houseman, later told police that the "moody" Alexander often proclaimed, "I know I will never find another wife as good as Aleta"; one can only imagine the pain this must have caused Anne Nagel. Stevenson's wife claimed Alexander spent much time before the fireplace, morose and writing poetry. On Sunday, December 6, 1936, the anniversary of Aleta's suicide, Alexander morbidly visited the yard on Woodrow Wilson Drive where she had shot herself. And on that date, Stevenson, according to later testimony, "grappled" with the hysterical Alexander, to get shells away as the actor vowed to kill himself.

Saturday night, January 2, 1937. The newlyweds had taken down their Christmas tree. Anne later told reporters of Ross' mood that night on the ranch:

> He was light-hearted. We planned a honeymoon trip to New York and he had already made arrangements with his manager. You know we never had a real honeymoon.

Cornelius Stevenson's wife would tell Detective Lieutenant W. G. Marr of Alexander's final actions:

> Sometime between 7:30 and 8:30, he took the pistol and said he was going out to kill a duck for dinner. But he met the hired man who had already killed it, and returned. Then he went out again and told Cornelius to call him from the barn when dinner was ready...

As Anne sat knitting in the house, Ross Alexander went to the barn, scrambled atop a chicken coop and brooder house with a flashlight and a gun—and shot himself in the head. Newspaper accounts reported the gun to have been a .22 caliber target pistol, but Henry Fonda remembered it even more grimly: "A year and a month after Aleta's death, Ross took that same rifle, put it in his mouth and blew his head off."

"SUICIDE'S WIDOW IN COLLAPSE" headlined the *Los Angeles Examiner* January 4, 1937. It was reported how butler Stevenson, finding the body, brought her the news; how she became "hysterical"; how she "fought with officers to allow her to rush to her husband's body"; and how she "moaned" in anguish, "The least you could have done was to have let me see Ross before they took him away." The body was taken to the W. M. Strother Mortuary, 6240 Hollywood Boulevard—the funeral parlor which, over the decades, handled the wakes of such celebrities as Peg Entwistle (who had jumped off the HOLLYWOODLAND sign in 1932), Bela Lugosi, and Brian Donlevy.* It was there that the inquest took place, at 9:30 A.M. January 6, 1937. Anne (who had been under the care of physicians at her grandmother's house), Cornelius Stevenson and Detective Capt. Bert Massey all testified. The coroner's jury took two minutes to issue a formal verdict of suicide.

**In recent years, the old Strother Mortuary had served as a theater. The building was recently demolished.*

Nagel testifies at the Hollywood inquest regarding the suicide of Ross Alexander. They had been married less than four months when he shot himself (Photofest).

Ross Alexander was buried at Sunrise Slope, Forest Lawn, Glendale, Friday, January 8, 1937. Louella Parsons expressed her sympathy for Anne, "who so suddenly and so cruelly was made a widow":

> Unfortunately, young Alexander, who made a large salary, saved nothing, and when he died he left only a meager $200—not

> enough to bury him—and a much-involved estate with lots of debts...

Actually, the April 22, 1937, tax appraisal of Alexander's estate totaled $2,085.09—$1,151.09 in cash and $860 in "Tangible Personal Property." Anne inherited claims against the estate ranging from Alexander's account at I. Magnin's clothing store, to such unpaid-for books as *Psychology of Sex*, *Impassioned Pygmies* and *Oscar Wilde*, to the funeral parlor bill for Aleta Alexander.

The suicide of Ross Alexander was the first tragedy of a calamitous 1937 for Hollywood. Within that year, Jean Harlow died of uremic poisoning, Colin (*Frankenstein*) Clive died of alcoholism/consumption and Ted Healy was beaten to death (possibly by a never-punished Wallace Beery).

Anne Nagel, only 24 years old, never got over it. Over three years later, in filling out a Universal questionnaire, she listed *Here Comes Carter* her favorite role—the film she had made with Alexander when they fell in love. Nor did Warner Bros. forget Alexander (whose final film, *Ready Willing and Able*, in which he co-starred with Ruby Keeler, was released months after his death). In fact, Alexander's suicide indirectly ushered in a new Warner Bros. figure who signed in 1937—and went on to big things: Ronald Reagan, who was signed by the studio because his voice was "considered similar" to Ross Alexander's.

Warner Bros. loyally kept Anne busy in 1937 just as they had kept Alexander busy after the suicide of his first spouse. Anne played in such '37 fare as *The Footloose Heiress* (an ironic title and role, considering her personal situation); she also went on loan-out that year to Monogram (*The Hoosier Schoolboy*, *A Bride for Henry*) and Republic (*Escape by Night*). It was all a horrible strain. Anne herself admitted she had "lost all interest" in her work after Alexander's suicide. Warner Bros. dropped her. She got leads at Monogram in such pictures as *Under the Big Top* (1938) and (another ironic title) *Should a Girl Marry* (1939).

Then came an overture from Universal City.

Nineteen thirty-nine was a monumental year in Universal's history, the year of such hits as the Rathbone/Karloff/Lugosi/Atwill *Son of Frankenstein*, the Deanna Durbin *Three Smart Girls Grow Up* and the Marlene Dietrich/James Stewart/Brian Donlevy *Destry Rides Again*. A new Universal was rising from the ashes of the Laemmle reign (which had toppled in 1936) and the miserably uninspired rule of usurper Charles R. Rogers (which had collapsed in 1938). The new regime, under Nate Blumberg and Cliff Work, would breed the crazy, imaginative existing Universal product of the '30s with an all-new, awesomely slick (and sometimes cutthroat) efficiency.

"Anne Nagel Termed," read a page one *Hollywood Reporter* headline of June 28, 1939. Anne joined such ladies as Constance Moore, Helen Parrish and Anne Gwynne—all pretty enough to be photogenic at eight o'clock in the morning, and all durable enough to survive the 6-day weeks and 18-hour days necessary to produce all this escapism. "Given a contract at Universal," proclaimed a "U" PR release, "she cites this opportunity for a fresh start as one of the high periods of her life."

Universal introduced Anne Nagel to the public:

> Anne plays the piano, sews and reads when she can't find a partner who will give her worthy opposition in a game of Ping-Pong... Her more strenuous diversions are swimming and riding. Tracking down and purchasing old phonograph records to add to her collection, said to be one of the largest and most unique in Hollywood, provide Anne with an unusual and absorbing hobby. And she is kept busy settling disputes between "Itchy" and "Lady," her cat and Dalmatian pooch, respectively. In music she prefers light opera, semi-classics and musical comedies... Her reading tastes include adventure, mysteries and the classic love stories... Anne's favorite actor is Spencer Tracy; her favorite actress, Helen Hayes... Being a pianist herself, she chooses Chopin as her favorite composer...

There was little time for hobbies over the next three years. Anne played in every type of escapism the studio offered: actioners like *Legion of Lost Flyers* (1939), with Richard Arlen and Andy Devine; musicals like *Argentine Nights* (1940), with the Ritz Brothers, the Andrews Sisters, Constance Moore and George "Superman" Reeves; and comedies like the W. C. Fields/Mae West *My Little Chickadee* (1940), with Anne as Miss Foster, the school marm. Nineteen forty saw her also starring in two Universal serials: *Winners of the West*, with Dick Foran, and *The Green Hornet*, with Anne as heroine Lenore Case—a role she reprised in 1941's 15-chapter *The Green Hornet Strikes Again*, this time opposite Warren Hull, who had replaced the original's Gordon Jones as the masked radio crimefighter.

And, of course, there were horror movies. The first was the Karloff-Lugosi *Black Friday*, which was keeping Anne busy as the third anniversary of Ross Alexander's suicide arrived. We first see Anne in this melodrama as Sunny Rogers, nightclub chanteuse, singing in the dubbed voice of Constance Moore from Universal's 1939 *Charlie McCarthy, Detective*. Mad doctor Ernest Sovac (Karloff) has performed a life-saving brain transplant on his English professor crony George Kingsley (Stanley Ridges), giving him part of the brain of gangster Red Cannon. Karloff's surgery unleashes a Jekyll/Hyde monster (and a superb Ridges performance). Anne's Sunny, erstwhile lover of mobster Cannon, is scared enough by his new reincarnation to betray him and run away with rival thug Eric Marnay (Lugosi) and Red's long-stashed half-million dollars. But Kingsley/Cannon finds out, smothers Bela in a closet, and kills Sunny ... himself doomed to be killed by "creator" Karloff as he tries to strangle the doctor's daughter (Anne Gwynne). Framing this flashback story at beginning and end: Karloff's last mile to the electric chair.

Black Friday was an example of slick Universal efficiency of the era: Shooting began December 28, 1939, and ended January 18, 1940; the final cost was $126,000 ($7,000 under budget). For 9 of the 18 days' shooting, director Arthur Lubin worked the company until 10:00 P.M.; one Saturday, they worked until 3:15 A.M. Sunday. The pace was so hysterical that Karloff, a founder of the Screen Actors Guild, refused at various times to work more than eight hours on any one day.

Yet spirits were high. Boris and Bela posed with the chorus girls on the night-club set; Bela brought his prized stamp collection to the studio to show to Anne. And Boris, Anne and co-star Anne Gwynne were all on hand, keeping perfectly straight

Bela Lugosi shows his stamp collection to Nagel during the shooting of Universal's *Black Friday*, 1940.

faces as Dr. Manly P. Hall "hypnotized" Bela for that infamous PR stunt in which the Hungarian (supposedly) truly believed he was suffocating.

Another curiosity about *Black Friday*: When Anne Nagel screams, it's in the voice of Anne Gwynne—who dubbed it in after Anne's death scene was shot.

Black Friday opened March 21, 1940, at New York City's Rialto Theatre. It rates as the final Universal for Karloff and Lugosi together—a fascinating fluke that didn't pair the stars for a single scene, yet survives as an exciting melodrama.

Anne's team spirit at Universal shows only too well in the fantasy comedy *The Invisible Woman*, which top-billed Virginia Bruce (in the title spot) over a last-legs John Barrymore (as the mad doctor who unleashes her). Anne had a virtual bit as Jean, one of Miss Bruce's fellow models. One of the "other" models was Maria Montez—who, within a year, would aggressively campaign her way to top Universal stardom while good-natured Anne withered on the vine. At any rate, the true star of this picture was John P. Fulton's special effects, which won an Academy nomination.

Then came *Man Made Monster*.

Original title, *The Mysterious Dr. R.* Director: George Waggner. Source material:

The Electric Man, a story by H. J. Essex, Sid Schwartz and Len Golos (revamped by Waggner under the *nom de plume* of Joseph West). Original berth at Universal: a 1935 project designed for Karloff and Lugosi. New *raison d'être*: to supply a trial run for Lon Chaney, Jr., fresh from his stage and screen triumph in *Of Mice and Men* and now trying out for a Universal contract. Result: one of Universal's fastest-moving, most richly entertaining shockers.

First of all, there's the 34-year-old Chaney as "Dynamo Dan," carnival performer-turned-guinea pig for mad Atwill's dream of creating a race of electrical supermen. He's as apple pie–appealing as the original Dan, with his shy crush on Anne's heroine and his teaching tricks to Corky the dog; he's later powerfully impressive as the Electric Man, glowing with the John P. Fulton special effects halo and sporting the Jack P. Pierce shrivel-faced makeup. *Man Made Monster* provides a perfect showcase for the Chaney pathos.

Then there's top-billed Lionel Atwill as mad Dr. Paul Rigas, playing just as passionately as if he was back on Broadway in 1920, starring in *Deburau*, ripping into his *Man Made Monster* dialogue:

> SAMUEL S. HINDS: Sometimes I think you're mad!
> ATWILL: *I am!* So was Archimedes, Galileo, Newton, Pasteur, Lister and all the others who dared to dream... Who can tell what *tomorrow's* madness may be?

A Universal favorite since his classic portrayal of one-armed Inspector Krogh in *Son of Frankenstein*, "Pinky" Atwill plays Rigas with a mad flamboyance and a sexual leer that must be seen to be believed. Charles Bennett, screenwriter of such classics as Hitchcock's *The Thirty-Nine Steps* and the De Mille epics of the '40s, was a pillar of the Hollywood "British Colony" of the Golden Age; shortly before his death in 1995, Mr. Bennett spoke with me about Atwill:

> I didn't like him. Atwill was a personal pornographer! He used to have a studio at his house out in Pacific Palisades, where he made and showed "blue" movies of naked women—and naked men. I didn't appreciate that. Why, the British Colony never really approved of Atwill—any more than we approved of Errol Flynn!

And there was Anne Nagel's heroine, June Lawrence. The girl has everything: she's pretty (remember that wonderful closeup in the garden, where she's holding the flowers?); is a devoted niece to her scientist uncle, Samuel S. Hinds; has a feisty personality (volleying wisecracks with reporter hero Frank Albertson with all the precision of a Warner Bros. alumna); has sex appeal (as when, in Albertson's convertible, she promises him some "real cooperation"); possesses a crusading sense of right (working to free Chaney when Atwill pins Hinds' murder on him); and, of course, displays a cat's curiosity (seeking Atwill's laboratory records—in her nightgown, naturally).

Anne Nagel's June is no scream-and-faint glamourpuss, but a real, warm character who—for once—doesn't just aim a howl and a curled upper lip at the horror heavy. There's even a nice dose of pre–World War II idealism, as Anne's June persuades her

***Man Made Monster*, 1941: Nagel at the mercy of "the maddest doctor of them all," Lionel Atwill.**

reporter fiancé to forsake a Pulitzer Prize–winning story and to burn the records of the diabolic Atwill (whose "Electrical Supermen" concept smacks of Nazi propaganda). Come the finale, the couple stares into the fireplace flames as Corky the dog whines approval, and as Anne gives her beau a sensually adoring look that makes us think he's going to be rewarded, amply and delightfully, for his sacrifice!

Man Made Monster "wrapped" at Universal Saturday, December 14, 1940. Chaney, winning his contract, took part in a ceremony on the old *Phantom of the Opera* stage as a plaque was dedicated to his father's memory—with a publicity bonanza for the son. Atwill took his leer and cat eyes home to Pacific Palisades where, nights later, he hosted that infamous Yuletide "orgy" which almost sank his career.

Man Made Monster opened at New York's Rialto Theatre the week of March 18, 1941. *Variety* called it:

> a shocker that's in the groove for horror fans. It makes no pretense of being anything but a freakish chiller, going directly to the point and proving mighty successful... Young Chaney looks like he is on his way ... backed up by Lionel Atwill in one of his better characterizations... Miss Nagel has improved lots in the past year... Unbilled pooch, used importantly, also deserves mention.

Nagel as a Universal Studio attraction, 1940 (Photofest).

"GEO. WAGGNER PULLS HIGH-VOLTAGE LEVER" headlined *The Hollywood Reporter* (3/24/41), speculating that the "all-around excellent production" of *Man Made Monster* was responsible for the Universal seven-year producer/writer/director contract Waggner had just signed. Before year's end, Waggner would be director and associate producer of *The Wolf Man*. Indeed, Waggner, Chaney, Atwill, Fulton, Pierce and Salter would all go on as legends of Universal 1940s horror—as would Evelyn Ankers, who joined Universal one month after Anne completed *Man Made Monster*.

Anne was flanked by Richard Arlen and Andy Devine in such Universal 1941 fare as *Mutiny in the Arctic*; worked for Waggner again in *Sealed Lips*; had a small role as circus star "Madame Gorgeous" in W. C. Fields' *Never Give a Sucker an Even Break*; and starred in *Road Agent* with Dick Foran, in which she sang *sans* dubbing. Yet Anne was getting lost in the factory of Universal.

Then came her embarrassingly small bit in *The Mad Doctor of Market Street*, produced by Paul (*House of Frankenstein*, *House of Dracula*) Malvern, directed by Joseph H.(*Gun Crazy*) Lewis, and completed at Universal July 19, 1941. Hardie Albright visits the title fiend (played by Atwill with his usual unsavory relish) to offer himself as a guinea pig to the maniac's life-sustaining experiment; Anne, as Mrs. Saunders, the guinea pig's wife, races to his rescue, in tears and slouch hat, sitting in a police car and speaking her single line of dialogue:

> "I had to come all the way from Sundayvale. I didn't realize what he planned to do until—until he didn't come home last night."

It's indeed too-late-to-the-lab; Anne weeps over the corpse—and is never seen again. By the time Una Merkel, Claire Dodd, Nat Pendleton, Richard Davies and John Eldredge enter the film on an ocean liner, Anne is out of the picture. And by the time the stars are shipwrecked on a South Seas island, where Atwill poses as "God of Life," one has almost forgotten Anne was even in the 61-minute movie.

Universal previewed *The Mad Doctor of Market Street* in Los Angeles as a decidedly anti-climactic 1941 New Year's Eve attraction. Wrote *The Hollywood Reporter*:

> a chiller-diller that can be used as a filler... The title role is of the sort that invites overacting, an invitation Lionel Atwill gladly accepts... Much of the ship-fire footage smacks of stock which photographer Jerome Ash tries vainly to match... Hardie Albright appears briefly as the first victim of the do[illegible] and Anne Nagel is his grief-stricken wife.

It was a sad, comedown bit for Anne—in a slapdash (but fun) "B" which *Variety* would label "strictly a tail-ender." The limited footage of an hysterical Anne, crying over a dead husband, almost seemed a tasteless reminder of her 1937 tragedy.

Anne's Universal sojourn ended with the 15-chapter serial *Don Winslow of the Navy* (1942); Claire Dodd had the femme lead, while Anne played the supporting role of Misty. Universal had chewed her up and spat her out even more exploitatively than they would Anne Gwynne and Evelyn Ankers, who temporarily stayed on as Anne departed the lot.

As her Universal contract expired, Anne went east, touring vaudeville in *The Hollywood Sweater Girl Revue*. The show visited movie houses in Boston, Providence and New York, where it played Broadway's Loew's State Theatre, supporting the Charles Boyer/Margaret Sullavan Universal feature *Appointment for Love*. *The*

Hollywood Sweater Girl Revue closed at Loew's on the night of December 3, 1941; the next day, Anne went to her hometown of Boston—and got married. The groom was 29-year-old Lieutenant James H. Keenan of the U.S. Army Air Corps, and a Municipal Court clerk performed the December 4, 1941, "surprise ceremony" that barred everyone except the bride (who, the press reported, wore "a short raccoon coat and a black velvet dress"), groom and two witnesses. Pearl Harbor followed three days later.

Back in Hollywood, Anne starred in the 1942 Columbia serial *The Secret Code*, co-starring with Paul Kelly. However, her most famous movie of 1942 was PRC's *The Mad Monster*, a grim but lively 74-minute zinger apparently concocted after PRC studied Universal's *Man Made Monster* and *The Wolf Man*. Anne, as in *Man Made Monster*, is the daughter of a doctor—this time George Zucco. "Petro," our Mad Monster, is played (well) by future Universal Frankenstein Monster Glenn Strange in a role presumably penned as a homage to Lon Chaney, Jr.—a simpleton (*à la Of Mice and Men*) who transforms via the madman's experiments (*Man Made Monster*) into a hairy monster (*à la The Wolf Man*). Sinister Cinema's video catalogue best sums up Strange's Mad Monster: "Ever seen a werewolf in Oshkosh before?"

It's George Zucco's show—a wonderfully flamboyant performance, barnstormed in a silver toupee, complete with bravura dialogue ("Yes, I know you want to join your brothers and howl at the moon!"), demonic cackling and whip-lashing of Petro. Anne valiantly copes with her own dialogue ("It's as if he's possessed by a demon!"), but Sam Newfield's direction and the PRC production values hardly do her justice. Although *The Mad Monster* was shot only a little more than a year after *Man Made Monster*, Anne looks much older; in some shots, she even looks like she might be Anne Nagel's ugly duckling sister.

Anne joined Gail Patrick, Nancy Kelly, Gertrude Michael and Tala Birell in Monogram's 1943 *Women in Bondage*, then was offscreen for several years, following her husband to various military camps. She returned in 1946 in Republic's Vera Hruba Ralston vehicle *Murder in the Music Hall* (billed 17th in the *Film Daily Yearbook* credits). Thereafter, amidst rumors of marital discord, she landed jobs ranging from bits in such films as MGM's *The Hucksters* (1947) to a lead in Film Classics' *The Spirit of West Point* (1947), starring Army football stars Glenn Davis and "Doc" Blanchard.

If the roles weren't spectacular, the news headlines were. A December 23, 1947, headline read: "ANNE NAGEL SUIT CHARGES SURGERY LEFT HER BARREN." Anne claimed that during an appendectomy she underwent October 14, 1936, as bride of Ross Alexander, the surgeon "removed other organs and so made it impossible for her ever to bear children"—all without her knowledge, consent or authorization. The surgeon was prominent Hollywood physician Dr. Franklyn Thorpe, who, in 1936, had been involved in divorcing Mary Astor in the sensational "diary" scandal. Anne, who claimed she didn't learn until January of 1947 why she couldn't conceive, demanded damages of $350,000. Dr. Thorpe sought a dismissal of the suit, claiming Anne had given him her "specific consent" and cryptically stating that she was "well aware of the nature of the surgery." No news of a settlement could be found, but based on Anne's later financial situation, it seems hardly likely that she received any settlement.

She played in *Don't Trust Your Husband* (1948) and returned to Universal for a bit in *Family Honeymoon* (1948), with Claudette Colbert and Fred MacMurray. Nineteen forty-nine saw her (barely) in MGM's *The Stratton Story*. Her final feature film: RKO's *Armored Car Robbery* (1950). Her role: a grieving widow.

On May 22, 1951, Anne went to court to secure a divorce from Lt. Col. Keenan. The *Los Angeles Times* reported:

> She testified that he gave her a radio for her birthday, then put his foot through its face, took the needles out of her knitting and raveled it, then gave her a cocker puppy for a peace offering—but would not permit the animal in the house. He then gave the pup away.

Keenan pleaded for a reconciliation attempt, so Superior Judge Ingall W. Bull agreed to delay signing the decree until "the colonel and the lady could talk face to face." However, as Anne's lawyer, Caryl Warner, was later quoted in the *Los Angeles Herald Express*:

> They went to their former home in the valley to divide up some of their personal belongings. There was quite a dispute. In fact, it was a helluva fight!

So Judge Bull signed the interlocutory decree May 25, 1951.

Anne Nagel seemed to disappear in the following years. Then, on February 6, 1957, she returned to court, trying to block Keenan's attempt to make the six-year interlocutory divorce decree final. She claimed she and Keenan had reconciled immediately after the divorce, and her testimony prevented the divorce from becoming final. Then she requested $400 per month separate maintenance. "He said we could reconcile on condition I would not drink, and to this day I have not," testified Anne.

Keenan begged to differ. According to the *Los Angeles Times*, he "said his wife embarrassed him by drinking to excess and that he 'only looked out for her well-being, by reason of the fact that she had no funds' after she was released from a hospital for treatment of alcoholism."

The court denied Anne's temporary alimony request. The Keenans finally divorced in the late summer of 1957.

In the fall of 1957, Screen Gems released *Shock!*, the famous package of old Universal horror shows, to television. As *Black Friday*, *Man Made Monster*, and *The Mad Doctor of Market Street* found new audiences, Screen Gems engaged Anne to play Mrs. Buffalo Bill on the TV series *Circus Boy*. Her leading man: Dick Foran, whom she had played opposite at both Warner Bros. and Universal.

There would be no comeback, however, for this lonely, haunted, alcoholic lady. Anne Nagel spent her final years "in retirement," living on South Kenmore Avenue in Los Angeles. She developed liver cancer. On June 5, 1966, following surgery, she entered the Sunray North Convalescent Hospital. The divorced, childless and largely forgotten actress died there July 6, 1966—almost 30 years after elopement with Ross Alexander, whose suicide had tormented her all those years. Reports of her age ranged from 50 to 54; the Motion Picture Relief Fund served as informant for her death certificate.

The Rosary was recited for the actress, who had wanted to be a nun, at the Pierce Bros. Chapel, 5959 Santa Monica Boulevard, 8:00 P.M. Sunday night, July 10. At 9:00 A.M., Monday, July 11, 1966, there was a Requiem Mass at St. Basil Catholic Church, 628 South Harvard Boulevard in Los Angeles. The body was taken to Holy Cross Cemetery in Culver City (where her *Black Friday* co-star Bela Lugosi is interred in his Dracula cape), and Anne Nagel was buried there.

There is no marker.

The Films of Anne Nagel

1932

Hypnotized (World Wide, Mack Sennett)

1933

College Humor (Paramount, Wesley Ruggles)
I Loved You Wednesday (Fox, Henry King)
Sitting Pretty (Paramount, Harry Joe Brown)

1934

Search for Beauty (Paramount, Erle C. Kenton)
Coming Out Party (Fox, John G. Blystone)
Stand Up and Cheer! (Fox, Hamilton MacFadden)
She Learned About Sailors (Fox, George Marshall)

1935

George White's 1935 Scandals (Fox, George White)
Doubting Thomas (Fox, David Butler)
Reckless Roads (Majestic, Burt Lynwood)
Redheads on Parade (20th Century–Fox, Norman McLeod)
Music Is Magic (20th Century–Fox, George Marshall)

1936

Here Comes Trouble (20th Century–Fox, Lewis Seiler)
Everybody's Old Man (20th Century–Fox, James Flood)
Bullets or Ballots (Warner Bros., William Keighley)
Love Begins at 20 (Warner Bros., Frank McDonald)
Hot Money (Warner Bros., William McGann)
China Clipper (Warner Bros., Ray Enright)
Polo Joe (Warner Bros., William McGann)
King of Hockey (Warner Bros., Noel Smith)
Down the Stretch (Warner Bros., William Clemens)
Here Comes Carter! (Warner Bros., William Clemens)

1937

Guns of the Pecos (Warner Bros., Noel Smith)
The Three Legionnaires (*Three Crazy Legionnaires*) (General Pictures, Hamilton MacFadden)
The Case of the Stuttering Bishop (Warner Bros., William Clemens)
The Hoosier Schoolboy (*Forgotten Hero*) (Monogram, William Nigh)
Escape by Night (Republic, Hamilton MacFadden)
The Footloose Heiress (Warner Bros., William Clemens)
A Bride for Henry (Monogram, William Nigh)
The Adventurous Blonde (Warner Bros., Frank McDonald)
Devil's Saddle Legion (Warner Bros., Bobby Connolly)

1938

Saleslady (Monogram, Arthur G. Collins)
Mystery House (Warner Bros., Noel Smith)
Under the Big Top (Monogram, Karl Brown)
Gang Bullets (Monogram, Lambert Hillyer)

1939

Convict's Code (Monogram, Lambert Hillyer)
Should a Girl Marry? (Monogram, Lambert Hillyer)
Unexpected Father (*Sandy Takes a Bow*) (Universal, Charles Lamont)
The Witness Vanishes (Universal, Otis Garrett)
Call a Messenger (Universal, Arthur Lubin)
Legion of Lost Flyers (Universal, Christy Cabanne)

1940

My Little Chickadee (Universal, Eddie Cline)
Ma, He's Making Eyes at Me (Universal, Harold Schuster)
Black Friday (Universal, Arthur Lubin)
Hot Steel (Universal, Christy Cabanne)

Argentine Nights (Universal, Albert S. Rogell)
Diamond Frontier (Universal, Harold Schuster)
The Green Hornet (Universal serial, Ford Beebe and Ray Taylor)
Winners of the West (Universal serial, Ray Taylor and Ford Beebe)

1941

The Invisible Woman (Universal, Eddie Sutherland)
Meet the Chump (Universal, Eddie Cline)
Man Made Monster (Universal, George Waggner)
Mutiny in the Arctic (Universal, John Rawlins)
Sealed Lips (Universal, George Waggner)
Never Give a Sucker an Even Break (Universal, Eddie Cline)
Road Agent (*Texas Road Agent*) (Universal, Charles Lamont)
The Green Hornet Strikes Again (Universal serial, Ford Beebe and John Rawlins)

1942

Stagecoach Buckaroo (*Ghost Town Buckaroo*) (Universal, Ray Taylor)
The Mad Doctor of Market Street (Universal, Joseph H. Lewis)
The Mad Monster (PRC, Sam Newfield)
Don Winslow of the Navy (Universal serial, Ford Beebe and Ray Taylor)
The Dawn Express (*Nazi Spy Ring*) (PRC, Albert Herman)
The Secret Code (Columbia serial, Spencer Gordon Bennett)

1943

Women in Bondage (Monogram, Steve Sekely)

1946

Murder in the Music Hall (*Midnight Melody*) (Republic, John English)
Traffic in Crime (Republic, Les Selander)
The Trap (Monogram, Howard Bretherton)

1947

Blondie's Holiday (Columbia, Abby Berlin)
The Spirit of West Point (Film Classics, Ralph Murphy)
The Hucksters (MGM, Jack Conway)

1948

Homecoming (MGM, Mervyn LeRoy)
One Touch of Venus (Universal-International, William A. Seiter)
Don't Trust Your Husband (*An Innocent Affair*) (United Artists/Nassar, Lloyd Bacon)
Every Girl Should Be Married (RKO, Don Hartman)
Family Honeymoon (Universal–International, Claude Binyon)

1949

Prejudice (New World/Motion Picture Sales, Edward L. Cahn)
The Stratton Story (MGM, Sam Wood)

1950

Armored Car Robbery (RKO, Richard Fleischer)

SHORT SUBJECTS

1937

Romance Road (Warner Bros.)

1941

Hollywood Meets the Navy (Republic)

1948

Pal's Return (RKO)

LOUISE CURRIE

It's probably the most delirious scene in all of the Monogram horror canon.

The climax of *The Ape Man* finds Bela Lugosi, in makeup that makes him look part-gorilla, and a swallow-coat that makes him look part-penguin. He's lunging about his cellar laboratory, the Edward Kay musical score roaring away like a mad circus overture. A "gorilla" (Emil Van Horn in his ape suit) leaps and jumps in his cage, turned on by the mayhem, and by the leading lady—blonde, lovely Louise Currie, teetering in her high heels as she lashes furry Bela with a long black whip.

The lady bears scrutiny. This is not the usual sassy-mouthed garter-snapper of Monogram. Louise Currie is tall (or at least seems so in those black high heels); she has a look of Katharine Hepburn–style aristocracy, with high cheekbones, lovely eyes, great legs and blonde hair that bounces on her shoulders. She's a classy lady (and a good actress), and her sincerity actually makes you care if Bela's Ape Man gets his hairy paws on her.

The ape, lovesick for Louise, kills Bela. Police kill the ape. Louise and hero Wallace Ford clinch for the camera.

"Screwy idea, wasn't it?" asks "Zippo," the simpleton who's capered through *The Ape Man* as Greek Chorus. He rolls up a car window; written on it: THE END.

Based on her work in *The Ape Man*, and her follow-up performance as a temporary zombie in Monogram's *Voodoo Man*, with Bela, John Carradine and George Zucco, Louise Currie easily wins the crown of Best (and Loveliest) Actress of the Poverty Row Horrors.

The honor bestowed might sound like a dubious one. After all, there are those who label Lugosi's *The Ape Man* his "most demeaning" role. *Voodoo Man* (while allowing Bela dignity as a goateed wizard) features the spectacle of John Carradine as a bongo-playing half-wit and George Zucco as a voodoo high priest in war paint and feathers, chanting to "Ramboona." And some Freudians out there are still pondering the deeper meanings of Louise and that *Ape Man* whip.

Happily, however, Louise Currie has a refreshing affection for her Monogram shockers of 50 years ago, great respect for Bela Lugosi and happy memories of the shooting of these penny dreadful (and perennially popular) movies. Indeed, Louise's charm, beauty and vivacity are part of the reason these movies enjoy such attention today, and she prefers them to the bits she did in films like *Citizen Kane*. While her best roles were played for the small studios, she has lived like a major movie star—enjoying a beautiful villa in Beverly Hills as, in later years, she operated her own Melrose Avenue Interior Decoration shop. Of course, beside her Monogram horrors, she's remembered for her appearance as a society debutante in RKO's *You'll Find Out*, which pitted Kay Kyser's band against Karloff, Lugosi and Peter Lorre, as well as playing the ever-imperiled heroines of the popular Republic serials *Adventures of Captain Marvel* (1941) and *The Masked Marvel* (1943). Yet it seems that the Monogram films are her favorites.

"Monogram called me their Katharine Hepburn," Louise Currie says today, with laughter but also a little pride. It was, indeed, a delightful collaboration.

***Chapter opener:* Louise Currie publicity shot.**

It was the Christmas season of 1988. Louise Currie, almost 40 years after her last film, had returned with her husband, John V. Good, from a holiday visit to her daughter in Santa Barbara. She came home with a nasty throat infection, yet she cheerfully insisted on doing the interview when I called her—pleading indulgence for "this terrible voice."

Born in Oklahoma City, educated at Sarah Lawrence College in Bronxville, New York, Louise came to California to study at Max Reinhardt's famous drama school in Hollywood. Her beauty instantly won her movie offers, which Louise turned down ("I didn't want to start trying to get jobs if I didn't know my trade"). However, after various stage roles and training with Reinhardt, Louise signed with agent Sue Carol (who wed her most famous client, Alan Ladd, and guided his career). She availed herself to the movies as she settled happily at 22240 Pacific Coast Highway (called Roosevelt Highway during the war years), right on the ocean.

> So beautiful. We owned a house at Malibu at that time—a wonderful place to live. It was gorgeous. There were so many days, even in winter, when it would be warm and lovely on the beach...

Louise's first releases were the 1940 PRC Westerns *Billy the Kid Outlawed* and *Billy the Kid's Gun Justice*. Then came RKO's *You'll Find Out*, which premiered at New York's Roxy Theatre November 14, 1940—complete with a personal appearance by star Kay Kyser and His College of Musical Knowledge. This musical curio pitted radio star Kyser and His College (including Ginny Simms, Ish Kabibble, Harry Babbitt and Sully Mason) vs. Boris Karloff, Bela Lugosi and Peter Lorre, in an "old house" filled with leading lady Helen Parrish and her debutante girlfriends. Though unbilled in *You'll Find Out*, Louise sparked much footage as one of the debutantes: "Where are the men?" she asks in her entrance, enjoying prominent closeups and angles from director David Butler. Louise remembers the "quite intelligent" and "very nice-looking" Karloff, the "quiet and unassuming" Lugosi and the "very small and very ... peculiar!" Peter Lorre:

> *You'll Find Out* really was fun; it was light-hearted, the whole idea was a spoof, and everybody was happy. I think that Kay Kyser was madly in love with Ginny Simms... It was quite a romance. He didn't marry her (he later married Georgia Carroll), but he and Ginny had quite a romance at the time of *You'll Find Out*. So they were *very* happy!
>
> Boris Karloff, interestingly enough, was very quiet. He didn't participate too much—he was rather a recluse, I'd almost say. I felt you didn't just run up and start chatting with him! I remember having long chats with Lugosi about his family life, and I met his wife; he was a very educated, polished, interesting man. It's amazing that he got into the horror end of it; he could easily have been a serious actor, have gone another direction. We had long conversations... I don't remember having too much contact with Peter Lorre; he was a strange little fellow—sort of as he portrayed!

Recently discovered home movies show the company of *You'll Find Out* happily at play; meanwhile, on a neighboring RKO soundstage, Orson Welles was making film history as producer/director/star/co-writer of *Citizen Kane*. Sue Carol got both Alan Ladd and Louise parts as members of the reporter squad in the bowels of "Xanadu" in the film's climax.

"If you could have found out what 'Rosebud' meant," says Louise as a bespectacled reporter, "I bet that would have explained everything."

Louise enjoyed working for Welles, observing his "remarkable" direction as the *wunderkind* selected his dazzling camera angles from "way up" on the camera boom. However, his painstaking methods wore her down:

> The thing I never liked about pictures was sitting around between takes for hours on end—to me, that was a waste of time. It was more stimulating for me to work than do nothing. A lot of people enjoyed the sitting, and played games, and got into all kinds of things. I really didn't. I'd read a book, to try to pass the time, but I enjoyed working faster—because I felt we were really accomplishing something.

Louise found a pace far more to her liking in Republic's 1941 12-chapter serial *Adventures of Captain Marvel*. The popular choice of many film buffs as the best cliffhanger ever made, the serial presented the exploits of Billy Batson (Frank Coghlan, Jr.), who—thanks to the ancient "Shazam" (Nigel de Brulier), met in an underground Siamese tomb—can transform into the formidable Captain Marvel (Tom Tyler, in a superhero costume so tight that, as shooting neared its end, Coghlan and co-star Billy Benedict presented Tyler with a jockstrap).

"That wasn't disrespectful," Coghlan told Tom Weaver in a *Comics Scene* interview, "but with his tight Captain Marvel outfit, we thought it would help!"

It was Captain Marvel vs. the masked arch-villain the Scorpion; Louise was Betty, ever-endangered secretary to the Malcolm Archaeological Expedition. Louise was in awe of the thrills-and-chills engineered by directors William Witney and John English; enjoyed the camaraderie with Coghlan and Benedict; and admired the "sensational" special effects of the legendary Howard and Theodore Lydecker and the famous stunt work of ace double Dave Sharpe—who, at one point, doubled for Louise herself. In a *Serial World* interview with Gregory R. Jackson, Jr., Louise recalled the climax of Chapter One, in which a dynamited bridge sent her station wagon plunging into a river. A Lydecker miniature provided the explosion, but...

> I remember they wanted me to be submerged in the station wagon that went into the water and then I was to be brought out. Well, I decided that really wasn't part of my talent and I said I didn't think I should do that. The station wagon was supposed to go completely into the water and I could just visualize myself drowning until they finally rescued me! So I became a little stubborn at that moment and told Hiram S. Brown, Jr., the producer, that I wouldn't do it. Finally, we agreed.

Dave Sharpe donned female attire and doubled Louise in the scene. Louise told Jackson that, years later, she met producer Brown at a party in Acapulco:

> I asked, "Do you remember when you asked me to get into that terrible water?" and he laughed and said, "Well, you were perfectly right; you shouldn't have done it." And so we had a lot of fun reminiscing.

Meanwhile, Louise was freelancing all over Hollywood, from Universal to RKO to Columbia. And ultimately, she ventured to 4376 Sunset Drive—the home of Monogram Studios:

> As for Monogram—yes, I got kind of a kick out of it! For one thing, in everything I did at Monogram, I had a leading role, which made it much more interesting for me.
>
> Monogram called me their Katharine Hepburn! I don't know if they referred to the "look" as much as I had gone to Sarah Lawrence College, and studied with Max Reinhardt...

And, on December 16, 1942, Monogram began shooting the thriller which (for horror fans) survives as Louise Currie's most famous film, described by Tom Weaver in his book *Poverty Row HORRORS!* as "a Golden Turkey of the most beloved kind": *The Ape Man*, starring Bela Lugosi.

> What a mess I've made of things!
>
> —Bela Lugosi, as *The Ape Man* (1943)

Amelita Ward was first announced as leading lady of *The Ape Man*, but it was Louise who ended up in the clutches of Lugosi. Louise was delighted to be acting again with Bela, who had been so charming on *You'll Find Out*:

> It was amazing that I even got to know Lugosi, because we worked so fast, and constantly. But on *The Ape Man*, and later *Voodoo Man*, I found him a very intelligent, extremely interesting man. I remember long chats with Lugosi about his family life, and I enjoyed meeting his wife again, whom I'd met on *You'll Find Out*.

Produced by "Jungle Sam" Katzman, directed by William "One Take" Beaudine, *The Ape Man* presents Louise as Billie Mason, a newspaper photographer who wears "Opening Night" perfume, wisecracks with élan and joins reporter Wallace Ford in a search for missing Dr. James Brewster (Lugosi). What they find: Lugosi in ape man makeup; Emil Van Horn, as the ape, whose scene-stealing antics include pouring straw over his own head in his cage while Lugosi tries to hold center stage; Minerva Urecal as Lugosi's I-talk-to-the-ghosts spiritualist sister Agatha (whose name her onscreen brother can't quite pronounce); and Ralph Littlefield as Zippo, *The Ape Man*'s "Greek chorus," who dashes in and out in a porkpie hat, offering dippy comments, taking credit as author of the story, and ending the hokum with the infamous Poverty Row curtain line, "Screwy idea, wasn't it?"

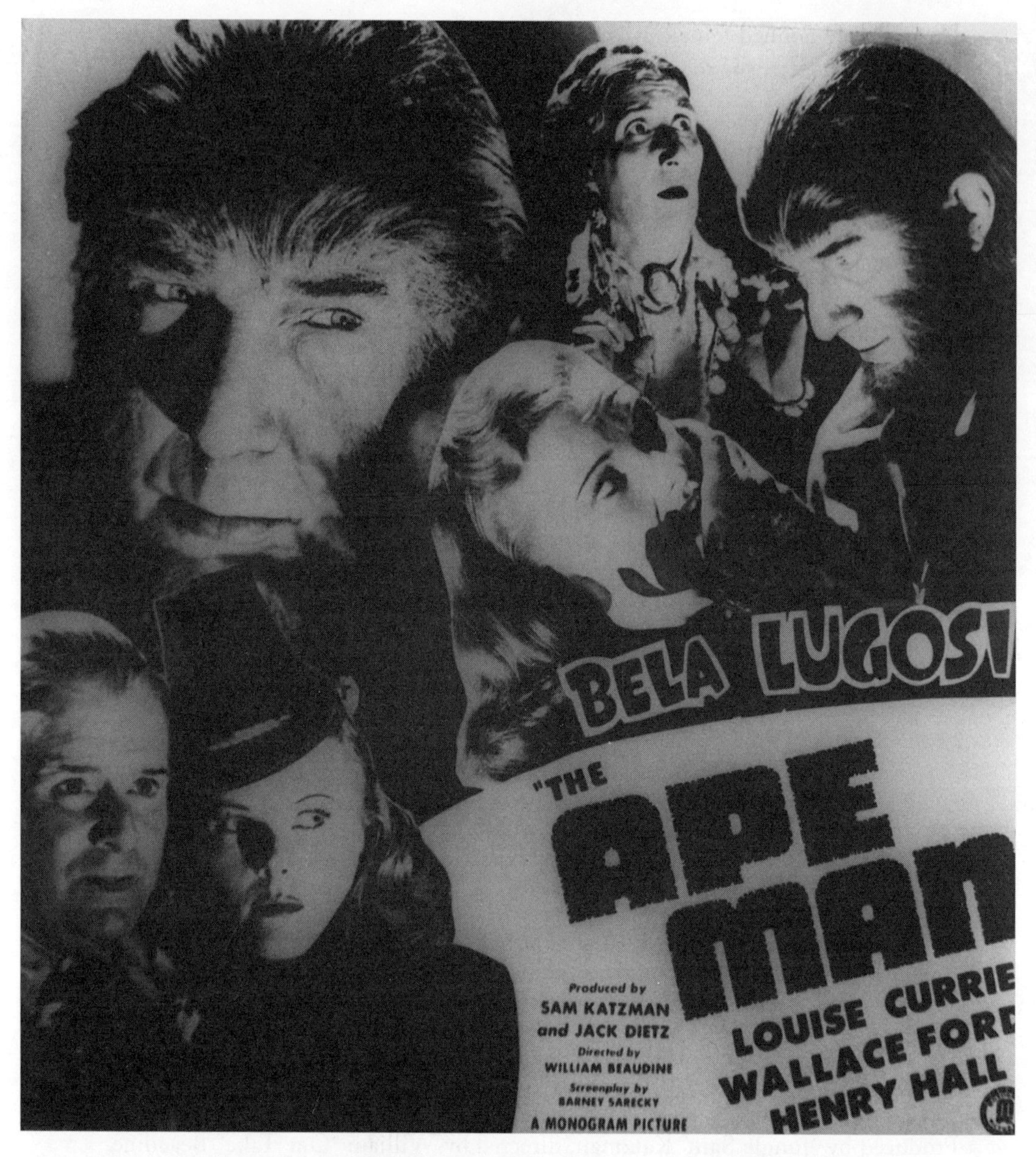

Currie wears a swashbuckling chapeau in this poster art for *The Ape Man*, 1943.

Several things save *The Ape Man*: Lugosi's usual, touching sincerity; that outrageous Edward Kay score; Van Horn's emoting (in the same passionate style he gave "Satan," his gorilla monster of Republic's *Perils of Nyoka* serial); and Louise, whose Billie is the most classy beauty ever to sashay through a Monogram soundstage. In the tradition of Hollywood's screwball comedy reporters, she charmingly trades quips with slightly overage hero Wallace Ford:

> FORD: Well, there's something screwy about the whole thing. I can feel it in my bones.

LOUISE: Maybe it's rheumatism!

The actress' 1940s fashion flair is charming, and she is especially attractive at the climax, as she searches the house in a long coat, high heels and a high, black hat with plume, that looks like it came from a swashbuckling costumer:

> Of course, things were cheaper; in the Monogram pictures I wore my own clothes, because sometimes in the cheaper films, if you get it out of wardrobe, you don't do very well!

It's all-out mayhem at the end of *The Ape Man*: Bela knocking off that hat and carrying Louise to his basement laboratory, Louise fighting back as she pelts Bela with a whip. The ape, who's become a fan of Louise's charms, breaks loose from his cage and mauls Bela to death as Louise races up the stairs to Ford and the police—who shoot the ardent ape.

> The climax of *The Ape Man* had to be pretty scary, because that's what they wanted. It was kind of difficult to film, because you had to make it quite realistic. You couldn't be too casual about it; it had to be scary to scare the audience—which I think it did!
>
> William Beaudine ... was a wonderful director, a wonderful man—quiet, kind, and not tempestuous, like some directors could be. He was very well-liked by all his cast. In *The Ape Man*, there was Wallace Ford, an awfully nice man and a good actor; Emil Van Horn, the "ape," a very nice young chap.... When you worked with people like that, a film became much more fun.

The Ape Man opened in March of 1943 at the Colony Theatre on Hollywood Boulevard, on a double bill with the East Side Kids' *Kid Dynamite*. "Louise Currie brightens the proceedings noticeably in the femme lead," reported *Daily Variety*. *The Ape Man* lumbered on to become one of Bela Lugosi's most infamous horror films. In his 1974 Lugosi biography, *The Count*, Arthur Lennig wrote that Lugosi "seems almost shy and embarrassed shuffling around the laboratory, as if he wished that no would have to see him." Over 20 years later, in Midnight Marquee's 1995 anthology *Bela Lugosi*, Mark A. Miller wrote, "Never before or after was Bela Lugosi cast in so demeaning a role," calling the script "a stink bomb" and opining that Bela's performance was "beyond redemption."

For Louise, however, *The Ape Man* needs no apology. She thinks Bela did "a brilliant job," and recalls the star showing no shame in his work:

> I think Lugosi was intrigued with the Ape Man role. It was difficult, but then again, it challenged him. That was part of his game, doing roles that were odd and unusual.

Louise also can personally vouch for the film's scare power: she took her little boy (then six or seven) to the Hollywood preview. "My son had dreams that had him waking up screaming for years; dreams of the ape capturing his mother!"

Indeed, thanks to Bela's love for acting, and Louise's charms, the film has its power. In a cover story on *The Ape Man* in *Cult Movies* #18, publisher Buddy Barnett hails the film's "fun, wonderful and bizarre little moments," and advises the reader:

> The next time you watch *The Ape Man*, don't be embarrassed, but just sit back and let the joy flow over you. You'll feel rejuvenated.

Nineteen forty-three also saw Louise in another famed serial: Republic's *The Masked Marvel*. This time the hero's identity was a mystery—was it Rod Bacon, Richard Clarke, David Bacon or Bill Healy? (Actually, stuntman Tom Steele played the hero throughout the 12 chapters.) Louise was Alice, the heroine, menaced by the evil Japanese spy/saboteur Mura Sakima (Johnny Arthur). Spencer Bennet directed; even the cast was in the dark during shooting as to who the hero truly was. Louise told Gregory Jackson, Jr.:

> As an actress, I think my part was far better in *The Masked Marvel*; I'm in almost all the scenes, my part is larger, and I make a bit more sense. I wonder, when you look at *Captain Marvel*, why I'm even in it. I guess they wanted a female to be rescued rather than a male at the end of each chapter... So for acting I think I enjoyed the part I was given to play in *The Masked Marvel*, but for the finished product, I think *Captain Marvel* was a better serial overall.

> Ramboona never fails!
>
> —George Zucco, in *Voodoo Man* (1944)

Voodoo Man—Louise's third and final screen union with Lugosi—is also one of Bela's most infamous films. Actually, Bela enjoys a fine showcase role as Dr. Richard Marlowe who, in wizard's robe and goatee, tries to transfer "life" into his wife, dead for 20 years. Abetting Bela in this zinger: John Carradine as Toby, a bongo-playing moron who leers at the female zombies; George Zucco as Nicholas, gas station attendant by day, war painted and feathered high priest of "Ramboona" by night; and Louise as Stella, wise-cracking sister of the leading lady (Wanda McKay). As this tart-tongued honey, kidnapped by Carradine and (temporarily) made a zombie by Bela, Louise again looks smashing both in her entrance in a convertible (sporting an odd, attractive Foreign Legion style hat) and in her diaphanous zombie robes, wandering in a trance across fields, her eyes gaping.

"Wasn't that funny?" laughs Louise today of her *Voodoo Man* melodramatics.

Alas, poor *Voodoo Man*; when it began shooting October 16, 1943, even its talent force seemed hell-bent on mocking it.

First of all, there was John Carradine, whose portrayal of the moronic Toby, stroking the tresses of a female zombie, must be seen to be believed. UPI Hollywood correspondent Frederick C. Othman filed an October 20, 1943, report, ACTOR TRADES MOVIES FOR SHAKESPEARE TOUR, noting how Carradine ("who earns better than $3,000 a week in the pictures and still doesn't like 'em") was playing in *Voodoo Man* by

Currie in the clutches of Pat McKee (left) and John Carradine; Bela Lugosi leers. ***Voodoo Man*, 1944.**

day while starring as Hamlet (with his own Shakespearean company) at the Pasadena Playhouse by night. Othman pressed for an interview as "the $3,000-per-week half-wit practiced voodoo rhythm on Monogram Studio's idea of a Haitian drum." Carradine, whose *Voodoo Man* check would help finance his San Francisco premiere as Hamlet on October 24, orated:

> My advance ticket sale in San Francisco has been excellent and I have every hope of never coming back to the movies.

Carradine's wild, over-the-top, frighteningly abandoned acting as Toby makes one suspect the actor was mocking Hollywood—performing as if he thought the only person who would pay to see *Voodoo Man* would have the I.Q. of poor Toby. Of course, after a brief Shakespearean triumph, Carradine *did* come back to movies (about 100 more of them!); for years he labeled *Voodoo Man* his "worst film." (He later deferred to 1966's *Billy the Kid Versus Dracula*, directed by *Voodoo Man*'s William Beaudine.)

Meanwhile, that day on the set, plump, cornfed co-producer Sam Katzman interrupted the Carradine interview to proclaim of *Voodoo Man*:

> I call this a moron picture. I have made a number of these films and I claim there must be something wrong with anybody who goes to see 'em... Just look at me, making all this money and with a fancy house and swimming pool. Do I deserve it? For making moron pictures?

Katzman ran off at the mouth, apparently before the cast, crew and his assistant Barney Sarecky (who, as the reporter noted, "was urging him to quit talking"); nevertheless, Katzman continued:

> This is a cockeyed business. We dream up these hokey stories and we hire some actors and a fine director like Bill Beaudine. Then the money flows in as if we were great geniuses. We're not. We're just lucky to be sitting in the right seats.*

And, as for "Bill" Beaudine, he eventually got into the act too, publicly pondering why *Voodoo Man* was being rushed to completion—since, in his opinion, nobody out there was anxious to see this one!

Yet Louise, again, has happy memories of the melodrama, and *Voodoo Man*'s most notorious performer:

> John Carradine—he was an excellent actor, and quite an interesting man, also. He was so tall and lanky—I enjoyed him!
>
> There was the benefit of a film made in a small studio—you worked together, you pulled together, you tried harder. A smaller studio, like Monogram, was more of a family, and you pulled to do a good film in a short amount of time, so it would be a standout.

Voodoo Man braved release Monday, February 21, 1944. The judgment of the *New York Post* probably pleased Sam Katzman: "This picture isn't content to portray zombies; it gives the impression of having been made by them." Leonard Maltin's *TV Movies* calls *Voodoo Man* a "campy B film"; in *Poverty Row HORRORS!*, Tom Weaver compares Lugosi, Carradine and Zucco to the Three Stooges. Yet it's remarkable to watch Bela, John and George throwing themselves (for better or worse) into their roles, and Louise—sleek, attractive, and one beautiful zombie—helps make *Voodoo Man* fun, almost in spite of itself.

Louise appeared in such films as United Artist's *Forty Thieves* (1944), a Hopalong Cassidy oater with William Boyd; Universal's *Christmas Holiday* (1944), with Deanna Durbin; and *Sensations of 1945*, with W. C. Fields (who relied on blackboard

**One suspects Katzman reveled in being caricatured in* Voodoo Man *as "S.K." (Ralph Ince), chief of Banner Pictures (the name of Katzman's production company). Come the film's fadeout, there's this exchange between S.K. and Ralph (Michael Ames, aka Tod Andrews), the screenwriter/hero, who's just submitted a script based on the film's plot:*

> S.K.: *Who do you see playin' the part of the Voodoo Man?*
>
> RALPH: *Say, why don't you get that actor...uh* [trying to remember the name] ... *Bela Lugosi? It's right up his alley!*

and cue cards for dialogue). She especially enjoyed playing a lady thief in 20th Century–Fox's *Second Chance*, and heavies in *Backlash* and *The Crimson Key* (all 1947). By the early 1950s, however, Louise and her husband, John V. Good, who himself had acted in such films as *Hitler's Madman* (MGM, 1943) and Val Lewton's *Mademoiselle Fifi* (RKO, 1944), decided the acting industry was not a good vocation for people whose major desires were a happy marriage and raising their children. Good became an architect—and Louise, who had been a decorator "just for fun" for her friends, began her own interior decoration business.

Come the late 1980s, Louise Currie still headed her very successful interior decoration business, which bore her name at 8469 Melrose Place, Hollywood. (The company recently closed after 40 years as a thriving salon.) She and her husband had long enjoyed a magnificent villa in Beverly Hills; they also owned a home in Palm Springs. (John Good recently passed away.) Certainly, Louise Currie has the distinction of having one of the most happy marriages (and enviable lifestyles) of any major or minor star of her day.

Near the close of our interview, Louise reflected on the enduring fame of the horror films—and, notably, her old colleagues Karloff and Lugosi:

> I think Karloff and Lugosi are so popular today because their roles were so much more unusual. They weren't just playing straight character parts, but something so imaginative—and the way they portrayed these parts had so much imagination. Of course, they also were very fine actors, and they took their work seriously.

She had coped gallantly and graciously with her laryngitis, going way beyond the call of duty as our interview ended. The sweet and classy quality that Louise radiated in *The Ape Man* and *Voodoo Man* clearly was a genuine part of her personality, and I expressed my fervent opinion that she was truly one of the most charming ladies to grace 1940s horror.

"I appreciate that," said Louise Currie, sincerely. "And I love hearing it, of course!"

The Films of Louise Currie

1940

Billy the Kid Outlawed (PRC, Peter Stewart, aka Sam Newfield)
Billy the Kid's Gun Justice (PRC, Peter Stewart, aka Sam Newfield)
You'll Find Out (RKO, David Butler)

1941

The Pinto Kid (Columbia, Lambert Hillyer)
Hello Sucker (Universal, Edward Cline)
Tillie the Toiler (Columbia, Sidney Salkow)
Citizen Kane (RKO, Orson Welles)
Look Who's Laughing (RKO, Allan Dwan)
Double Trouble (Monogram, William West)
Dude Cowboy (RKO, David Howard)
Bedtime Story (Columbia, Alexander Hall)

1942

Call Out the Marines (RKO, Frank Ryan and William Hamilton)
The Bashful Bachelor (RKO, Malcolm St. Clair)
Stardust on the Sage (Republic, William Morgan)

1943

The Ape Man (Monogram, William Beaudine)
Around the World (RKO, Allan Dwan)

1944

Voodoo Man (Monogram, William Beaudine)
Million Dollar Kid (Monogram, Wallace Fox)

Forty Thieves (United Artists, Lesley Selander)
Christmas Holiday (Universal, Robert Siodmak)
Sensations of 1945 (United Artists, Andrew Stone)
Practically Yours (Paramount, Mitchell Leisen)

1945

Love Letters (Paramount, William Dieterle)

1946

Gun Town (Universal, Wallace Fox)
The Bachelor's Daughters (United Artists, Andrew Stone)
Wild West (*Prairie Outlaws*) (PRC, Robert Emmet Tansey)

1947

Backlash (20th Century–Fox, Eugene Forde)
Three on a Ticket (PRC, Sam Newfield)
The Crimson Key (20th Century–Fox, Eugene Forde)
Second Chance (20th Century–Fox, James S. Tinling)
The Chinese Ring (Monogram, William Beaudine)

1948

This Is Nylon (Nylon/Apex Film Corp.)

1949

And Baby Makes Three (Columbia, Henry Levin)

1951

Queen for a Day (United Artists–Stillman—Arthur Lubin)

SHORT SUBJECTS

1941

Orchids to Charlie (Elizabeth Arden/Fine Arts Studios featurette)
The Reluctant Dragon (RKO/Disney, Alfred L. Werker, Hamilton Luske, Jim Handley, F. Beebe, Erwin Verity and Jasper Blystone)

1942

Tireman, Spare My Tires (Columbia short, Jules White)

1943

A Blitz on the Fritz (Columbia short—J. White)
His Wedding Scare (Columbia short—Del Lord)

SERIALS

1941

The Green Hornet Strikes Again (Universal serial, Ford Beebe and John Rawlins)
Adventures of Captain Marvel (aka *Return of Captain Marvel*) (Republic serial, William Witney and John English)

1943

The Masked Marvel (Republic serial—Spencer Gordon Bennet)

Peggy Moran

THE MUMMY'S HAND
WITH
DICK FORAN · PEGGY MORAN
WALLACE FORD · Cecil KELLAWAY
EDUARDO CIANNELLI · GEORGE ZUCC
TOM TYLER
A UNIVERSA
Picture
UNIVERSAL
Original Story by Griffin Jay · SCREENPLAY BY GRIFFIN JAY AND MAXWELL SHANE DIRECTED BY CHRISTY CABANNE · ASSOCIATE PRODUCER: BEN PIVAR

Universal's 1932 *The Mummy*, starring Boris Karloff and Zita Johann, is a classic melodrama, a dreamy reincarnation romance, one of Hollywood's greatest fantasy films.

Comparing *The Mummy* to Universal's later *Mummy* sequels of the 1940s is like comparing Ancient Egypt to Perth Amboy.

Yet what horror buff worthy of the name can claim they don't enjoy those crazy, wildly paced, 60-minute sequels? "Kharis" (no longer "Im-Ho-Tep," as he was in Karloff's day) was a formidable monster, first played by Tom Tyler in *The Mummy's Hand* (1940). Gaunt, stiff and ominous, "B" cowboy star Tyler was a fine Kharis—although a bit upstaged by George Zucco's "Andoheb," a wonderfully villainous Egyptian high priest. Mummy and high priest perished in the wild finale of *The Mummy's Hand*, but both were back with a vengeance in *The Mummy's Tomb* (1942).

"The fire that sought to consume Kharis," crooned an especially aged and palsied Zucco, "only seared and twisted and maimed."

To bolster the horror, Kharis returned in the seared, twisted, maimed and chubby form of Lon Chaney, Jr.—now with one good eye to guide the Mummy's one good arm and one good leg. He just kept-a-comin' in *The Mummy's Ghost* and *The Mummy's Curse* (both 1944).

There was something sadly appealing and wonderfully spooky about 3700-year-old Kharis—that one-eyed, lovelorn ragbag, stalking across Universal's back lot under a full moon, performing his weird, shuffling, melancholy dance to the rhapsodic strains of Hans J. Salter's music. What was Kharis' special charm? Perhaps it was his romanticism, as the Mummy devotedly sought to fulfill his destiny for Amon-Ra. Maybe it was his bad luck; he had the pitiful misfortune to be entrusted to a leering-eyed parade of Egyptian priests and acolytes. Zucco, Turhan Bey, John Carradine, Martin Kosleck—a rogue's gallery of Hollywood's finest heavies all betrayed Kharis in hopes of the joys of the flesh.

However, for many fans of the *Mummy* series, there was one absolute: Kharis had an incredible fetish for carrying off heroines in negligees.

Indeed, to get his hands on that silk nightie (and the gal inside it), that old Mummy stopped at nothing. He lumbered into tents. He pulled his ancient body up a trellis. He crashed a Cajun casino. He was incorrigible. Yet one could hardly blame him: The *Mummy* sequels boasted some of the most beautiful horror heroines ever to check their mascara at Universal.

There was Elyse Knox in *The Mummy's Tomb*, a wholesome blonde whose All-American beauty lured Turhan Bey from his sacred duties. Lush Ramsay Ames in *The Mummy's Ghost* had the flamboyant blessings of those white streaks blazing through her brunette tresses, growing more stark each time the Mummy crossed her path; who could blame Carradine for forsaking old Kharis in hopes of eternal life with Ramsay? And in *The Mummy's Curse*, there was Virginia Christine rising from the swamp in horrific mummy-in-mudpack, only to emerge later from a pool as a sexpot in black wig, false eyelashes and sultry stares.

However, the distinction of being the first heroine to don a negligee, tempt

***Chapter opener:* Poster art for *The Mummy's Hand*, 1940.**

Kharis and be carried off into the night by him was Peggy Moran. She was just Kharis' type: pert, vivacious, shapely. She had lovely legs (which were a bit plump, but that was the fashion in the '40s) and (perhaps her trademark) an aristocratic nose—hailed by writer Doug McClelland as "the sauciest skislide nose that side of Kay Kendall." Like her Universal colleagues Anne Gwynne, Evelyn Ankers, Anne Nagel, *et al.*, she was amazingly versatile and exhaustively overworked—cheesecake, publicity tours and 22 films in less than three years, supporting everyone from Abbott and Costello to Johnny Mack Brown to Deanna Durbin. Peggy would be spared the traumas that faced many of her compatriots. In 1942, she married Henry Koster, Universal's prized director of the enormously popular Durbin pictures. She retired (he insisted), and as Koster went on to movies like *Harvey*, *The Robe* and *The Virgin Queen*, Peggy happily raised their two sons and enjoyed her on-the-sidelines role as wife of one of Hollywood's most in-demand directors.

Today a widow, Peggy Moran is still perky, vivacious and attractive—many of the qualities that made her famous are still there to be seen. *The Mummy's Hand* haunts her constantly—and she doesn't mind a bit.

"I always wanted to be an actress," says Peggy, who was born Marie Jeanette Moran in Clinton, Iowa, on October 23, circa 1918. Her father was Earl Moran, a calendar artist and magazine illustrator whose specialty was pin-up art. (In recent years, Peggy was a guest at a memorabilia show at the Beverly Garland Hotel in North Hollywood, and saw for sale one of her father's paintings of Marilyn Monroe.) Peggy's mother was "an ex–Denishawm dancer" who gave up her career for marriage and raising Peggy and her brother, David.

The Morans moved to Hollywood. Peggy's parents divorced when she was five; Earl moved back to New York and Peggy stayed west, graduating from John Marshall High School in 1937. ("Don't count back the years—forget that part!" laughs Peggy today.) While Mrs. Moran was on jury duty, a judge noticed Peggy, told Mrs. Moran her daughter was pretty enough to be in the movies, said he knew a talent scout and, sure enough, a screen test was made at Universal.

Universal didn't sign her. Now more determined than ever, Peggy stormed Warner Bros.:

> I walked into the studio, I didn't even have an agent at the time, and I met the casting director. He said, "What can I do for you?" and I said, "I'd like to be under contract!" Well, that got the biggest laugh! He laughed so hard, and I said, "What's so funny?" He said, "You'd like to be under contract? So would thousands of other girls! But come on, I'll introduce you around." And I got a contract there!
>
> I believed in myself, implicitly, and that's what built my faith later. I became very much a believer in things. And the one thing you have to believe in is yourself. I was so innocent, I didn't know any better. And that's the best—I think you have to have your own good self-image.

The six-month contract at Warner Bros. tossed Peggy into a variety of product: *Gold Diggers of Paris* (1938), with Peggy capering as a showgirl supernumerary in the last of the Busby Berkeley Gold Digger musicals; the James Cagney/Pat O'Brien *Boy Meets Girl*; the Bette Davis/Errol Flynn *The Sisters*, both with Peggy in a bit as a telephone operator; and the short subject *Campus Cinderella*, with Peggy as a co-ed. Dropped by Warners, the freelancing Peggy got her first billing as a Southern girl in Columbia's *Girls' School* (1938), directed by John (*The Lodger*) Brahm. She won her first major role as the heroine of Republic's Gene Autry oater *Rhythm of the Saddle* (1938).

Then came *Ninotchka*. "Garbo Laughs" was the legendary ad copy for this MGM classic, co-starring Melvyn Douglas, directed by Ernst Lubitsch—and featuring, as the Commissar, a bearded Bela Lugosi.

> I remember my agent took me over to MGM, and I had to stand there with a whole line of girls. I didn't know what we were being picked out for—as it turned out, it was for the three cigarette girls. Well, the director, Ernst Lubitsch, came in, he took one glance, and he picked me first—"You" and "You" and "You!" So fast!

So Peggy was the first cigarette girl, a giggling, leggy Paris beauty—one of the many bon-bons in this confectionery, lavish romance.

> Garbo always had a standing screen; she acted behind it so that the rest of the set wouldn't be watching. You never saw her. So I only saw her when I actually had to do a scene with her, where I came through the door and faced her. That as the only time I saw her!
>
> When *Ninotchka* showed in my hometown of Clinton, Iowa (a very small town), the theater had on its marquee, "Clinton's Own Peggy Moran, with Garbo in *Ninotchka*!"

Before *Ninotchka* was released in November 1939, Peggy had won a contract at Universal. She made her debut in *Little Accident*, a Baby Sandy vehicle released October 27, 1939. She was now a Universal starlet who, like Anne Gwynne, Constance Moore and Anne Nagel, was expected to be able to do anything and everything—and look lovely while doing it:

> I did everything! Once they signed me up at Universal, I worked so hard. The pictures I made were done in two or three weeks; we'd start shooting at eight in the morning until eight at night, sometimes without dinner. I'd have a few days in between, and then they'd have me in *another* picture. I called myself always "the Queen of the Bs"!
>
> On many of these pictures, I had to do *physical* things. I had to skate backwards (try practicing skating backwards!)... I had to have mud thrown in my face ... all kinds of things. I'd come home and be so tired that my mother would have to put me on the couch and rub my back and I just cried from being so tired.

> People think working in pictures is playing. Oh boy, it wasn't! I was really worn out!

There was consolation. On *First Love* (1939), in which Deanna Durbin received her first on-screen kiss (from Robert Stack), Peggy (in a bit role) met Henry Koster—Universal's German *wunderkind* who had directed such Durbin box office smashes as *Three Smart Girls* (1936) and *100 Men and a Girl* (1937). They soon fell in love. Peggy recalls a joke that "Bobby" (as she called Koster, as did his friends) once made about her charming "ski nose":

> My future husband was a great teaser. He said, "You know, you're a beautiful girl—you look like a cross between Loretta Young and Bette Davis." (I didn't, but he said it!) "But from the profile," Henry said, "you look just like Donald Duck!"

Unfortunately for Peggy, Koster was at the time unhappily married (although planning a divorce). To try to make the situation easier, Joseph Pasternak, Universal producer of many of Koster's films (and a close friend), squired Peggy around town, to such nightclubs as the Trocadero and Ciro's. She was lovely and vivacious and—while devoted to Koster—had many sparkling evenings in Hollywood:

> Once, when I was doing a picture with the Andrews Sisters at Universal, *Argentine Nights* (1940), Deanna Durbin asked me to double-date with her and Vaughn Paul (whom she later married). Deanna said, "Would you go out with us? We have somebody from Canada, and we want you to double-date with us." I went to the Andrews Sisters and said, "Oh, Deanna Durbin wants me to go out double-dating with her tonight! What will I wear? I don't know what to put on! I don't have anything!" I didn't have time to shop, the way they worked me. And the Andrews Sisters said, "You come home with us tonight!" They took me to their apartment in Hollywood, and they dressed me all up—with furs, with shoes, with jewelry! They just had such fun dressing me up. And my date that night ... Bert Parks! We had fun that night.

Then came *The Mummy's Hand.*

> "Should Kharis obtain a large amount of the fluid, he will become an uncontrollable monster, a soulless demon with the desire to kill and kill!"
>
> —Eduardo Ciannelli (as the High Priest) in *The Mummy's Hand*

In 1940, Peggy was leading lady in Universal's two most profitable "Bs" of the year. The first was *Oh, Johnny, How You Can Love*, a comedy co-starring Tom Brown (and, in a bit role as a mechanic, Laird Cregar). The other box office winner: *The Mummy's Hand.*

There was little sense of folklore in the works as Peggy showed up at 6 A.M.

Wallace Ford (left), Peggy Moran, and Dick Foran in *The Mummy's Hand*, 1940 (courtesy Doug McClelland Collection).

each day for makeup and hairdo. As Michael Brunas, John Brunas and Tom Weaver wrote in *Universal Horrors*:

> With a budget set at a tight $80,000, *The Mummy's Hand* went before "Woody" Bredell's cameras at the end of May 1940... Rampant cost-cutting is evidenced by the film's utilization of stock shots (chiefly from *The Mummy*), hand-me-down sets (most notably the extravagant temple set left over from James Whale's *Green Hell*), a musical score lifted almost entirely from *Son of Frankenstein*, a cast boasting no horror names (fifth-billed George Zucco hadn't yet become firmly established in the genre) and a Rush! Rush! shooting schedule that left little time for aesthetic nuance.

Poetry? No. Yet somehow, a crazy, comic book–style folklore did emerge in *The Mummy's Hand* as Peggy (as Marta Solvani) joined rowdy archaeologists Dick Foran and Wallace Ford and her magician dad "The Great Solvani" (Cecil Kellaway) on a trip to the Temple of Karnak on the Hill of the Seven Jackals. Director Christy Cabanne provided breakneck pace, the Universal back lot gave a fine masquerade as

Egypt, and there was crackerjack villainy from George Zucco, as the evil Karnak priest, Andoheb. Finally, there was, of course, the Mummy—played by Tom Tyler, "B" Western star who, in 1939, had turned villain as Luke Plummer in John Ford's classic *Stagecoach*. (The stiffness Tyler played in his Jack P. Pierce makeup was tragically prophetic: He died in 1954 at age 50 of a heart attack, following years of crippling arthritis.)

Peggy's memories of *The Mummy's Hand* have their own mist of time about them. Still, she vividly remembers Foran ("very friendly"), Ford ("very funny"), Kellaway ("such a sweet fellow") and Zucco ("very nice"). And, as for Tom Tyler's Mummy:

> Because we did *The Mummy's Hand* so fast, and I was pushed from one picture to the other so quickly, I never actually met the actor Tom Tyler without his makeup on. He had to come in at four in the morning, I think, to the makeup man to get "bound up" and all that. By the time he had all that makeup on, he couldn't even talk ... so we sort of nodded to each other...
>
> So I was really kind of afraid of him, you know? He gave me an eerie feeling! You'd rehearse your lines at home, but you can't rehearse a scream—the neighbors would hear you, or something! So, I remember I didn't know what I was going to do about the scream.
>
> Well, we shot the scenes I had to do with him—I was on the back lot of Universal, with caves there, and we'd shoot those scenes at night, sometimes at midnight! It was dark, I was *really* afraid of him. And when he picked me up, and I had to look up at him, and had to scream, I had *no* problem—that I do remember!

Naturally, the sight of Peggy in her nightgown causes George Zucco's pinball eyes to light up with lechery; he forgets Kharis and offers her (and himself) the always-popular gift of eternal life. Foran and Ford save the day: Ford shoots Zucco (the high priest taking a tumble down the temple steps) and Foran burns up the Mummy. Yet the Mummy was destined to come back, as Lon Chaney, Jr., for those tana leaves and nightgowns; and even Zucco, ancient and trembling, would show up for the next two sequels.

Completed in June 1940, *The Mummy's Hand* came in at $84,000—$4,000 over budget. Released September 20, it spawned a series, and has become Peggy Moran's calling card with horror fans.

Before 1940 was out, Peggy starred in *One Night in the Tropics*, the film bow of Abbott and Costello:

> They were wonderful. Especially Lou! He was cute! Abbott was a little more distant; he was always on the phone, gambling on the horses or something. But Lou was very nice. Yeah, we had fun together.

Her final 1940 release was Universal's *Trail of the Vigilantes*, a popular comedy/western starring Franchot Tone. Peggy had dated Tone:

> There was a clip in a magazine, a picture taken in a nightclub, me dancing with Franchot Tone. One of the other couples dancing was Betty Grable, with somebody, and she's looking over, turning her head, looking at Franchot Tone, and he's looking very devotedly at me. The caption had some comment: "Betty Grable's looking at Franchot Tone, but he's too taken up with Peggy Moran." Naturally, I cut *that* one out!

Peggy's other horror film of her Universal days (and nights) was *Horror Island* (1941). Directed by George Waggner (who had just completed *Man Made Monster*, and later that year would hit bonanza with *The Wolf Man*), this 60-minute, $93,000 potboiler saw Peggy as heiress Wendy Creighton, joining a treasure hunt for a $20,000,000 fortune to a 400-year-old castle off the Florida coast. Also in on the fun: hero Dick Foran, a peg-legged Leo Carrillo and—as "Panama Pete, the Phantom"—Foy Van Dolsen, a formidable presence in his cape and slouch hat. Shot in a madcap 12 days, with Waggner sometimes working the company until midnight, *Horror Island* used sets from *Tower of London*, employed a Hans J. Salter musical score scavenged from other horror films (with the main title borrowed from Universal's 1940 Marlene Dietrich/John Wayne *Seven Sinners*)—and emerged as a slick little film nicely boasting chills and comedy.

The pace never let up. On July 25, 1941, Peggy was crowned "Queen of Aluminum" by Los Angeles Mayor Bowron—the climax to a pot-and-pan collection for national defense metal. Peggy received her aluminum crown flanked by a "mountain" of the pots and pans, musical and comedy acts and an honor guard of Boy Scouts. Also in 1941, Peggy appeared in Chicago on stage in *The Sweater Girl Revue*; she and Peter Lind Hayes acted a scene from Emlyn Williams' melodrama *Night Must Fall*.

Peggy carried on in 1941 Universal fare like *Hello, Sucker* (with Hugh Herbert) and *Flying Cadets* (with William Gargan). Nineteen forty-two saw her in such B product as *There's One Born Every Minute*, a Hugh Herbert comedy (footnoted in film history as the screen debut of Elizabeth Taylor), and *Drums of the Congo*, with Stuart Erwin and Ona Munson. Her final Universal film was a curiosity: In 1942's *The Mummy's Tomb*, Dick Foran (in old age makeup) tells the saga of *The Mummy's Hand* (with lots of clips), and refers to his late wife. We see a framed picture of Peggy—her portrait touched up to give a "mature" appearance! Shortly thereafter, Lon Chaney's Kharis shows up to slay Foran and send him off to join his "Marta."

Joe Pasternak engaged Peggy to replace an ill Ann Rutherford in Pasternak's first MGM musical, *Seven Sweethearts* (1942). On October 30, 1942, Peggy married Henry Koster—who very definitely wanted her to retire from acting.

> I married on my husband's condition: "I don't want you to work in pictures any more. I don't want all the electricians pinching you on the set!"

As it was, Peggy did do one more film: Republic's 1943 *King of the Cowboys*, with Roy Rogers and Smiley Burnette. She learned after shooting began that she was pregnant; a baby boy, Nicolas, was born in August of 1943.

Peggy says she never really missed acting—the exhaustive schedules, the publicity appearances and the cheesecake art. She has one grim story about the last:

> "Cheesecake"—oh, yes, billions of pictures. Bathing suit pictures. Whenever you had any time off from a film, you did bathing suit pictures. And during the war, I got a letter from the soldiers. There was a picture of me in a newspaper, leaning—didn't have my name or anything, just the picture. And the soldiers wrote, "We recognize that this is you. And we're sending it to you because we found this picture in the knapsack of a dead Jap." And they wrote, "I guess they have the same taste that we have." I'm so glad we won the war—I would have hated to have that Jap come over here and start looking for me!

Henry Koster continued a very impressive directorial career with such films as *The Bishop's Wife* (1948), *Harvey* (1950), *No Highway in the Sky* (1951), *The Robe* (1953), *The Virgin Queen* (1955), *Flower Drum Song* (1961) and *The Singing Nun* (1965).

> My husband said that, when I gave up my career, he'd use me in every one of his pictures. What he meant was, he had a bust made of me by sculptor Yucca Salamunich, and that appears in every picture he did. Like Hitchcock put himself in his pictures, my bust is somewhere in all of my husband's pictures! Even in *The Robe*—they changed just the hairdo!

The Kosters had a very happy marriage; when he was directing a film, she'd have lunch with him every day. Their son Nicolas (now deceased) was a San Francisco psychiatrist; their second son, Peter, is an L.A. probation officer. On September 21, 1988—after almost 46 years of marriage—Henry Koster died at the age of 83.

Today, Peggy Moran Koster lives in Camarillo, California. She's an active member of the Science of the Mind Church and attends nostalgia conventions, including FANEX 12 in 1998—where her popularity (and the popularity of her films) amazes her.

> Those "B" pictures are shown now all over the world—and the audiences don't know they're "B" pictures, necessarily. They like them—they prefer them to these very modern, sophisticated pictures. And I get fan mail from all over! I get at least several letters a week!

Kharis—wherever he is—can hardly be surprised.

The Films of Peggy Moran

1938

Gold Diggers in Paris (Warner Bros., Ray Enright)
Boy Meets Girl (Warner Bros., Lloyd Bacon)
Girls School (Columbia, John Brahm)
The Sisters (Warner Bros., Anatol Litvak)
Rhythm of the Saddle (Republic, George Sherman)

Peggy Moran Koster in the early 1980s (courtesy Doug McClelland Collection).

1939

Ninotchka (MGM, Ernst Lubitsch)
Little Accident (Universal, Charles Lamont)
First Love (Universal, Henry Koster)

1940

Oh, Johnny, How You Can Love (Universal, C. Lamont)
The Big Guy (Universal, Arthur Lubin)
Danger on Wheels (Universal, Christy Cabanne)
West of Carson City (Universal, Ray Taylor)
Alias the Deacon (Universal, C. Cabanne)
Hot Steel (Universal, C. Cabanne)
I Can't Give You Anything but Love, Baby (Universal, Albert S. Rogell)
Argentine Nights (Universal, A. S. Rogell)
The Mummy's Hand (Universal, C. Cabanne)
Strike Up the Band (MGM, Busby Berkeley)
Spring Parade (Universal, H. Koster)
Slightly Tempted (Universal, Lew Landers)
One Night in the Tropics (Universal, A. Edward Sutherland)
Trail of the Vigilantes (Universal, Allan Dwan)

1941

Horror Island (Universal, George Waggner)
Double Date (Universal, Glenn Tryon)
Hello, Sucker (Universal, Edward Cline)
Flying Cadets (Universal, Erle C. Kenton)

1942

Treat 'Em Rough (Universal, R. Taylor)
There's One Born Every Minute (Universal, Harold Young)
Drums of the Congo (Universal, C. Cabanne)
Seven Sweethearts (MGM, Frank Borzage)

1943

King of the Cowboys (Republic, Joseph Kane)

Short Subjects

1938

Campus Cinderella (Warner Bros., Noel Smith)

A picture of Peggy Moran, altered to make her look "mature," appears in Universal's 1942 *The Mummy's Tomb*. A clip in which Miss Moran was "a singing extra" in *Strike Up the Band* appears in the MGM 1974 compilation, *That's Entertainment!*

Evelyn Ankers

Halloween … the night that bonfires burn and witches fly on broomsticks and spirits run amok.

In this century's mythology, with Hollywood's Wolf Man and Mummy and Invisible Man and Dracula and Frankenstein's Monster the most celebrated of bogeymen, perhaps the most hallowed spot for All Hallow's Eve is the legendary back lot of Universal City, California.

Midnight. A full moon. High in the mountains which loom over the studio, little tendrils of mist appear. They float down, swirling about the cobbled streets of the old back lot Tyrolean village—where, over 65 years ago, the villagers marched with their torches to pursue the Monster in *Frankenstein*. And it is here, this Halloween night, that the ghosts of the cinema's most beloved nightmares gather for their revels.

In a silvery glow, the ghosts take form in the streets. The village is festooned with garland wreaths and candlelit jack o'lanterns leer atop poles as the festivities begin. The spirit of Franz Waxman leads the spectral band in the rousing march from *Bride of Frankenstein*.

The spirits applaud, respectfully. There has appeared the shade of Carl Laemmle, Sr., who founded Universal City in 1915—still tiny and wizened and smiling, a bit dazed by the Universal of today, the nation's third largest tourist attraction. In his shadow is "Junior" Laemmle, producer of the greatest horror films of all time, yet scarcely more a ghost now than he was the final 40 years of his life, when he haunted Hollywood as one of the movies' most colossal has-beens.

A warm reception greets the grim ghost of Lon Chaney, Sr., free for the night from his anonymous crypt at Forest Lawn, Glendale. Long gone is the back lot Notre Dame Cathedral, where the Man of a Thousand Faces leered from a gargoyle in 1923's *The Hunchback of Notre Dame*. However, still standing on the old "Phantom Stage" is the original Paris Opera House set of 1925's *The Phantom of the Opera*. Chaney leaves the back lot revelers to visit this historic old set.

The first bonfire goes up in flame. The revelers cheer. And there enters, dramatically, the sardonic ghost of "Jimmy" Whale, with swagger and cheroot, still playing the English aristocrat, and sporting the elegant suit he wore the day he drowned himself in his Pacific Palisades pool in 1957. Universal's bitter, homosexual "ace" director of *Frankenstein*, *The Old Dark House*, *The Invisible Man* and *Bride of Frankenstein* had penned a sad, rambling suicide note which, in a wicked irony, had paraphrased the Monster's classic curtain line in Whale's misanthropic masterpiece *Bride of Frankenstein*—"We belong dead."

The crowd is growing … Claude Rains … Dwight Frye … Jack P. Pierce. The band rips into the "Faro-La, Faro-Li" song from *Frankenstein Meets the Wolf Man*.

A new cheer arises, for here is the cadaverous ghost of Colin Clive, smoking a cigarette, and garbed in his laboratory smock from *Frankenstein* and *Bride of Frankenstein*; the hypersensitive actor, remembered by *Frankenstein* leading lady Mae Clarke as having the face of Christ, was crucified by alcohol in 1937. Perhaps tonight, Clive will reprise his classic, long lost *Frankenstein* line for the crowd: "In the name of God! Now I know what it feels like to *be* God!"

***Chapter opener:* Evelyn Ankers (courtesy Ronald V. Borst/Hollywood Movie Posters).**

Another bonfire lights. Joining hands around it is Elsa Lanchester, once again in her *Bride of Frankenstein* makeup and costume. Soon she leaves the party and hikes with friends to Universal's lake, seeking an angry, hissing swan such as the one in London's Regents Park that was her inspiration for the vainglorious Female Monster.

Edward Van Sloan ... Maria Ouspenskaya ... John Carradine...

The music and crowd grow louder. There's Lionel Atwill, Horror's cat-eyed voluptuary, chuckling, smoking and sporting the monocle, constable uniform and wooden arm he cocked to salute in *Son of Frankenstein*. He enjoys a folk dance with the spirit of Ilona Massey, just as they did at the Festival of the New Wine in *Frankenstein Meets the Wolf Man*, as revelers gossip once again of the Yuletide "orgy" Atwill allegedly hosted at his Pacific Palisades house, and which nearly destroyed his career.

Basil Rathbone ... Glenn Strange ... George Zucco...

There is a respectful (but restrained) welcome for the burly ghost of Lon Chaney, Jr., Universal's 4-F portrayer of the Wolf Man and the Monster and Count Alucard and the Mummy. He keeps a strange distance from his father, who has silently rejoined the party; instead, Lon Jr. makes a beeline for the punchbowl.

Tod Browning ... Edgar Ulmer ... Karl Freund ... and, in her filmy gown, Egyptian headdress and wig from *The Mummy*, Zita Johann...

The festivities are nearing a climax. And now, in the middle of the square, appear the hosts of this Hallow's Eve celebration—Karloff and Lugosi. "Dear Boris," in his 1931 Monster guise, with his cigarette, sly grin and a cup of punch, delights the revelers with his British humor; "Poor Bela," tall and resplendent in the Dracula cape in which he was buried, smoking his cigar, enjoying the gypsy music, emotionally wipes away a tear at the warmth of the reception.

However, there must be a Queen for the Festivities.

And she is, of course, Evelyn Ankers, Universal's blonde and beautiful "Queen of the Horrors," leading lady of *The Wolf Man*, *The Ghost of Frankenstein*, *Captive Wild Woman*, *The Mad Ghoul*, *Son of Dracula*, *Weird Woman*, *The Invisible Man's Revenge*, et al. Her lovely face is always a joy in close-up, be she registering chic fear, romantic allure or simply my-girdle-is-killing-me; she is a charming actress with modern lady sophistication, yet fairy tale princess magic...

Lon Chaney, Jr., fresh from the punchbowl, asks her for a dance. She turns him down flat.

Nevertheless, as the festivities peak, the celebrants merrily request that Evelyn signal the start of the torchlight parade, to be led by Karloff and Lugosi through the village streets, up Universal's highest hill, to light the climactic Halloween bonfire.

And Evelyn Ankers smiles, tosses back her blonde hair—and screams.

> I was under contract to Paramount Pictures, and I had a bowling team—"Dick Denning's Demons." We were having a final tournament one night at the Sunset Bowling Alley, there were 53 teams, and "Dick Denning's Demons" were way up in front. Evelyn Ankers and I had the same publicity agent, and he thought, "Gee, this is great. I'll see if I can't arrange a meeting." So he told me she was anxious to meet me, and told *her* I was

> anxious to meet *her*—when, in reality, neither one of us had even heard of the other!
>
> So I'm bowling, and there's Evie Ankers, sitting in the bleachers with her mother, and all dressed up in a tight black silk dress, and a big picture hat, and high heel shoes—anything but a bowling costume! Finally, the publicity agent came down and said, "Look, Evie's really getting upset up there. Here you've been anxious to meet her, and you haven't even come up and said hello." So I said, "You told me that she was so anxious to meet *me*—so she can sit up there for a bit until I get through with this game!"
>
> Anyway, I got through, and went up and met her, and said, "How about joining us in bowling?"—never thinking for a *minute* that she would do it, because she's all dressed up!
>
> And she said, "Oh, sure. I'd love to!"
>
> Well, she came down, in her tight black dress and big hat; she kicked off her high heels; she grabbed the ball, having never been a bowler—and she ripped her black silk dress, right up the side!
>
> But, as fate would have it—she hit a strike. And I thought, if this gal could do that, she's got something!
>
> —Richard Denning, in an interview with Gregory William Mank, June 1990

On Wednesday, January 8, 1941, Universal City signed a new actress to a seven-year contract.

In those days, Universal was a crazy circus, a rip-roaring carnival going full blast under the San Fernando Valley mountains. *The Film Daily Yearbook* clocked Universal's 1941 output at an incredible 59 feature films—along with serials, musical shorts and Walter Lantz's Woody Woodpecker cartoons. In the center ring were Universal's top attractions: soprano sensation Deanna Durbin; legendary comic W. C. Fields; and a pair of former burlesque comics about to win fame, fortune and enormous Universal clout: Abbott and Costello.

Also in the major spotlight were Marlene Dietrich (who had scored a magnificent comeback in Universal's 1939 *Destry Rides Again)* and Irene Dunne and Loretta Young, who visited Universal now and then on special contracts for reverential pampering.

And leaping back and forth from main ring "As" and sideshow "Bs" were the more serviceable, less lofty contractees: leading men Richard Arlen, Buster Crabbe, Broderick Crawford, Dick Foran, Robert Cummings, Allan Jones and Robert Stack; starlets Jane Frazee, Nan Grey, Anne Gwynne, Irene Hervey, Constance Moore, Peggy Moran, Helen Parrish and Maria Montez—whose beauty (as well as ambition and temperament) soon coronated her as Universal's Queen of Kitsch.

There were the "curiosities," like Baby Sandy and the Andrews Sisters.

And, of course, there was the Chamber of Horrors. Boris Karloff, Universal's Frankenstein Monster, was gone, shaking with stage fright, about to open on Broadway in *Arsenic and Old Lace*. However, still harmlessly relaxing in Universal bungalows were such actors as Bela Lugosi, Lionel Atwill and George Zucco. Also, the studio was picking up its option on another horror name: the son of "The Man of a

Thousand Faces," who had triumphed as the retarded Lennie in 1939's *Of Mice and Men* and had just had a Universal horror trial run in *Man Made Monster*: Lon Chaney, Jr.

Come January 8, 1941, Evelyn Ankers, of the London stage and cinema, and of Broadway, joined the Universal fold.

Less than two weeks after signing her contract, Evelyn was the featured romantic lead (opposite Richard Carlson) in Abbott and Costello's new film, *Hold That Ghost*. Evelyn played Norma Lind in her very first Hollywood film, and might easily have been upstaged by Joan Davis, the Andrews Sisters, Ted Lewis and His Orchestra and, of course, Bud and Lou, but for her beauty, poise—and the various wild screams she sounded in the course of the comedy's 86 minutes.

Hold That Ghost was a crazy set, but Evelyn was very much her own lady. So raucous were Bud and Lou in their pie fights and on-set antics that Evelyn (as she recalled) kept her back to the wall at all times.

In August of 1990, 89-year-old Arthur Lubin, director of *Hold That Ghost*, recalled Evelyn for me as he relaxed at his Hollywood Hills house:

> In those days of the movies, Evelyn Ankers had just what the moviegoers so much wanted to see—beauty, and gentleness. I did two pictures with her at Universal, *Hold That Ghost* and *Eagle Squadron* [1942]. She was a darling girl, always on time on the set—and she always looked well-groomed. Everybody loved her.

Evelyn was all-actress—and all-lady. *Hit the Road* was a vehicle for the "Little Tough Guys" Huntz Hall, Billy Halop, Gabriel Dell, *et al.* During shooting, she defied her character's name of Patience Ryan, lambasting the boys for ridiculing and defying the director, German refugee Joe May. And on the same picture, she escaped a romantic overture from Mr. Hall ("acne and all," she recalled) on the deserted set—by issuing a quick, firm knee to his groin.

By the time Richard Denning met Evelyn Ankers at the bowling tournament that night, "Evie" was fully established at Universal City. Only 23 years old, Miss Ankers already had an adventurous (and traumatic) life behind her. It was a life which Mr. Denning learned about as he courted the actress Universal would promote as "the unofficial globe-trotting champion of Hollywood."

> Evie grew up under so many difficulties as a girl. She learned to survive through grit and determination. She was born in Valparaiso, Chile, of English parents. She had a ten-year-older brother Derek, and her Dad ran off when Evie was still a child. He was a very relaxed, charming, "gay caballero"; he wound up in Spain, and had a lady friend over there, and then went to England and lived his whole life off some woman He never accepted any responsibility for raising a family, or anything else. So something Evie never really had was a father…
>
> So "Mom" had to make a living, and Evie became one of those child actresses whom the mother kept pushing and push-

> ing and pushing—Evie *never* really liked the business. Her mother was not only excited about her career, she became dependent on her career...
>
> —Richard Denning

August 17, 1918, always has been the publicized date of the birth of Evelyn Ankers. The Universal publicity mill indulged itself, issuing releases about her adventurous "mining engineer" father and her mother, "the first white woman" to venture into "savage South American jungles," where she met up with "unruly natives, hair-breadth escapes in mountain torrents and landslides." There was also some true horror for the child. As Doug McClelland reported in his piece on Evelyn Ankers in Leonard Maltin's late-lamented *Film Fan Monthly* (October 1968): "Whisked all over South America during childhood, Ankers had seen her father, a mining engineer, shot in the stomach by a worker he'd discharged. Another time, he had his horse shot under him by the henchman of a rubber magnate."

After Father deserted his family, Mrs. Ankers pinned her hopes on her beautiful daughter. At the age of ten, Evelyn made her dramatic debut: the title role in *The Daughter of Dolores*, presented on the stage in Colombia. Perhaps inspired by a "roving fortune teller, high in the Chilean Andes" (again courtesy of Universal publicity) who told little Evelyn she would "go far," Mrs. Ankers soon took off for England, with her talented daughter in tow, in hopes of attracting a major producer.

Universal made much of the fact that Evelyn ("who, by the way, pronounces it 'Ee-v-elyn'," noted a PR release) attended the Latymer School in London, as well as the Golophyn School and the Tacchomo School of Music and Dramatic Art. However, as Richard Denning says, "She didn't have a great education, scholastically," due to her mother's exhaustive traveling and career planning. Evelyn's real desire was to become a ballet dancer; in fact, she danced on the very first "live" British television show, telecast in 1934.

It was 18-year-old Evelyn's "arresting blonde beauty," however, that supposedly caught the eye of the great Alexander Korda; he signed her, and Evelyn Ankers' first film was *Belles of St. Mary's*, an MGM release of 1936, never booked in the United States. Evelyn was one of a flock of school girls. "After seeing myself in my first film, *Belles of St. Mary's* in 1936," she told Doug McClelland, "I decided I needed a *lot* more training and was accepted by the Royal Academy of Dramatic Art."

The next years were very busy ones: training at RADA; playing on the London stage with Vivien Leigh in *Bats in the Belfry*; acting in such Korda films as *Rembrandt* (1936, with Charles Laughton and Elsa Lanchester, with Evelyn as a dinner party guest). Evelyn was a socialite in *Wings of the Morning* (1937, starring Henry Fonda and Annabella, and Evelyn's first color film); lady-in-waiting to Flora Robson's Elizabeth I in *Fire Over England* (1937, with Raymond Massey, Vivien Leigh, Laurence Olivier, Leslie Banks and Robert Newton); another lady-in-waiting, this time to Marlene Dietrich in *Knight Without Armour* (1937); and a skier in *Over the Moon* (1938, with Merle Oberon, Robert Douglas and Rex Harrison). Her first lead was as Dorothy in Fox-British's 1938 *Murder in the Family*, a "quota quickie" which also featured Jessica Tandy, Roddy McDowall and Glynis Johns. Between 1936 and 1938, Evelyn appeared in 12 British films. Major celebrity almost came her way when

MGM considered her for the female lead in 1939's *Goodbye Mr. Chips*; however, red-haired Greer Garson won the role, quickly becoming *the* class act of MGM during the war years.

A film offer took Evelyn and Mother back to Buenos Aires in 1939; when it failed to come through, Evelyn headlined her own radio show, *The Evelyn Ankers Hour*—as a singer. Once again, top stardom loomed when Gabriel Pascal called Evelyn back to England for *Major Barbara*; however, the war scuttled production, and Deborah Kerr eventually won stardom in the role Evelyn was originally to play. Mother and Evelyn then decided the best bet was America, but both received a shock when, en route on a Holland-American liner, they were stopped by a Nazi submarine. After a *tête-à-tête* between the captains, the liner continued for America.

Success followed—on Broadway. On March 26, 1940, the melodrama *Ladies in Retirement* opened at Henry Miller's Theatre, starring Flora Robson. Evelyn had landed the role of the maid, Lucy Gilham, who, in her big moment, prophetically let out a wild, bloodcurdling scream which shook the theater—and the audience. "Go to see it and get the hell scared out of you!" proclaimed Walter Winchell of the *New York Daily Mirror*. *Ladies in Retirement* ran 151 performances in New York, then took off for Los Angeles. (Columbia would produce a 1941 film version starring Ida Lupino, with Evelyn Keyes in the Ankers stage role of Lucy.) During the play's L.A. engagement, Evelyn's beauty (and scream) inspired contract overtures from Universal, Warner Bros, and 20th Century–Fox. Evelyn originally accepted the Fox offer and was promptly announced for *Scotland Yard*, to star George Sanders.

Sanders had other ideas. The cynical star claimed the script was offensive to Scotland Yard (and the entire nation of England to boot); he went on suspension. John Loder replaced him, and in the confusion, Nancy Kelly replaced Evelyn. In the realm of Alice Faye, Linda Darnell and Betty Grable, Evelyn was quickly adrift.

However, Universal's offer still held. The lot needed a leading lady for Abbott and Costello's *Hold That Ghost*, and Evelyn said good-bye to Fox and hello to Universal come January 1941.

By Christmas of that year, Evelyn had found her special "niche" at Universal—one originally confining, yet one which eventually assured her of movie immortality.

> Did Evie enjoy working with Abbott and Costello? No, they kept goosing her all the time. And that didn't go over too well—she was this almost "stuffy" English girl, in one of her early films. Of course, they were difficult to work with—and then Evie met an equal to them in Lon Chaney, Jr.!
>
> As for Basil Rathbone and Nigel Bruce on the *Sherlock Holmes* picture—oh yeah, she enjoyed them. They had a great sense of humor, especially Nigel Bruce, and he could identify with Evie's English background. They had a lot of fun. One time, I came on their set, I was in the Navy (before I went into submarines) and I had my tight dress-blues on. Nigel and Evie were sitting talking, and I came over, just to say hello. Nigel, seated, turned around to me and said to Evie, "Oh, my dear girl! Your husband has the most enormous ... er ... er ... *personality* that I think I've ever seen!" (I don't think I could equal that today!)

On the set of *Hold That Ghost*, 1941, Lou Costello vies with Evelyn Ankers in revealing a glimpse of stocking.

Deanna Durbin? Yes, Evie enjoyed her. She thought Deanna was a great gal. No problems. But, see, Evie never really liked acting. Period. She didn't like the work, she didn't like to have to get up at five in the morning and all that. So it was a real strain on her. Evie was a wonderful, wonderful gal, but she had a very strong personality, and a very definite temperament—she could take just so much.

—Richard Denning

On December 9, 1941—one decade and three days after the official release of *Frankenstein,* and two days after Pearl Harbor—Universal City hosted a special press preview of *The Wolf Man*. The studio was proud of its "All-Star Horror Film," produced and directed by George Waggner, scripted by Curt Siodmak, scored by Charles Previn, Frank Skinner and Hans J. Salter, and starring Claude Rains, Warren William, Ralph Bellamy, Patric Knowles, Bela Lugosi, Maria Ouspenskaya, Evelyn Ankers and Lon Chaney.

"Previewed at the studio for a press and professional audience," reported *Motion Picture Herald,* "which displayed no enthusiasm for the enterprise."

Yet, to Universal's joy, *The Wolf Man,* which opened at New York city's Rialto Theatre on December 20, 1941, became the hit of the season. The $180,000 production reaped a $1,000,000 domestic gross, coronated Chaney, Jr., as Universal's "New Master Character Creator"—and bequeathed the studio a horror film which, over the decades, has become a major part of Universal's awesome monster mythology. Too, *The Wolf Man* gave the horror genre Evelyn Ankers. As Gwen Conliffe, fated to be the love of poor, doomed Lawrence Talbot, Evelyn sparked many moments of *The Wolf Man*:

• There is her enchanting introduction: Chaney, adjusting the giant telescope in his father's observatory, aiming it into the back lot Tyrolean town, and spying Evelyn through the window of her second story bedroom, trying on earrings and coyly posing before her mirror (more than one horror fan has wished that Chaney had adjusted his telescope about three minutes earlier)...

• There is the flirtatious first meeting of Chaney and Evelyn in Gwen's father's antique shop, as she shows him the silver wolf's head cane ... Evelyn's distinction of being the first player to recite the infamous "Even a man who is pure in heart..." ditty (believed for years to have been true German folklore, but actually concocted by Curt Siodmak, who laughs, "It's amazing how fertile one's imagination becomes when a check is attached to the job!") ... the fog-shrouded visit to the camp of Bela the gypsy (Lugosi), with Larry and Jenny Williams (Fay Helm), and its aftermath—as Larry is bitten by the wolf which has torn out Jenny's throat ... the gypsy carnival, where Chaney gives Evelyn the pentagram, and she runs off alone as a terrified gypsy warns Chaney, "There's a werewolf in camp!"...

• And of course, there's the classic climax, Chaney's Wolf Man baying in the foggy forest, the musical score blasting away; Evelyn, bravely loping in her high heels past the gnarled, horrific trees and through the epic fog, her blonde hair bouncing on her shoulders, trying to find her Larry; Maria Ouspenskaya's marvelous old Maleva warning her, "Come with me or he will find *you*!" ... the Wolf Man attacking Evelyn, bestially fondling her, snarling in her face as she screams wildly, hysterically, magnificently ... and, finally, Evelyn, in the arms of fiancé Knowles, looking past the anguished face of Rains' John Talbot, who has killed his own son with the silver-headed cane, seeing the transformed face of the Wolf Man, and gasping the film's curtain line—"Larry..."

As *The Wolf Man* filmed October 27 to November 25, 1941, Evelyn was having a fatalistic fright in real life: her association with six-foot, 220-lb., alcoholic, "sexually

HIS HIDEOUS HOWL A DIRGE OF DEATH!
Not a 'Thing'...but a mortal man—a living horror...with its unearthly body a twitching tomb of strange desires!
The WOLF MAN
with
CLAUDE RAINS
WARREN WILLIAM
RALPH BELLAMY
PATRIC KNOWLES
BELA LUGOSI
MARIA OUSPENSKAYA
EVELYN ANKERS
and the new master character creator
LON CHANEY
as "The Wolf Man"

Poster art for *The Wolf Man*, 1941.

confused" (so says Curt Siodmak) and (by most accounts) violently disturbed Lon Chaney, Jr. The meeting was hardly auspicious.

Evelyn wrote the foreword ("The B and I") for her friend Doug McClelland's 1978 book *The Golden Age of "B" Movies*. There she recorded her first meeting with the redoubtable Chaney on *The Wolf Man*—and his first words to her.

"So you're the gal who swiped my dressing room," growled Chaney. "You took it away from Broderick Crawford and me—I think that was a hell of a thing to do!"

Evelyn, concerned, asked the front office about the "plush, new dressing room" just awarded her, which she shared with Anne Gwynne—and learned why she had inherited it:

> Someone told me that every Friday or Saturday night, Lon and Brod Crawford would take bottles into their dressing room, get loaded, and then somehow manage to hang the furniture from the ceiling and brawl... The cleaning crew was treated to a sight resembling a World War II battlefield.

The boisterous Chaney, arriving on-stage in full Wolf Man regalia (courtesy, of course, of makeup genius Jack P. Pierce), loved creeping up behind Evelyn, tapping her on the shoulder and—when she turned around—baring fangs and grabbing her. ("He had to hold me, or I would have ended up in the rafters!")

Yet Chaney wasn't the only trial of *The Wolf Man*. The fog machine (one of the

Ankers reads the palm of a Spanish gypsy extra between scenes of *The Wolf Man*, 1941. The original caption on this publicity photo claimed that Ankers served as an interpreter for the Spanish-speaking extras on the set.

true stars of the picture) was so strong in its wafting chemicals that Evelyn, while filming the climax in the forest, passed out cold on the "forest" floor—and nobody noticed! "It would have been a short career," Evelyn wrote, "if they hadn't tripped over me at last."

However, Evelyn's real menace on *The Wolf Man* was not Chaney, nor the fog machine. It was a 600-pound bear, held on a chain by a gypsy (Kurt Katch) in the carnival episode, originally featured in the uncut print fighting a human-form Larry Talbot. As Evelyn wrote in McClelland's *The Golden Age of "B" Movies*:

> The bear ... decided that he wanted to know me better. I was unaware of what was happening behind me. The next thing I knew, Lon took off, as did everybody else. I turned, wondering what the commotion was all about and where my leading man had gone, and saw the bear coming after me!
>
> I never ran so fast in all my life. With the bear coming close behind me, I shot up a ladder into the rafters, where an electrician

> grabbed my hand and pulled me on top his platform. He then blinded the bear with a hot floodlight. The trainer finally caught up with the animal, retrieved his chain, reprimanded him, and gradually got him back down onto the stage. After I scrambled down myself (it was much harder going down, believe me), they told me I had *flown* up!

(Universal, of course, had its revenge on the ebullient bear, cutting him entirely from the release print of *The Wolf Man.*)

All in all, *The Wolf Man* was a melodrama off-screen for Evelyn too. "When it was over," she wrote, "I was relieved and happy that the gray hairs didn't show among the blonde."

"Evelyn Ankers is a lovely, intelligent heroine," noted *The Hollywood Reporter* in reviewing *The Wolf Man.* Yet no one fully realized then just how dynamically Evelyn was filling out the cycle of Universal horror heroines. The "leading ladies" had been a fascinating lot, a striking, sometimes kinky parade of beauties and talents, often almost as eccentric as the horror shows themselves.

And now came Evelyn Ankers. She took the Universal heroine into a new, real realm—while retaining a touch of the Never-Never Land quality of Helen Chandler from *Dracula,* the poetics of Zita Johann from *The Mummy* and the magic of Valerie Hobson in *Bride of Frankenstein.* She was beautiful, stunning in her Vera West wardrobes, her '40's glamour style (did *any* actress ever wear hats so charmingly?) and low-key performances perfectly suited to the new, rapid pace of Universal's war years horror movies. Of course, in one wonderful aspect, Evelyn was far more flamboyant than her predecessors: None of the Universal ladies of the celebrated '30s could match Evelyn's lush, classic, full-throated scream.

A few historians have expressed regret that Evelyn wasn't around to grace the horrors of the epic 1930s. Truly, however, it was the 1940s which best suited her—and most needed her. She gave sparks of both class and sex appeal to Lon Chaney (especially in *The Wolf Man*), immeasurably aiding an actor whose great forte was a bovine sincerity.

And after all—can one imagine arch, cheroot-smoking "Jimmy" Whale directing headstrong, no-nonsense Evelyn as he did Valerie Hobson in *Bride of Frankenstein*—and ordering her to wear no underwear under her costume?

> We eloped to Las Vegas—September 6, 1942. We celebrated monthly anniversaries. Gosh, until we were married about 25 years, we still exchanged monthly anniversary cards...
>
> Less than three weeks after we were married, I enlisted in the Navy, eventually winding up in submarines for three years. And then Evie had to work to support her mother, and me, because my service salary wasn't commensurate with what I was getting in the picture business...
>
> —Richard Denning

Even before *The Wolf Man* premiered, Evelyn was at work on *The Ghost of Frankenstein,* which began shooting at Universal just days after Pearl Harbor, through the 1941 Christmas and 1942 New Year holidays—and just after Richard Denning had discussed marriage with her. (When Denning first met Evelyn, she was engaged to actor Glenn Ford.)

In *The Ghost of Frankenstein*, Evelyn played Elsa Frankenstein, daughter of Ludwig (Sir Cedric Hardwicke); her place in Universal's Frankenstein genealogy would have made her granddaughter to Colin Clive and Mae Clarke/Valerie Hobson, niece to Basil Rathbone and Josephine Hutchinson, cousin to Donnie Dunagan. She was at her most beautiful in this fourth of the studio's Monster sagas, which features one of Evelyn's most memorable vignettes: Sitting in Ludwig's study on a stormy night, studying Henry Frankenstein's records of Life and Death, she sees a monstrous shadow on the wall, turns to see Chaney's Monster and Lugosi's Ygor spying at the rain-slashed window—and screams.

Chaney, as the Monster, was no more charming to work with than before; almost frightening in its realism is the scene where Chaney uses Evelyn as an evening-gowned battering ram against a locked laboratory door. By now, Lon was lamenting that lugging the statuesque Evelyn about in monstrous poses was too strenuous, and demanded the studio create a special strap to tie her to him, reducing his strain in lifting her—hence the creation of Universal's "Evelyn Ankers Strap." Add this to Chaney's constant whining about the makeup, and one can understand why Jack P. Pierce (according to Chaney) used to stick his makeup pencil in his eye and mouth.

Released Friday, March 13, 1942, *The Ghost of Frankenstein* boasted a splendid cast: Hardwicke, Lugosi, Ralph Bellamy, Lionel Atwill, even Universal's Frankenstein lucky charm Dwight Frye in a bit role as a villager. Evelyn did a promotional tour for *Ghost*, and later recalled, with embarrassment, discussing Hollywood and life with "a charming, cultivated man, quiet-mannered and a little shy." Only afterwards did Evelyn learn she had been talking with Bela Lugosi—who was so brilliant as bearded, broken-necked old Ygor that Evelyn hadn't even recognized him! (Ilona Massey would inherit Evelyn's role of Elsa in 1943's *Frankenstein Meets The Wolf Man*.)

Life went on at Universal: publicity interviews ... "cheesecake" photos ... and, of course, one movie assignment after another, with barely time to shop for new hats, or escape to the Racquet Club in Palm Springs.

Evelyn's best role of 1942 was as Kitty, the self-sacrificing Limehouse gal of *Sherlock Holmes and the Voice of Terror*. It was a dramatic showcase for Evelyn, festooned with a Cockney accent, a stirring patriotic speech to the bar denizens, and a great death scene at the treacherous hands of "Nazi" Thomas Gomez (shot on the old *Dracula* set). She had great fun working with Basil Rathbone and Nigel Bruce, the latter flirting with her outrageously at every opportunity.

It was in the course of 1942 that Evelyn received the only loan-out of her Universal sojourn, and it hardly was auspicious. MGM borrowed her for a seventh-billed performance as Celia Wellsby, daughter of card-cheat Henry Travers in *Pierre of the Plains*, a North Woods actioner starring John Carroll and Ruth Hussey.

Also in 1942—on Sunday, September 6, in Las Vegas—Evelyn became Mrs. Richard Denning. Her blonde, athletic husband, born Louis Albert Denninger in Poughkeepsie, New York, had signed with Paramount in 1936, playing small parts in

Ankers atop the globe (Universal Studios' symbol) on the set of *The Ghost of Frankenstein*, 1942.

such De Mille epics as *The Buccaneer* (1938), *Union Pacific* (1939) and *North West Mounted Police* (1940), supporting Betty Grable in *Million Dollar Legs* (1939), scoring on loanout to Columbia in *Adam Had Four Sons* (1941) and winning true stardom as Dorothy Lamour's saronged love in Paramount's Technicolor *Beyond the Blue Horizon* (1942). "The fan mail was coming in," chuckles Denning today, "and everything was hotter than a pistol!" The war changed all that as Denning entered the Navy. Evelyn

The Ghost of Frankenstein, **1942: Ankers, Sir Cedric Hardwicke, Lon Chaney, Janet Ann Gallow.**

now faced the responsibility of not only absorbing the financial shock of Denning's lost Paramount pay, but—as ever—the full support of her mother. "Her mother didn't want Evie to get married," says Denning, "because, to put it bluntly, she thought this might be the end of her meal ticket."

Nineteen forty-three. Eight Universal feature credits for Evelyn Ankers. *All by Myself* was one of Evelyn's favorites, a slick comedy in which Evelyn, as Jean Wells, blackmails Patric Knowles into posing as her fiancé. Rosemary Lane top-lined the billing, and Felix Feist directed. Evelyn later picked Feist as her favorite director: He had read-throughs of the script before shooting, gave plenty of rehearsal time, and developed a rapport among the players.

In June of 1943, Universal released the infamous *Captive Wild Woman*, first of the Paula the Ape Woman sagas. John Carradine leered his first starring role as Dr. Sigmund Walters, transforming a gorilla into Acquanetta—who reverts to ape when sexually jealous. In this most lurid of Universal melodramas, Evelyn was star-billed as Beth Colman, girlfriend of circus lion-tamer Milburn Stone (cast reportedly because he resembled famed Clyde Beatty in the cat-taming scenes so generously lifted from Universal's 1933 *The Big Cage*). *Captive Wild Woman* is a wild 60 minutes, packed

Ankers does publicity "leg art" for *Sherlock Holmes and the Voice of Terror*, 1942 (Photofest).

with guilty pleasures for this writer: Evelyn (who never looked lovelier in gorgeous hat and hip-hugging suit), archly flirting with Stone as soon as he's back from the jungle; the rococo Carradine, his slouch hat rakishly cocked, parading about the circus grounds, showing off his left profile like a mad Shakespearean; the unintentionally funny scene of the diminutive Stone, in a moment of triumph, picking up and twirling his considerably taller leading lady; and the classic horror vignette with a kinky twist: Evelyn, tossing in her bed at night, awakens to find in her boudoir not a male monster—but a female beast!

Still, *Captive Wild Woman* is one of my favorite Evelyn Ankers shows—primarily for the climax. Carradine traps Evelyn (who's sporting a lovely bonnet and Vera West wardrobe) in his laboratory, smirking about using her glands as Cheela the Ape (Ray "Crash" Corrigan in his ape suit) freaks out in her (his) cage. In closeup, a sly, wicked little hint of a smile flickers on Evelyn's face, and she unleashes the rampaging gorilla on Carradine—thereby avenging what he's done to poor Acquanetta's sexual promise.

In November 1943, Universal released *Son of Dracula*, directed with morbid élan by Robert Siodmak (brother of Curt, who worked on the script until Robert fired him and brought in Eric Taylor). This time, the studio's lovely blonde Louise Allbritton (in a black wig) had the top femme spot as Southern belle Katherine Caldwell, two-timing Chaney's pudgy Count "Alucard" to gain immortality for her and her lover (Robert Paige). Evelyn had a light assignment as her sister Claire, who shares none of Katherine's evil fascinations; she doesn't even scream in the picture. Nor did *Son of Dracula* give Evelyn screen time with her old *vis-à-vis* Chaney, who performed one of his more famous atrocities on the set (i.e., creeping up behind Robert Siodmak and smashing a vase over his bald head).

It was about this time that Evelyn, who so long had suffered the Chaney indelicacies, got a bit of revenge on him—through her husband. Universal hosted a dinner to show off its Grand Guignol attractions, and Seaman Denning, who would soon to ship out on submarines, joined his wife there. As fate decreed, Evelyn, Richard and Chaney all found themselves at the same table. Denning remembers the meal very well:

> Well, I was home, on leave from the Navy, and I had my beautiful dress blues on, which I never wore except on very special occasions! At this point, I was still with Naval Officer Procurement in downtown Los Angeles. So Chaney made some crack [*Denning performs an excellent imitation of a slurred-voice, in-his-cups Chaney*]: "Of course, you're wearing the uniform, which looks *beautiful*—but you're not at sea, or doing anything to win the war!"
>
> I said, "Well, I wouldn't say that. I do what my superior officers assign me to do, and that is, right now, recruiting WAVEs so that men can be released to go to sea. And I figure that's better than just not being in the service, and making a good living as an actor, and letting your career be furthered while those of us who have to go into the service, or chose to go into the service, allow you guys to go on in pictures."
>
> So Chaney gave me a dirty look and said, "Oh, well, that's not a very nice attitude to have. I *can't* make the service." And I said, "Well that's your problem, not mine." And the thing kept escalating...
>
> Finally Chaney said, "Aw, drop dead"—and threw some of his food on my nice, new, tailor-made uniform! And that flipped me off. We were having dessert, ice cream, and I picked up my ice cream and I just splatted it right in his face—just shoved it in his face! Of course, that did it! He got up, and I got up, and we

> were going to really go for it! And Evie screamed, and they calmed us down. And I never saw him again!

Evelyn's final shocker of 1943 was *The Mad Ghoul*, which surrounded her with George Zucco (superb as the mad doctor who lusts after her), David Bruce (in the withered, heart-seeking title spot) and Turhan Bey (as her fiancé). The climax found Evelyn on the old "Phantom Stage," lip-synching to a Lillian Cornell record (Universal had betrayed its promise that Evelyn could perform her own singing, even after she had rehearsed for weeks), but naturally performing her own scream as Bruce's Ghoul staggered out of the wings. In her Introduction to *The Golden Age of "B" Movies*, Evelyn expressed what a "pleasure" it was to work on *The Mad Ghoul* with Zucco, Bruce and Milburn Stone (her lion-taming boyfriend in *Captive Wild Woman*, here playing a detective). "All three were great troupers and, best of all, they were gentlemen, quite a unique characteristic in Hollywood in those days."

On September 20, 1943, Universal City released this PR release:

> With three years of intensive training behind her, Evelyn Ankers, blonde Universal actress, is now stepping into the "big time." During the past year, studio executives have handed Evelyn roles of steadily increasing importance, among them the part of the "other woman" in Deanna Durbin's *His Butler's Sister*...
>
> In addition to acting and dancing, Miss Ankers has a fine soprano voice, plays the piano, accordion and banjo. She rides exceptionally well, is a fine tennis player, skis, bowls, skates and fences. Her pet indoor hobby is collecting souvenirs, her favorite being a charm bracelet which she started with a 50-year-old gold hunchback charm given to her by her grandmother.

However, Universal City would not make good on its promise to promote Evelyn into the "big time." Before 1944 was over, Evelyn would have left the Universal lot forever.

Evelyn Ankers' final year at Universal was, perhaps, her most versatile; still, it was also perhaps her most frustrating, and one that ultimately embittered her against Hollywood.

Evelyn's first release was *Ladies Courageous*, Walter Wanger's salute to the Women's Auxiliary Ferrying Squadron, "officially" sanctioned by the U.S. Army Air Force. Loretta Young, Geraldine Fitzgerald and Diana Barrymore all had the sparky roles; Evelyn was Wilhelmina Van Kronk, a Teutonic WAF. The role was of little worth, but the film was pivotal in Evelyn's career; MGM had wanted her for the plum part of slatternly maid Nancy, in support to Ingrid Bergman and Charles Boyer, in *Gaslight*, based on Patrick Hamilton's hit play *Angel Street*. Universal declined to "loan out" Evelyn, forcing her into *Ladies Courageous*, so MGM allowed a newcomer named Angela Lansbury to play the role—and win an Oscar nomination.

Then came *Weird Woman*, best of Universal's *Inner Sanctum*s, with Evelyn in one of her flashiest roles: Ilona Carr, Other-Woman-from-Hell, out to destroy the superstitious bride (Anne Gwynne) of her old flame (Lon Chaney, hilariously miscast as a

Richard Denning, in his navy uniform, visits wife Evelyn Ankers on the set of *His Butler's Sister*, 1943.

brilliant college professor/author). Based on Fritz Leiber's *Conjure Wife*, directed by Reginald LeBorg, *Weird Woman* saw Evelyn throwing herself at the married Chaney, dispatching a lovesick co-ed (Lois Collier) to create a scandal with him, sending off the co-ed's madly jealous boyfriend (Phil Brown) to attack Chaney (the boyfriend gets shot instead), driving poor old Ralph Morgan to suicide, and attempting to drive Gwynne mad with voodoo chant phone calls. But the tables are turned, and the wicked Evelyn goes hysterical, wakes up screaming, jumps out a bedroom window in her high heels and runs across the top of an arbor, falls—and hangs herself on a vine.

Elizabeth Russell, the infamous "Cat Woman" of RKO's *Cat People*, was a heavy in *Weird Woman*—and warmly remembers Evelyn. "As for Evelyn Ankers, she was beautiful and (I think) the real star of the film..."

Follow the Boys found Evelyn (along with most of Universal's contract players, including Chaney) as "The Hollywood Victory Committee"; meanwhile, off-screen, she was busy at the Hollywood Canteen and the USO. *Pardon My Rhythm* was a Gloria Jean comedy, directed by Felix Feist, with Evelyn as Patric Knowles' jealous fiancée; the *New York Times* noted it in Evelyn's obituary as her favorite film.

It was back to horror in *The Invisible Man's Revenge*, starring Jon Hall; Evelyn was Julie, daughter of the English couple (Gale Sondergaard and Lester Matthews) whom Invisible Man Hall believed cheated him. The real stars of this one were the John P. Fulton special effects, John Carradine as mad Dr. Drury of Thrustlewood, and

Ankers with George Zucco in *The Mad Ghoul*, 1943.

Ankers swoons in the clutches of David Bruce in a publicity photo for *The Mad Ghoul*, 1943.

his invisible dog, Brutus. By this time, Evelyn's weekly Universal salary had hit $700 (Chaney was earning $2000 weekly).

The infamous *Jungle Woman* followed—sequel to *Captive Wild Woman*, and a popular choice as Universal's all-time worst horror film. Acquanetta spoke lines, J. Carrol Naish got bogged in the mess and actually gave a rank performance, director

Reginald LeBorg did what he could, and *PM* slammed the film as "an out-and-out steal on unsuspecting moviegoers, being mainly old footage ... from *Captive Wild Woman* with a few new inserts added." Aside from the finale scene in a morgue, with the cast huddled around Paula's hirsute cadaver, Evelyn (reprising her role of Beth) sat through this 60-minute opus in an interrogation room, in a perfectly lovely sombrero bonnet, her legs crossed, understandably looking as if she wished she could escape the set and her girdle and go splash in a pool.

Much more felicitous was *The Pearl of Death*, a tip-top *Sherlock Holmes* thriller, with one of Evelyn's most delicious performances: villainess Naomi Drake, mistress of disguise (a Cockney dishwasher, a poor little match girl and a bespectacled clerk) and uneasy heartthrob of the Creeper (Rondo Hatton). Widely applauded as one of the very best of the Rathbone-Bruce series, it was a showcase for Evelyn, as she wickedly sashayed through the melodrama, out to snare the Borgia Pearl.

All the while, Universal gave no rest to Evelyn. At one point, the actress found herself named "Rodeo Queen" of a Western Cattleman's association, and the studio dispatched her to a stockyard of sheep and calves to sit atop a boxcar—and pose in a cowgirl suit!

Meanwhile, Evelyn was keeping a secret from the Universal hierarchy: She was pregnant. Rightly suspecting they would drop her contract if they knew the truth, Evelyn blamed her growing weight on "female problems"—only to find herself cast as stripper Bonnie Latour, oomphing "Just Because You Made Those Goo-Goo Eyes at Me" in *Bowery to Broadway*, starring Susanna Foster. In the midst of Evelyn's 1890s striptease burlesque bumps, the baby kicked—and the "stripper" gasped.

There would be one more Universal show before the studio learned the truth, and, indeed, terminated the contract: *The Frozen Ghost*, an awful "Inner Sanctum" potboiler with Evelyn as girlfriend of Chaney's hypnotist, "Gregor the Great." The movie's main attraction is noting how Vera West helped Evelyn conceal her delicate condition. Shot early in the summer of 1944, the 12-day production would not be released until the summer of 1945—and prove a decidedly non-glorious Universal swan song for Evelyn Ankers.

Evelyn settled in Malibu to await the birth of the baby; in Octoberof 1944, Diana Dee Denning was born. No longer in the Universal fold, Evelyn had to support her baby daughter, her mother and her overseas husband. The ensuing years would be tough ones: Evelyn visited Republic to star in *Fatal Witness* (1945); cavorted at PRC in the title role of *Queen of Burlesque* (1946); and returned to Republic to co-star with Albert Dekker in *The French Key* (1946), as a nightclub chanteuse.

Meanwhile, Richard Denning returned home from the war and saw his daughter for the very first time. Both Richard and Evelyn managed to land parts in 20th Century–Fox's juvenile-targeted *Black Beauty*, shot late in 1945 and released in the summer of 1946; in the beloved horse story, Evelyn lost her real-life husband to Mona Freeman. (On the same picture, a fire scene flamed out of control, singeing Richard's hair and blistering his ears.)

However, all the heat that had been sparked back in 1942 via Denning's *Beyond the Blue Horizon* had been extinguished during War Years. The Denning family moved into a house trailer in Paradise Cove. Richard worked as a lobster fisherman.

In August of 1946, weeks after *Black Beauty*'s release, Evelyn became a U.S. citizen. Denning and Anne Gwynne accompanied her to the "swearing in" ceremony.

Soon Denning's career picked up; he played in such features as Paramount's *Seven Were Saved* (1947) and Film Classics' Cinecolor *Unknown Island* (1948), in which the leading man discovered dinosaurs (actually "animated" by men sporting prehistoric suits). Denning also replaced Lee Bowman opposite Lucille Ball on CBS radio's *My Favorite Husband* (which had premiered July 5, 1948). Evelyn kept working too, safeguarding the family's security with paychecks for such fare as Republic's *Spoilers of the North*, a saga of salmon fishing, starring Paul Kelly.

However, as a concerned wife and mother, Evelyn's patience with Hollywood was wearing very thin. It would take Sam Katzman, the infamous low-budget producer of Lugosi's Monogram horrors, to detonate the explosion which ultimately lowered the curtain forever on Evelyn Ankers' career.

> Evie was doing a picture, *Last of the Redmen*, for Sam Katzman and Columbia, with Jon Hall. They were up in the mountains on location, and they were hot and dusty and thirsty and tired and everything that goes on with location work. Sam Katzman was known for his "economical" productions!
>
> Anyway, Evie got to the end of her tether, which was not unusual for Evie. They kept looking around for Sam Katzman and his nephew Lenny and they couldn't be found. The word came, "They had to go down the hill—business..." So Evie's sitting there waiting, and Sam and Lenny come up—and they're eating ice cream sundaes! And Evie's hungry, and it's before lunch. She says, "I'm sure the rest of us would like some of that." And Lenny said, "Well, we just got it for ourselves; we're going to break for lunch pretty soon." And that set Evie off. She really let it all hang out. She called them some very unfavorable names, and it was a real stand-off!
>
> Well, I'm sure what happened was, whenever anybody referred to Sam or Lenny about Evie's performance and attitude on that picture, it was totally negative. And that didn't bother her one little bit, because she already had had it in the business. But by this time, my career was getting started again, so Evie thought, "Oh well—who needs it?"
>
> —Richard Denning

Whatever the blackballing power of Sam Katzman, Evelyn was soon oblivious to it. She finished off 1947 with a showy role in Columbia's *The Lone Wolf in London* as a musical comedy star/thief/murderess. For Eagle-Lion, Evelyn was a nightclub operator in 1949's *Parole, Inc.*, flanked by Michael O'Shea and a soon-to-be-bald Turhan Bey.

Then came one of her best roles: Gloria James, the English aviatrix ("nicely played by Evelyn Ankers," noted the *New York Times*), seeking a hidden valley where, for 20 years, she had imbibed from a magical fountain of youth in RKO's 1949 *Tarzan's Magic Fountain*. Lex Barker was the ape man, Brenda Joyce was Jane and Albert Dekker and Charles Drake played villains out to snare Evelyn's elixir. Blonde

Evelyn went "dark brown" in this melodrama, to heighten the effectiveness when her Gloria went *Lost Horizon* and became old and gray.

The grand feature finale: Columbia's inept 1950 *The Texan Meets Calamity Jane*, with Evelyn as the latter—a sadly ignominious ending to a sometimes impressive feature film career.

Evelyn was fed up with Hollywood; what she most dearly wanted was to be a good wife and mother. Fortunately, Richard Denning's career allowed Evelyn to stick to her guns.* He co-starred with Barbara Britton as TV's crime-solving *Mr. and Mrs. North* (CBS, 1952–1953; NBC, 1954), with Evelyn guesting on the show a couple times; worked throughout the 1950s in many films, including such science fiction fare as Universal-International's *Creature from the Black Lagoon* (1954), Allied Artists' *Target Earth* (1954), Columbia's *Creature with the Atom Brain* (1955, written by Curt Siodmak), AIP's *Day the World Ended* (1956, directed by Roger Corman), and Warner Bros.' *The Black Scorpion* (1957); he also had a major role in 20th Century–Fox's "DeLuxe Color and CinemaScope" *An Affair to Remember*. Denning took Evelyn and daughter Dee with him to England as he starred as television's *The Flying Doctor* (syndicated, 1959).

Evelyn had done a bit of television throughout the 1950s: "Sam and the Whale," with Cecil Kellaway, on *Cavalcade of America* (ABC, 9/29/53); *General Electric Theatre* (CBS, 1953); *Screen Director's Playhouse* (NBC, 1955); *20th Century–Fox Hour* (CBS, 1956); and, her reported last, *Cheyenne* (ABC, 1/28/58). Meanwhile, her greatest and most demanding fan, her mother, had died in Hollywood in 1954.

The Dennings were faithful members of the Beverly Hills Lutheran Church, and after the England adventure on *The Flying Doctor*, Evelyn performed her last acting, in a Lutheran-sponsored featurette: *No Greater Love* (1960), with the former "Queen of Horrors" as a converted nurse. Denning's steady employment on TV (as *Michael Shayne, Private Detective*, NBC, 1960–1961; the "Karen" segment on *Ninety Bristol Court*, NBC, 10/64–1/65, and its spin-off, *Karen*, 1/65–9/65) and the movies (United Artists' *Twice-Told Tales*, starring Vincent Price, 1963) soon allowed the family to enjoy homes in both Corona del Mar, California, and Maui, Hawaii. Having long ago paid her dues, Evelyn had the right to be outspoken on Hollywood—and she was. In Doug McClelland's 1968 *Film Fan Monthly* profile, Evelyn recalled Universal ("It was always nerve-wracking and a tremendous effort for me"), claimed she was happy it was all behind her, vowed never to act again—and harpooned Hollywood in general:

> As far as the picture business, as a whole, is concerned, both my husband and I feel it has completely gone to "pot"—in more ways than one. He and I—Dick especially—have both turned down scripts for movies and plays because we felt they had been written under the influence of LSD. Maybe we are squares, but we also can't stand the filth and perversion they are now show-

**The March 28, 1950,* Hollywood Reporter *noted that Evelyn had won the leading female role in the new TV series* Ding Howe and the Flying Tigers, *which was to star Richard Denning; the series never came to pass.*

> ing as "entertainment." Consequently, we just don't go to the movies any more, and that's also one of the main reasons we want to move over to Hawaii permanently, to get away from it all, to live a life more like we think God intended us to live: quiet, clean, healthy, but most of all peaceful—away from the man-made rat race!

As such, it was a dream-come-true when Denning won the part of the Governor (originally offered to Lew Ayres) on CBS's *Hawaii Five-O*, shot, of course, in Hawaii. The show premiered September 26, 1968, and would run for 12 seasons, finally winding down in 1980 and beginning a whole new life in reruns. The *Hawaii Five-O* producers offered Evelyn the role of the governor's wife; she would have no part of it.

Evelyn delighted in the beauty of Hawaii. The Dennings' daughter, Dee, a graduate of San Diego State College (and harboring no interest at all in show business), eventually settled in Hawaii too, and delighted Evelyn and Dick with two granddaughters. Evelyn, who had seen so much temperament, indulgence and heartbreak in her Hollywood years, felt enormously blessed. So many of her Universal colleagues had faced tragic endings in their personal lives; her legendary leading man, Lon Chaney, his voice nearly destroyed by throat cancer, his body sadly bloated, had shambled miserably through his final movies, confessing a terrible fear of becoming a "has-been" before his death in 1973. Evelyn had won a happy ending seemingly worthy of a melodrama heroine.

"Apparently the good Lord had other plans for me," Evelyn officially eulogized her career in *The Golden Age of B Movies*, "and knew that eventually I'd be much happier away from it all on our beautiful Maui."

> Evie's illness lasted over two years. It started with internal cancer. She went all through the chemotherapy ... just horrible. Near the end, Evie said, "I just want to go up to our country place in Haiku and be out there alone with you and wait until the Good Lord calls me."
>
> So we were there, in the country in Haiku, from May until the end. We both prayed that the Lord would take her and relieve her, because I was giving her shots every half-hour for the pain, and it was horrible. She got down to about 97 pounds. So weak, you know. Yet, I think the greatest time of our marriage was those last three months. We were alone, at our country place; we had plenty of time to think about the 43 years of being together: the good, the bad, the prosperous, the not-so-prosperous, the things we had gone through together. And we felt closer, I think, in those last months than we did even on our honeymoon. This is a feeling you only get after sharing your life, your joys, your problems, everything, together...
>
> —Richard Denning

August 1985. Near the end, Dee joined her father with her dying mother; "It was wonderful for Evie and for Dee-Dee," says Denning.

The end finally came August 29, 1985. Evelyn Ankers was buried at the Makawao Veterans Cemetery on her beloved Maui. The cinema colony, remembering her considerable talent, perhaps envying her lifestyle and happiness, mourned.

And the world of horror, fantasy and science fiction eulogized her as "Queen of the Horror Films."

Richard Denning is today happily remarried, with six stepchildren, and divides his time between Hawaii and California. He's very proud of his daughter Dee: "She's just a wonderful wife, mother and everything else. I dearly love her." Denning is also proud that Dee is planning to write a full-scale biography of Evelyn Ankers.

> Evie and I were very blessed. We were both active in the church, and to this day, my God and my Savior are the most important things in my life. I always feel I have the help of a supernatural power, and a couple of angels thrown in for good measure. Evie and I always had God as our unseen partner. And that was probably our greatest help.

When so many of us began watching *Shock Theatre* as children, perhaps we loved Evelyn Ankers because she looked like the beautiful princesses in the fairy tale books we slowly were outgrowing. As we grew older, we admired her loveliness, and thrilled time and again to the sensation of her scream; and, as the old Universal melodramas became lifelong friends to so many of us, we fully perceived her talent, her versatility and the true magic she gave to *The Wolf Man*, *The Ghost of Frankenstein*, even *Captive Wild Woman*.

Perhaps, too, some of us sensed the depth and character that sparked her best performances, and that ironically led Evelyn to forsake Hollywood, avoid the tragic finales of so many of her contemporaries and live the life that she believed "God intended" her to live.

Still, today, over a decade after her death, more than half-a-century after her best movies were made, Evelyn Ankers' legacy to horror and fantasy shines more brightly than ever.

And, after All Hallow's Eve at Universal City, after the beloved ghosts have dispersed into the realm of videocassettes and late show revivals, there will always echo, over the old Universal sound stages and high into the mountains, "I never drink—wine" ... "It's alive!"...

And Evelyn Ankers' scream.

Richard Denning died in October 1998 as this book went to press.

The Films of Evelyn Ankers

1936

Belles of St. Mary's (MGM, James Fitzpatrick)

Rembrandt (London–United Artists, Alexander Korda)

Land Without Music (aka *Forbidden Music*) (Capitol-General, Walter Forde)

1937

Wings of the Morning (Fox-British, Harold Schuster)

Fire Over England (London–United Artists, William K. Howard)

Knight Without Armour (London–United Artists, Jacques Feyder)

Over the Moon (London–United Artists, Thornton Freeland)

1938

Murder in the Family (Fox-British, Al Parker)
The Villiers Diamond (Fox-British, Bernard Mainwaring)
The Claydon Treasure Mystery (Fox-British, Manning Haynes)
Second Thoughts (aka *Crime of Peter Frame*) (Fox-British, Al Parker)
Coming of Age (Geo. Smith–Columbia, Manning Haynes)

1941

Hit the Road (Universal–Joe May)
Bachelor Daddy (aka *Sandy Steps Out*) (Universal, Harold Young)
Hold That Ghost (Universal, Arthur Lubin)
Burma Convoy (Universal, Noel Smith)
The Wolf Man (Universal, George Waggner)

1942

North to the Klondike (Universal, Erle C. Kenton)
The Ghost of Frankenstein (Universal, Erle C. Kenton)
Eagle Squadron (Universal, Arthur Lubin)
Pierre of the Plains (MGM, George B. Seitz)
Sherlock Holmes and the Voice of Terror (Universal, John Rawlins)
The Great Impersonation (Universal, John Rawlins)

1943

Keep 'Em Slugging (Universal, Christy Cabanne)
Captive Wild Woman (Universal, Edward Dmytryk)
All by Myself (Universal, Felix Feist)
Hers to Hold (Universal, Frank Ryan)
You're a Lucky Fellow, Mr. Smith (Universal, Felix Feist)
Son of Dracula (Universal, Robert Siodmak)
The Mad Ghoul (Universal, James Hogan)
His Butler's Sister (Universal, Frank Borzage)

1944

Ladies Courageous (Universal, John Rawlins)
Weird Woman (Universal, Reginald LeBorg)
Follow the Boys (Universal, Edward Sutherland)
Pardon My Rhythm (Universal, Felix Feist)
The Invisible Man's Revenge (Universal, Ford Beebe)
Jungle Woman (Universal, Reginald LeBorg)
The Pearl of Death (Universal, Roy William Neill)
Bowery to Broadway (Universal, Charles Lamont)

1945

The Frozen Ghost (Universal, Harold Young)
The Fatal Witness (Republic, Lesley Selander)

1946

Queen of Burlesque (PRC, Sam Newfield)
The French Key (Republic, Walter Colmes)
Black Beauty (20th Century–Fox, Max Nosseck)
Flight to Nowhere (Screen Guild, William Rowland)

1947

Spoilers of the North (Republic, Richard Sale)
Last of the Redmen (Columbia, George Sherman)
The Lone Wolf in London (Columbia, Leslie Goodwins)

1949

Parole, Inc. (Eagle-Lion, Alfred Zeisler)
Tarzan's Magic Fountain (RKO, Lee Sholem)

1950

The Texan Meets Calamity Jane (Columbia, Ande Lamb)

1960

No Greater Love

SHORT SUBJECT

Evelyn Ankers appeared in *Screen Snapshots* No. 6 (Columbia, 1943).

According to *The Billboard* (4/29/44), Evelyn played in the "first television film to be shot with top-bracket players," produced by Universal the week of April 22, 1944, at Don Lee's video station W6XAO. Oliver Drake produced, Patrick Michael Cunning directed and the cast also included Turhan Bey, Jon Hall and Frances Langford.

Maria Ouspenskaya

The Wolf Man.

Fog, one of the true stars of this classic horror movie, swirls about mournfully as Lon Chaney's Wolf Man, leering and roaring, fondles the wildly-screaming Evelyn Ankers. Claude Rains, as Sir John Talbot rushes through the mist, his eyes shining through the fog as he raises the silver wolf's-head cane and beats the Wolf Man to death. The milestone Frank Skinner/Charles Previn/Hans J. Salter musical score thunders savagely with each fatal blow of the cane ... under Universal's full moon.

Through the fog, there has come the rattle of a carriage, driven by Maleva, the old gypsy woman—Maria Ouspenskaya. Maleva, whose son Bela (Bela Lugosi) had been a werewolf, and who had bitten Chaney's Larry Talbot, quaveringly recites her prayer:

> The way you walked was thorny,
> through no fault of your own.
> But as the rain enters the soil,
> the river enters the sea,
> so tears run to a predestined end.
> Your suffering is over.
> Now you will find peace for eternity.

Her theatricality is wonderful, her mysticism strangely, entirely convincing. And as Chaney's beast turns slowly back into Larry Talbot, as Rains' Sir John stares in anguish at the cane with which he had beaten his son to death, as Evelyn Ankers' Gwen sees the thing that attacked her in the night and sighs "Larry!" Maria Ouspenskaya's Maleva rides her gypsy carriage out of the film, carrying with her the legend of the werewolf—and the allegiance of countless horror fans.

The characterization is a classic: Maria Ouspenskaya's Maleva, of both *The Wolf Man* and the sequel, *Frankenstein Meets the Wolf Man.*

From her very first Hollywood film—Goldwyn's 1936 *Dodsworth*, for which she won a Best Supporting Actress Academy nomination—Maria Ouspenskaya was a striking, unforgettable show business original. The five-foot, 90-lb., wizened alumna of the Russian Art Theatre, who off-screen sported a monocle and carried herself with an imperial Russian regality, could play anything within her type; indeed, her second Oscar-nominated performance, as Charles Boyer's charming grandmother in 1939's *Love Affair*, was about as far from Maleva as one could get. "Madame" (as her drama pupils addressed her) dedicated her life to the theater. Never married, never caring for possessions, she lived her life like a Mother Abbess of Drama, running an acting school in New York and, later, Hollywood.

Somehow, Maleva, the stoic, silently-suffering gypsy seer, was Maria Ouspenskaya's perfect role.

It's pitiful to realize that the true monster which finally destroyed her was a lit cigarette.

***Chapter opener:* Maria Ouspenskaya in a publicity shot for *The Wolf Man*, 1941.**

Maria Ouspenskaya was born in Tula, Russia, on July 29. The year? That's a mystery; traditional reference books list her birth year as 1876; one even gives 1867. However, according to her early Hollywood publicity, her death certificate and her grave marker at Forest Lawn Cemetery, Glendale, the actress was actually born in 1887. This would have made her 54 years old when she played Maleva in *The Wolf Man*—and almost five years younger than her screen "son," Bela Lugosi!

The 1887 date is credible; her early years might have aged anyone prematurely. A coloratura soprano, the first ambition of "Madame" was to be a singer. She studied at the Warshaw Conservatory until she ran low on funds. She enrolled at Adasheff's School of Drama, Moscow, paying the bills by singing in a church. After graduation from the theater school, she toured in a stock company.

Nineteen eleven. Maria was one of 250 applicants who auditioned for the famed Moscow Art Theatre. It was the realm of Konstantin Stanislavsky, who created his "method" of naturalistic acting. Maria was one of the few selected from the 250 hopefuls. In the next ten years, Madame created over 100 stage roles in such plays as *The Three Sisters*, *The Cherry Orchard*, *The Lower Depths* and *The Brothers Karamazov*. She also became one of Stanislavsky's drama instructors.

Meanwhile, she was living (according to later Universal PR) "through more than her share of suffering ... two revolutions, famine and other privations..." Madame remembered the Russian Revolution, when she was playing in two productions simultaneously—and caring for a critically ill sister. According to a 1939 clipping:

> Because of her sister's critical condition, it was Miss Maria's task to keep from the invalid the fact that outside their frosty windows an empire was crumbling, a people facing starvation and want. This was her most trying role... They had one stove. The temperature was below zero in all but the sickroom. There the tiny stove burned brightly, fed, one by one, by the valuable volumes of the Ouspenskaya Library! When the books were gone, the furniture followed... And when the furniture of all but the invalid's room was burned, the doors between the other rooms were splintered and fed to the valiant little stove...

According to the clipping, the crisis passed—and Madame ensuingly responded to all praise of her acting with the words, "But you should have seen the performance I gave one winter in Moscow!"

Madame played in several Russian-made films, such as *Nichtozhniye* (*Worthless*, 1916), which featured Michael Visaroff (who later played the innkeeper in 1931's *Dracula*), and *Tsveti Zapozdaliye* (*The Flowers Are Late*, 1917)—based on a Chekhov story, and starring Olga Baclanova (fated to star as the evil Cleopatra in 1932's *Freaks*). In 1922, Stanislavsky toured his company throughout Europe and the United States, performing Byron's *Cain* and Gogol's *The Inspector General*. In January 1923, Madame first played New York in an all-Russian production of Tolstoy's *Tsar Feodor Ivanovitch*. Stanislavsky led his company on a second U.S. tour in 1924, and—after it closed—Maria Ouspenskaya decided to stay in America and not return to Russia.

"It was the reverse gypsy in me," said Madame. "I got myself settled in America and I've never had the slightest inclination to get away from it."

There was one problem: She was about to be deported by immigration authorities, for she had no job. Hence, Richard Boleslawski (who later directed such Hollywood films as *Rasputin and the Empress*, *Les Misérables* and *The Garden of Allah*) offered her a teaching post with his American Laboratory Theatre. Madame gratefully accepted and would make her mark in the American theater not only as an actress, but as a teacher.

Saturday night, October 11, 1924. New York was a dream come true for any playgoer. *Ziegfeld Follies* was playing at the New Amsterdam Theatre, *George White's Scandals* was at the Apollo and *Earl Carroll's Vanities* was at the Music Box. The Marx Brothers starred in *I'll Say She Is* at the Casino; Ed Wynn headlined *The Grab Bag* at the Globe; *Abie's Irish Rose*, *What Price Glory?* and Jeanne Eagels in *Rain* were all playing to full houses. Lionel Atwill was reprising his recent triumph, *The Outsider*, at the Bronx Opera House; and, for moviegoers, Broadway offered such diversity as De Mille's *The Ten Commandments*, Douglas Fairbanks' *Thief of Baghdad*, and John Ford's *The Iron Horse*.

On that Saturday night, at the Greenwich Village Theatre, Maria Ouspenskaya made her official New York debut as Paris Pigeons in *The Saint*, directed by Richard Boleslawski. The star of this religious pageantry was Leo Carrillo, as a restless seminarian; however, as the *New York Times* reported,

> The cheers of Saturday night's audience were rather for Maria Ouspenskaya, stepping from the ensemble of the Moscow Art Theatre to play her first role in English—and to play it, to the astonishment of every one, easily and even colloquially...

The Saint ran 17 performances, and Madame proceeded with a noteworthy career on Broadway. She played Fiametta, the Blind Woman, in a revival of *The Jest* (Plymouth Theatre, February 4, 1926, 78 performances), starring Basil Sydney and Alphonz Ethier in the roles played in 1919 by John and Lionel Barrymore. Arthur Hopkins (who had directed the original) supervised the revival, and the *New York Times* saluted Madame's "smoldering quality."

The Witch (Greenwich Village Theatre, November 18, 1926, 28 performances) seemed prophetic for the actress who later created *The Wolf Man*'s Maleva. Madame played Herlofs-Marte, a witch "hounded by town guards and an inflamed populace." As a church bell ominously tolls, she crawls for shelter to Anne Pedersdotter (Alice Brady). As the *New York Times* reported,

> eventually the town guards track her by spots of blood, pull her from her hiding place, twist her arms until she confesses, and carry her off to her doom. Miss Ouspenskaya summons all the terror and panic in that incident.

This melodrama ended with Anne being challenged to touch the body of her dead husband to prove she is not a witch; Alice Brady scored as she revealed her witchery with "a diabolical scream."

Maria Ouspenskaya carried on: as Curtis, Petruchio's cook in Basil Sydney's modern dress version of Shakespeare's *The Taming Of The Shrew* (Garrick Theatre,

Ouspenskaya in her Broadway debut, *The Saint*, 1924.

October 25, 1927, 175 performances); the *New York Times* reported that she made "an effective cartoon" of her role.

When Boleslawski's American Laboratory Theatre disbanded in 1929, Madame founded her own school: The Maria Ouspenskaya School of Dramatic Arts. She always followed Boleslawski's philosophy:

> The actor's art cannot be taught. He must be born with ability. But the technique through which his talent can find expression—that can and must be taught.

She also found time to work in the theater: In 1930, she played in *The Cherry Orchard* and returned to Broadway as Fraulein in *The Passing Present* (Ethel Barrymore Theatre, December 7, 1931, 16 performances). On opening night, a wild wind rattled the Ethel Barrymore Theatre (appropriately, *Frankenstein* had just opened in Times Square!), spooking many of the actors—but not Madame.

Then, come Saturday night, February 24, 1934, Madame opened at the Shubert Theatre in what became her greatest Broadway success, and her entree to the movies: *Dodsworth*. This Sidney Howard adaptation of the Sinclair Lewis novel featured a large

Ouspenskaya (left) with actress Margo, who was visiting "Madame" on the set of *Dodsworth*, 1936.

cast: Walter Huston as Sam Dodsworth, retiring Midwest automobile manufacturer; Fay Bainter as his vain adulteress-wife Fran; Nan Sunderland (in real life, Mrs. Walter Huston) as Edith, the woman who consoles the heartbroken Dodsworth; Kent Smith (later the perplexed Oliver of Val Lewton's *Cat People* and *The Curse of the Cat People*) as Kurt, the young European nobleman whom Fran wishes to marry; and Maria Ouspenskaya as Baroness von Obersdorf—Kurt's mother, who brought down the house as she told off the selfish Fran and forbade her marriage to her son.

"Maria Ouspenskaya makes one of her rare and memorable appearances as a German countess," reported Brooks Atkinson in the *New York Times*. "Although the scene is brief, this gifted actress burns it into the memory with the flame of her extraordinary artistry."

Dodsworth ran 317 performances. Madame followed with *Abide with Me* (Ritz Theatre, November 21, 1935, 36 performances); she was Emma, a housekeeper who fatally shoots the evil husband of her employer.

Meanwhile, Samuel Goldwyn paid $160,000 for the rights to *Dodsworth* and engaged two players from the original Broadway production to reprise their roles (under William Wyler's direction): Walter Huston and Maria Ouspenskaya. All Hollywood took notice of the five-foot, silver-haired dynamo—complete with monocle in her right eye—as she arrived in the movie capital.

"Sam Goldwyn's most prestigious film to date," wrote A. Scott Berg of

Dodsworth in his best-selling *Goldwyn: A Biography*. Released September 18, 1936, the film finds Huston as the retiring automobile tycoon who takes a European vacation. Fran (Ruth Chatterton), his cockatoo of a wife, goes along—telling people she's 35 years old, flirting, having an affair with a roué (Paul Lukas), apologizing for her husband's boisterous personality, tinting her hair and trying to hide the news she's become a grandmother. Inevitably, the marriage collapses. Dodsworth is heartbroken.

In today's feminist age, many audiences often regard *Dodsworth* with sympathies askew. Director Wyler, trying for political correctness in later years, insisted that Ruth Chatterton "only wanted to play her as a selfish bitch, and I kept trying to make her see that Mrs. Dodsworth had a very good case for behaving the way she did... She'd been a good wife for 25 years, and raised their children..."

If so, then Maria Ouspenskaya's performance must cause feminists to writhe in agony. As the venerable Baroness von Obersdorf, mother of the titled young Kurt (Gregory Gaye) whom Fran wishes to marry, Madame makes a dramatic entrance on a snowy morning, with a cane almost as tall as she is, and with a shining cross hung around her neck—and takes on Fran Dodsworth in what was, originally, the showstopping scene of the play and film:

> BARONESS: Even if there were not the—religious question... There is the question of children, too... Can you give them to him?
>
> FRAN: Well, what makes you think I couldn't?
>
> BARONESS: I am so much older than you are, my dear. You will forgive if I observe that you are older than Kurt!... I should think of my own happiness, if I were you... Have you thought how little happiness there can be for the *old* wife of a *young* husband?

Come the finale, Sam runs away to his beautiful woman (Mary Astor) who consoled him after Fran left him; Fran is left alone and screaming on a ship; and Maria, with one scene, had become a major Hollywood character actress.

Nineteen thirty-six was the first year of the Academy's Best Supporting Actor and Actress category, and Madame was one of the original contestants, vying for the honor with Beulah Bondi (*The Gorgeous Hussy*), Alice Brady (*My Man Godfrey*), Bonita Granville (*These Three*) and Gale Sondergaard, who was also making her screen debut (*Anthony Adverse*). *Daily Variety* predicted that Madame and Ms. Sondergaard were "about even" as favorites to win the Academy Award; Gale Sondergaard took home the prize. (Walter Huston won the New York Critics Award and an Oscar nomination.)

Originally, Madame saw her Hollywood sojourn as a lark, an experiment in her acting craft, and she returned to New York—playing Polymnia in *Daughters of Atreus* (44th Street Theatre, October 14, 1936, 13 performances), which introduced Eleonora Mendelssohn to American audiences. The ever-impressed *New York Times* hailed: "As the beloved nurse of the family, Maria Ouspenskaya has the voice and the command of style that give the classics a purpose on the stage..."

As Madame settled back into her 27 West 67th Street, New York City school, Hollywood serenaded her with offers. Her *Dodsworth* performance had won her top acclaim, as had her teaching. Anne Baxter, an alumna of Madame's school, later recalled Madame's exercises—such as the day Madame challenged her, "You are the yellow flame of a candle, blowing in the wind, whispering to the dark beyond the window":

> If I have any dramatic imagination, she developed it... I studied with Madame for three years, and at the end of that time anybody in our class could recite *Jack and Jill* and dream it up until you'd think they were doing *Jekyll and Hyde*!

It was MGM that enticed Madame's Hollywood return via 1937's *Conquest*, Metro's $3,800,000 Garbo vehicle, in which Madame played crazy Countess Pelagia—who accuses Charles Boyer's *Napoleon* of cheating at cards. "You are cheating, you little corporal, you!" she shouts, brandishing her cane and overturning the table. Madame spoke of her co-stars:

> I found Miss Garbo very easy to work with. She is friendly and has irresistible charm. She was born with so much that cannot be learned. I think her a very great artist. Mr. Boyer was simple and easy in his relations with others, but absorbed at all times in his character. It was artistically and personally a joyful experience to work with them.

While acting in *Conquest*, the monocled Madame took a dip in the Pacific three times a day. Indeed, swimming became a favorite hobby; as the late actor Thomas Beck told Roger Hurlburt (Entertainment/Feature writer for the Fort Lauderdale *Sun-Sentinel*):

> Whenever I wasn't at the studio, I would be at the beach. Maria would often join me for a swim. I remember that she would calmly begin treading water, always with a cigarette in her mouth, puffing away, and talking about what I was doing, what role, and that sort of thing. She gave advice and tutored lots of actors in those days. When the cigarette burned down and the ash went "ffft" in the water, she would slowly paddle ashore, light up another and wade back out...

For a time, Maria commuted back and forth from her New York school to Hollywood. There were three Ouspenskaya performances in 1939, Hollywood's golden year:

Love Affair, from RKO, was a classic Irene Dunne/Charles Boyer romance, directed by Leo McCarey and featuring Madame as Mme. Marnay, Boyer's delightful grandmother. Back in New York after completing *Love Affair*, Madame wrote to a friend and enthused about Boyer, McCarey, and her plane trip:

> Charles Boyer is simply a beautiful, charming pal of mine. He said to me last that it seems that it's our destiny to play together.

> The director was understanding, creative and kind. In other words, I enjoyed this work this time very much. I liked the part too, and I enjoyed flying above the clouds. Believe me, I will find every slightest excuse to avoid the train for the sake of a plane...

Love Affair placed Madame in the Best Supporting Actress Academy race of 1939, along with Olivia de Havilland (*Gone with the Wind*), Geraldine Fitzgerald (*Wuthering Heights*), Edna May Oliver (*Drums Along the Mohawk*), and—the winner—*Gone with the Wind*'s Hattie McDaniel. (Cathleen Nesbitt played Grandmother in McCarey's 1957 *An Affair to Remember*, starring Cary Grant and Deborah Kerr; Katharine Hepburn plays the grandmother in the recent Warren Beatty–Annette Bening 1994 version of *Love Affair*.)

The Rains Came, from 20th Century–Fox, was a "disaster" epic starring George Brent and Myrna Loy; Madame played the Maharani of Ranchipur. The earthquake special effects won an Oscar. (In the 1955 remake *The Rains of Ranchipur*, starring Lana Turner and Richard Burton, Eugenie Leontovich inherited Madame's role.)

Judge Hardy and Son, from MGM, was another of Louis B. Mayer's favorite series, with Madame as Mrs. Valduzzi; she and Egon Brecher (the sinister Major-domo in 1934's Karloff/Lugosi *The Black Cat*) act the roles of immigrants facing eviction—saved by Mickey Rooney's Andy.

Meanwhile, on September 18, 1939, the first semester officially began at the Maria Ouspenskaya Private Studios of Dramatic Arts, Hollywood. Now based in the film colony, Madame and her school offered courses in Diction, Ballet, Rhythmic Physical Control, Voice Production, Stage Makeup, and Sketching. Come the second year of study, Madame provided her students with full-length productions.

Madame supervised personally, with carefully selected faculty. The tuition tab for this wealth of dramatic expertise: $50 per month.

In the midst of 1939, *Photoplay* offered its readers a little profile of Maria Ouspenskaya:

> She is a lovely little lady, Madame Ouspenskaya, quiet, friendly, cheerful, free from temperament and jealousy... She is not 70, as has been reported, but just a little over 50. She is a talented pianist. When she is not playing in pictures she supervises a dramatic school... Russian-born, she is now an American citizen and proud to be. She would like to keep on acting "for years and years—until I actually am as old as I appeared to be in *Love Affair*." When you congratulate her on a scene, she only smiles...

About this time, Madame offered her own definition of talent:

> Well, first, I should say a capacity for hard work. Second, perhaps, an ability to get the most out of one's five senses. And then, thirdly, an agreement—a contract between one's self and God—that's talent.

There were half-a-dozen film appearances for Madame in 1940. She played Franziska Speyer, the wealthy widow who donates the necessary funds to research

Charles Boyer, Maria Ouspenskaya and Greta Garbo in *Conquest*, 1937.

syphilis in Warner Bros.' biopic *Dr. Ehrlich's Magic Bullet*, starring Edward G. Robinson, and directed by William Dieterle. MGM's opulent *Waterloo Bridge*, a remake of Universal's 1931 James Whale tragedy, starred Vivien Leigh (in Mae Clarke's old role of prostitute Myra) and Robert Taylor (succeeding the original's Douglass Montgomery) as the soldier who loves her. Mervyn LeRoy directed, and Madame played Madame Olga Kirowa, a ballet mistress with the martinet style of Brian Donlevy's Sgt. Markoff of *Beau Geste*. She stayed at MGM for *The Mortal Storm*, an early anti–Nazi drama with Madame as Mrs. Breitner, who helps her son (James Stewart) escape the storm troopers; the anti–Nazi theme continued at 20th Century–Fox with *The Man I Married*, starring Joan Bennett, Francis Lederer and Madame as Frau Gerhardt, widow of a concentration camp victim. There was RKO's *Beyond Tomorrow*, with Madame as housekeeper Madame Tanya, caring for three oldsters (Harry Carey, Charles Winninger and C. Aubrey Smith), all of whom share Christmas dinner with two strangers who fall in love (Richard Carlson and Jean Parker). RKO's *Dance, Girl, Dance*, was a curiosity—the dual story of ballerina Maureen O'Hara and stripper Lucille Ball. Maurice Moscovich originally was cast as "a temperamental dance maestro," but he died suddenly after four days' shooting. Unable to replace Moscovich with a man, RKO hired Madame—and renamed the character "Madame Basilova"!

In its Christmas 1940 issue, in a story on actors who were artists, *Time* featured Ginger Rogers' charcoal sketch of Madame.

Ouspenskaya in costume for *Waterloo Bridge*, 1940.

Her drama school was flourishing. One of Madame's pupils in the early 1940s was Marie Windsor, who became the tall brunette vamp of so many movies and TV shows. In 1995, Ms. Windsor shared with me her memories of Ouspenskaya:

> The first thing I noticed about Madame was how tiny she was—
> I'm so tall. But she took over a room when she entered, and she

> didn't have to do a thing! She *glowed*! I remember the monocle, and, boy, did she smoke—all during the classes, all the time—a chain smoker. And she wore a big Indian silver ring with kind of little bells on it—I called it a "jingle bell ring." And a couple of times, when I was doing scenes, she'd jingle this ring and say, "Marie! Marie! You must feel it here! *Here*!"—and she'd keep pounding her stomach with her ring!
>
> Madame was great in developing the imagination. She'd make the girls change purses, and then we'd have to put our hand inside the purse and close our eyes and figure out with our fingers what the contents were. And she was good at having us creating in our own imagination heat, and cold—all Stanislavsky.
>
> In my career as an actress, I used Madame's technique all the time. And I was very touched by the fact that she made me feel I was one of her favorites. I was very fond of her.

One of Windsor's classmates was Frances Rafferty, who became an MGM starlet and one of the stars of TV's *December Bride*. She recently told me:

> My first impression of Madame? I was scared to death! She made us stand up—about ten of us—and she had us all recite "Mary Had a Little Lamb." We each were to recite it to get the attention of the group—how could we command this attention? Well, of course, everybody was orating and carrying on, and then Madame began to tell us the more quiet the tone, the more attention you got. She was wonderful.
>
> Madame was the old school Russian disciplinarian. If we really goofed a scene, or lost concentration, we'd have to recite the alphabet backwards! Oh, yes—"Z, Y..."—I've never forgotten it!
>
> In truth, though, she was very sweet. She had a wonderful, wry sense of humor, in her descriptions of things, she would use humor—oh!—brilliantly. I'd been a dancer, and I would fly through scenes, you see—so she wouldn't let me play anything but old ladies, so that would slow me down! I learned from Madame my whole method of performing—that it all came from inside, from within. That, to me, is the spearhead of her teaching.

Meanwhile, in 1941, Madame gave her most celebrated performance: Maleva, the old Gypsy woman of *The Wolf Man*.

> The Legend of the Damned
>
> In many a distant village there exists the legend of the Werewolf or Wolf Man... A legend of a strange mortal man with the hair and fangs of an unearthly beast ... his hideous howl a dirge of death.
>
> —from the coming attraction trailer for *The Wolf Man* (1941)

Her presence is immense. In a role especially designed for her by Curt Siodmak, Maria Ouspenskaya makes her entrance in *The Wolf Man* on a cart, arriving in the autumn sunshine of Universal's back lot Tyrolean village. Her cursed son Bela (Bela Lugosi) is with her; Lon Chaney and Evelyn Ankers watch their strangely sad, foreboding procession. In her first glimpses in the film—on the cart, at the gypsy camp that night of the full moon, in the forest after Chaney's Larry Talbot has killed her son Bela with the silver-headed cane (and was bitten), and at Talbot Castle—Madame's Maleva is strangely mute, a mystic presence.

When she finally speaks, it is to the priest (Harry Stubbs) in the chapel, as Bela's coffin is brought to the crypt.

"Bela has entered a much better world than this," she quavers—"at least so your ministers always say, sir."

Then she lifts the lid of the casket and looks at her dead, lycanthrope son:

> The way you walked was thorny,
> through no fault of your own...

Later, after the gypsy carnival, Larry Talbot finally meets Maleva in her tent, and she chants:

"Whoever is bitten by a werewolf and lives—becomes a werewolf himself!"

Chaney is dismissive—and slightly hysterical—but she persists. She puts a charm around his neck, and sends him away.

"Go now—and Heaven help you!"

More than anyone in the cast, Maria Ouspenskaya gives *The Wolf Man* its power, its sense of classical Greek tragedy. As the film continues, her appearances are superbly dramatic ... rescuing Chaney's Wolf Man, caught in a trap, with her "The way you walk is thorny..." prayer; challenging Claude Rains' arrogant Sir John when he scorns her "witch's tales"; trying to persuade Evelyn Ankers' Gwen to escape the foggy forest on the climactic night of the hunt.

"I've got to find him!" says Evelyn.

"Come with me or he will find *you*!" says Madame.

The Wolf Man does find Gwen; she screams, and Sir John beats the monster to death with the silver-headed cane Larry had used to kill Bela the gypsy. Once again, Madame has arrived at the tragic scene in her carriage, with its hanging lantern; in the fog, she appears, almost like a saint. And she recites once more:

> The way you walked was thorny,
> through no fault of your own...
> Now you will find peace for eternity.

And, before the shocked eyes of Rains' Sir John, Evelyn Ankers' Gwen, and the audience, Lon Chaney returns to human form—and finds his own eternity as a horror star.

"Wherever a good, old-fashioned killer diller of a murder meller will go," reported *Variety* after Universal previewed its new melodrama December 9, 1941, "*The Wolf Man* should do a thumping business." Indeed it did, becoming Universal's million-dollar hit of the season.

Ouspenskaya reads the palm of Evelyn Ankers in this publicity shot from the set of *The Wolf Man*, 1941 (courtesy Ronald V. Borst, Hollywood Movie Posters).

And Maleva became Maria Ouspenskaya's greatest performance in the movies, a characterization as vital to the horror genre as Larry Talbot himself. Not only does the performance contain color, theatricality and power—Madame's Maleva features a very real spirituality, which is so vital a feature of the classic horror films. Her prayers, her chants and her very presence send chills up the spine—akin to those felt when Karloff's Frankenstein Monster reaches for the rays of the sun, when Isis answers Zita Johann's prayer to save her from the Mummy; it's a performance that sparks with a religious fervor. Madame invested Maleva with a spiritual passion—a testimony not only to horror movies (often the most faith-filled of movie genres), but to Maria Ouspenskaya herself.

On Christmas Day 1941, *The Shanghai Gesture*, from United Artists, had its world premiere at New York City's Astor Theatre. It featured one of Madame's more aberrant roles—"The Amah," silent maidservant of Mother Gin Sling (Ona Munson). Madame had not one word of dialogue in this Josef von Sternberg–directed melodrama.

Maria was part of the all-star cast of Warner Bros.' *Kings Row* (1942), as Madame Von Eln, gentle grandmother of Paris; her scenes with child actor Scotty Beckett are filled with warmth and charm. In this deluxe soap opera based on the Henry Bellamann novel, she perishes a dope addict—long before Ronald Reagan has his legs amputated by Charles Coburn, and wakes up with his famous "Where's the rest of me?" scream.

Madame returned to Universal for 1942's *Mystery of Marie Roget,* 60 minutes of Poe *à la* Universal, with Maria playing Mme. Cecile Roget, grandmother this time to Maria Montez. In the book *Universal Horrors* by Michael Brunas, John Brunas and Tom Weaver, actress Nell O'Day remembered that she and Madame played scenes with Lisa the leopard. A solicitous assistant cameraman asked Ouspenskaya if she was afraid of the cat.

Madame's reply: "I am not afraid of any-sing!"

Then, on October 12, 1942, Universal began shooting *Frankenstein Meets the Wolf Man*. Reunited were many talents from *The Wolf Man*: producer George Waggner; star Lon Chaney, Jr., reprising his anguished Larry Talbot; Bela Lugosi, promoted here from the werewolf gypsy to a blind Frankenstein Monster, with dialogue; and Patric Knowles, up from the gamekeeper of the 1941 film to obsessed male lead scientist Dr. Frank Mannering. Even some of the minor players came back—such as Doris Lloyd (Jenny Williams' vengeful mother of *The Wolf Man*) as a benign nurse, and Tom Stevenson (the slaughtered gravedigger of *The Wolf Man*) reincarnated as one of the grave robbers of the opening. The movie is one of the most beloved shockers ever produced.

"A nice little old lady with a steel spine," was how Patric Knowles remembered Madame in an interview with Gary Don Rhodes' late-lamented Bela Lugosi Fan Club. In the film, Chaney's Talbot, freed on a night of the full moon from his tomb, escapes a hospital in Wales and goes seeking Maleva. Madame's expression when she first sees the resurrected werewolf is chilling—and unforgettable. Larry Talbot begs for her aid.

"I will guard you," promises Madame's Maleva, taking Chaney's face in her hands, "and take care of you as I took care of my own son."

Maleva promises Larry Talbot, "I know a man who has the power to help you," so it's off to Vasaria, where, indeed, *Frankenstein Meets the Wolf Man*. The audience meets Baroness Elsa von Frankenstein (a gorgeous Ilona Massey), the jolly mayor (Lionel Atwill), villager Rudi (Dwight Frye)—and, of course, the Monster (Lugosi).

Rex Evans (behind the counter), Lon Chaney, Jr., Maria Ouspenskaya, and (on table) Martha Vickers in *Frankenstein Meets the Wolf Man*, 1943.

We have such spectacles as the musical "Festival of the New Wine" (crashed by the Monster); Knowles, Miss Massey and Madame hunting for the lycanthrope and the Monster in the ruins; and—of course—the moonlit Monster vs. Wolf Man climax.

If a time machine existed for horror fans, many would line up for a ride back to Universal City in the autumn of 1942 and a peek at the *Frankenstein Meets the Wolf Man* set: to see and hear Lugosi delivering dialogue as the blind Monster (before all references to his blindness were cut by the editor, along with the dialogue, because, as Curt Siodmak said, "it sounded so Hungarian funny...!"); to be on the back lot and the Phantom Stage for the shooting of the "Faro-La, Faro-Li" musical number, sung by Adia Kuznetzoff; to see the climactic battle of the "Twin Titans of Terror."

However, perhaps no day of shooting was as dramatic as Thursday, November 5, 1942. On that day, Lon Chaney and Madame were riding on a carriage when an accident happened. *The Hollywood Reporter* noted, "Madame Maria Ouspenskaya suffered a fractured ankle yesterday when a coach being used in *Frankenstein Meets the Wolf Man* ran over her foot..." Louella Parsons, in the *Los Angeles Examiner*, was more dramatic:

> A really terrible accident at the Universal Studios occurred while making *Frankenstein Meets the Wolf Man*. Maria Ouspenskaya and Lon Chaney, Jr., were riding in a wagon when it overturned and fell on both of them, breaking Madame Ouspenskaya's leg

> and ankle. She is now in the hospital and at her age this is an extremely serious accident. Lon Chaney, Jr., was not as badly injured...

Photoplay reported Louella's account, and Madame recuperated at Cedars of Lebanon. On that same fateful day, Bela Lugosi collapsed on the set in Frankenstein Monster makeup, the *Reporter* noting that the star was suffering from exhaustion "brought on by Lugosi packing around the 35-pound Monster makeup..."

Madame left Cedars of Lebanon Monday, November 9.

Frankenstein Meets the Wolf Man has always provided horror fans with a mystery: What happened to Maleva? She's last seen, gently reprimanding Ilona's statuesque Elsa for calling Chaney "insane":

"He is not insane. He simply wants to die"—and she walks off.

Did she perish in the flood waters from the exploding dam? According to Siodmak's shooting script, she was supposed to show up in the climax, amidst the mayhem of the battling horrors and the dynamited dam, and escape in her carriage with Knowles and Massey. Perhaps it was the accident that prevented the scripted final action from being shot.

It was all over November 11, 1942. Released in March 1943, *Frankenstein Meets the Wolf Man* was a box office volcano. Once again, Madame's Maleva gave the melodrama a mystical touch that is powerful, profound and richly dramatic.

By 1943, Madame's film career was in a decline. In his book *Maria, Marlene ... and Me* (Shadbolt Press, 1993), actor/critic Dean Goodman remembers his days as a student and confidante in Madame's school. Goodman was a "pet" of Madame's, and she'd often chat with him over a glass of vodka, talking of her theater adventures in Russia and reflecting on why her film offers were dwindling. According to Goodman, Madame claimed she'd battled with director Mervyn LeRoy on *Waterloo Bridge*—she'd wanted to bring sympathetic touches to her role of the ballet mistress, and LeRoy wanted her to play her as a monster. Madame had even gone to Louis B. Mayer to plead her case. Mayer backed LeRoy 100 percent, and Madame claimed she was labeled as "difficult" ever since. Goodman continued:

> Madame early gained another kind of reputation which restricted her work in Hollywood. She was so good an actress that she literally stole most of the scenes she was in, albeit legitimately, and certain actresses were reluctant to have her in their pictures. Garbo and Myrna Loy were said to be among those who, after single experiences (in *Conquest* and *The Rains Came*, respectively) declined to work with her again.

Goodman also provided this insight:

> I don't think she particularly liked women. She was plain, some might even say ugly, and perhaps she had her sex jealousies. She never married, but she flirted with every man who crossed her path and charmed many of them.

After the release of *Frankenstein Meets the Wolf Man*, Madame decided to go East for what would be her final Broadway appearance. The play was *Outrageous Fortune* by Rose Franken, who had such success with the play *Claudia* (and who also directed *Outrageous Fortune*); Madame shared star-billing with Elsie Ferguson. The play opened at the 48th Street Theatre November 3, 1943, with Madame as Mrs. Harris, a matriarch.

Madame's devotion to the theater (and her fellow actors) became heroically apparent the last week of the play's run: She had developed lobar pneumonia—but insisted on playing the show's final five performances.

"If a soldier sneezed, would he refuse to go into battle?" she demanded.

Even though the play was scheduled to close that Saturday night, Madame completed the seventy-seventh and final performance—with a 104° temperature. Between her scenes, she fell onto a cot in the left wing of the theater, cared for by an attendant and given Sulfa drugs frequently.

"I am an artist," said Madame, "and when you love what you do, you find the force and energy to do it through love and will power."

At the curtain call of *Outrageous Fortune*'s last performance, Madame received "a rousing round of applause"—and then moved to Mt. Sinai Hospital to recuperate. It would be her final New York stage performance.

In her final years, it was more difficult to accept Madame's 1887 birthdate. The July 8, 1944, *Los Angeles Examiner* noted she was "critically ill" at Cedars of Lebanon, yet once again she rallied—and sought continually permission to act for the soldiers in the Aleutians!

> I am not afraid of anything, and I am seldom sick. Discomfort means nothing to me—you should have toured Russia in the old days!

Few film appearances remained. She was Queen of the Amazons(!) in RKO's *Tarzan and the Amazons* (1945), with beefy Johnny Weissmuller, curvy Brenda Joyce as Jane and the original "Boy," Johnny Sheffield. She made her color film debut as Madame Goronoff in Republic's 1946 musical *I've Always Loved You*, directed by Frank Borzage. Nineteen forty-seven found Madame in a "Wild Bill" Elliott western, Republic's *Wyoming*, in which she played Maria, "faithful family servant" to Vera Hruba Ralston. Her final film was Warner Bros.' 1949 *A Kiss in the Dark*. As Mme. Karina, one of the occupants of an apartment house bought by concert pianist David Niven, Madame had a scene where she became inebriated on champagne—and confessed she would rather be loved than be known as the great piano teacher that she is.

While she had closed her own school, Madame taught at several acting academies in Hollywood in her final years, including the American Repertory Company, whose student body was comprised largely of ex–G.I.s.

Thursday, December 1, 1949.

Madame was in bed at her apartment, 1600 North Martel Avenue, in Hollywood. It was shortly after midnight. She was smoking a cigarette.

A friend, Mrs. Inez Simmons, who was staying with Madame that night, discovered the bed in flames. She dragged Madame from the fire, put out the blaze unaided and called Madame's personal physician. Dr. Marion J. Dakin subsequently admitted his patient to St. Joseph's Hospital, Burbank, where she was suffering from "extreme shock" and "second and third degree burns about the legs and body."

Originally, there was hope for her recovery; the *Los Angeles Herald Express* headlined that Madame had been "Saved from Death in Flaming Bed." Yet her condition was grim.

Her final days also sadly reflected the indignities of the life of an actor. Apparently Madame had no medical insurance or nest egg to provide for medical treatment. Hence, the venerable actress, in her critical condition, was shipped all the way across the San Fernando Valley to the Motion Picture Country Home Hospital. It was there, Saturday morning, December 3, 1949, that Maria Ouspenskaya died.

The death certificate gave her age as 62; the coroner's office gave her age as 68. Cause of death: a cerebral hemorrhage, due to shock and second and third degree burns.

On Tuesday, December 6, 1949, Swami Paramhansa Yogananda of the Church of Self-Realization conducted the funeral service at Pierce Bros. Hollywood Mortuary, 5959 Santa Monica Boulevard. One hundred fifty mourners came to the chapel, including actors Akim Tamiroff and Leonid Kinskey. "In the drama of life, she played her part well," eulogized Yogi Yogananda, who conducted the service with both spoken and chanted prayers.

"Bela has gone to a much better world than this," Madame's Maleva had said in *The Wolf Man*, "or so your ministers always say, sir."

After the funeral, the body was cremated at the Chapel of the Pines (where the ashes of such stars as Lionel Atwill and Helen Chandler are, at last report, still in vaultage). Burial at Forest Lawn, Glendale, followed in January of 1950.

On January 13, 1950, the *Hollywood Citizen-News* reported Maria Ouspenskaya's estate to have totaled $358. This was broken down into a bank account of $64.62, a salary check of $93.70 and "property" worth $200—the last willed to Robert Abbot of Eagle Rock. There's a bizarre postscript to this sad accounting. In May of 1989, Collectors Bookstore in Hollywood offered in its "Collectors Showcase" auction catalogue this item:

> Maria Ouspenskaya Estate Items, 1930s–1950s, 13 × 16, 3 of her personal large scrapbooks w/newspaper clippings, 8 × 10 portraits, 3 pp. on *Frankenstein Meets the Wolf Man*: 8 × 10s of her w/Napoleon, *Rains Came*, 2 from Weissmuller Tarzan film, 23 other 8 × 10 candids and 8 × 10 negatives + 3 records of a 1940 interview & an interview by Bing Crosby on *Kraft Music Hall*; mostly all fine.

The suggested bidding price was "$300–$400." Madame's collectibles, over the decades, had matched or exceeded the original final worth of her total estate.

On January 20, 1950, there was a final interment service for Maria Ouspenskaya at Forest Lawn Memorial Park. The flat grave marker reads:

MARIA OUSPENSKAYA
"Our Beloved Madam"
July 29, 1887–Dec. 3, 1949

At the service, Eva Lorraine, Madame's friend of many years, read "The Divine Gypsy" from the book *Songs of the Soul*, written by Yogi Yogananda, who had conducted the funeral in December.

"It seems fitting to read to you Madame's favorite poem," said Miss Lorraine, "which was a source of divine inspiration to her. It was the one poem which touched her deeply."

The Films of Maria Ouspenskaya

Russian Films

1915

Sverchok Na Pechi (*The Cricket on the Hearth*)

1916

Nichtozhniye (*Worthless*) (Alexander Volkon)

1917

Tsveti Zapozdaliye (*The Flowers Are Late*) (Boris Sushkevich)

1919

Zazhivo Pogrebennii (*Buried Alive*) (A. Volkon)

1923

Khveska/Bolnichnii Storozh Khveska (*Khveska*, or *Hospital Guard Khveska*) (A. Ivanovsky)

1929

Tanka—Traktirshchitza (*Tanka, Innkeeper*) (B. Svetozarov)

American Films

1936

Dodsworth (Goldwyn/United Artists, William Wyler)

1937

Conquest (MGM, Clarence Brown)

1939

Love Affair (RKO, Leo McCarey)
The Rains Came (20th Century–Fox, C. Brown)
Judge Hardy and Son (MGM, George Seitz)

1940

Dr. Ehrlich's Magic Bullet (Warner Bros., William Dieterle)
Waterloo Bridge (MGM, Mervyn LeRoy)
The Mortal Storm (MGM, Frank Borzage)
The Man I Married (20th Century–Fox, Irving Pichel)
Beyond Tomorrow (RKO, A. Edward Sutherland)
Dance, Girl, Dance (RKO, Dorothy Arzner)

1941

The Wolf Man (Universal, George Waggner)
The Shanghai Gesture (United Artists, Josef von Sternberg)

1942

Kings Row (Warner Bros., Sam Wood)
Mystery of Marie Roget (Universal, Phil Rosen)

1943

Frankenstein Meets the Wolf Man (Universal, Roy William Neill)

1945

Tarzan and the Amazons (RKO, Kurt Neumann)

1946

I've Always Loved You (Republic, Frank Borzage)

1947

Wyoming (Republic, Joseph Kane)

1949

A Kiss in the Dark (Warner Bros., Delmer Daves)

SHORT SUBJECTS

1940

Chinese Garden Festival (Republic)
Screen Snapshots No. 3 (Cloumbia)

Clips of Maria Ouspenskaya from *The Wolf Man* appear in *The Howling* (1981).

Elizabeth Russell

In her horror films, she looked like a satanic Dietrich.

The arch beauty ... the blonde hair ... the long legs ... add the magic of Val Lewton's RKO horror unit, and this slinky, feline, remarkably striking actress evoked in the movies some Renaissance painter's concept of Lucifer's mistress.

Her name is Elizabeth Russell.

And, from the moment she first appeared as "The Cat Woman" in Lewton's *Cat People*, sashaying across the Belgrade Cafe on that snowy night, flashing a sexy, sinister smile at Simone Simon and purring "Moya sestra?" she was one of the most electrifying presences of the horror genre.

In the long-lamented Lewton unit, where the novel, brilliant producer always tried to mix beauty with terror, Elizabeth Russell became his talisman. She created a little parade of memorable characters: Mimi, the consumptive, death-fearing prostitute of *The Seventh Victim*; Kitty, the gin-loving floozy niece of Karloff in *Bedlam*; and—most indelibly—Barbara, the lonely, neurotic, drunken menace of *The Curse of the Cat People*, stalking little Ann Carter on the staircase in the climax of that incredibly sensitive fantasy.

Meanwhile, at Monogram, she was Countess Lorenz, the evil crone whom husband Lugosi keeps young with the spinal fluid of kidnapped brides in *The Corpse Vanishes*.

At Paramount, she was the ghost who haunted the Devonshire cliffside house in *The Uninvited*.

And, at Universal, she was the college wife whose eyes shot daggers at Anne Gwynne and Evelyn Ankers in *Weird Woman*, the studio's most enjoyable "Inner Sanctum" entry, with Miss Russell prowling through the potboiler (in the words of the *New York World-Telegram* critic) "as though any minute she was going to bite someone."

What was it about this blonde, former John Robert Powers New York City "long-stemmed American Beauty" model, that made her Hollywood's most provocative horror beauty of the 1940s? Maybe it was that decidedly feline glamour she exuded. Maybe it was because, in the era of healthy girl-next-door superstars like Betty Grable, Elizabeth Russell was a classic beauty, who had the eyes, the cheekbones, the aristocratic sensuality of the evil princess of a fairy tale; one could imagine her enjoying the lightning from her tower balcony on a stormy night. Perhaps it was the arrogance and irreverence she freely admits today that she harbored toward Hollywood. And certainly, it was the fact that this lady could act.

Today, Elizabeth Russell—a white-haired, still strikingly feline grandmother—is amused by her fame. The "Satanic Dietrich" of the 1940s lives in the 1990s with the Nazarene Nuns, in a Los Angeles convent not far from the old MGM Studios. Deeply religious, long free of the arrogance which compromised her career ("I've done penance for my lack of humility," she says), she is eager to do what she truly wanted to do all her life—write.

Ask Elizabeth Russell to explain her Hollywood career, and she laughs.

And try telling her she was "electrifying" in her old films (as do so many people

***Chapter opener:* Elizabeth Russell in a 1936 Paramount portrait.**

who serenade her with fan mail), and you'll get in response a gentle, beautiful smile she rarely had a chance to flicker in her days as the movies' most diabolic female.

She was born Elizabeth Convery in Philadelphia. Various reference books list her birthdate as August 2, 1916. She had a Catholic education, which she deeply appreciates today.

"The nuns gave me the classics," she says, "and I'd read Shakespeare aloud in class. 'Out, damn spot!'"

While Elizabeth was only a teenager, she met and befriended Rosalind Russell, who was attending Philadelphia's Rosemont College. Through Rosalind, Elizabeth met her brother John; in 1929, they eloped to Maryland and got married. They later had a son, John Knight Russell.

"It wasn't a gunshot wedding, or anything," says Elizabeth today. "It was just kid stuff. And it was just too soon, I guess, for either of us to get married."

Suddenly faced with the challenge of making a living, Elizabeth followed a tip from Rosalind's older sister, who suggested she try to become a John Robert Powers model. "My first job was $100, which seemed like a million in those days," she says. "The John Robert Powers agency gave me so much work, right off the bat, that I was a big success!"

> I made a lot of money and, I must say, I was in every rotogravure section of the Sunday newspaper! I did Chesterfield Cigarettes billboards, Old Gold Cigarettes in theater playbills, Leg Art, everything; I was a fashion model in *Harper's*, and *Vanity Fair*, and all those magazines; the columns of Ed Sullivan and Walter Winchell mentioned me every week.
>
> I worked very hard modeling. I had to model on Sundays; in the summer time, we had fur coats to model, and in those days, we didn't have air-conditioning. And we had those klieg lights, that burned your eyes if you looked at them.
>
> It was very exciting, looking back on it. But, like everything else, when you're young, you don't take any action—the action happens to you.

In 1936, a new action "happened" for Elizabeth: Paramount saw a screen test she had made, and offered her a contract. Her husband had not been working during these Depression days in New York, and they had separated, so Elizabeth decided to accept the Hollywood overture.

> I came to Hollywood with my son, who was practically a baby. I'd never been to Los Angeles; we came by train, and had come through a snowstorm, with the train banked up with snow. Then I woke up one morning on the train—and saw orange groves! It was like magic!
>
> At the station in Pasadena, there was a gent there to meet me with 12 American Beauty roses. They took the baby away from me, and somebody held him while they took pictures of me getting off the train!
>
> Well, this would turn anybody's head—and I was spoiled rotten!

Among the stars who drove daily through the Marathon Street gate of Paramount Studios were Gary Cooper, Mae West and Marlene Dietrich. Paramount placed Elizabeth in the studio school, where she was coached in acting, and took many glamour glossies of the new starlet. However, as she laughs today, Elizabeth simply refused to be impressed.

> Being so successful a model in New York had spoiled me—so I wasn't impressed with anybody or anything! Once, a studio still man was supposed to take me to this dinner party, that Adolph Zukor was giving... Well, I told this photographer that I thought they had an awful nerve, to ask me to a dinner party when I had to get up at four or five o'clock in the morning, as I was working—and I didn't think that was very nice of them! Well, of course, he told it to somebody—and it got to the front office!
>
> So I was constantly in rebellion. And, of course, I should have kept my mouth shut!

Meanwhile, Paramount cast its rebellious young starlet in *Girl of the Ozarks* (1936); she replaced Frances Farmer, whom Paramount had just loaned to Goldwyn for *Come and Get It*; her co-stars were Leif Erickson (who had just married Farmer) and Virginia Weidler. Elizabeth also played in *My American Wife* (1936), with Francis Lederer and Ann Sothern; *Lady Be Careful* (1936), with Lew Ayres, Mary Carlisle and Buster Crabbe; and *Hideaway Girl* (1937), with Robert Cummings, Shirley Ross and Martha Raye.

"I was foil for Martha's wit on the set," recalls Elizabeth, "and I think we might have been a team. She kept imitating everything I said. She had everyone in convulsions—including me!"

In the midst of these "B" films, Cecil B. De Mille shot a test of Elizabeth for the role of Calamity Jane in *The Plainsman* (1936). Elizabeth claims it was a ruse to scare Jean Arthur into signing for the part and stop holding out for more money.

Meanwhile, Elizabeth candidly admits, her lofty attitude worked against her at the studio. She wasn't reluctant to remind people that she had been making excellent money as a New York model, and recalls:

> Toward the end of my Paramount contract, I went to a party one night, and this man came over and sat next to me. He said, "You don't know me, do you? I'm a producer on the Paramount lot."
>
> "Oh," I said.
>
> And he said, "You know, I saw your screen test today. They showed it in the rushes. We were all there, your picture came on the screen, and somebody in the dark said, "Oh—Mrs. Rich Bitch!"

"And *that's* why they're not going to pick up your contract!" added the producer. Elizabeth soon was "at liberty."

A new contract offer followed—at RKO. Elizabeth remembers,

> Right after I left Paramount, I went to RKO. Billy Grady, the casting man at MGM, had taken this job at RKO, and he only signed me for six months because he knew he would be going back to MGM—and he wanted to take me with him. However, I didn't go under contract to MGM. He made a pass at me—and I ruffled his prima donna behavior. Once again, I was just dumb—I should have just said "No" and then kept my mouth shut!

Elizabeth played in one RKO film—*Annapolis Salute* (1937)—before her option lapsed. She had lampooned her share of sacred cows during this sojourn in Hollywood:

> I went to the races at Santa Anita one day, went into the dressing room, and sat down at the mirror next to this girl. She was fixing her hair, I was fixing mine, neither of us said anything and I got up and went out.
>
> Well, did I ever hear about that! This girl was Betty Miller, who also had been a model in New York, and was now on contract at Columbia under the name of Joan Perry. She was the girlfriend of Harry Cohn, Columbia's president, and later married him. "Elizabeth Russell never spoke to me!" she complained after that day at Santa Anita.
>
> And I said, "How was I supposed to know her? Her nose was bobbed, and she now has blonde hair!"

Her Hollywood visit also ended in divorce. On October 5, 1937, Elizabeth received a divorce from John Russell, telling the court (according to the *Los Angeles Examiner*) that "she borrowed money on which to live, because her husband refused to contribute toward her support and that of their son, John Knight Russell, aged four." In later years, Elizabeth admitted that the sight of her on the screen had so intimidated her husband that he'd developed a drinking problem.

Elizabeth went back to New York; began modeling again; acted with Esther Ralston in *Central Casting* at Brooklyn's Shubert Theatre; toured in summer stock; and acted on radio. She became very good friends with Maria Montez, then a New York model on the eve of Universal stardom, and with ZaSu Pitts, who persuaded her to return to Hollywood, where she joined ZaSu in *Miss Polly* (United Artists, 1941). She returned to RKO to play the "Girl on Plane" in *A Date with the Falcon* (1941), starring George Sanders—who played the mandolin, did the tango with Elizabeth and pursued her for years.

"George Sanders asked me to marry him six times," laughs Elizabeth today.

Then came her first horror film: Monogram's *The Corpse Vanishes* (1942).

"One of Poverty Row's most entertaining horror films of the '40s," writes Tom Weaver in his *Poverty Row HORRORS!* (McFarland, 1993) of *The Corpse Vanishes*, which began shooting Friday, March 13, 1942. The melodrama stars Bela Lugosi, who snares brides from the altar, sending each an orchid that produces the semblance of death. His motivation: to get the virgins' spinal fluid to make his wife, the Countess, young and beautiful again.

Bela Lugosi serenades Elizabeth Russell as Angelo Rossitto beholds her in *The Corpse Vanishes*, 1942.

Elizabeth was the vain, evil Countess Lorenz—racking up points as perhaps *the* top Woman-You-Love-to-Hate in Monogram's Lugosi series.

There are her introductory cries of anguish as Lugosi, back to the remote country house with a freshly kidnapped bride, prepares to inject her. "Look at me! Look at me!" cries the Countess (who, even in age makeup, looks far younger than Lugosi!).

There's her arrogance toward dwarf Angelo Rossitto, part of the "family" who assists Bela (Minerva Urecal is mother, giant Frank Moran brother!) as Bela serenades her at the organ with "Ave Maria": "Don't touch me, you gargoyle!" says Elizabeth to the dwarf!

There's her meeting of the nosy reporter (Luana Walters) who shows up hot on the trail of the missing brides: "You are not welcome here!" snaps Elizabeth—who then slaps her right across the face!

And there's her sneaking into the lady reporter's room that night, looking her over with an evil smile, and leering, "Such lovely skin! Some time you too will be a bride, hmmm?"—a scene today which seems a bit kinky as well as frightening.

Sleeping with Lugosi in side-by-side coffins, Elizabeth almost steals *The Corpse Vanishes*, staying vile and nasty to the film's bitter, outrageous end. Aged and moaning again by the finale, awaiting the life-rejuvenating injection, she sees Lugosi stabbed in the back by vengeful Minerva Urecal, who has lost both sons in Lugosi's service.

As the dying, eye-bulging Bela tries madly to stay alive long enough to get the injection for his beloved, Elizabeth's Countess enters the scene.

"Your hand is unsteady," henpecks Elizabeth!

Bela hits the floor, and finally so does the Countess—where an expiring Ms. Urecal drives the knife into her.

Elizabeth's memories of all this Monogram madness are mercifully vague. "A foreign actor who was nothing like he appeared on the screen" is her memory of the "very affable" Lugosi, while a recent viewing of the film left her amused.

"Where did I get that Russian accent?" she laughs. "I was as menacing as Lugosi was!"

Elizabeth, now back in Hollywood, was sharing a small bungalow on Walden Drive in Beverly Hills with Maria Montez, who was becoming one of Universal's top stars via such Technicolor escapism as *Arabian Nights* (1942).

> Maria and I were very close friends, because we came from the same Catholic Church background. At this time, Maria was fascinated with astrology, and she introduced me to a Hollywood astrologer named Carroll Righter, who became famous; Marlene Dietrich used to go to him, and all the stars. Maria and I both were hooked on astrology... Maria's curiosity came from the voodoo doctors in Santa Domingo, and mine trying to find the clue to all that religion that the Catholic nuns planted in my brain.

It was while on a double date with Maria Montez that Fate guided Elizabeth to the man most responsible for her impact in Hollywood.

> I was on a double date with Maria Montez. Her date was Peter Viertel, a writer, who later married Deborah Kerr; my date was Count Ledebur (a real Austrian count, and a casualty from Hitler's reign). Peter said, "You know, I have a friend at RKO who needs a woman for his new movie who looks like a cat. Why don't you go see him?"
>
> "You mean you think I look like a *cat*?" I asked.
>
> "Well," he said (trying to get out of it!), "they'll talk about you looking like a cat, so the audience will accept it. Go and see my friend right away tomorrow."
>
> So I went to see Val, and he took me right away for the Cat Woman!

There was an immediate rapport between Elizabeth and this husky, hypersensitive man with a Hemingway complex, a man with beautiful brown eyes who always carried a Boy Scout knife. *Cat People* scriptwriter DeWitt Bodeen had envisioned silent screen actress Jetta Goudal in the role, but Lewton personally selected Elizabeth for *Cat People*. His maiden RKO production began shooting July 28, 1942.

Perhaps no actress ever made so much of so little. The scene is the Belgrade Cafe, the snow is falling in the night outside, and a wedding party celebrates the marriage of Irena Dubrovna (Simone Simon) and Oliver Reed (Kent Smith). At a nearby table, the Cat Woman turns and looks at the smiling, laughing bride.

Russell (standing) greets her "sister," Simone Simon (seated center of right-hand bench) in the wedding party scene of *Cat People*, 1942.

"Look at that woman," says the Commodore (Jack Holt), the groom's boss. "Isn't *she* something."

"Looks like a cat," says wedding guest Carver (Alan Napier).

The Cat Woman walks to the table. She says "Moya sestra?" twice to the bride—and leaves, sashaying out into the snow.

In truth, the role was even smaller than that—considering that Lewton had Simone Simon dub the "Moya Sestra" line for Elizabeth. "They used Simone's voice for 'Moya sestra,'" says Elizabeth, "and do you know, later, Val Lewton told me that was the biggest mistake he ever made—letting her dub my line."

Two closeups, four dubbed words and less than ten seconds of screen time—yet, for horror fans, Elizabeth Russell's classic cameo is one of the little masterpieces of the terror genre. As captured by director Jacques Tourneur, there was something strikingly ambiguous in that closeup; something both beautiful and wicked. Is this a woman who can transform into a cat? Is she a lesbian? DeWitt Bodeen (who died in 1988) told me,

> Although the cafe meeting of Simone and Elizabeth Russell was very brief, some audience members read a lesbian meaning into

> the action. I was aware that could happen with the cafe scene, and Val got several letters after *Cat People* was released, congratulating him for his boldness in introducing lesbiana to films in Hollywood!

Premiering at the Rialto Theatre in New York on December 7, 1942, *Cat People* was one of the great sleepers of Hollywood history—saving RKO from bankruptcy after Orson Welles' *Citizen Kane* and *The Magnificent Ambersons* (the staircase of which was among the scavenged sets for this $134,000 production).

"Elizabeth had only one brief scene in the picture, but it was a wow," wrote Harriet Parsons in a "Keyhole Portrait" profile of Elizabeth in the *Los Angeles Examiner* (5/21/44), "and from then on she was a fixture in Lewton's films."

"It gave the impression of mystery," says Elizabeth Russell of her famous scene of over 55 years ago. "I read the script, and that's the way I did it—a strange, mysterious thing."

"I recall that after a horror sequence," remembered Mark Robson, editor of *Cat People* (and later a Lewton director), "we always tried to give the audience relief by going to something very beautiful, lyrical if possible." In Elizabeth Russell, Val Lewton could mix at once horror and beauty. She became good friends with her doomed (and smitten) producer:

> Val was a darling man. Oh, he never instructed the directors, he never complained about anything—but he really worked himself into a lather. Val was constantly on the set, and had the worried look all the time; he was always in there, perfecting the script the night before. Val cared too much about his work. He worried himself into a state—and it finally killed him.
>
> Val liked me, and I liked him. As a matter of fact, somebody said, "You know, Val has got a crush on you!" "Don't be silly," I said. "Yes, he has!" insisted this person. Well, I was in several of his pictures, and if he had a "crush" on me, he never lifted his finger or his eye to let me know about it.
>
> We were never lovers; we might have been, but since we were not, there was a closer bond. Val told me he had never cheated on his wife since they had been married. I wasn't about to dispel that sanctity.

As *Cat People* prepared for release, Lewton began shooting *I Walked with a Zombie*, in which Elizabeth might have been ideal as the beautiful zombie wife (played by Christine Gordon). However, Elizabeth was committed to *The Hangman*, an independent project produced by Seymour Nebenzal and directed by Douglas Sirk, based on the assassination of Nazi Reinhard Heydrich, and Himmler's barbaric vengeance against the village of Lidice. After completion, MGM bought the property, re-shot a few scenes, and released the movie as *Hitler's Madman* (1943).

Hitler's Madman plays like a horror film, complete with John Carradine's satanic Heydrich, Patricia Morison's doomed heroine and a finale in which the ghosts of the slaughtered villagers rise from the flames to plead with the audience to avenge their murder. Elizabeth played Maria Bartonek, a villager promised that her husband

(Richard Bailey), who has been arrested by the Gestapo, will return home for dinner. As she and her little children joyfully await him, he does indeed return "home for dinner"—carried into the cottage in a coffin.

Elizabeth remembers the talent staff of *Hitler's Madman* ("They were all European Jews"), Carradine ("a brilliant man, but a drunk") and her contract ("I got a big salary for *Hitler's Madman*").

On March 31, 1943, the *Hollywood Reporter* noted that Lewton was "seeking Elizabeth Russell to play the menace in *The Seventh Victim*." By the time the film began shooting May 5, 1943, Elizabeth's character was no "menace," but Mimi—a dying prostitute, whose apartment neighbors the room where satanist Jean Brooks keeps a noose hanging at all times. Elizabeth personally described her role as "the Ophelia-like creature who wandered through *The Seventh Victim*."

The finale of *The Seventh Victim* is classic Lewton—Jacqueline, who wants to die, meeting Mimi—who is terrified of it:

> MIMI: I'm Mimi … I'm dying … I've been quiet, oh, ever so quiet. I hardly move and yet it keeps coming all the time … closer and closer. I rest and rest and yet I am dying.
>
> JACQUELINE: And you don't want to die … I've always wanted to die. Always.
>
> MIMI: I'm afraid. I'm tired of being afraid … of waiting … I'm not going to wait! I'm going out … laugh, dance … do all the things I used to do.
>
> JACQUELINE: And then?
>
> MIMI: I don't know.
>
> JACQUELINE (enviously): You will die.

As Mimi goes out for the night, all glamorous, for an evening of fatal sin, we hear the chair fall over in Jacqueline's room—she finally has hanged herself.

In her black Cleopatra wig and those giant, haunted eyes, Jean Brooks (q.v.) gave a performance that illuminated Lewton's personal demons. Long lost and sought by film historians (she died in 1963), Ms. Brooks was a mystery to Elizabeth too:

> I never knew, and did not speak to her. When I saw her, I wondered where she came from. She had not been making the scene around town. Maybe I was jealous that she had the lead. As you can see, I had a very high regard for myself!
>
> My role was nothing—a small part. But Val and Mark Robson looked at *The Seventh Victim* after we finished it, and Val wrote me a letter and said, "You stole the picture, Russell!"

Indeed, Elizabeth Russell's star was rising in the wake of *Cat People*. On April 14, 1943, Paramount began shooting the much-heralded (and well-remembered) *The Uninvited*, in which Elizabeth actually played the title character—the ghost of Mary Meredith, haunting the cliffside house where Ray Milland and Gail Russell move in Devonshire, England.

> I had to pose for the painting in the film, which was in the "English" style of the time, with the clouds behind the woman and so forth. The painter was an Englishman named Kitchen, a charming man who had lost most of his stomach in World War I. I remember he gave a party, and Ronald Colman and Lillian Gish were there, and I was invited, as I was to pose for the painting—which today is in a Los Angeles museum.

The Uninvited had its problems (Gail Russell was so nervous in her star-making performance that a "No Visitors" sign went up on the sound stage). Elizabeth had her problems, too:

> So I posed at this studio before the picture began shooting (on salary all the while!). Then I was supposed to appear as the ghost of Mary Meredith, floating down the staircase of the cliffside house. It took much longer to shoot than they had hoped! First of all, I was suspended on a wire, like Mary Martin in *Peter Pan*; then, they made this whole suit for me, from the neck to the feet—and my knees couldn't bend. It took days to shoot the scene.
>
> All that—and I didn't have any speaking part!

On June 18, 1943, the *Reporter* announced, "Elizabeth Russell moves her fright kit over to Republic for another shiver-inducing role in *Mystery Broadcast*"—released as *A Scream in the Dark*. Elizabeth's role: Muriel, a villainess who marries men, kills them and collects the insurance.

Then on June 22, 1943, *The Hollywood Reporter* broke this news:

> RKO is reported to be talking to Elizabeth Russell about a term deal, under which she would be built as Hollywood's first femme shudder lume. If deal eventuates, she'll probably work under Val Lewton.

Alas, Elizabeth's agent held out for too much money—a fact she didn't know until some time later—and she lost her chance to win "Hollywood's first shudder lume" status.

"That's what happens to innocence abroad on its way up," rationalizes Elizabeth. "Oh, the 'what-might-have-beens'!"

Of course, Elizabeth was still a good friend of Val Lewton and would come to dinner at his house at 1217 Corsica Drive in the Pacific Palisades. Naturally, Lewton wanted Elizabeth for the inevitable sequel to *Cat People—The Curse of the Cat People*.

Shooting of this wonderful, moving fantasy began August 26, 1943, at RKO. The sequel lured back all three stars of the original: Oliver (Kent Smith) and Alice (Jane Randolph), married and living in Tarrytown, New York, have a shy, daydreaming little girl Amy (Ann Carter)—whose imaginary(?) playmate is the ghost of Oliver's dead first wife, Irena (Simone Simon). Neighboring the Reeds in the Headless Horseman country is a creepy old mansion, housing mad old actress Julia Farren (Julia Dean) and her sad, lonely and frightening daughter Barbara (Elizabeth). The

Farrens provide the only "horror" to be found in this sensitive little film: Ms. Dean when she narrates the story of the Headless Horseman to Amy; and Elizabeth, as she climactically stalks the child on a snowy winter's night, looking like Mortal Sin as she climbs up the old staircase, enjoying some of the best (and most chilling!) closeups of her career.

The Curse of the Cat People, scripted by the original's DeWitt Bodeen, was fated for many production twists and turns. Elizabeth had her own chills during the filming:

> I saw Val a few days before shooting and he told me not to memorize the dialogue because he was going to change it. But alas, my role came up and no new dialogue—and I wasn't prepared to shoot! I had to hurry and try to memorize it on the set, which was disastrous (no idiot cards in those days), with everyone watching from the front office! And me, holding up everything, because I didn't know my lines.
>
> What shook me was that someone finally told me Val was in the hospital—and neither the director, nor anyone else, knew what he had told me about *not* memorizing my lines! They thought I was making up an excuse!

The September 15, 1943, *Hollywood Reporter* had filed the news that the workaholic Lewton was ill. By that time, *The Curse of the Cat People*, under the direction of Gunther von Fritsch (noted in the trade paper as a director of "recent MGM shorts"), was way behind schedule. On Monday, September 20, 1943, the *Reporter* noted,

> Gunther von Fritsch bows out as director of *The Curse of the Cat People* as of this A.M., replaced by Robert Wise, who last week started directing a second unit when it became apparent that it would not be possible to make up the eight days behind schedule. Move was decided upon by Charles Koerner, Sid Rogell and Val Lewton.

Thus did Robert Wise, the film's editor, begin an Oscar-winning directorial career. As Elizabeth remembers,

> Bob was somewhat apprehensive about directing his first film. I told Bob, astrologically, that he was setting down his roots in a career and that it would be lasting. How about that! And do you know that, all these years later, in 1994, I saw Bob recently—and he remembered my astrological prediction?

With Wise as the new director, *The Curse of the Cat People* wrapped two weeks later, October 4, 1943. Yet the trouble was not over. After previewing the film, Lewton (who was becoming increasingly obsessive about his work) decided to personally write a new ending and re-shoot the climax of the picture. *The Hollywood Reporter* noted that Wise was putting the film back into production on Saturday, November 20, 1943, "for added scenes with Elizabeth Russell, Eve March and Ann Carter." The new ending: rather than have Irena's Ghost unlock a jammed closet door so little

Russell as the bitter, unloved daughter of mad actress Julia Dean in *The Curse of the Cat People*, 1944.

Amy can escape the mad Barbara, the villainess transformed before Amy's eyes into a vision of Irena—whom Amy addresses as "my friend." The love and trust disarm Barbara, who ceases her attack as Amy's family arrive on the rescue.

"The whole production is a novel and entrancing flight in film. Don't miss it," praised John T. McManus in his *PM* review after *The Curse of the Cat People* premiered at New York City's Rialto on March 3, 1944. Certainly it is one of Lewton's most poetic, original and memorable films—while Barbara Farren is probably Elizabeth's finest performance. As Ed Bansak wrote in his "Fearing the Dark: The Val Lewton Legacy" series in *Midnight Marquee* (#42):

> At last there is the possibility that things will turn out well for Amy. But Barbara Farren remains *The Curse of the Cat People*'s most tragic figure, Lewton's ultimate victim... What does the future hold for her? ... The *one* scrap of affection that entered her life by virtue of Amy's hallucination wasn't even meant for her. But so starved for love was this woman that she took whatever she could get. We get no indication that Amy will ever return to the Farren house to comfort Barbara. Barbara Farren

Russell in *The Curse of the Cat People*, 1944.

> will remain a recluse until the day she dies. And the final, most chilling suspicion is that such a day will come soon.

The Curse of the Cat People won some publicity for Elizabeth, as Harriet Parsons celebrated her in her "Keyhole Portrait" series in the *Los Angeles Examiner*:

> [S]he describes her screen self as "a female Bela Lugosi in a constant zombie state" ... off-screen Miss Russell is distinctly non-zombic ... she's a curvaceous, vivacious, blue-eyed, ash-blonde ... that she should be typed as a fright gal is highly ironic...

Ms. Parsons also reported that Elizabeth's 11-year-old son John had taken in a showing of *The Curse of the Cat People*:

> [W]hen he came home his mother asked him what he thought of her in the film... "You were kinda crude," was the startling reply ... for a few dreadful moments Liz thought she'd given birth to a critic ... but further questioning revealed Johnny had meant to say "cruel"...

From the sublime to the ridiculous: at long last, Elizabeth visited the hallowed grounds of Universal City, California, where she became part of that studio's horror legacy in *Weird Woman* (1944), the most delirious of the "Inner Sanctum" series. Based on Fritz Leiber's *Conjure Wife*, this little winner emerged as a chiller/soap opera: Brilliant college professor/author Norman Reed (a wildly miscast Lon Chaney) marries tropical bride Paula (Anne Gwynne), spawning the rabid jealousy of old flame Ilona (an eye-squinting, nostril-flaring Evelyn Ankers). Vampy Evelyn tries to drive the bride (and everyone else) crazy by preying on her voodoo fears. Elizabeth played Evelyn Sawtelle, ambitious, bitchy wife of a timid professor (Ralph Morgan), who becomes hysterically mad after her husband commits suicide (due to Ilona's machinations).

"Best 'meanie' in the cast is Elizabeth Russell," noted the *New York Journal-American* after *Weird Woman* braved the Rialto March 31, 1944, "who isn't the villainess at all."

Elizabeth remembers this crazy brew of voodoo and soap opera burlesque as being rather hysterical:

> One night on *Weird Woman*, we were working overtime, late—and we got hysterical, laughing. Lon Chaney would say a line, we would all laugh—the cast, the crew, the director, Reginald LeBorg—and we could not speak! We were trying to save time, late at night, but the whole unit was in tears, laughing!

Elizabeth played in Lewton's *Youth Runs Wild* (1944) as Mrs. Taylor, the uncaring, war-time factory-working mother of the film's sympathetic delinquent (Vanessa Brown). The film was disemboweled by the RKO front office.

Audiences saw her in small roles in such 1945 MGM fare as *Keep Your Powder Dry* (as a WAC sergeant), *Our Vines Have Tender Grapes* (starring Edward G. Robinson, Margaret O'Brien and Elizabeth's close friend Agnes Moorehead), and *Adventure* (of "Gable's Back and Garson's Got Him" fame), with Elizabeth as the "First Dame."

There would be one more Val Lewton horror film for Elizabeth—*Bedlam*, starring Karloff, directed by Mark Robson, and premiering at New York's Rialto on Good Friday, April 19, 1946. This moving costume melodrama features Elizabeth in the comic role of Mistress Sims, Karloff's gin-swilling niece, whom the villain supplies as new mistress for obese Lord Mortimer (Billy House) after Anna Lee becomes their personal and political enemy. Elizabeth and Karloff played together with terrific comic timing, but she has no warm memory of the horror superstar:

> The English were very "superior" to us. And Karloff, an Englishman, perhaps had a right to be that way—he was a very well-to-do actor. He was never affable with me.

Stirring, moving and frightening, *Bedlam* dropped the final curtain on Hollywood's Golden Age of Horror—a horror message picture, blessed by Karloff's powerhouse portrayal and Lewton's painstakingly passionate production. In a sense, it was the end of Elizabeth Russell's film career. She went back East as Lewton faced heartbreak at Paramount, MGM and Universal-International; in 1951, she called him from the East and learned Lewton had begun work with Stanley Kramer Productions.

Russell with Lon Chaney, Jr., in *Weird Woman*, 1944.

> I called Val and said, "I'm coming out," and he said, "I'm so glad. I'm just starting a picture, and I want you in it."

However, Lewton suffered a heart attack, was taken to Cedars of Lebanon Hospital—and died there at three o'clock in the morning of March 14, 1951. "I went to his funeral," says Elizabeth sadly.

Also in 1951—on September 7—Elizabeth's very close friend Maria Montez died of a heart attack while bathing in her home in France. She was only 33 years old.

For a time, Elizabeth continued acting. She played in two 1952 Monogram releases—the Cinecolor *Wild Stallion*, and the Bowery Boys' *Feudin' Fools*. Robert Wise cast her as a "Saloon Gal" in *So Big* (Warner Bros., 1953); Mark Robson supplied her final film job as "Frolick's Woman" in *From the Terrace* (20th Century–Fox, 1960). She acted in stock, and in 1954, starred with her *Hitler's Madman* star John Carradine in *A Bill of Divorcement* in Bedford, Massachusetts.

"*All the President's Men* (1976) would have found her as a kindergarten teacher," wrote Randy Vest in his excellent feature on Elizabeth in *Films in Review* (May 1981). "But the scene was scrapped at the last minute."

Her son came first. She never remarried. She soon abandoned acting for a clerk job at Houghton-Mifflin in New York, and later moved to Washington, D.C., where her son attended Georgetown University. She finally found the time to write, and has

Elizabeth Russell with the author, FANEX 3, Baltimore, 1990.

penned two plays: one about the life of Maria Montez, another entitled *The Ambassador*. She has much to express.

"They've had nothing but chaos since God was taken out of the schools," she says, "and they'll never have anything but chaos until they put Him back."

Deeply religious, she has taken a severe look at her own life:

> I analyzed myself. I took myself apart as if I stood apart from myself. I went through my life, and I said, "What did you do that for?" and "Why did you do that?" And everything in my life had been for a selfish reason.
>
> That really put me on my knees. And I went to Mass from the time I was 40, for 25 years, every day, to Communion. And it changed me.

In 1990, Elizabeth was a guest at the FANEX Convention in Baltimore. A short time later, she moved back to California to try to succeed in her lifelong dream to be a writer.

"They're all gone," marvels Elizabeth Russell of the Hollywood people she knew. "Maria Montez, Rosalind Russell, the astrologer Carroll Righter, George Sanders, George's brother Tom Conway, Val Lewton's gone." RKO Studios, where Elizabeth made her mark in Hollywood, has been out of business for 40 years. Even the house where Elizabeth visited Lewton in the Pacific Palisades is gone—torn from its foundation and moved away from the site where Lewton and his guests could see Catalina Island on a clear day.

There has been a more personal loss—her son died in 1993. Yet Elizabeth Russell is active: writing, marketing her scripts, proud of surviving the 1994 earthquake, full of faith, and remembered by her contemporaries. In 1993, Ruth Lewton, Val's widow, one year away from her own death, spoke with me of her husband's loving and loyal talent force at RKO of 50 years ago.

"And there was Elizabeth Russell," said Mrs. Val Lewton. "The woman who looked like a cat."

The Films of Elizabeth Russell

1936

Girl of the Ozarks (Paramount, William Sutton)
My American Wife (Paramount, Harold Young)
Lady Be Careful (Paramount, J. T. Reed)
Forgotten Faces (Paramount, E. A. Dupont)

1937

Hideaway Girl (Paramount, George Archainbaud)
Annapolis Salute (RKO, Christy Cabanne)

1941

A Date with the Falcon (RKO, Irving Reis)
Miss Polly (United Artists, Fred Guiol)

1942

The Corpse Vanishes (Monogram, Wallace Fox)
So's Your Aunt Emma (*Meet the Mob*) (Monogram, Jean Yarbrough)
Cat People (RKO, Jacques Tourneur)
Stand By for Action (MGM, Robert Z. Leonard)

1943

She Has What It Takes (Columbia, Charles Barton)
The Seventh Victim (RKO, Mark Robson)
Hitler's Madman (MGM/Angelus, Douglas Sirk)
A Scream in the Dark (Republic, George Sherman)

1944

The Uninvited (Paramount, Lewis Allen)
The Curse of the Cat People (RKO, Gunther von Fritsch and Robert Wise)
Weird Woman (Universal, Reginald LeBorg)
Youth Runs Wild (RKO, Mark Robson)
Summer Storm (United Artists/Angelus, Douglas Sirk)

1945

Keep Your Powder Dry (MGM, Edward Buzzell)
Our Vines Have Tender Grapes (MGM, Roy Rowland)
Adventure (MGM, Victor Fleming)

1946

Bedlam (RKO, Mark Robson)

1952

Wild Stallion (Monogram, Lewis D. Collins)
Feudin' Fools (Monogram, William Beaudine)

1953

So Big (Warner Bros., Robert Wise)

1960

From the Terrace (20th Century–Fox, M. Robson)

Simone Simon

July 28, 1942. It was the first day of shooting for *Cat People* at RKO Studios, Hollywood.

The production attracted a cat's curiosity. It was the maiden project of Val Lewton, young producer newly chosen to head RKO's horror unit. It was a production gauged to challenge Universal's supremacy as Hollywood's top horror studio. And it was, by all early reports, an avant-garde horror script, penned with brilliance by DeWitt Bodeen, who had tapped into Lewton's real-life phobia of cats.

However, the top gossip inspired by *Cat People* was its star, France's Simone Simon—making a "comeback" as "Cat Woman" Irena Dubrovna. As a 20th Century–Fox star of the late 1930s, Mlle. Simon had inspired her own ooh-la-la legend and lore, and a wake of wicked rumors: Simone walked a leopard on a leash. She was the love child of William Randolph Hearst and Marion Davies. She had been a Paramount stock company actress from Salem, Oregon, before she got the idea of affecting the "phony" French accent. She once tore her 20th Century–Fox dressing room to shreds during a storm of temperament. She played dramatic scenes only after dousing herself with perfume that inspired her performance. She was suffering from a mysterious illness, expected to kill her at any minute. She was really 45 years old.

Actually, the true saga of Simone Simon in Hollywood was so colorful that no such silly concoctions were necessary. She had arrived in the movie colony in 1935 as a major European discovery of 20th Century–Fox—only to see her career topple in a storm of alleged illness, ego and scandal. She had fled Hollywood and had sailed back to France—later described by *Whatever Became of...?*'s Richard Lamparski as "one of Hollywood's most spectacular failures."

Now, Simone was back—having played the small (but vivid) role of the witch girl from the mountains in RKO's *The Devil and Daniel Webster* (1941). Val Lewton had personally selected her to star in *Cat People*. Would she behave? Would the $140,000 "B" production crash under her Gallic temperament? Would she be Lewton's Waterloo?

Cat People, in fact, would come in under budget and schedule—and with a classic performance by Simone Simon. Only Elsa Lanchester's *Bride of Frankenstein* survives as a more-huzzahed female monster of the horror genre. Subtle, sexy and curiously tragic, Simone Simon's Irena was the true spark of Lewton's *Cat People*, which made show business history and spawned a sublime sequel, *The Curse of the Cat People*, with Simone lovely as Irena's gentle ghost.

Simone Simon departed Hollywood in the late 1940s. Today, maintaining a prestigious address in Paris, blind but still glamorous in her 80s, she is one of the last surviving legends of the Lewton unit at RKO. One is tempted fancifully to imagine that she truly has nine lives, so superbly did she star in *Cat People*—imbuing her role with beauty, tragedy and a dab of the Gothic tradition.

Simone Simon was born in Marseilles, France, on April 23, 1911 (1914 being the publicized birth year). According to her publicity, she spent her childhood years as an international traveler, living with her mother and stepfather everywhere from Mada-

***Chapter opener:* Simone Simon in *Cat People*, 1942.**

gascar to Paris, from Budapest to Turin and Berlin. In Paris, she studied sculpture, and was advised by "a winner of the Prix de Rome" sculptor to pursue drawing. She studied to be a fashion designer (shades of *Cat People*'s Irena Dubrovna), later switching to charcoal portraits.

It reportedly was a June day of 1931, at the Cafe de la Paix, where Simone, sipping mocha, attracted the eye of Russian exiled director Tourjansky—who told her she should become an actress. She tested for producer Adolphe Osso and made her film debut as Pierrette in *Le Chanteur inconnu*, which starred the famous opera singer Muratore. Simone followed up in Osso's *Un Fils d'Amérique* and *Le Roi des palaces*.

Marc Allegret then directed Simone in *La Petite Chocolatière*; Simone credited Allegret with responsibility for her success, especially after he teamed her with Jean Pierre Aumont in *Le Lac aux dames*. On the telephone from Paris, Miss Simone told me in 1994:

> Marc Allegret met me in 1931, when I worked in Paris in a "utility" part in one of his pictures. He gave me little parts in other pictures, then he made *Lac aux Dames* all around me, to make a star of me. He gave me the chance of my life. I owe him everything.

Miss Simon's *Le Lac aux dames* portrayal of "the elf-like Puck" made her a sensation at the Belgian premiere, where Simone made a personal appearance.

"After *Lac aux dames*," says Miss Simon, "practically all of the studios asked me to go to Hollywood."

Her career was going great guns in Europe; she had completed *Les Yeux noirs* for Tourjansky and *Les Beaux Jours* for Allegret; and had made her stage debut at the Bouffes-Parisiens Theatre. "I was very, very happy," she recalls. "I sang every night—I played in three musical comedies in three years there." Yet Hollywood was irresistible, and Simone Simon signed a 20th Century–Fox contract. In September of 1935, the five-foot, three-inch, 114 lb., brown-haired, blue-eyed Simone arrived in Hollywood—and 20th Century–Fox heralded her as Europe's "Tender Savage."

Simone was one of the first stars to contract with dynamic 20th Century–Fox. As the late 1930s arrived, a wonderful parade of stars and players would pass every morning through the Pico Boulevard studio gates: Shirley Temple, America's #1 box office star; Tyrone Power; Alice Faye; Don Ameche. Fox "Players" were on time, too: a short, stocky, bald Broadway actor who arrived early every morning sporting a white sailor suit and cap—emerging later in the day in toupee, girdle and lifts as Brian Donlevy; a cadaverous young actor in slouch hat and flowing cloak, smoking a long Russian cigarette, roaring Shakespeare at the rising sun and winning fame as John Carradine; and a pop-eyed Hungarian actor who would suffer a nervous breakdown because he so hated the *Mr. Moto* series Fox had launched for him—Peter Lorre.

The chief of 20th Century–Fox: a 33-year-old, buck-toothed, polo-mallet–swinging dynamo from Wahoo, Nebraska, named Darryl F. Zanuck.

Miss Simon took an apartment at the Garden of Allah ("an enchanting place ... it doesn't exist any more"), made sure she had a piano to play in her lodgings, and asked for an audience with her studio boss.

Simon as a 20th Century–Fox contract player, late 1930s.

I was very fond of Darryl Zanuck. I thought he was very bright, he was cute-looking, and if he hadn't been my boss, I certainly would have had a feeling for him. But, because he was my boss, I didn't—I just couldn't. If you look back, he had no idea what to do with actresses, really. He had good actresses there—Alice Faye, Loretta Young, Janet Gaynor—but he only did marvels with Tyrone Power, Warner Baxter, Don Ameche. He had no idea, I think with girls—though he tried.

Fox gave Miss Simon the deluxe star build-up, and announced two top properties for her: *A Message to Garcia* and *Under Two Flags*.

There would be trouble.

A Message to Garcia was Spanish-American War historical fiction, starring Wallace Beery and John Boles, and directed by George Marshall. Simone became "ill" (she had disliked her role, and told Zanuck he should give it to stock contractee Rita Cansino—later Rita Hayworth); Fox ultimately replaced her with Barbara Stanwyck.

Under Two Flags was a Foreign Legion adventure costumer, starring Ronald Colman and directed by Frank Lloyd (fresh from MGM's *Mutiny on the Bounty*). Simone landed the role of "Cigarette," a flashy part for which most actresses in Hollywood would have killed. On October 11, 1935, the *Los Angeles Examiner* announced that Simone was ill with influenza. (Simone personally claimed she became ill because Zanuck had forced her to ride a horse, which her doctor had forbidden her to do.) Eventually she was replaced as Cigarette—by no less than Claudette Colbert.

However, some insisted the true villain was not the flu, nor Zanuck, nor the horse—but Simone's temperament. Louella Parsons claimed Simone had been "temperament itself on the Fox lot," and that Frank Lloyd had "found it impossible to work with her." Columnist Robin Coons later reported:

> [Simone] landed in town on the wrong foot and stayed on it practically all the way. She hadn't been in Hollywood three days before she had tangled with the studio makeup man. Ernie Westmore was doing the usual experimental work on her hairdress but it ended in Simon-pure tantrum. This is sometimes known as Asserting One's Importance.

Finally, on April 16, 1936, the *Examiner* announced that the 0-for-2 Simone would star in *Girls' Dormitory*. Shooting began that spring, under the direction of Irving Cummings; the film premiered September 16, 1936, at the Grauman's Chinese Theatre and Loew's State Theatre in Hollywood. Simone Simon was now officially a Movie Star, and Zanuck approved a lavish publicity stunt: He had scores of "bathing beauties" spell out the name SIMONE SIMON for a dazzling aerial shot.

Simone's next film was *Ladies in Love* (1936); she took fourth billing under established Hollywood favorites Janet Gaynor, Loretta Young and Constance Bennett. Don Ameche and Paul Lukas were the leading men; the film is notable because of the presence of "Tyrone Power, Jr.," who would quickly become Fox's top male star.

Simone worked 16 days on Fox's *White Hunter*, co-starring Warner Baxter and directed by Irving Cummings, before suffering another attack of influenza. June Lang replaced her.

Meanwhile, perhaps inevitably, Simone emerged as 20th Century–Fox's French sexpot—a "sex kitten" with a pout, a petite but provocative figure and a baby doll voice. She later claimed Zanuck "bugged" her dressing rooms, and that some of her dressers were "stool pigeons" who reported her laments back to the front office. She also tolerated the aforementioned rumors—walking a leopard on a leash, being the love child of Hearst and Marion Davies, etc.:

> You know what happened? A few days after I had arrived in Hollywood, the publicity department sent me pages and pages of questions—each one more stupid than the other! One question was, "What is your favorite animal?" and I was so fed up, I wrote, "Panther." That's all—and they soon had me walking one on a leash! They wrote I poured perfume all over myself before dramatic scenes; in truth, I never even perfumed at the time.
>
> As for being the child of William Randolph Hearst and Marion Davies ... well, in the spring of 1937, Marc Allegret came to visit me. He laughed, "I have a good one to tell you, that I heard while having a manicure. Do you know you are the daughter of Marion Davies and Mr. Randolph Hearst? And that they named you Simone Simon after their ranch at San Simeon, and that you go to visit them every night—in hiding?" It was so funny! A few years later, during the war, I went to a party in New York, and one of Hearst's sons was introduced to me. Apparently he knew the story, because he said, "Hello, sis!"
>
> Another rumor—I was afraid to meet Indians in California. Hollywood—it was so out of this world!

Meanwhile, Zanuck starred Simone in *Seventh Heaven* (1937), a remake of the silent classic, directed by Fox's famed Henry King. Simone played Diane (the role which had won an Academy Award for Janet Gaynor); James Stewart played Chico and Gale Sondergaard was terrific as Diane's half-mad, whip-cracking sister. Simone fought the casting: "I never did want to do *Seventh Heaven*. I told Zanuck that it was a very short time to do a picture ten years after it had been a success."

On June 4, 1937, Zanuck pulled Simone out of *Danger—Love at Work*. Director Otto Preminger had objected to her casting due to her heavy French accent; Zanuck (according to Preminger's autobiography) viewed the early rushes, was displeased with her performance and replaced her with Ann Sothern (borrowed from RKO). Zanuck vowed "to find the right story" for the French star. On June 16, she sailed for France and a vacation—amidst rumors that she'd never come back. Come September 13, 1937, and Simone was back at Fox, reporting for the Walter Winchell/Ben Bernie comedy *Love and Hisses*. On October 14, she collapsed on the set with a 100°-plus temperature and went home in an ambulance; however, she finished the picture, which premiered New Year's Eve, 1937.

Meanwhile, Simone had received an unusual Hollywood compliment. In RKO's *High Flyers* (1937), a Wheeler and Woolsey comedy, Lupe Velez imitated Shirley Temple, Dolores del Rio—and Simone Simon.

As Simone remembers, Zanuck was sincere in his effort to make her a major star:

> Once Zanuck called me to his office, and he was very cute; he stood there, those two teeth showing in the front, his cane in one arm; he showed me the palm of his hand and he said, "I know I've got something with you, but I don't know what to do

***Opposite:* Simon on the tennis court.**

> with it. Tell me!" Well, I offered him three or four pictures, taken from books; I mentioned directors I wanted to work with: Rouben Mamoulian, Anatole Litvak, William Wyler. Zanuck said to me, "No. Mamoulian is through, Litvak hasn't done anything, Wyler is not box office." I wanted to do *Pygmalion* (which was wrong of me, because I wouldn't have been good in it); I wanted to do *Wuthering Heights*...
>
> Well, I wasn't very humble! But I wanted to do beautiful things—and Zanuck turned everything down.

Come January of 1938, Zanuck presented her *Josette*, especially tailored for her talents. Don Ameche and Robert Young were her leading men, the supporting cast boasted Bert Lahr, Joan Davis and Tala Birell, and Allan Dwan directed. But if *Josette* was the climax of her Fox stardom, it was also the climax of her illnesses: on February 2, 1938, Simone collapsed again—this time with pneumonia and a 103° temperature. She was taken to Cedars of Lebanon Hospital, her condition was reported as "critical" and Fox insisted she had become so ill because of her "refusal to take a few days' rest that would have tied up a production in which she was appearing."

She finished *Josette*. Zanuck announced a new property for her, *The French Doll*. She was also slated for *Suez* and *The Baroness and the Butler*.

Then the bomb exploded—Hollywood's "Gold Key Scandal," with Simone Simon as the star.

It all began on the night of April 22, 1938, when word leaked from the office of District Attorney Buron Fitts that Simone had claimed that a forger had siphoned at least $15,000 from her bank account and possibly as much as $5000 from her personal account. Early on April 23, 1938 (Simone's 27th birthday), police arrested Sandra Martin, Simone's 32-year-old brunette secretary. "Weeping hysterically," Ms. Martin confessed that she had financed her penthouse bungalow at 1225½ South Beverly Glen Boulevard, $3000 worth of furniture, an $850 diamond ring, $350 worth of silver fox furs, 75 pairs of gloves and drawers full of silk stockings and fancy lingerie by robbing her boss:

> My salary was $87.50 every two weeks. I made out the checks and had Miss Simon sign them, then went back to the typewriter and made them read $287.50...

The very next day, April 24, 1938, Sandra—now with a lawyer—denied everything. "How could I confess? I'd done nothing to confess," vowed Sandra. She made it clear she was out to "get" Simone Simon, in words possibly remembered four years later by Val Lewton:

> She was like a cat ... as long as you smoothed her, she purred; when you stopped ... she scratched!

Sandra Martin waged an epic battle—depicting Simone as a French voluptuary who threw wild parties. Indeed, she claimed she had a recording made at one such frolic, where Simone could be heard carrying on in epic depravity. Sandra Martin promised her recording "would blow the lid off the movie colony."

The trial was a carnival. The tidbit which truly captivated the press was the news that Simone allegedly had given a solid gold key (or keys) to her home to a lover (or lovers—"It was her way of saying 'Merry Christmas,'" sniped the *Examiner*). As Simone departed the court room one day, reporters mobbed her, crying for her to divulge the lover's name.

"Wouldn't you like to know?" Simone smiled.

Meanwhile, all this gossip about the sexy French star and her amours so aroused a 17-year-old Providence, Rhode Island, boy that he came crashing through the second story boudoir window of Simone's West Los Angeles home in the middle of the night of May 2, 1938. "The actress coolly summoned her butler," reported one clipping of the event, "and sat up in bed clad only in a silk nightie." Police arrested the boy, who said he'd wanted to protect Simone from "kidnapers"; later, he claimed he wanted to borrow money from her to study witchcraft in South Africa, hoping to "end all wars through the application of witchcraft." Police filed an insanity complaint and requested the boy be held for observation in the Psychopathic Hospital.

On July 19, 1938, the sentence came down for Sandra Martin: She had to serve nine months in the county jail and ten years' probation. If she ever divulged any of Simone's secrets, or spoke about the gold key, she would have to serve the full sentence. As to the gold key recipient(s), only one name was ever divulged: George Gershwin, a convenient name, since the composer had died in the summer of 1937.

Twentieth Century–Fox had enough of the Simone Simon Follies; Zanuck finally dropped her contract. Yet the cat landed on her feet: Just before the contract lapsed, Simone received a cable from Jean Renoir, offering her the co-starring role (with Jean Gabin) in Émile Zola's *The Human Beast*.

Simone's departure from New York Harbor on the liner *Normandie* was not without incident. She eluded a mob of autograph seekers, who chased her, screaming insults. On the ship, IRS officials demanded to see her passports and income tax receipts. Before Simone set sail, she had to pay the agents $4000.

"I think I *never* come back here!" pouted Simone.

In Paris, Simone indeed landed the top female spot in *The Human Beast*, which turned out to be highly acclaimed and a great boost to her tarnished career.

Escaping the war in Europe, Simone returned to the United States, was said to be sampling hats in the East—and opened in the fall of 1939 in New Haven in a musical play called *Three After Three*, co-starring Mary Brian and Mitzi Green and featuring Stepin Fetchit. It was a rip-off of Fox's 1938 *Three Blind Mice*, with Simone the leader of a trio of ladies hunting husbands. The play did sell-out business in Boston, Baltimore and Philadelphia (where it opened Christmas night, 1939). Simone, however, was not impressed by her own performance.

"I wanted to quit, but they wouldn't let me," she later told Boston critic Elliot Norton. "I should think they would have been glad to get rid of me, I was so bad!"

After braving Chicago and Detroit, *Three After Three* closed on the road in March of 1940, never reaching Broadway.

While *Three After Three* was touring in December 1939, Louella Parsons "scooped" that Cecil B. De Mille had offered Simone the plum role of "Louvette" in Paramount's *North West Mounted Police*. Louella doubted if the play producers would release her; either they didn't, or De Mille changed his mind; Paulette Goddard got the part in the 1940 Technicolor epic, which also starred Gary Cooper, Madeleine Carroll and Robert Preston.

Simone headed for Hollywood; began dating; and guest-starred on Rudy Vallee's radio show (5/30/40). She got her mother to the movie capital to live with her, and began studying for U.S. citizenship. Eventually, she won the role of the Witch Girl from the Mountains in RKO's *All That Money Can Buy*, aka *The Devil and Daniel Webster*, starring (respectively) Walter Huston and Edward Arnold.

> My part of the witch girl in *The Devil and Daniel Webster*, directed by William Dieterle, was very short—and one of my big disappointments. I did that picture to meet the beautiful actor, Walter Huston—and while I got to meet him during the shooting, I never had a scene with him!

The Devil and Daniel Webster emerged as a wonderful piece of Americana, and Simone's performance as the Witch Girl is truly enchanting.

Simone began a series of personal appearances; when RKO's *Mexican Spitfire at Sea* braved the RKO Boston Theatre, Simone was in the stage show, along with flamenco dancer Carmen Amaya, comedian/harmonica player Gil Lamb, the dancing and piano-playing team of Buck and Bubbles, and Christiani's "top-notch acrobatic troupe." It was reported she sang with "bewitching style."

Then Val Lewton joined RKO.

Dark-eyed, burly, 38 years old, highly-strung and brilliantly imaginative, Val Lewton began his first production at RKO with passion. As he sat in his office, enjoying tea and strawberry jam, he ping-ponged ideas with director Jacques Tourneur and writer DeWitt Bodeen for *Cat People*. It was a story of sex problems—a young bride cannot make love to her husband—dressed up and masquerading as a horror movie, festooned with the legend of cat-women from Serbia, who worshipped the Devil and surrendered to sexual passion by tearing their men to shreds. Is the young bride frigid? Is she a lesbian? Is she, in fact, a cat woman? The talents of *Cat People* would present their tale with wonderful ambiguity. And as it evolved, one actress instantly inspired his creation of Irena Dubrovna, the cat woman.

"Val told me from the first to write the part around Simone Simon," remembered DeWitt Bodeen. "He seemed confident that he would be able to get her."

On July 6, 1942, *The Hollywood Reporter* announced that Simone would "cut short" a personal appearance tour in the East to accept the starring role in *Cat People*. Naturally, there was speculation whether Mlle. Simon would bring her legendary temperament back to Hollywood with her:

> When I arrived on the train, the publicity department had gone completely haywire—the photographers arrived with a hat, made like the head of a panther! And they wanted me to put that on my head! I had a reputation of being temperamental—I never knew why—but this became part of my temperamental legend, because when they said, "Will you please, Miss Simon, put that on your face?" I said, "I certainly will *not* put that on my face! If

Simon in a publicity pose for *Cat People*, 1942.

> you want, you can photograph me with it in my hand." So they said, "Oh, there she goes again!"

The movie that would capture the imaginations of a world-wide audience and save RKO began shooting July 28, 1942. The $141,659 budget forced the use of the Central Park Zoo set, left over from an Astaire/Rogers dance picture; the great staircase in Irena's brownstone was a survivor from Welles' *The Magnificent Ambersons*.

Family-man sophisticate Val Lewton found Simone mesmerizing. "I think Val was intrigued with Simone Simon," Mrs. Val Lewton told me in 1993, over 40 years after her husband's death (and a year before her own). "She was an intriguing lady. So French, so different. And she was awfully nice to me—she really was." Simone warmly remembers Lewton:

> Val Lewton, I think, was a perfect man. He was so different from all the people I met in Hollywood, and the people I worked with there. He was so courteous, and gentle, and polite, and well-intended toward people. He was very kind, you know, and very faithful in his friendships.
>
> I have a very funny letter from Val. During one of the pictures I did with him, he had invited me for lunch at the studio. The letter says: "Dear Simone: It's no doubt in my mind that your English is improving, because I had a message from my secretary that a 'Mitzi Moon' was apologizing, because she couldn't come for lunch. I couldn't imagine who that 'Mitzi Moon' was—and then I figured it was 'Miss Simon'!"

Simone's "scandalous" Hollywood past captivated Lewton, who loved Simone's worldly jokes, her high spirits and her jokes about her "falsies"—which she referred to as her "eyes." Indeed, she enchanted most of her co-workers—at least the male ones. As the late DeWitt Bodeen (who also served as the film's dialogue director) wrote in *Films in Review* magazine (April 1963):

> Simone Simon arrived ... and loved her part. She already knew and loved Jacques Tourneur. She loved Val; she loved Mark Robson; she loved me. She wanted to know immediately who her leading man was to be, and when she met Kent Smith, she loved him. Simone was, and is, one of the most lovable actresses I've ever known. Men never have any difficulty with her...
>
> She was unique, she was Continental, and she was a real movie star. She also distrusted women. Miss Randolph wisely avoided her, as did Elizabeth Russell, who had a brief but memorable role as the cat-faced woman who recognizes Simone as "her sister" in the cafe wedding party scene.

Indeed, the animosity between the feline, brunette Simone and the foxy, blonde Jane was one of the delights of *Cat People*. Jane Randolph (q.v.) paints a whole different portrait of La Simon as a vain, trouble-making diva; if so, this clash of female personalities was perfect for the film: Simone as the sexually-confused bride, Jane as the sophisticated co-worker "Ollie" turns to in his sadness.

As far as Simone Simon is concerned, however, there was no trouble on the *Cat People* set:

> I did love everybody in *Cat People*, because everybody was aiming sincerely to do our best with what little we had. Jacques Tourneur was a very nice man—the contrary of a showing-off person, who hardly had time to direct us—yet directed us

> beautifully. Kent Smith and I got together very well, and Jane Randolph was a very nice girl. I remember Elizabeth Russell, naturally, because she was so striking! In the short scene, where she appeared to me at the wedding dinner, she had been made up beautifully. And that was typical of Val—he had that girl in that bit, then took her to better parts in other pictures, including *The Curse of the Cat People*, in which she had a very large part as the mad girl. That's what I mean when I say Val was faithful; once he was glad with the work of someone, he never forgot it.
>
> All of us did *Cat People* in such a hurry—three weeks, Monday through Saturday. We either rehearsed twice and shot once, or rehearsed once and shot twice. The only thing I was afraid of was that the people would laugh at us. It was such a strange story—and could have been taken in the wrong style.

Cat People averted an early crisis when the RKO front office almost fired Tourneur for not being graphic enough in his directorial style; Lewton agonized over every inch of the film. Clearly, Simone was an inspiration to the Lewton unit, and DeWitt Bodeen remembered:

> There was only one woman connected with the production Simone liked and trusted—Babe Egan, the wardrobe woman, who worked in terror of being required to do more than sew on a button, since she actually couldn't sew a stitch. She had been a set musician in the days of the silents, when emoting stars wanted mood music to background their scenes, and she had also been an Orpheum headliner, and had toured Europe with her all-girl band, "Babe Egan and Her Redheads." Now, through pull, she had got herself a job as wardrobe woman, there being nothing open in the music department. One day, when I went to Simone's portable dressing room, between shots to cue her in her lines for the next scene, I found her blithely sewing a torn hem in Babe's skirt. Simone, the practical Frenchwoman, could acquit herself with needle and thread, and sewed on her own buttons—and kept Babe's secret.

On August 12, *The Hollywood Reporter* noted that Lewton had two units shooting around the clock on *Cat People*: work with Simone, Kent Smith and Tom Conway by day, and the Jane Randolph-in-Central Park episode all night. *Cat People* wrapped August 21, 1942, ahead of schedule, and at a cost of $134,959.46—over $6000 under budget. Hollywood cynics hoping that Simone Simon would sink the show were disappointed.

The October 6, 1942, preview of *Cat People* at RKO's Hillstreet Theatre, a downtown L.A. movie house popular with delinquents and drunks, was unforgettable. "The preview was preceded by a Disney cartoon about a little pussy cat," wrote DeWitt Bodeen, "and Val's spirits sank lower and lower as the audience began to catcall and make loud mewing sounds. 'Oh, God!' he kept murmuring, as we wiped the perspiration from his forehead." As the title *Cat People* filled the screen, there were (in Bodeen's words) "whoops of derision and louder meows." Suffering at the preview, meanwhile, was Simone Simon:

> I was with a girlfriend of mine, who happened to be the wife of the producer of *The Human Beast*. We went to the preview, she was on my left—and that poor girl! I pinched her every time I was going to appear! I was scared to death! "Here I come! Oh my God! I hope they don't laugh!" I was so afraid the people would laugh at me. She's a friend of mine still, and she says, "I'll never forget that evening—you pinched me so!"

The Hillstreet audience stopped laughing; they were "enchanted," in DeWitt Bodeen's words, as would be millions of audiences over the decades. On December 7, 1942, *Cat People* opened at New York City's Rialto Theatre and became one of the greatest surprise hits of show business history. Fifty years after its release, Danny Peary wrote in his book *Guide for the Film Fanatic*:

> Simone Simon is perfectly cast... One fascinating image has Irena crouching at the bottom of her bedroom door, like a *cat in heat*, while her sexually frustrated husband stands on the other side... Simon gives an erotic, sympathetic performance ... cinematographer Nicholas Musuraca does wonders with light and shadows—the crisscross pattern over Irena's door makes apartment seem like a cage. A classic...

There's Simone's wonderful reciting of the "Marmaluke" legend of her native Serbia, inside her darkly-lit apartment ... the horror on her face when Elizabeth Russell, as the chillingly feline "Cat Woman," greets her in the Belgrade Cafe on that snowy wedding night with the words "Moya Sestra" (meaning "My sister"—that's Simone herself dubbing Miss Russell's two famous words) ... the crazy, almost vicious little smile on her face when she toys with the little bird her bridegroom has bought her—and the guilt that replaces it when she realizes she has killed the canary ... the eerie cheesecake scene where she strips off her stockings in her dark bathroom, next to the bathtub (with its cat-claw legs!) after stalking Alice in Central Park and (as hinted) slaying several sheep to satisfy her bloodlust after Alice jumps on the bus...

Of course, what audiences remember most vividly are those "Irena vs. Alice" episodes. The infamous "walk" through Central Park has an almost viciously satisfying edge to it: Miss Randolph's Alice, all gussied up in her black chapeau and long beige coat and high heels, having just spent the evening schmoozing with Irena's husband over coffee as he poured out his marital woes, running faster and faster as Irena follows her (as a woman—later as a cat?); those bus brakes almost knocking Alice out of her high heels (and the audience out of its seats!) as the bus arrives to her rescue...

Most celebrated is the pool scene, sparked by the same sexual tension. Alice is in her bathing suit, stripped of any figure-flattering foundations,* her blonde coiffure

**In* The Celluloid Muse, *by Charles Higham and Joel Greenberg, the late Jacques Tourneur noted of Miss Randolph and the swimming pool vignette: "My only complaint about that scene was that the girl threatened in the pool wasn't feminine or diminutive enough. She was built like a wrestler! Too bad!"*

drenched, her makeup washed off in the water, at a loss for all her dry, sophisticated cool as she bobs in the pool, the cat sound and shadow inspiring her hysterical screams—until Irena switches on the light and emerges from the shadow with her sly, vengeful, cat-who-swallowed-the-canary grin. Jane might be surprised to learn that Simone gives her the bouquets for that classic scene:

> Jane Randolph acted beautifully, when she was supposedly scared in the pool by the panther. She was wonderful in that scene! She did the fright so beautifully! They don't give her enough credit. The only thing I did in that scene was turn on the light. And my shot was taken separately from her—she wasn't in the pool any more!

Later there is Irena's climactic anguish when Oliver announces he's leaving her—and she slits the fabric on the sofa with her fingernails ... the odd look on her face as she moves into psychiatrist Tom Conway for a kiss—just before transforming into a cat...

Cat People was a sensation, eventually earning $4,000,000 internationally. Simone Simon had found her role—one which appealed to the imaginations of millions and won her a place in the Hall of Fame of Classic Horror Performances.

Hollywood's award to Simone for the *Cat People* triumph: *Tahiti Honey* (1943), a Republic "B" which co-starred her with Dennis O'Keefe and Michael Whalen. "Simone Simon delivers several songs," reported *Variety*, "the best being the title number, which is far from a hit."

Simone told interviewer Roy Frumkes that Ernst Lubitsch offered her the role of the flirtatious maid in *Heaven Can Wait*, the Technicolor fantasy 20th Century–Fox produced in 1943 starring Don Ameche, Gene Tierney and Laird Cregar (as the Devil). Simone claimed she rejected the job—both because she didn't want to act with Miss Tierney ("who looked a little bit like me but was much more beautiful"), and because "I hated to go back through the small door into the studio where I was once treated like a big star." Signe Hasso played the maid.

On June 8, 1943, the *Los Angeles Examiner* reported Simone to be "running strongest of all" for the role of "Three Martini" in De Mille's *The Story of Dr. Wassell*, which would star Gary Cooper. The role had been assigned to Veronica Lake, who withdrew after becoming pregnant; Elena Verdugo (q.v.) was also a contender; in the end, Carol Thurston played Three Martini.

Val Lewton, meanwhile, had produced *I Walked with a Zombie*, *The Leopard Man*, *The Seventh Victim*, and *The Ghost Ship* (four films in ten months)—and then came *The Curse of the Cat People*. One of Lewton's most personal works, it's a perfect sequel to *Cat People*. Kent Smith's Oliver and Jane Randolph's Alice have wed; they live in the Headless Horseman countryside of Tarrytown, New York, with their lonely little daughter Amy (Ann Carter). For neighbors, in a creepy old mansion is a mad old actress (Julia Dean) and her sad, dangerously bitter daughter Barbara (Elizabeth Russell). Making friends with the unhappy Amy: the ghost of Irena, played by Simone.

The fantasy began shooting at RKO August 26, 1943. "Simone Simon is a ghost in *The Curse of the Cat People*," related the September 2, 1943, *Hollywood Reporter*, "and Val Lewton's biggest problem is to materialize her in a dress which is ethereal yet will pass the Hays Office." Tell Simone Simon how beautiful she is in *The Curse of the Cat People*, and she laughs.

> Well, they better have tried to make me beautiful—because I had nothing else to do! Good God! They did the film to make profit out of the first *Cat People*, to milk it. I should never have done that.

Major troubles clawed at *The Curse of the Cat People*; hypertense Lewton was hospitalized; director Gunther von Fritsch was replaced by editor Robert Wise on September 20, 1943, due to von Fritsch's falling behind schedule. The film wrapped October 4, 1943; on November 20, Lewton recalled Ann Carter, Elizabeth Russell and Eve March (as Amy's schoolteacher) to shoot a revised ending. (There was also one unfortunate cut: Amy imagines Irena, whose snapshot she had found among her father's things, dressed like a fairy tale princess she saw in one of her books. With this scene snipped from the release print, Simone's low-cut tight medieval gown seems silly—albeit charmingly sexy.)

Simone reportedly behaved throughout the troubled shooting of the sequel. She never revealed, at the time, her major problem with *The Curse of the Cat People*:

> A gentleman producer had wanted me to do a picture with him, which Linda Darnell eventually did instead of me. He said he would take me only if I turned down *The Curse of the Cat People*. "If you do another B picture," he told me, "you're through with A pictures." I was so grateful to Val for *Cat People*, that I couldn't let him down.
>
> So by doing *The Curse of the Cat People*, I missed that A picture—but I don't regret it. I couldn't have said to Val, "Sorry, boy—you gave me this beautiful part in *Cat People*, but now I will let you down to do an A picture." He would have understood—but he never knew it. I never told him.

"Have you ever expected thunder and lightning, then waked to find it the loveliest of days, with the last hint of the stars disappearing over the horizon? It's like that with *The Curse of the Cat People*...," wrote John T. McManus in the New York newspaper *PM* after the film premiered at the Rialto Theatre March 3, 1944. Most critics axed the movie (the *New York Journal-American* sniped that Simone impersonated a ghost "with nicely tinted fingernails"), yet it did great business—a movie way ahead of its time. The Christmas Eve episode, in which Irena's spirit transforms the yard of the Reed home into a winter wonderland to delight Amy, is charming, while the climax—in which the inimitable Miss Russell, looking like Sin Incarnate, stalks little Amy up the Gothic staircase—is one of the great fright scenes in the Lewton canon.

Actually, Simone Simon perfectly runs the thematic gamut for Val Lewton in *Cat People* and *The Curse of the Cat People*. In the original, she is the epitome of the

Simon as the gentle, singing ghost of Irena in *The Curse of the Cat People*, 1944.

Lewton victim, the lost soul fearing the worst in herself, destroyed by her lack of faith in her own goodness and worth (as, tragically in life, was Lewton). In the sequel, however, Death has made her a happy, beautiful singing angel—a talisman of the "Death is Good" theme that permeated Lewton's work. Karloff's *The Body Snatcher* is the virtuoso performance in Lewton's horror classics; but Simone Simon's

Irena (both alive and dead) is the character who best represents the remarkable depth and poetry of this incredibly sensitive producer.

Simone's 1944 *Johnny Doesn't Live Here Anymore*, directed by Joe May (*The Invisible Man Returns*, *The House of the Seven Gables*), didn't get a nod from the New York critics. Worse, Simone, while at Monogram, told police on Christmas Eve, 1943, that her $1000 beaver coat, $50 French clock and a leather dressing case had been stolen from her dressing room.

Lewton followed *The Curse of the Cat People* with a juvenile delinquency film, *Youth Runs Wild* (1944)—then starred Simone for the third and final time as *Mademoiselle Fifi* (1944), "based upon the patriotic stories of Maupassant." Robert Wise directed; Simone played Elizabeth Rousset, "a fiercely patriotic laundress" who saves her "superior" coach companions by giving her sexual favors to a Prussian officer. She eventually kills him; come the finale, the funeral cortege bears the Prussian's body as the bell rings in the village—Simone's Elizabeth and the village priest hiding at the top of the bell tower. The garter belt-and-whip-evoking title made many believe *Mademoiselle Fifi* was a sex farce; it failed at the box office, and didn't even receive a Broadway opening.

Simone was announced for a guest appearance on Bela Lugosi's short-lived, 1944 radio series, *Mystery House*. On December 16, 1944, Edith Gwynn of *The Hollywood Reporter* informed the movie colony,

> Simone Simon is selling all her California possessions, including her car... She'll live in New York permanently...

In September 1945, Simone appeared at Philadelphia's Walnut Theatre in *Emily*, as an invalid who stayed in bed the entire play; it never made it to Broadway.

She went to Europe, where she was always good for the headlines; a great stage success in Paris in *Petite Bonheur*; a rumored engagement to William Rothschild; a later romance with Alec Weisweiler, who ran one of France's largest racing stables; escaping injury in a 1954 airliner crash. She also won acclaim in European films such as *Temptation Harbor* (1947), *La Ronde* (1950, directed by Max Ophuls) and *Pit of Loneliness* (1951, in which she played a lesbian).

There would be no more U.S. comebacks; in 1951, Val Lewton, Simone's most ardent Hollywood champion, died at age 46. She lived in Europe much of the time, maintaining for many years an address in New York City. On April 19, 1961, MGM announced that Simone had signed to play Brigitte Bardot's mother in *The Private Life of Brigitte Bardot*, to be filmed in Paris, but the film never came to pass. In 1968, Richard Lamparski wrote in *Whatever Became of...?*:

> She is still a Parisian, and has yet to marry or change her name by marriage, although her friendship with a Frenchman with several million dollars and a wife is well-known in theater and social circles. Her favorite pastime is playing gin rummy. She appeared in Paris in the play *La Courte Paille* opposite Jean Meyer, but friends say it is only an exercise in ego. She wanted to prove that she was still attractive and as good an actress as people remember. She was.

The years passed. Simone appeared in *La Femme en bleu* (1973) as a madam. In the late 1970s, DeWitt Bodeen looked her up in Paris and found Simone a happy and successful artist.

The 1982 remake of *Cat People*, directed by Paul Schrader with Nastassja Kinski inheriting the Irena role, did nothing to shoo Simone back into the Hollywood limelight she had shunned five decades ago—even though this silly, graphic and pretentious film made Lewton's original (and Simone's performance) shine all the more. On Halloween 1984, Simone received the Medal of Paris from Prime Minister Jacques Chirac.

In 1993, Roy Frumkes took a plane to Paris to meet Simone Simon, at her invitation. "My thrill at tracking her down," wrote Frumkes in *Perfect Vision* magazine, "was intensified by the fact that, at age 82, and practically blind, she performed like a true femme fatale and played a game of verbal cat and prey with me, which she won." Frumkes found her living in Victorian splendor, the windows offering "a spectacular view of the Arc de Triomphe." Hollywood's now-octogenarian Cat Woman flirted charmingly with Frumkes, but, in the end, belied her femme fatale legend, stating that she had been loving the same man for 43 years. "We've grown old together," said Simone. "Maybe nobody else wants him! Nevertheless he's still attractive, and I enjoy him."

So Simone Simon goes on. "I was wonderful!" she laughs today of her screen image of half-a-century ago, "and I still am. I grow younger every day." She is, perhaps, all the things Irena Dubrovna might have been had she escaped the Curse of the Cat People.

The Films of Simone Simon

1931

Le Chanteur inconnu (French)
Mam'zelle Nitouche (French)

1933

Tire-au-Flanc (French)

1934

Le Lac aux dames (French, distributed by Franco-American, Marc Allegret)

1935

Les Yeux noirs (*Dark Eyes*) (French, distributed by Frank Kassler, V. Tourjansky)
Les Beaux Jours (French)
Prenez garde à la peinture (French)

1936

Girls' Dormitory (20th Century–Fox, Irving Cummings)
Ladies in Love (20th Century–Fox, Edward H. Griffith)

1937

Seventh Heaven (20th Century–Fox, Henry King)
Love and Hisses (20th Century–Fox, Sidney Lanfield)

1938

Josette (20th Century–Fox, Alan Dwan)

1939

La Bête humaine (French, Jean Renoir)

1941

All That Money Can Buy (*The Devil and Daniel Webster*) (RKO, William Dieterle)

1942

Cat People (RKO, Jacques Tourneur)

1943

Tahiti Honey (Republic, John H. Auer)

1944

The Curse Of The Cat People (RKO, Gunther von Fritsch and Robert Wise)
Johnny Doesn't Live Here Anymore (Monogram, Joe May)
Mademoiselle Fifi (RKO, Robert Wise)

1946

Petrus (French)

1947

Temptation Harbor (British)

1950

Donne senza nome (*Women Without Names*) (Italian)

La Ronde (French, Max Ophuls)

1951

Olivia (*Pit of Loneliness,* French)

1952

Le Plaisir (*House of Pleasure*) (French, Max Ophuls)

1955

Double Destin (French)

1956

The Extra Day (British)

1973

La Femme en bleu (Films La Boetie–Elefilms–Italia International Corp., Michel Deville)

Simone Simon can be seen in distant long shots in *Under Two Flags* (20th Century–Fox, 1936), in which she was replaced by Claudette Colbert.

Jane Randolph

They are two of the greatest moments of 1940s Hollywood Horror, both sparking the same movie—and both sparked by the same actress.

Val Lewton's *Cat People*. It's late at night, and our "ingenue," Alice Moore, played by Jane Randolph, tall, blonde, chic, in a long beige coat and terrific '40s hat, walks home nervously through a Central Park traverse. She's terrified. The staccato of her high heels beats faster and faster. She's convinced a bestial creature is stalking her.

Suddenly comes a shriek of bus brakes. "You look as if you'd seen a ghost!" cracks the bus driver.

"Did *you* see it?" gasps Alice.

Later, she visits the pool below her apartment house. In the low, dark room, she hears a bloodthirsty growl—and dives into the water. The growling becomes ferocious, the shadow of a great cat flickers on the wall, and Alice screams wildly...

"Gee whiz, honey," says a clerk, who has rushed to the pool at Alice's scream, and sees her robe. "It's torn to ribbons!"

Nineteen forty-two's *Cat People* was one of the most novel successes of Hollywood history. The sly, brilliant shock tactics of the fastidious Lewton, the tragedy of Simone Simon's feline performance, the subtlety of Jacques Tourneur's direction, the depth of DeWitt Bodeen's screenplay—all made *Cat People* threaten to revolutionize a genre. Yet the film remained unique, surviving as a brilliant curiosity in the realm of cinema horror.

One of the most striking novelties of *Cat People* was the "ingenue" Alice, as realized by RKO contractee Jane Randolph. A Reinhardt-trained Shakespearean actress, Miss Randolph was no wilting flower, *à la* Fay Wray of the '30s; nor did she resemble the fairy tale beauty Evelyn Ankers, Universal's "Queen of Horror" of the '40s. Jane Randolph's Alice of *Cat People* was a professional woman—at ease with the men in her office, smoking cigarettes, bright, witty, with a sophisticated sex appeal which threw Simone Simon's implied frigidity into even sharper focus.

However, in one department, Miss Randolph was the classic horror ingenue—as she screamed wildly in the classic swimming pool sequence, menaced by the cat creature's growls in the shadows.

Jane Randolph's Hollywood sojourn ended with Universal-International's beloved *Abbott and Costello Meet Frankenstein* (1948), in which she played Joan Raymond, sexy insurance investigator. She wed wealthy Spaniard Jamie del Amo and lived a happy life in Europe and America. Now a widow, dividing her time between homes in Switzerland and Los Angeles, Miss Randolph spoke with me as *Cat People* hit the 50th anniversary of its premiere.

Jane Randolph was born in Youngstown, Ohio, in 1919, living in Canton and attending DePauw University. Her first job was with a judge in Chicago, working in his office one summer; then she took off for Hollywood, to study drama with Max Reinhardt. "That was what I *wanted* to do," she says.

Miss Randolph remembers the celebrated director:

***Chapter opener:* Jane Randolph feeds Glenn Strange a snack between takes on the set of *Abbott and Costello Meet Frankenstein*, 1948.**

> I think Reinhardt was one of the most wonderful people I've ever met ... just fantastic, and I was very lucky—he liked me... He put me in everything he did out here: Shakespeare, a lot of Noël Coward, and all the plays Thornton Wilder wrote...

Meanwhile, Miss Randolph attracted the attention of Warner Bros. (where Reinhardt had co-directed, with William Dieterle, the 1935 film *A Midsummer Night's Dream*) and joined the talent-grooming school there, too:

> I was at Warner Bros. under contract for six months, and went to school every day. I sat on a set every day, watching Bette Davis work, watching them make *The Maltese Falcon*, and *The Man Who Came to Dinner* ... so I was busy all day and worked with Reinhardt at night! A long day!

Almost immediately, Miss Randolph won her first role: a bit in 1941's *Manpower*, starring Marlene Dietrich, Edward G. Robinson and George Raft. It was a memorable experience for Jane—especially meeting the legendary Dietrich:

> I hadn't been at Warners but a week or so, and they said, "You're going to be in *Manpower*." It was a very short scene, but it was interesting to be with Marlene Dietrich. She would come on the set in the morning, and she'd been up since four, she couldn't sleep, so she always come with a cake—she'd bake a cake for everyone! Doing things that you would never think Marlene would do... She was great with everybody on the set, because she would buy marvelous presents for the cameraman and the whole crew—she would buy watches—she really spent her money... I don't think a lot of people do that!

RKO Studios, 780 Gower Street, Hollywood, was then in the tempest of Orson Welles' *Citizen Kane* and *The Magnificent Ambersons*. "Showmanship in the Place of Genius" was the new motto of the financially imperiled lot, which now desperately dispatched talent scouts to find fresh faces for the new program of pictures designed to lure the masses. It was Jane's performance in a play at Reinhardt's that won her a stock contract at RKO Studios. She arrived just about the time that Val Lewton, David O. Selznick's longtime production aide and story editor, joined the studio as an associate producer. While touring the lot, Jane discovered that Dorothy (*Citizen Kane*) Comingore had failed to report for a test for *Highways by Night*, so Jane volunteered to replace her in the test—and won the lead.

Highways by Night was a 63-minute "B" melodrama about truck racketeering, directed by Peter Godfrey (Poole the butler in MGM's 1941 *Dr. Jekyll and Mr. Hyde*) and starring Richard Carlson. "It was a nice experience to do," says Jane of her role as Peggy Fogarty, poor girl whose family is at the mercy of gangsters. *Variety* called the 1942 release "filler fodder," but predicted that the new leading lady "could show to better advantage with more suitable material."

One of Jane's first jobs at RKO was the lead in the short *Hollywood Starlets* (1942). Playing herself, she is "taken in hand" by RKO, and her training is the subject of the reel. Jane gets dramatic instruction, learns about grace, how to kiss and meets Tim Holt, Fibber McGee and Molly, George Sanders and James Craig. In *The Falcon's Brother* (1942), starring the real-life brothers George Sanders and Tom Conway, she learned a lot about movie-making—as well as a lot about Conway and Sanders:

> Tom was just an angel—a dear, sweet person ... so nice, so polite... I think everybody just adored him. George really wasn't very nice—and he *wasn't* nice to work with! When I first met George on *The Falcon's Brother*, we were doing stills (and he was always "on-the-make" for every girl that he ever worked with). So Tom said, "Look, leave this girl alone, she's a nice girl." And George didn't like that—so he was very mean to me the whole picture [*laughing*]! You'd have a closeup with him, and it's kind of nice if somebody looks at you. He'd play with his suspenders, and look down, or pick something up on the floor. You know, he knew all those things distract you, especially when you haven't worked that much... We had a lot of girls, models from New York in that movie, and he was always on the make for every one of them!
>
> Also, what George did to Tom in *The Falcon's Brother.* He upstaged his brother ... tried to outact him, and everything. It was hard for Tom... And that director [Stanley Logan] was an Englishman, so he and George got along just like twins. He never screamed at George—everything George did was marvelous! George always felt he was superior. And he treated people that way. So who needs that?
>
> Years later, I saw George, and I asked him about Tom. He just acted like he didn't know who he was. I said, "I hear he's ill. Where is he?" George said, "Out at the Motion Picture Home." I said "Do you go out?" and he said, "No." I think that's terrible! Tom died out there...

Fortunately, such misadventures only made Jane appreciate the happy, upbeat, wonderfully efficient RKO lot all the more:

> I was very busy, because the publicity department liked me (I was very fortunate) and they kept me busy doing something all the time. The people were so nice in publicity. The girl who was head of the wardrobe department was marvelous, and I would say the camera crews, everybody there, were just exceptional. And so nice always to me—that's a big help.

"Nice" is the word Jane uses most frequently in describing her RKO compatriots—and one of the "nicest" was Val Lewton.

Painstakingly preparing his maiden production at the studio, Lewton was searching for the right actress to play Alice Moore, co-worker of draftsman Oliver Reed (Kent Smith)—bridegroom of our infamous "Cat Woman" (Simone Simon). DeWitt Bodeen's script was a bold, offbeat sex saga in horror movie clothing: Boy meets Girl; Boy weds Girl; Girl refuses to allow Boy to have sexual relations with her; Boy falls for Other Girl at work; Wife jealously stalks Other Girl. Festooning the plot, however, was Bodeen's wonderfully wicked folklore of Irena Dubrovna, cursed descendant of the "Marmalukes" of Serbia—the "Cat Women" who slay the men who arouse their passions.

Jane won the role of Alice; *Cat People* began shooting at RKO July 28, 1942, on a paltry budget of $141,659. The cast was a strange mixed bag of talent. France's Simone Simon (q.v.), former 20th Century–Fox attraction who had departed Hollywood in a blaze of temperament and scandal, but had returned after war broke out in Europe, played Irena. Kent Smith, an All-American type Lewton had noticed bicycling to the studio every day, was cast as Oliver. Tom Conway, Jane's gallant friend from *The Falcon's Brother*, played the sinister psychiatrist, Dr. Judd. Jack Holt (Al Capp's inspiration for "Fearless Fosdick") took care of an old RKO commitment by playing "the Commodore," boss of Oliver and Alice. Six-foot, five-inch Britisher Alan Napier, Lewton's friend (and, decades later *Batman*'s TV butler), was cast as a co-worker. Finally, sinister-looking beauty Elizabeth Russell (q.v.) won the cameo of the "Cat Woman" who greets Irena on the latter's snowy wedding night in the cafe.

Jacques Tourneur (Lewton's pal and collaborator on the second unit shooting of the storming of the Bastille scenes in MGM's 1935 *A Tale of Two Cities*) was director; Nicholas Musuraca was behind the camera. It was a happy company. However, as shooting progressed, a strange phenomena took place: Simone Simon and Jane Randolph, rivals in the movie, became rivals on the set.

> I think Jacques Tourneur was a marvelous director, but he had a lot of trouble with Simone Simon, because she's a very difficult girl. Terrible! If I was in makeup in the morning, and she walked in, she was furious, because she didn't want to wait one second for anybody! I hadn't done very many movies (doing a play is different), and she was always upstaging me. Jacques Tourneur *really* bawled her out, in French. He really bawled her out, and she didn't like that either. She was very difficult with everyone!

Family man sophisticate Lewton, always on the set to supervise, found Miss Simon fascinating: he saw her as a globe-trotting siren, and loved her worldly humor, risqué high spirits and jokes about her "falsies" she professionally affected. Miss Simon apparently knew he was captivated—and according to Jane, took advantage:

> One night Jacques Tourneur, and Val Lewton, and Bodeen and all—we were going home, and we were all in a room, talking. And Simone came in and said, "Oh, my car doesn't start." I said, "Do the lights go on?"—and she looked at me, frightened, you know, because she hadn't thought about that. We all went out to the car, and it was DeWitt or Val, one of them, who started the car—it started right away. Then she said, "Oh, well, I'm hungry!" And these men want to get home to their wives and have dinner! So we all piled her in a car and went up to the drive-in on Sunset Boulevard and ordered her something to eat. Then she didn't eat it—she picked at it. So we finally took her back to the studio and left. But she would do things like that. All day long!

Jane recalls that Simone Simon's naughty behavior climaxed in the famous Belgrade Cafe scene, where Elizabeth Russell purrs "Moya Sestra" (actually in Miss Simon's dubbed voice):

> We were sitting at a table in a cafe and Simone *deliberately* took her drink, just spilled it down the front of her whole pale blue silk suit. Well, that stopped production for the rest of that day—they had to send the suit out to be cleaned, they had to change everything to another set ... it cost a lot of money. Well, she'd do things like that.

What generations remember most vividly about *Cat People* are the two great shock sequences—both focusing on Jane's terror as Irena (presumably) stalks her. The Central Park traverse scene is unforgettable: the sound of Jane's tapping high heels, the shriek of bus brakes (masterminded by editor Mark Robson, later a Lewton director, and heralding the trademark of sudden shocks in other Lewton thrillers—thereafter known as "busses"), and the wonderfully palpable rising terror of Jane's Alice. While the memory of Jane in her long beige coat and large, dark 1940s chapeau is indelible for many fans, she jokes about the scene now.

"I look at *Cat People* today," laughs Jane, "and I'm not so mad about that *hat*!"

The masterpiece vignette of *Cat People* is the pool episode. Representatives from RKO visited the Royal Palms Hotel in downtown Los Angeles (not far from the old bungalow court where William Desmond Taylor had been murdered) to find a pool sufficiently claustrophobic for Lewton and Tourneur. The bloodthirsty growl in the shadows (causing Randolph's Alice to jump into the pool); the shadow on the wall of a great cat (which Tourneur later claimed was the shadow of his fist); and the phenomena of Alice, our chic heroine, becoming a wild, screaming hysteric as she bobs helplessly in the water, all contribute to perhaps the most famous scene in the Lewton canon.

"It's very frightening," says Miss Randolph of her most famous moment in Hollywood, "and that's why they always show that scene in film schools."

Cat People "wrapped" at RKO August 21, 1942, at a cost of $134,959—almost $7000 under budget. All in all, it had been a happy adventure for Jane—who warmly remembers her doomed producer:

> On *Cat People*, I saw Val Lewton every day. He couldn't have been nicer—a really nice man. I was always sorry when I moved to Spain, and wasn't here for so many years, that I never saw him. He always had a lot of things to talk about.

On Monday, December 7, 1942, *Cat People* premiered at New York City's Rialto Theatre—and proved one of the most incredibly popular successes of movie history. The film saved RKO from bankruptcy (along with the success of *Hitler's Children*), and Jane won her share of praise: *The Hollywood Reporter* noted that she "does her best screen work," *Motion Picture Herald* called her "pleasingly unaffected" and *Variety* prophesied, "She aims herself for even better casting." In retrospect, Jane's Alice is a very important performance in the Lewton legacy: She's the first of the most intelligent, refreshing beauty parade of horror heroines of "Golden Age" horror films.

Randolph walks through Central Park, stalked by a cat woman in *Cat People*, 1942 (Photofest).

Randolph, Tom Conway and Kent Smith (on a staircase left over from Orson Welles' *The Magnificent Ambersons*) in *Cat People*, 1942.

Lewton perhaps should receive some posthumous honor from feminists for his depiction of women in horrors: from nurse Frances Dee in his next terror film, *I Walked with a Zombie*, to crusader Anna Lee (q.v.) in his last, *Bedlam*, the producer presented women who were bright, adventurous and attractive.

Jane Randolph's only 1943 release was RKO's *The Falcon Strikes Back*, directed by Edward Dmytryk (fresh from Universal's *Captive Wild Woman* and destined for bigger things), starring Tom Conway and Harriet Hilliard (Mrs. Ozzie Nelson) and featuring fellow RKO starlet Rita Corday (soon to land the Widow Marsh role in Lewton's *The Body Snatcher*).

Jane Randolph's Alice of *Cat People* is so refreshing that it's a joy to find her reprising the role in Lewton's sequel *The Curse of the Cat People* (1944). Alice has wed widower Oliver (Kent Smith again), forsaken her career and is now a happy, fulfilled, high-heel wearing housewife—and a caring, sensitive mother to their troubled child, Amy (Ann Carter). The family lives in a cottage in pastoral Tarrytown, New York (home of Washington Irving's "Headless Horseman")—near the eerie domicile of a dotty old actress (Julia Dean) and her neurotic daughter (Elizabeth Russell). And finally, there's the ghost of Irena (played again by Simone Simon, in an ethereal, low-cut, falsies-flaunting gown) who is the playmate of troubled Amy. Miss Randolph recalls *The Curse of the Cat People*:

Alice (Jane Randolph) and Oliver (Kent Smith) cower under the ghost of Irena (Simone Simon) in this publicity shot for *The Curse of the Cat People*, 1944.

> I was back in Ohio at my grandmother's, when RKO called me and said, "You have to come right back." They sent the script, and I read it, but I wasn't crazy about it—I didn't think it was as good a story, but there was not much you could do about it…

The Curse of the Cat People began shooting August 26, 1943, under the direction of Gunther von Fritsch. He reportedly was "too slow," so editor Robert Wise made his directorial bow, replacing von Fritsch after 18 days of filming. Jane remembers the tense atmosphere:

> I know it was a big problem—there was always a big problem on the set. So Bob Wise, who was the cutter (and very nice), took over. I don't think the problem was the original director, but the whole thing—which was too bad. They had made so much money with *Cat People* that they wanted to do a sequel right away. I think DeWitt Bodeen was writing still, all the time, every night. And since Simone had been so difficult on *Cat People*, she didn't have as big a part in the sequel...

The Curse of the Cat People "wrapped" October 4, 1943, and opened in New York City on March 3, 1944. It's one of Lewton's most personal works, and one of the most sensitive of Hollywood fantasies; James Agee, critic for *Time* and *The Nation* (and a champion of Lewton's work), hailed it for being "full of the poetry and danger of childhood." The snowy Christmas Eve episode, the neighboring spooky mansion and its macabre occupants all give *The Curse of the Cat People* some of Lewton's most haunting dynamics.

Jane Randolph departed RKO after *The Curse of the Cat People*. She recalls the financial woes which wracked the studio during the War Years:

> There was a big strain at RKO at that time; they were having financial problems, and, boy, the producers would walk on the set and everybody would get pretty nervous. If you were overtime, you worked at night, and they were always worried about everything. That was before Howard Hughes bought RKO...

Jane went on to adventures (and misadventures) at various other studios. One of the latter took place at 20th Century–Fox, on 1944's *In the Meantime, Darling*:

> Otto Preminger was the director—and just like his Nazi portrayals. Sadistic! He'd say, "Wouldn't you like to come by after work and have a drink with me and some caviar?" I'd say, "No, I can't, I have to go home, I have a date." He asked me about three times, I said, "No, thank you"—and that's when he became very mean. I had one big long scene, a whole page of dialogue, and after I'd done it about 30 times, he just kept making me do it and do it and do it—just to be mean. The camera crew almost walked off the set!

Miss Randolph reported to Republic for two 1945 releases. The first was *Jealousy*, directed by Gustav Machaty, with a colorful "horror name" cast: John Loder (star of RKO's *The Brighton Strangler*), Nils Asther (*The Man in Half Moon Street* and *Bluebeard*), Karen Morley (*The Mask of Fu Manchu*) and Michael Mark (Little Maria's father in *Frankenstein*). The other Republic was *A Sporting Chance*. She worked with the Bowery Boys (1946's *In Fast Company*), William Boyd's Hopalong Cassidy (1946's *Fool's Gold*) and played Marina Lamont, the villainess in Universal's final serial, 1946's *The Mysterious Mr. M.*

After a trio of Eagle-Lion action films—1947's *Railroaded* and *T-Men*, and 1948's *Open Secret*—as well as some radio and television work in New York, Jane landed what would be her farewell performance, and one of her most famous: Joan Raymond, insurance investigator of U-I's *Abbott and Costello Meet Frankenstein* (1948).

This grand comic finale to Universal's once-awesome Monster saga began shooting at Universal City February 5, 1948, on a budget of $759,524, under the working title of *The Brain of Frankenstein*, and with Charlie Barton directing. Miss Randolph signed for four weeks at $350 per week, taking last featured billing in the cast of Bud and Lou, Lon Chaney as the Wolf Man, Bela Lugosi as Dracula, Glenn Strange as Frankenstein's Monster and Lenore Aubert (q.v.) as evil Dr. Sandra Mornay. (U-I originally considered Dorothy Hart, then Ella Raines for the part of Joan before signing Miss Randolph.)

It was a wild set, with pie fights and practical jokes, and Randolph got a real work-out in the film: vamping Costello, dancing with Lugosi (and falling under his vampiric spell) at the masquerade ball, and helping hero Charles Bradstreet set fire to the back lot pier to destroy Strange's Monster—hence winning the cinema distinction of aiding and abetting the final destruction of Universal's beloved Monster.

> *Abbott and Costello Meet Frankenstein* was fun! I can remember all these years later ... it was great fun. Abbott and Costello were marvelous to work with ... no tension. They were extremely funny, always clowning around; even if it wasn't part of the script, they were clowning. Terrific ... Glenn Strange as Frankenstein—he was marvelous! Every time we'd go out and do stills, out in the truck or out any place, I'd laugh so, because it seemed so ridiculous! Sure, I remember Bela Lugosi (a nice person), and Lon Chaney, and director Charlie Barton, who was easy to work with. I see people in Europe all the time who say, "Oh, I saw you in *Abbott and Costello Meet Frankenstein*!

The movie finished shooting March 20, 1948—slightly over schedule and budget. On April 9, the studio recalled Jane for an added scene—her first appearance in the film, in the insurance office, with Frank Ferguson and Howard Negley. Charlie Barton had it all "in the can" by 11:30 that morning.

Abbott and Costello Meet Frankenstein previewed at Los Angeles' Forum Theatre Friday night, June 25, 1948—one of the biggest hits in Universal's history, and a wonderfully funny farewell to the studio's beloved goblins.

It was also the final movie of Jane Randolph. Today, she feels her film career never took off because of poor representation—and her refusal to "play ball" with the big shots:

> My problem was I never had a good agent. And when David Selznick asked me to please have dinner with him, I refused three times. (I probably should have gone to dinner with him!)

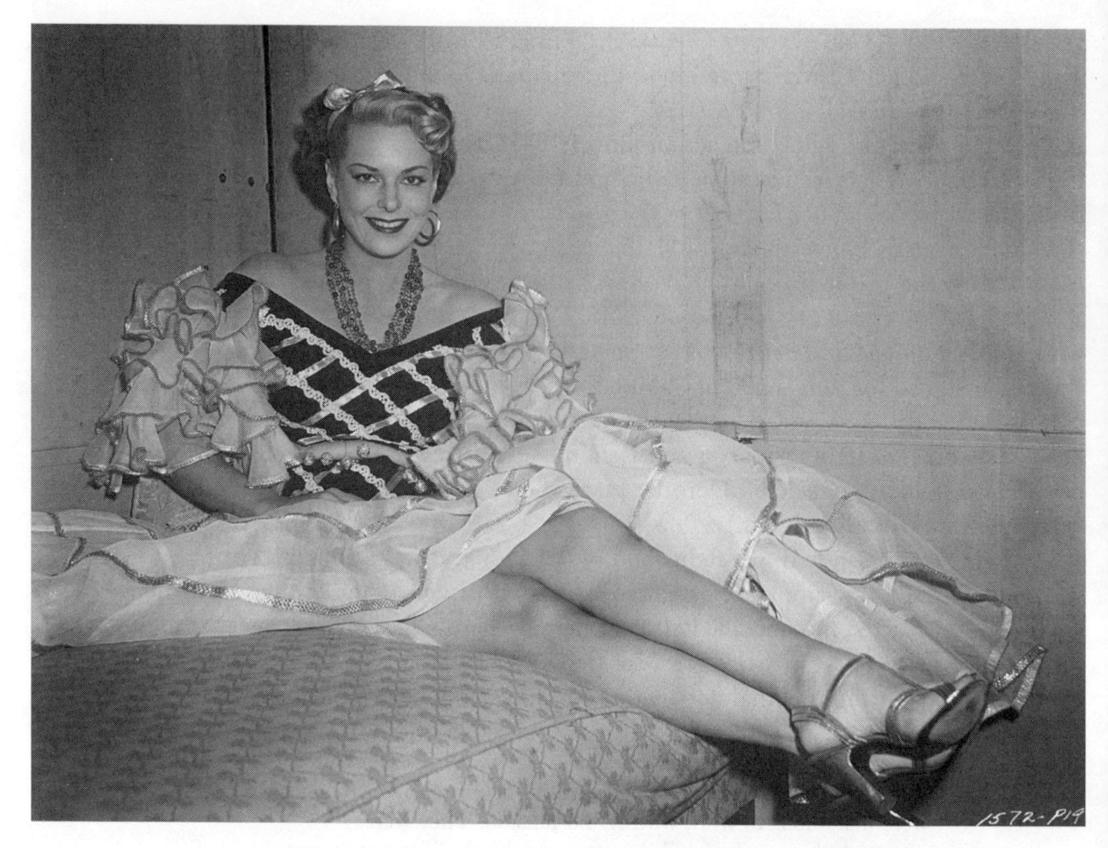

Randolph relaxes during a break on the set of *Abbott and Costello Meet Frankenstein*, 1948.

> He liked what I did because I'm sort of the Ingrid Bergman type, and he liked that. He called me and finally his secretary said, "You realize who Mr. Selznick is?" I said, "Yes, but I don't want to have dinner with him." And he never called again [*laughing*]! It was probably stupid, but that's the way I felt.

She also married. On April 20, 1948—11 days after shooting her added scene for *Abbott and Costello Meet Frankenstein*—Jane wed Jaime del Amo, described by the *Los Angeles Examiner* as a "wealthy sportsman and scion of an early California family." Del Amo was former Spanish vice consul in Los Angeles, owner of "Del Amo Ranch Enterprises" and oil producing operations; his family owned one of the largest old Spanish land grants in Los Angeles. The couple eloped at midnight in del Amo's chartered plane, and wed in Las Vegas. Jane entered a lavish new lifestyle, living much of her time in Switzerland, France and Spain. She had a daughter, to whom she is very close; Mr. del Amo died about 30 years ago.

Today, Jane Randolph del Amo travels the world. She keeps an apartment in West Los Angeles, not far from the studios where she acted half-a-century ago.

> I like Switzerland, because I live there in the winter, and I ski every day, all winter. That's very good, very healthy. I come back to Los Angeles now because my daughter is here, and I have

> friends here that I've had for years. It's nice to be back here. I go on water color painting workshops a lot. I just went up to Carmel to paint for a week. Absolutely breathtaking.

Paul Schrader remade *Cat People* for Universal release in 1982. In homage to the original (and Jane Randolph's most famous Hollywood episode), Schrader retained the pool scene, but with a distinct difference. In the 1982 *Cat People*, the imperiled Alice—played by Annette O'Toole—is topless.

The Films of Jane Randolph

1941

Manpower (Warner Bros., Raoul Walsh)
Dive Bomber (Warner Bros., Michael Curtiz)

1942

The Male Animal (Warner Bros., Elliott Nugent)
Highways by Night (RKO, Peter Godfrey)
The Falcon's Brother (RKO, Stanley Logan)
Cat People (RKO, Jacques Tourneur)

1943

The Falcon Strikes Back (RKO, Edward Dmytryk)

1944

The Curse of the Cat People (RKO, Robert Wise and Gunther von Fritsch)
In the Meantime, Darling (20th Century–Fox, Otto Preminger)

1945

A Sporting Chance (Republic, George Blair)
Jealousy (Republic, Gustav Machaty)

1946

In Fast Company (Monogram, Del Lord)
Fool's Gold (United Artists, George Archainbaud)
The Mysterious Mr. M (Universal 13-chapter serial, Lewis D. Collins and Vernon Keays)

1947

Railroaded (Eagle-Lion, Anthony Mann)
T-Men (Eagle-Lion, Anthony Mann)

1948

Open Secret (Eagle-Lion, John Reinhardt)
Abbott and Costello Meet Frankenstein (Universal-International, Charles T. Barton)

SHORT SUBJECT

1942

Hollywood Starlets (RKO)

Anne Gwynne

In the rip-roaring World War II days and nights of Universal City, California, the coronated "Queen of the Horrors" was the blonde and bounteous Evelyn Ankers (q.v.).

However, if Evelyn was queen, there most certainly was no contest for princess: Evelyn's close friend and dressing room sharer, Anne Gwynne.

Indeed, in horror film circles, fans might well debate retrospectively who truly deserved the crown as Queen. Evelyn, of course, had the classic credit of *The Wolf Man* and her famed repertory (*The Ghost of Frankenstein*, *Son of Dracula*, *The Mad Ghoul*, *The Invisible Man's Revenge*), as well as *Sherlock Holmes* and "Inner Sanctum" films. She had the beauty of a fairy tale princess and her spine-tingling scream was a classic in itself.

Yet, in examination, Anne Gwynne comes closer to challenging "Evie's" throne than one might originally imagine. True, Anne's horror credits included *The Black Cat* (1941), a rather feeble horror/comedy, and *The Strange Case of Doctor Rx* (1942), in which Anne posed helpless in the grasp of a killer ape in a scene never actually glimpsed in the movie. However, while Evelyn never acted with "King" Karloff, Anne did three times: *Black Friday* (which also featured Lugosi), *House of Frankenstein* and RKO's *Dick Tracy Meets Gruesome*. While Anne didn't rack up the individual films with various Universal goblins, she co-starred with Dracula, the Wolf Man, Frankenstein's Monster and a hunchback in *House of Frankenstein* (although her episodic role sentenced her only to appear in the Dracula vignette). While Evelyn was spared ever having to act in serials, Anne trouped her way through cliffhangers, including the popular *Flash Gordon Conquers the Universe*. And while Evelyn "aged" a bit in her Universal sojourn, from the refreshingly lovely heroine of *The Wolf Man* to the foxy (but rather girthy) glamourpuss of *The Mad Ghoul* only two years later, Anne remained strikingly fresh and lovely, with Betty Grable legs and a charm all her own.

Like Evelyn, Anne Gwynne worked in virtually every feature commodity Universal could offer—joining the studio a year-and-a-half before Evelyn arrived, and acting with Deanna Durbin, Abbott and Costello, singing, dancing and playing everything from farce to melodrama to Westerns. Of course, the two actresses worked together a number of times, notably in *Weird Woman*, most popular of Universal's "Inner Sanctums," a horror soap opera that sparks mainly due to Anne and Evelyn battling over Lon Chaney.

Both ladies made dozens of films for Universal City; both were mercilessly overworked by the studio; and neither lady maintained a high-profile career after Universal.

The strange checks and balances remained over the years. While Evelyn boasted of her very happy marriage to actor Richard Denning and a dream retirement in Hawaii, Anne was widowed in 1965, and lived alone, working as a secretary in the San Fernando Valley near Universal. But while Evelyn Ankers died in 1985, Anne Gwynne is a survivor, although reportedly a very ill one—refusing interviews with most journalists who seek her memories of the Universal legendary years when she was truly "Princess of the Horrors" with no real desire to topple her friend Evelyn's throne.

***Chapter opener:* Anne Gwynne relaxes with John Carradine on the set of *House of Frankenstein*, 1944.**

> Sure-to-Win Gwynne: On that we bet our last dime. The tenacity, the determination, the do-or-die spirit that permeates Anne's blonde loveliness will reap her a golden harvest one day, you mark our words...
>
> —"Round-Up of Pace Setters" by Sara Hamilton, *Photoplay*, October 1941

She was born Marguerite Gwynne Trice in Waco, Texas, on December 10, 1918. Her parents later moved to St. Louis, Missouri, and Anne studied at Stephens College in Columbia, Missouri, where she pursued drama. Anne reportedly appeared in a 1936 St. Louis promotional film; when her father, who worked for Catalina Swimwear, attended a Los Angeles convention the summer after Anne's freshman college year, he took his daughter along. Result: Anne got a job modeling swimsuits, attended the Bliss-Hayden Little Theatre evenings and was soon acting in little theater productions of such plays as *Stage Door*, *The Colonel's Lady* and *Inside Story*.

Anne appeared in a newsreel entitled *Swimming Under Water* and a charity short with Edgar Bergen and Charlie McCarthy before her momentous interview at Universal. As Richard Lamparski reported in *Whatever Became of...?*:

> One day she had an appointment at Universal in the morning and at Warner Brothers after lunch. Anne never made it to her second date. After a 30-minute interview, she was signed to a contract which began at $75 a week in June of 1939.

In his book *Universal Pictures*, Michael Fitzgerald (a close friend of Anne's) claims she "obtained a contract with Universal after the shortest interview on record (47 seconds) and no screen test." *Photoplay* (October 1941) provided the most dazzling account of all:

> Anne was signed to a long-term contract after the shortest interview imaginable. It consisted of exactly three questions.
>
> "Have you ever acted on the stage professionally?" She was asked.
>
> "No," said our Annie.
>
> "Have you ever been in pictures?"
>
> "No."
>
> "Would you like to be in pictures?"
>
> "*Yes*," howled Anne and signed the paper.

Anne made her Universal debut as Kitty in *Unexpected Father*, a vehicle for Baby Sandy, which premiered at New York's Palace Theatre in August 1939. Also in the cast: Mischa Auer, Dennis O'Keefe, Shirley Ross and Anne Nagel (q.v.)—who had also signed with Universal in June of 1939.

Before long, Anne was averaging seven pictures a year for Universal—"sometimes two or three at a time," she remembered. She acted in everything—from Deanna Durbin's *Spring Parade* (1940) to *Flash Gordon Conquers the Universe*. And it was in late 1939 that she began her first horror feature: *Black Friday*, starring Karloff and Lugosi.

Anne played Jean, daughter of Dr. Ernest Sovac (Karloff), who, on one Friday the 13th, transplants the brain of a gangster into the head of his dying friend, English professor George Kingsley (Stanley Ridges)—with predictably melodramatic results. Lugosi was a gangster, Anne Nagel was the nightclub chanteuse, and Arthur Lubin worked the company late into the night to bring in the film in 18 days and a cost of $124,000.

In an interview with Michael Fitzgerald in *Fangoria* (#115), Anne remembered the star of *Black Friday*—Boris Karloff:

> What an actor; what a *man*! I had a key scene with Boris, the one where I'm urging him to take Stanley Ridges back home from New York. Well, we shot the entire scene with the camera on Boris. Arthur Lubin was the director, and for some reason I've always felt that he didn't like me. He said "Wrap!" but Boris came to my rescue and said, "*Don't do this to her*. Give Anne a close-up." Which is exactly what Lubin had to do, and it's in the picture! ... Most actors wouldn't think of it, or do it if they *did* think of it, but Boris Karloff I'll always admire. He was not only a fine actor who could play just about anything, but a really terrific human being. He is sorely missed.

Anne joined Karloff, Anne Nagel and Stanley Ridges the day the press watched Lugosi supposedly hypnotized to play his *Black Friday* death scene. Anne told Fitzgerald about Lugosi:

> Again, he was a very nice, pleasant fellow. But he was a foreigner who didn't speak English that well, so my relationship with him was just pleasantries, nothing much to speak of...

As for the hypnosis story, Anne gives a definite opinion: "All hype. All for publicity. I didn't believe it—it was all a put-on for the camera and the press. The studios always did those sorts of things."

While *Black Friday* has its admirers, many regard the film as a fluke—and can't forgive it for not pairing Karloff and Lugosi in a single scene. Anne, despite her scream and presence, needed a better thriller to establish her as a scream queen.

Anne didn't get such a break in 1941's *The Black Cat*—shot from February 17 to March 10, 1941, on a $176,000 budget. No relation to the Karloff/Lugosi masterpiece of 1934, nor Poe's tale, this *The Black Cat* is an old house comedy/thriller starring Basil Rathbone, Broderick Crawford (one of Anne's favorite leading men), Lugosi, Gladys Cooper ("It seemed as though she was slumming, working in this picture," Anne told Fitzgerald), Gale Sondergaard ("Rather reserved, but striking—a real beauty"), Hugh "Woo Woo" Herbert and Alan Ladd ("That little insecure man, in person, didn't seem to have it").

"An uninspired burlesque masquerading as a horror movie," write Michael Brunas, John Brunas and Tom Weaver in *Universal Horrors*, "it remains one of Universal's most misrepresented thrillers."

Anne kept working away for Universal, night and day, in any role in which she was needed. As *Photoplay* reported:

> Her studio gives her a gold star daily for cooperation. Anne will cheerfully break a date to make publicity pictures any time she's asked. She never wastes a minute foolishly, but studies and watches other players at work.
>
> She rides well, swims, lives with her mother in a Hollywood apartment and works, works, works. That's why we know she'll win. Her one bright consoling thought is that no one so far has comforted her with, "Oh well, Gwynne and bear it."

Ironically, the very traits that *Photoplay* saluted were the ones that ultimately worked against Anne Gwynne as the studio took her for granted. As she told Richard Lamparski (*Whatever Became of...?*) decades after the fact:

> I wish I had been more insistent on better pictures. Maria Montez complained about absolutely everything and told me not to be so cooperative. They made her a star, and I'm sure her demands had a lot to do with it...

Indeed, Montez joined the studio as a bit player almost a year-and-a-half after Anne began there, but aggressively became one of the lot's top attractions. Anne took everything Universal threw at her, in a spirit of camaraderie, trusting it would lead to better things; meanwhile, Universal exploited her to the limit, even marketing paper cut-out dolls of Anne (along with likenesses of such studio starlets as Helen Parrish, Ann Gillis, Jane Frazee, Peggy Moran and Anne Nagel).

As fans bought the October 1941 issue of *Photoplay*, Anne went into *The Strange Case of Doctor Rx*. Patric Knowles played private investigator Jerry Church; Anne was his mystery writer/amateur detective wife, Kit; in the course of this 66 minute "B," they encounter a bespectacled red herring named Dr. Fish (a jolly but wasted Lionel Atwill), Bongo, a brain transplant-craving killer gorilla (Ray "Crash" Corrigan) and a madman so fearful (revealed to be Samuel S. Hinds) that he turns his male victims to white-haired, hopelessly insane idiots. It sounds impressive, but is actually more a poor man's *Thin Man* comedy than a horror show; Anne, in a nightgown, posed for PR shots with Corrigan's gorilla (a scene never glimpsed in the movie!).

Still, as Anne told Fitzgerald in *Fangoria*, she had "fun, fun, fun" making the film, largely due to the ad-libbing that director William Nigh encouraged (and, with an incomplete script, needed). The late Patric Knowles told the authors of *Universal Horrors* that Anne was "a great joy," and that he would have welcomed a series of Jerry-and-Kit Logan Church detective films—"Yes, if Anne Gwynne was the lady."

By this time, Anne was settled into the former dressing room of Lon Chaney and Brod Crawford (who had lost the quarters due to their affectionate drunken brawls, which regularly trashed the spot) with Evelyn Ankers, who had joined Universal City in January 1941. Evelyn's work in British films, as well as the London and Broadway stage, probably encouraged Universal to award her instant stardom, without the bit parts that Anne had endured. While Anne might have been the contender for Universal's top horror leading lady, in *Black Friday* and *The Black Cat*, Evelyn immediately became the Universal Horror Queen via *The Wolf Man* (1941), which began shooting just as Anne was finishing up the far-inferior *The Strange Case of Doctor Rx*.

Gwynne, Universal's TNT girl—"Trim, Neat & Terrific"—on the set of *The Strange Case of Doctor Rx*, 1942.

Nineteen forty-two saw Anne as the leading lady in Abbott and Costello's *Ride 'Em Cowboy*; she looked charming in her cowgirl suit, performed her own steer-roping stunt and enjoyed working with the comics, as well as Dick Foran and Johnny Mack Brown. Anne told Bob Furmanek and Ron Palumbo in their book, *Abbott and Costello in Hollywood*:

Gwynne (left) as Pearl, the tragic chorine of *Broadway*, 1942. On the right is Janet Blair.

> These two fellows were old burlesque boys; they knew the ropes. They were so fresh and delightful and funny. They weren't burned out and they *loved* doing what they were doing. Every time somebody laughed, they were in ecstasy. There was a genuineness about them... Even when I saw them working on other pictures, they were delightful.

Anne gave perhaps her best performance as Pearl, the chorus girl/murderess of *Broadway* (1942), which starred George Raft, Pat O'Brien and Janet Blair. The film not only gave Anne a showcase in which to show off her beautiful legs, but revealed just how much depth and emotion she could convey as an actress.

Nineteen forty-three saw Anne in such Universal fare as *Top Man*, a musical starring Donald O'Connor and Susanna Foster (q.v., fresh from *Phantom of the Opera*), and *Frontier Badman*, starring Diana Barrymore, Robert Paige and—as "Chango, the Mad Killer"—Lon Chaney. Meanwhile, Anne became one of the top leggy pin-ups of World War II; she was romantically linked with cowboy actor Tom Keene; and on January 22, 1943, the *Los Angeles Examiner* reported she was wearing "a diamond engagement ring" from Capt. Charles Sales of United States Field Artillery. However, the marriage never took place and Anne for the time remained single—and wary of the Hollywood "wolves" who flocked to her door.

Anne had second billing in Universal's "Inner Sanctum" entry, *Weird Woman* (1944); she was excellent as the superstitious bride Chaney brings back from the tropics—and who is menaced by madly jealous Evelyn Ankers. Anne responded to Michael Fitzgerald's *Fangoria* inquiry about Chaney:

> Well, now you've got me. I have nothing but glowing things to say about Boris Karloff, and only praise for Bela Lugosi, but Lon Chaney was something else, although we actually got along fine together. But he would pull practical jokes on people—and they did become quite cruel. He never bothered me at all—it was Evelyn who incurred his wrath. They worked together more often, and yet they couldn't stand each other, sort of like the way Jon Hall and Maria Montez never got along...

Anne also stated she felt Chaney "wrong" for his role of a brilliant, dashing college professor/author in *Weird Woman*—and how tough it was for her and Evelyn Ankers to play enemies in the movie. As Reginald LeBorg told Tom Weaver in his book, *Interviews With B Science Fiction and Horror Movie Makers* (McFarland, 1988):

> Evelyn Ankers was a very sweet girl and a very good actress, but, no, she wasn't very happy about her part in *Weird Woman*. She was a good friend of Anne Gwynne's, and she had to play Gwynne's enemy in *Weird Woman*—to torment her... When Ankers had a scene with Gwynne that was rather macabre, she couldn't do it very well because she loved Gwynne so much that she *couldn't* be mean to her. I gave her a few pointers, and after three or four takes she did it very well.

As Elizabeth Russell (q.v.), who played one of her best neurotic roles in *Weird Woman* recalls, the "three or four takes" often erupted into wild hilarity. Yet in the finished film, Anne plays with apparently total sincerity, and her escalating terror—as Evelyn plagues her with voodoo-chant phone calls—again gives evidence of just how fine an actress she could be.

Nineteen forty-four audiences also saw Anne in *Moon Over Las Vegas* and *South of Dixie*, both with David (*The Mad Ghoul*) Bruce as leading man; she was the star of *Murder in the Blue Room*, which offered a ghost in a derby (Robert Cherry) and Anne singing "One Starry Night" (her voice dubbed by Martha Tilton). She was lovely, too, in *Babes on Swing Street*.

Of course, the 1944 Anne Gwynne performance horror fans remember most vividly is Rita, the American newlywed, who almost becomes a bride of John Carradine's Dracula in *House of Frankenstein*.

Built around the contract of Boris Karloff, the Monster Rally offered Karloff as mad Dr. Gustav Niemann, J. Carrol Naish as homicidal hunchback Daniel, Lon Chaney in his third appearance as the Wolf Man, Carradine as Dracula, Glenn Strange as the Frankenstein Monster and Elena Verdugo (q.v.) as the gypsy girl who loves the Wolf Man enough to kill him (and be killed in return). Along for the ride: Lionel Atwill as Inspector Arnz and George Zucco as Professor Bruno Lampini, original owner of the traveling "Chamber of Horrors" which Karloff takes over to wreak his macabre revenge.

Shooting began under the title of *The Devil's Brood* on April 4, 1944. Anne's fee for the show reveals the inequity suffered by studio starlets: At Universal for five years, Anne received a "flat fee": $3000. Compare this to Karloff's $20,000, Chaney's $10,000 and the $7000 taken home by both Carradine and Naish, and the $3500 paid to Peter Coe, who played her bridegroom (and who had been at the studio for less than a year). Then again, Anne's three grand was a lot better than the $250 per week paid free-lancing Elena Verdugo and Glenn Strange.

Because of the contract Karloff had with Universal, Anne, Carradine, Peter Coe and Lionel Atwill didn't start work until Thursday, April 27; director Erle C. Kenton had already shot the climax of the picture, and Chaney, Elena Verdugo, George Zucco and Glenn Strange all had finished their work on the film. Karloff and Naish completed their work two days later, Saturday, April 29, and Kenton devoted the last seven days of shooting to the Dracula episode (which appears in the first third of the film).

As Rita, the bride of Carl Hussman (Peter Coe) and daughter-in-law of the Burgomaster (Sig Rumann), Anne creates her finest performance in a horror film. "It's like being wrapped in the arms of a gigantic ghost," sighs Anne's Rita, who has insisted that her spouse, father-in-law and Inspector Arnz (Lionel Atwill) all accompany her to the Midnight Horror Show.

After Karloff has resurrected Dracula, and dispatched him out to seek revenge against the Burgomaster (who had sent him to prison), Dracula arrives in his coach and invites the Hussmans to join him. Instantly, Anne and Carradine create a macabre chemistry, striking sexy sparks at the inn, as the Count shows the bride his ring:

Gwynne, featured in exotica never actually glimpsed in *House of Frankenstein*, 1944.

> ANNE: I see glimpses of a strange world—a world of people who are dead, and yet alive.
>
> CARRADINE: It is the place from which I've just returned.
>
> ANNE: It frightens me.
>
> CARRADINE: (giving her the ring): Wear it. It will drive away your fears… I will come for you before the dawn.

Pioneering the way for the cinema's sensual vampiric victims (for which Hammer Studios fans would later attempt to take credit!), Anne, under the Dracula spell, transforms from the All-American apple pie beauty of her first scenes to a sighing, soon-to-be succubus. In a chillingly effective shot, Anne stands by a window, back to the camera in shadow, and sighs longingly:

> It's a wonderful night. The darkness beckons to me. Another world. The world I see is far away, and very near. A strange and beautiful world...

Anne turns from the shadow, walks into the light, and continues—"in which one may be dead—and yet alive." As she intones the tag of this speech, she leans over a lamp—and its reflection makes her face seem to glow with evil. It's a superb moment.

Of course, it all leads up to a Wild West–style chase, Carradine driving a coach with Anne inside, Lionel Atwill's gendarme cavalry and lumpy Coe all in horseback pursuit. Pursued by the heroes, Carradine in turn is pursuing Karloff's Chamber of Horrors wagon which contains his coffin. To escape the police, Karloff and Naish ruthlessly dump the Count's casket. Carradine's coach crashes, he races to his coffin at the crest of the hill—and screams as the dawn shrivels this diabolic playboy to a skeleton. Anne (not a hair out of place, despite the chase and crashed coach!) is rescued from the carriage; the Dracula ring falls from her finger—and she hugs Peter Coe for her last shot in the picture.

Anne only worked nine days on *House of Frankenstein*; Kenton completed the film right on its 30-day schedule on Monday, May 8, 1944, as Anne, Carradine and Coe all went to Sherwood Forest, near Malibu (and near the lake where Karloff's Monster met "Little Maria" in *Frankenstein*), for their final shots in the chase. Anne told *Fangoria* about her role:

> The part was nice, but not great. I had fun with it, but I'm only in the first 25 minutes and then zap, I'm off for the rest of the film! That's not good showmanship... John Carradine was a good choice for Dracula; both Bela Lugosi and Lon Chaney were too heavy for the part. I felt that my scenes with Carradine were some of the best acting I ever did, and of course the picture plays often on television—I wish I had a piece of those Universal horror films!

By the time *House of Frankenstein* opened at New York's Rialto Theatre on December 15, 1944, Anne was off the Universal lot. Actor James Craig (who had acted in *Black Friday*) had encouraged Anne to put her career in the hands of agent Harold Rose, and to do so, Anne secured her release from Universal—departing at the same time as Evelyn Ankers, who had married Richard Denning and who left to have their daughter, Dee.

"They said they would see that I went places," said Anne. "Well, I went places, all right—out the door to Poverty Row!"

Indeed, 1946 audiences saw Anne in only two pictures: *Fear*, a *Crime and Punishment*–style tale released by Monogram, and *I Ring Doorbells*, released by PRC.

There were consolations. On December 19, 1945, the *Examiner* reported that Anne was engaged to Hollywood lawyer Max Gilford, who proposed to Anne on his yacht in Balboa harbor. ("The moon was wonderful," said Gilford, "and so was Anne.") On Christmas Eve of 1945, the *Examiner* noted that Anne had just signed a "$1000 a week, seven-year contract" with Consolidated Studios. Shortly afterwards, Gilford married Anne (his third wife); Evelyn Ankers was maid of honor, and the bridesmaids included Lois Collier and Peggy (Moran) Koster.

In 1946, Anne was beside Evelyn Ankers when Evelyn received her citizenship papers. On July 28, 1946, Anne gave birth to a seven-and-a-half-pound daughter, and announced she would name her Barbara Gwynne; on September 30, 1948, she and Gilford became parents of a seven-pound, six-ounce baby boy.

Meanwhile, Anne's career declined, despite some interesting assignments. She played Tess Trueheart in RKO's *Dick Tracy Meets Gruesome* (1947); she thought the film "so cute" and "probably one of the better jobs I had in the freelance field," but was disappointed to have so little screen time with Karloff's Gruesome. Nineteen forty-seven also saw her in Screen Guild's *Killer Dill* and Republic's *The Ghost Goes Wild* ("Yuck... Edward Everett Horton, such a fine actor, behaving so silly in that schlock"). And Anne co-starred with John Howard in what she calls "the very first filmed TV series," *Public Prosecutor*, shot in 1947 and 1948.

She worked for Allied Artists and Lippert, but the pace wore her down; on June 11, 1949, columnist Dorothy Manners ran this notice:

> Anne Gwynne, who has made 50 "B" films, has put her foot down on making another. Says she won't even do a nervous "A."

In fact, she did some very nervous "Bs" throughout the 1950s, including Gene Autry's *The Blazing Sun* (Columbia, 1950). But the real heartbreaker for Anne was 1957's *Teenage Monster*, which offered Anne a mother role, along with veteran stunt man Gil Perkins (*King Kong*, *Frankenstein Meets the Wolf Man*) in Jack P. Pierce makeup as the title terror. Anne pulled no punches in discussing the film with *Fangoria*:

> Oh, do you have to bring *that* up? It was absolutely the worst thing I ever did, the worst thing I ever *could* have done ... that was a very bad movie... And to top it off, the producers turned around three years later, and re-released it under the title *Meteor Monster*. It was still the same picture, the same bomb. I refuse to look at it... After how that turned out, I simply said, "No more."

Anne took a long sabbatical from show business. Her husband died in 1965, and she eventually came back for a Head and Shoulders commercial, and a very small part as Michael Douglas's mother in 1970's *Adam at 6 A.M.*

Meanwhile, Anne's daughter, billed as Gwynne Gilford, has acted in such films as *Beware! The Blob* (1972) and *Fade to Black* (1980); Gwynne Gilford's husband is Robert Pine, who acted in such films as *Munster, Go Home!* (1966) and *Empire of the Ants* (1977), as well as playing the sergeant on TV's *CHiPs*.

In the early 1980s, *Whatever Became of...?* author Richard Lamparski invited several of his favorites, including Anne and her Universal compatriots Susanna Foster and Gale Sondergaard, to (as Anne recalls) "sign our name in cement at his home in the hills near Universal." In his 1976 edition, Lamparski had reported that Anne "lives alone in the San Fernando Valley. To keep herself occupied, she does secretarial work for a metaphysician." And he quoted her as saying:

> It was a busy, happy time in my life, and I have no regrets, but I must admit that every now and then I wonder what might have happened if I'd kept that appointment at Warners.

In 1985, Anne suffered a blow when she learned that her dressing room companion, matron of honor and longtime friend Evelyn Ankers had died of cancer in Hawaii. It was also at this time that Anne began appearing regularly at Michael Fitzgerald's Universal Reunion Parties, which attracted such celebrities as Acquanetta and Lucille Lund (q.v.), as well as the now-late Reginald LeBorg, Peter Coe and Robert Paige.

Aside from her friend Fitzgerald, Anne has almost entirely avoided interviews in recent years. In the early 1990s, fans were saddened to hear that Anne had suffered a major stroke at her home, where she reportedly was incapacitated for a lengthy time before anyone found her. This major illness, along with her long-time reticence and a certain sad-eyed wistfulness she displayed at the Universal reunions, make fans pessimistic that she'll ever return to the limelight.

At Christmas time of 1994, Evelyn Ankers' daughter Dee wrote to me that she had visited Los Angeles—and had looked up Anne Gwynne. Dee and Anne had a tearful, emotional reunion—remembering the days Anne and Evelyn shared at Universal, when the Queen and Princess of Horror bequeathed fans so many wonderful movie memories.

The Films of Anne Gwynne

1939

Unexpected Father (Universal, Charles Lamont)
Little Accident (Universal, C. Lamont)
Oklahoma Frontier (Universal, Ford Beebe)
Charlie McCarthy, Detective (Universal, Frank Tuttle)

1940

Honeymoon Deferred (Universal, Lew Landers)
Framed (Universal, Harold Schuster)
Man from Montreal (Universal, Christy Cabanne)
Black Friday (Universal, Arthur Lubin)
Bad Men from Red Butte (Universal, Ray Taylor)
Sandy Is a Lady (Universal, C. Lamont)
Spring Parade (Universal, Henry Koster)
Give Us Wings (Universal, C. Lamont)
Flash Gordon Conquers the Universe (Universal 12-chapter serial, Ford Beebe and Ray Taylor)
The Green Hornet (Universal 13-chapter serial, F. Beebe and R. Taylor)

1941

Nice Girl? (Universal, William A. Seiter)
Washington Melodrama (MGM, S. Sylvan Simon)
The Black Cat (Universal, Albert S. Rogell)
Tight Shoes (Universal, A. S. Rogell)
Mob Town (Universal, William Nigh)
Melody Lane (Universal, C. Lamont)
Road Agent (Universal, C. Lamont)

1942

Don't Get Personal (Universal, C. Lamont)
Jail House Blues (Universal, A. S. Rogell)
Ride 'Em Cowboy (Universal, A. Lubin)
The Strange Case of Doctor Rx (Universal, William Nigh)
You're Telling Me (Universal, C. Lamont)

Broadway (Universal, W. A. Seiter
Men of Texas (Universal, Ray Enright)
Sin Town (Universal, R. Enright)
Keeping Fit (Universal short subject, *America Speaks* series, A. Lubin)

1943

We've Never Been Licked (Universal, John Rawlins)
Frontier Badman (Universal, William McGann)
Top Man (Universal, C. Lamont)

1944

Ladies Courageous (Universal, J. Rawlins)
Weird Woman (Universal, Reginald LeBorg)
Moon Over Las Vegas (Universal, Jean Yarbrough)
South of Dixie (Universal, J. Yarbrough)
Babes on Swing Street (Universal, Edward Killey)
Murder in the Blue Room (Universal, Leslie Goodwins)
House of Frankenstein (Universal, Erle C. Kenton)

1946

I Ring Doorbells (PRC, Martin Mooney)
Fear (Monogram, Alfred Zeisler)
Glass Alibi (Republic, W. Lee Wilder)

1947

The Ghost Goes Wild (Republic, George Blair)
Killer Dill (Screen Guild, Lewis D. Collins)
Dick Tracy Meets Gruesome (RKO, John Rawlins)

1948

Panhandle (Allied Artists–Champion, Lesley Selander)
Enchanted Valley (Eagle-Lion, Robert Emmet Tansey)

1949

Arson, Incorporated (Screen Guild/Lippert, William Berke)

1950

The Blazing Sun (*The Blazing Hills*) (Columbia)
Call of the Klondike (Monogram, Frank McDonald)

1951

King of the Bullwhip (Howco-International, Ron Ormond)

1952

Breakdown (Realart/Jack Broder Productions, Edmond Angelo)

1955

Phantom of the Jungle (Lippert, a three-part *Ramar of the Jungle* TV show spliced into a feature)

1960

Teenage Monster (*Meteor Monster*) (Howco, Jacques Marquette)

1970

Adam at 6 A.M. (National General, Robert Scheerer)

ILONA MASSEY

It's the climax of *Frankenstein Meets the Wolf Man* —"such a climax," hailed *The Hollywood Reporter*, "as no picture ever had before."

The desolate Frankenstein ruins, atop a mountain crag, below a dam—and a rising full moon. In the laboratory, Patric Knowles' Dr. Frank Mannering is preparing to drain the life electrically from Lon Chaney's Larry Talbot and Bela Lugosi's Monster—each unconscious and strapped to an operating table. However, the same lure that so tortured Colin Clive, Basil Rathbone and Sir Cedric Hardwicke now overpowers Knowles...

"I can't destroy Frankenstein's creation!" says Knowles. "I've got to see it at its full power!"

The unholy machines flash and roar and crackle, awakening Baroness Elsa Frankenstein—Ilona Massey. She sits up in bed, with her blonde braids and beauty mark and clingy white nightgown. Putting on a censor-pleasing wrap, Miss Massey sashays to the laboratory in her high heels, and beholds the electrified Monster that destroyed her father and grandfather.

"Frank! You're making him strong again!"

Lugosi's Monster opens his eyes—and sees Ilona's Elsa. He grins wickedly, as if the electricity has restored his potency in more ways than one.

"Don't pull that switch!" yells Mannering.

Too late. Elsa Frankenstein has yanked the lever to try to stop the blasphemy, and the equipment explodes. The Monster breaks his operating table bonds. He knocks out Mannering and scoops up Elsa.

Meanwhile, a full moon has arisen. Talbot transforms into the Wolf Man—and attacks the Monster, who drops the leading lady as "The Beast Battle of the Century" begins...

Everything about *Frankenstein Meets the Wolf Man* was sensational—including the Leading Lady.

Frankenstein had given us Mae Clarke, wistful, flowery, as Elizabeth. *Bride of Frankenstein* featured Valerie Hobson as Frankenstein's fiancée, looking like a Christmas angel. *Son of Frankenstein* saw red-haired, ethereal Josephine Hutchinson as Elsa von Frankenstein. And *The Ghost of Frankenstein* had co-starred Evelyn Ankers as Elsa, granddaughter of Clive's Monster Maker, niece of Rathbone's Wolf von Frankenstein and daughter of Hardwicke's Dr. Ludwig Frankenstein—a role Evelyn played at the apogee of her fairy tale princess beauty.

Ilona Massey, inheriting the Elsa Frankenstein role from Miss Ankers in *Frankenstein Meets the Wolf Man*, was something else again. The Frankenstein faithful now had a sexpot—the Hungarian blonde diva, MGM's "Singing Garbo" of *Rosalie* and *Balalaika*, always an eyeful with her blonde hair, lush, ample figure, sparkling bedroom eyes and—just below the right corner of her mouth—a genuine beauty mark.

It was a colorful career for Ilona Massey in Hollywood, to say the least; her leading men ranged from Nelson Eddy to the Marx Brothers. Just as colorful was the tinge of notoriety that surrounded this beautiful woman from the time she arrived at

Chapter opener: **Massey makes her Hollywood debut in the MGM musical extravaganza *Rosalie*, 1937.**

MGM in 1937, a personal European discovery of Louis B. Mayer. After only two films, her career almost collapsed forever after an in-house Metro sex scandal that nearly blackballed Ilona into Hollywood exile.

Ilona battled back from her early scandal; she won acclaim as a concert singer, Broadway star, movie attraction (including a comeback at the very lot that had blackballed her); showed herself to be a dynamic dramatic actress; and she proved herself a devoted American citizen and a devout anti-Communist. It was, in fact, her most passionately played role, against the people who had terrorized her family and her homeland.

Thus it is that one of Hollywood's most glamorous women—and most notorious sirens—is buried today at Arlington National Cemetery.

Ilona Massey's beginnings were hardly glamorous. The true family name, Hajmassy, translates as "garlic." And when the actress was born on June 16, 1910 (1912 was also publicized; Ilona personally preferred 1916), it was in one of the poorest neighborhoods of Budapest, Hungary. As Ilona told the *New York Times* in 1952:

> My salvation is that I have known misery and hunger. In my youth in Budapest, I didn't know the taste of meat until I was seven years old. That's how poor my family was. If I'm well-fed, well-dressed and have a home, what else is there for me to want?

Typesetter Frank Hajmassy and his wife Lidia put Ilona through high school, but couldn't afford the singing lessons that their music-loving daughter craved. After high school, Ilona worked as a salesgirl—primarily, according to G. Richard Wilkinson's profile of her in *Films in Review* (January 1971), "to earn the money a Dr. Laszlo required to prepare her for an audition at the Vienna Folks Opera." Meanwhile, she loved the movies—and idolized MGM's Jeanette MacDonald and Nelson Eddy: "To me they were the most talented and beautiful artists of our time."

Ilona's audition succeeded, and she made her debut with the Vienna Folks Opera in Puccini's *Tosca*. The director of the Vienna State Opera noticed her almost immediately—and Ilona joined the world-famous "Statsoper." Her Statsoper years, 1934 to 1936, were memorable ones, and she married for the first time—to Nicholas Szavozd, "a Hungarian capitalist," and reportedly heir to 4000 acres. Ilona and Nicholas wed and divorced within a year; supposedly her in-laws were unhappy that Nicholas had wed a lady outside their class, and had vowed to disinherit him if he didn't divorce his bride.

She also made her film debut—in two 1935 Austrian films: *Knox und die lustigen Vagabunden* and *Der Himmel auf Erden*. Ilona told Mr. Wilkinson that, on the subject of these two European pictures, she remembered "practically nothing."

Meanwhile, Metro-Goldwyn-Mayer Studios, Hollywood, studio of MacDonald and Eddy, was at the zenith of its glory. Louis B. Mayer, who would be 1937's top-paid man in the United States ($1,300,000), embarked on a European trip to buy talent for Leo the Lion. In his 1960 book *Hollywood Rajah: The Life and Times of Louis B. Mayer*, former *New York Times* film critic Bosley Crowther described Mayer's adventure in Carlsbad, where the mogul met "a lovely blonde Hungarian, Ilona Hajmassy,

Massey as a very alluring Baroness Elsa Frankenstein in *Frankenstein Meets the Wolf Man*, 1943.

whose cool and delicate beauty captivated Mayer." Crowther claimed Ilona was "by way of being a particular protégée of the director of the Vienna Statsoper," and that she became Mayer's "favorite dancing partner":

> Everyone there that year remembered, or heard about, one charming episode that occurred during a lively rumba session.

> Miss Hajmassy was wearing an evening gown of conspicuously fragile construction, and in the middle of a strenuous dance with Mayer a shoulder strap broke, thus permitting the exposure of a great deal more than was normally intended of the actress' smooth poitrine. After a moment of hesitation, she rushed off to seek repairs.

Ilona's version: Mayer came to the Statsoper one night when she sang the off-stage role of the High Priestess in *Aïda*, and ran backstage right after the opera to offer an MGM contract. At any rate, Mayer shipped his European collection of three dozen "finds" (including Hedy Lamarr) back to Culver City. Ilona sailed on the *Normandie* from Cherbourg to the United States with her Aunt Thesesa and sister Dodo. In the summer of 1937, Ilona Hajmassy—all 164 lbs. of her—arrived at MGM.

Metro changed her name to Ilona Massey, provided $300 worth of English lessons and singing coaching per day, slapped her with a strict diet and presented Ilona with her first film: *Rosalie*, co-starring Nelson Eddy, Eleanor Powell, Frank Morgan, Ray Bolger, Edna May Oliver and George Zucco. This $2,000,000 musical (based on a Ziegfeld show, with a new score by Cole Porter) featured Ilona as Brenda, girlfriend to Rosalie (Miss Powell)—the tap-dancing princess of a European country fancifully called Romanza.

Ilona's true glory in *Rosalie* comes in the Festival of Romanza. A soprano note sounds in the night—and Ilona enters, blonde and bounteous, tightly corseted, looking like Mortal Sin in a black gown with an endless train, spangled with stars, and cut to show off her legs. She sashays through the set, a little elf cavorting around her playing a flute, fountains ejaculating as she sings "Spring Love Is in the Air." It is true MGM kitsch—and only a prelude to Eleanor Powell's big "Rosalie" number, in which the dancer leaps across a series of giant drums as thousands of extras watch, a chorus sings and Nelson Eddy beholds Eleanor in rhapsodic closeup.

On December 16, 1937, MGM previewed *Rosalie* at the Village Theatre in Westwood. *Variety* reported:

> Super-musical extravaganza is *Rosalie*, the most lavish, ornate, tinseled and glittering production which has come from Hollywood... It is a 250-pound elf, a mastiff playing with a ball of twine, an elephant doing a toe dance... There is interest in the first screen appearance in America of Ilona Massey, whom Metro has been grooming... She is a very attractive young woman, possessing considerable self-assurance and a voice of wide range...

Rosalie was MGM's big Broadway attraction for Christmas 1937. On December 23, 1937, Ilona joined Louis B. Mayer and many of the stars of *Rosalie* on the *Good News of 1938* radio show to tub-thump the musical, which became one of MGM'S top moneymakers of 1937-1938. "Ilona Massey, attractive newcomer, sings beautifully," reported *Photoplay*.

Meanwhile, the November 5, 1937, *New York Times* had reported that MGM was preparing *Madame Pompadour* as a lavish star vehicle for Ilona. (The same story announced that MGM would remake Tiffany's 1930 *Journey's End*, with Robert Montgomery inheriting the late Colin Clive's role of the alcoholic Captain Stanhope, and the original's James Whale directing again). Neither it nor *Madame Pompadour* was filmed. Still, Ilona enjoyed major publicity, as a personal threat to Jeanette MacDonald, but Ilona denied it ("Miss MacDonald did not have to look out for anyone," saluted Ilona). Ilona proved herself very popular with all who knew her. Stella Zucco, widow of great character actor George Zucco (who was featured with Ilona in *Rosalie*) recalled on New Year's Eve, 1992:

> Ilona Massey was a wonderful girl. Perfectly beautiful! She was one of my favorites—not like Hedy Lamarr! They came over from Europe together, and had shared an apartment in Hollywood, and Ilona walked out—Hedy was impossible! But Ilona was a very good talent, I think—and very nice.

She was charming, and on July 8, 1939, this testimony appeared on the movie pages of the *Los Angeles Examiner* from a Mr. Jim James:

> I am a worker at MGM and my wife is in the wardrobe department, and we both nominate Miss Massey to take top place along with Marion Davies and Binnie Barnes as the three finest women to ever set foot in a movie studio.

By that time, Ilona finally had won her second MGM role: *Balalaika*, a 1939 musical spectacular of the Russian Revolution, which officially co-starred Ilona opposite Nelson Eddy, and was directed by Reinhold Schunzel. She played Tanya Marakova, whose violin-playing Bolshevik father (Lionel Atwill) gets involved in an assassination plot against the royal father (C. Aubrey Smith) of Prince Peter Karagin (Eddy). Eddy's big moment came when he sang "Silent Night" in army trenches; Ilona's glory shone when, in black skin-tight gown slit up the leg, and fishnet stockings, she sang "Tanya"—a masterpiece of MGM musical nonsense.

"I'm Taaan-ya" sings Ilona, flashing her eyes lasciviously at the camera.

"Don't do that with your eyes!" musically admonishes a gaggle of chorus boys in top hats and tails.

Ilona ventures into the cabaret audience, sits at a table, shows off her legs and drinks champagne; Cossack dancers join in, the chorus boys hoist Ilona up and carry her through the crowd, she hits an outrageously high note...

Anyway, Ilona does it with charm—and she loved working again with her old idol, Nelson Eddy. "I'd always thought stars were out to take scenes, not give them away," said Ilona. "But that's what Nelson Eddy did."

Balalaika was the Christmas 1939 attraction at New York's Radio City Music Hall. The *Balalaika* trailer hailed Ilona as "the star who will make this year's Big Entertainment News!" and *Variety* hailed her performance, reporting that *Balalaika*...

> ...should catapult her into the sacrosanct marquee division. Miss Massey has just about everything for visual and oral cinematic appeal. A beauty of much personal charm... Miss Massey will

> become a b.o. personality by word of mouth chiefly on the comparison to the Dietrich-Garbo qualities...

MGM prepared several Ilona Massey projects: *Waterloo Bridge* (which James Whale had filmed at Universal with Mae Clarke in 1931); a musical revamping of *Romance*, the 1930 Garbo film; a lavish original Technicolor musical, *New Orleans*; and the Countess role in the anti-Nazi drama, *Escape*.

Then—literally and figuratively—it all came to a crash. On August 25, 1939, Louella Parsons had reported that she would be "greatly surprised" if Ilona did not marry Sam Katz, an MGM executive producer, after his divorce was final. In February of 1940, MGM dispatched Ilona to Idaho to add glamour to a film premiere. Also on hand was Alan Curtis—former Chicago taxi driver and New York model who had become a rising Hollywood leading man. Ilona, Curtis, Senator Carl Brown and his wife and one "Bill Parker of Hollywood" were driving in a snowstorm when Parker, driving the car, had to swerve off the road to avoid a head-on collision. The senator's wife broke her arm and suffered a cut head. Ilona and Curtis began a romance.

The romance hardly made a hit at MGM. A month after the Idaho accident, MGM was still heralding big plans for Ilona— including *Incident in Java*, to co-star Ilona with an "already signed" Robert Taylor. Meanwhile, Ilona enjoyed a concert tour in South America.

Then—suddenly—Ilona Massey was off the lot. In his 1993 book *Merchant of Dreams: Louis B. Mayer, MGM and the Secret Hollywood*, Charles Higham included this report on Ilona:

"She was pushed out of MGM because her lover, Sam Katz, found out, by the presence of a hat in her front hall, that she was having an affair with the actor Alan Curtis."*

"I was blackballed," Ilona told Richard Lamparski in a radio interview (circa 1970):

> I was the black sheep. And one of the producers said to me at that time—and I shall not mention his name, because he's deceased, and let sleeping dogs sleep—he said, "You will crawl on your hands and feet to come back for us to give you a job, and we shall not do it." I said, "Mr. 'K,' I assure you, that you will never see the day that I do that"—which he didn't...

Vivien Leigh came to MGM to star in *Waterloo Bridge*. Norma Shearer took the Countess role in *Escape*. *New Orleans*, *Incident in Java* and the remake of *Romance* were scrapped by MGM. And, in 1940, Ilona Massey did not appear in a single movie.

The power of the studios could be monolithic, and there was gossip that MGM would kill off any chance Ilona had to continue a Hollywood career. However, late in 1940, she signed to star in *New Wine*, a biopic of Franz Schubert—played by none other than Alan Curtis. The 1941 United Artists release was directed by Reinhold Schunzel (who had directed *Balalaika*); Ilona sang "Ave Maria."

**Over the years, gossip has also claimed that MGM executives Eddie Mannix and Benny Thau were Ilona's lovers.*

The climax of her musical stardom: Massey in MGM's *Balalaika*, 1939.

Ilona was the principal soloist at the Hollywood Bowl Easter Sunrise Service of 1941.

On March 26, 1941, Ilona and Alan Curtis wed at the Westwood Hills Congregational Church. The *Los Angeles Examiner* ran a large photo of the newlyweds, Ilona gorgeous in a rose-colored hat, tailored beige suit and blue blouse, with a bouquet of orchids at her shoulder. The ceremony was simple—attended only by Curtis's brother and mother, and Ilona's aunt.

Producer Edward Small defied MGM and gave Ilona the lead in *International Lady* (1941), as a German spy pursued by both U.S. and British secret services. The melodrama flanked her with two major leading men: George Brent and Basil Rathbone (one of the actors Ilona respected most in Hollywood); a colorful supporting cast featured Gene Lockhart, Martin Kosleck and her friend George Zucco.

In May of 1941, Ilona and Alan Curtis were the "guests of honor" on Louella Parsons' Friday night CBS radio program. In July of 1941, it was announced that Eddie Small would produce *Bella Donna* for Ilona, but the plan fell through. In August, Small claimed to be starring Ilona in the flashy role of the unspeakably evil wife of *A Gentleman After Dark*, which would have co-starred her with Brian Donlevy and Preston Foster. Ilona reportedly had reservations about playing the mother of a teenager; Miriam Hopkins played the villainess (whom Olga Baclanova had played in the 1929 version, *Forgotten Faces*). Then Small claimed he had bought *Up in Mabel's Room* to co-star Ilona and Louis Hayward; when that film premiered in 1944, neither star was in it.

The year 1942 brought rumors of marital discord with Curtis—and also brought Ilona to Universal City for two pictures. The first was *Invisible Agent*, starring Jon Hall as the Invisible Man (a spy) and Ilona as British spy Maria Sorenson, a Mata Hari heroine whose espionage helps foil Nazi Sir Cedric Hardwicke and Japanese Peter Lorre. The producer was Frank Lloyd, who had won an Academy Award for 1933's *Cavalcade* and directed such epics as MGM's 1935 *Mutiny on the Bounty*; the director was Edwin L. Marin, who had helmed Lugosi's *The Death Kiss* (1932) and Metro's 1938 *A Christmas Carol*. There were many names familiar to the fans of *Shock!* Theatre, including associate producer George (*The Wolf Man*) Waggner; screenplay writer Curt Siodmak (between *The Wolf Man* and *Frankenstein Meets the Wolf Man*); and John P. Fulton, who copped an Oscar-nomination for his special effects. There was even some stunt work provided by Eddie Parker, who would double Lugosi in *Frankenstein Meets the Wolf Man*.

Ilona hated *Invisible Agent*. In fact, she told Mr. Wilkinson in his 1971 *Films in Review* piece that she "disliked the latter so much that she can scarcely remember what it was about" and "can't remember what her role in this film was." The role ranged from cheesecake (when she begins to get undressed, the peeping Invisible Man sneezes; "Gesundheit," says Ilona, before giving a coy gasp) to comedy (when Nazi underling J. Edward Bromberg tries to woo her over dinner and the Invisible Man throws mashed potatoes on him; Ilona laughs) to ridiculous dramatics (Ilona, complete in flyer's cap, piloting a bomber in the explosive climax). Certainly she looked very silly, dangling in mid-air, supposedly hoisted by Hall's Invisible Man—a bit of "movie magic" reportedly accomplished by Fulton attaching strong, invisible wires through Ilona's clothes to her corset.

Audiences loved *Invisible Agent*'s mixture of fantasy and propaganda. Of Universal's four sequels to *The Invisible Man*, *Invisible Agent* was the most successful: negative cost, $322,291; international gross, $1,041,500.

Ilona's reward for top-billing Universal's big moneymaker: *Frankenstein Meets the Wolf Man*.

Publicity portrait of Massey for *Invisible Agent*, 1942.

It's always a bit odd to watch *Frankenstein Meets the Wolf Man*, see the titles form from the vapors of a smoky laboratory test tube, and see the star billing:

Ilona Massey
&
Patric Knowles

"Poor Bela" shows up in the supporting cast, beneath Lionel Atwill, who played the jolly Mayor of Vasaria; Chaney gets special "And LON CHANEY as The Wolf Man" billing later in the titles. Yet Ilona bequeaths *Frankenstein Meets the Wolf Man* such class, beauty and sex appeal that its hard to begrudge her the billing.

The first official shooting day of *Frankenstein Meets the Wolf Man* at Universal City was Monday, October 12, 1942. Right up to the eve of shooting, Universal had planned to star Chaney as *both* Wolf Man and Monster. On October 13, *The Hollywood Reporter* ran this notice (beside a review of *The Mummy's Tomb*):

> ONE MONSTER IS ENOUGH,
> SO LUGOSI DOES THE OTHER
>
> Bela Lugosi goes to Universal to portray the Monster in *Frankenstein Meets the Wolf Man*, which went into production yesterday with Lon Chaney as the Wolf Man. Chaney was originally scheduled to portray both roles, but producer George Waggner decided the idea was not feasible because of the intricate make-ups required for the parts and the terrific physical strain of playing both roles.

(Of course, Lugosi signed on for the role he'd scorned in 1931, with some compensation: In the Siodmak script, the Monster was blind—and had dialogue. Post-production editing would remove both dialogue and references to the blindness.)

October 15, 1942: Lionel Atwill, playing the Mayor of Vasaria, was found guilty of perjury in regards to his celebrated 1940 Yuletide orgy at his Pacific Palisades house, and received a five-year probationary sentence.

November 5: Maria Ouspenskaya (q.v.), reprising her Maleva from *The Wolf Man*, was seriously hurt when a cart she and Chaney were riding overturned.

Also on November 5: Sixty-year-old Lugosi collapsed on the set—a collapse a doctor blamed on the Jack P. Pierce Monster makeup and costume. Director Roy William Neill shot around him as Bela was sent home to recover.

And, in the midst of all this real and make-believe melodrama, Ilona had deep troubles of her own: She and Alan Curtis had separated August 19. On October 22, 1942, the second week of *Frankenstein Meets the Wolf Man*'s shooting, Louella Parsons reported that Ilona and her husband of one year and seven months (who, while Ilona was busy on *Frankenstein Meets the Wolf Man*, was himself acting with John Carradine and Patricia Morison in *Hitler's Madman*) would divorce.

Yet Ilona Massey had fun on *Frankenstein Meets the Wolf Man*—and looked absolutely beautiful. She loved working with Lon Chaney and told James Miller in an interview in *Varulven* magazine (#4):

> I think Lon Chaney is one of the nicest, sweetest people in the world. It was a great deal of fun. You know it took four hours to put on his makeup and when it was on, it was hot under the lights, it was very difficult for him to eat. He mostly had soup which he sipped through a straw and just for fun, we put hot peppers in it! We had a lot of fun ... everyone had fun in the picture.

We first see Ilona's Baroness Elsa Frankenstein in the office of Mayor Lionel Atwill; she's stunning in a beige suit, wrap-around fur and large black bonnet. Chaney (who wants to get his lycanthrope hands on the Frankenstein records, to end his

Lon Chaney's Wolf Man and Bela Lugosi's Monster battle over Ilona Massey in this publicity shot for *Frankenstein Meets the Wolf Man*, 1943.

cursed existence) enters—and the two stars create an instant sexual chemistry. Ilona's eyes sparkle as she looks Chaney's Lawrence Talbot up and down— and one can almost see Lon blush! Atwill (naturally) picks up on the attraction, sputters, chomps on his pipe and exits, leaving the two to talk—and for Chaney to show more sex appeal than he ever had before or ever would again in his career.

"Lon Chaney was, of course, a dear man," said Ilona. "I never had any difficulty with my co-stars, but Chaney was something special."

Indeed, Ilona and Chaney appear in many candid shots together from the film: sitting with Chaney's German Shepherd "Moose" (who appeared in the film in the gypsy camp), listening to records together, being entertained by a magician...

Bela Lugosi had reason to enjoy working with Ilona. She shared his native Hungarian language; besides, his first two wives had been Hungarian—and both had been named Ilona! The actress told James Miller she liked working with Bela:

> Yes, he was a very nice man, but by then he was getting old, and most of his stunts were done by a stunt man and not by him.

Ilona shared the scene with Lon, Bela, Knowles, Atwill, Dwight Frye (as villager "Rudi") and 500 extras in the famous "Festival of the New Wine" episode, a blend of interiors shot on the "Phantom Stage" and actual night exteriors shot on Universal's back lot Tyrolean village. Curt Siodmak provided the lyrics and Hans J. Salter wrote the music for the "Faro-La, Faro-Li," song, delivered by Adia Kuznetzoff, as "The Festival Singer," with eye and teeth-flashing gusto:

> Come one and all and sing a song,
> Faro-La, Faro-Li!
> For life is short, but death is long,
> Faro-La, Faro-Li!

The singer delivers what turns out to be the final verse to Ilona and Chaney, with the unfortunate line, "And may they live *eternally*!"—which the death-seeking werewolf hardly wishes to hear. As delightful as Kuznetzoff is, one wonders if anyone at Universal considered changing Siodmak's script so that *Ilona* sang the song! It would have dramatically suited the tale (the villagers magnanimously welcoming Frankenstein's daughter back to the village by having her sing for them); it would have been effective if Larry Talbot (so suave to the Baroness up to this point) had become hysterical in her face as she sang to him; and the whole episode might have seemed almost a homage to Ilona's big "Festival of Romanza" song in *Rosalie*. It probably would have lured some non-horror audiences, who wanted to hear Ilona sing, to buy a *Frankenstein Meets the Wolf Man* ticket.

As it is, Ilona does have a wonderfully festive dance with Atwill, who (whatever his perjury travails at the time) couldn't resist the twinkle in his eyes as he merrily twirls Ilona about, effusively kissing her hands after the dance ends. Lugosi's Monster crashes the party, sending the villagers into hysterics as the Baroness clutches Patric Knowles' Dr. Mannering and Chaney escapes in a horse-drawn cart, the Monster kicking wine barrels at the villagers.

Ilona, Knowles and Madame Ouspenskaya visit Talbot and the Monster at the ruins. The leading lady finds the lost records, and later warns Knowles of the horrors suffered by her family...

To no avail.

Of course, come the climax, Ilona, in her nightgown, is the gorgeous pawn in the battle of Monster and Wolf Man. Ilona's screams are probably the worst of the Frankenstein series (she screams, not surprisingly, like an opera singer trying to save

Ilona Massey, Lon Chaney, Jr., and Chaney's dog "Moose," all getting along fine on the set of *Frankenstein Meets the Wolf Man*, fall of 1942.

her voice!). The Monster and the Wolf Man battle it out in spectacular fashion, finally perishing as the dam explodes and the water crashes down on them, Ilona and Knowles watching the cataclysmic finale to the strains of Hans J. Salter's finale music.

"Personally, I love horror films," said Ilona, "and that's why I did this one. I thought it would be wonderful to do a horror film. I really enjoyed it."

Frankenstein Meets the Wolf Man premiered at New York's Rialto Theatre March 5, 1943; not a single major reviewer noticed the emergency editing, which removed Lugosi's Monster dialogue ("because it sounded so Hungarian funny!" said Curt Siodmak) and references to his blindness. Over the decades, Lugosi's Monster has become one of the most beloved "bad" performances of the genre, and the film one of the most popular of all horror movies.

Leading ladies of the first four Universal Frankenstein films added their charm; Ilona Massey gave *Frankenstein Meets the Wolf Man* a true glamour. Patric Knowles (in the *Bela Lugosi Newsletter*) summed it up best when he recalled Ilona: "A joy to look at and work with."

On December 16, 1942, before *Frankenstein Meets the Wolf Man* premiered, Ilona won a divorce from Alan Curtis. She cited his drinking:

> He kept me awake nights and my health became very bad and I was forced to see a physician. He would come home at two in the morning and refused to tell me where he had been...

"Did he make disparaging remarks about your family?" asked Ilona's attorney.

"Yes," said Ilona. "He insulted my mother, and he never even met her."

Ilona kept the Brentwood house, while Curtis retained the ranch in Mendocino. (Curtis joined Universal, playing in such films as 1944's *Phantom Lady*, the hero of 1944's *The Invisible Man's Revenge* and Abbott and Costello's 1945 *The Naughty Nineties*. He died in New York City in 1953 at the age of 44, a victim of liver disease.)

Melodrama fans recall Ilona Massey primarily because of her rendezvous with the Monster and the Wolf Man (Ilona herself inferred that it was, along with *Balalaika*, her favorite film). However, *Frankenstein Meets the Wolf Man* seemed the cinematic kiss of death for the diva. Her efforts to escape MGM's blackball seemed ultimately to have failed, while the marriage that had led to her MGM exile had collapsed.

So Ilona fled Hollywood for Broadway—and *The Ziegfeld Follies*, which opened April 1, 1943. The musical extravaganza was a smash hit, co-starring Milton Berle and Arthur Treacher and running 553 performances. She left the show to tour British New Guinea with the USO, and also enjoyed a triumphant Latin America singing tour.

Then, on October 23, 1944, the *Los Angeles Examiner* announced that Ilona was signing a new Hollywood contract—with MGM! Louis B. Mayer welcomed Ilona back in *Holiday in Mexico*, a Technicolor songfest starring Jane Powell, Walter Pidgeon and Xavier Cugat and his Orchestra. The 1946 release was a great showcase for Ilona, who sang an opera sequence and was lavishly costumed. (She supposedly was a substitute for first-choice Jeanette MacDonald.)

The comeback looked promising, but, in fact, Ilona only made three more films before leaving Hollywood. She co-starred again with Nelson Eddy in Republic's color *Northwest Outpost* (1947), supported by Hugo Haas, Elsa Lanchester and Joseph Schildkraut. Also for Republic, she played a dance hall hostess in *The Plunderers*, a 1948 Western co-starring Rod Cameron, Adrian Booth and Forrest Tucker. And there was *Love Happy* (1949), an Artists Alliance/United Artists release (produced by Mary

Pickford!) starring Groucho, Chico and Harpo Marx, Vera-Ellen—and Ilona as a Russian princess who smuggles diamonds inside a sardine can. *Love Happy* perhaps is best-remembered today for the brief appearance of another stunning blonde—Marilyn Monroe.

Meanwhile, on Sunday afternoon, May 19, 1946, Ilona sang at the *Los Angeles Examiner*–sponsored "I Am an American" Day patriotic spectacle at the Hollywood Bowl; on July 26, 1946, she took the oath of allegiance to become a citizen. In March of 1947, Ilona succeeded in bringing her mother to the United States—later telling a congressional committee that she had bribed Hungarian officials $2000 to get her mother out of the country.

In 1950, Ilona began a radio show, *Top Secret*. And she scored on early television as a dramatic actress. On May 15, 1950, she appeared on CBS-TV's *Studio One* in "The Ambassadors," returning to *Studio One* November 27, 1950, for "The Shadow of a Man" and February 26, 1951, for a restaged version of "The Ambassadors." She starred on CBS's *Video Theatre* ("Purple and Fine Linen," January 15, 1951); played the highly dramatic role of a drug-addicted wife and mother on NBC's *Cameo Theatre* ("The Third Time," July 30, 1951); and guest-starred on ABC's *Faith Baldwin Playhouse* ("The Sleeping Beauty," October 6, 1951) and NBC's *Curtain Call* ("The Liar," August 22, 1952).

On January 6, 1952, Ilona wed Charles Walker, "Manhattan antique jeweler," in New Rochelle, New York. The following month—February 13, 1952—she began her own ABC-TV series, *Rendezvous*, in which she played Nikki, owner of a Paris night club. Ilona was light-hearted about her "vamp" image as she told the *New York Times*: "A woman is a woman. Playing the part of a siren just comes naturally. It's no strain at all."

However, the role Ilona believed in most deeply—and the one she played most passionately—was an anti-Communist. On July 28, 1951, at the height of the Hollywood Witch Hunt melodramas, Ilona led 50 protesters picketing the Park Avenue headquarters of the Russian Delegation to the United Nations. Ilona's placard read, "Please, everyone, help destroy the cruel barbarians." The Russian delegation was outraged, protesting to the U.N. and denouncing Ilona and her protesters as "hooligans."

On August 23, 1954, Ilona risked reprisals against her family in Hungary by testifying before a congressional committee in New York. In pink dress, pink shoes, pink stockings and "sparkling diamonds and amethysts," she told how her family had been "murdered and robbed" under the Communists. She related how she had lived as a child, under Bela Kun's terror-regime, on a diet of rotted cornbread; that she had learned that "Hungarian and Russian Communists had killed one of her cousins, raped another, sent a nephew to Siberia, ordered her sister into the county poorhouse and confiscated a rich 32-acre farm the family had bought with her movie earnings."

Ilona sobbed on the stand as she testified, and sealed her professional doom in increasingly liberal Hollywood when she declared:

> It would be a good thing for all the Hollywood reds to be sent to Hungary for a taste of their own medicine—only I don't think anyone would go!

On March 1, 1955, an anonymous caller telephoned Ilona's mother and told her that Ilona was dead—"You'll read all about it in the papers," said the voice. The *Los Angeles Examiner* inferred it to be a retaliation against her anti-Communist testimony.

On April 24, 1955, Ilona opened a new "supper club act" at the Chi-Chi in Palm Springs. And then, on July 14, 1955, only 24 hours after her Mexican divorce from Charles Walker came through, Ilona wed for (officially) the fourth time. The groom was Ret. Air Force General Donald S. Dawson, former administrative assistant to President Truman. Dawson had a ten-year-old daughter, Diana, by a previous marriage, and Ilona said, "It has made me happy to have this new side to family life that I have never enjoyed before."

Although Ilona vowed to retire after this marriage, she was busy; she starred in a production of *Tonight or Never* at the Pasadena Playhouse in the summer of 1956. She kept politically active, too; on the night of November 4, 1956, Ilona led a candle-carrying picket line before the Soviet Embassy in Washington, D.C., protesting the Russian attack on Hungary. She led further anti-Communist demonstrations in New York and Hollywood.

In the spring of 1959, Ilona made one more movie: *Jet Over the Atlantic*, in which she played a vainglorious opera diva who turns to religion when she learns there's a bomb on her plane. The cast was filled with such veterans as Virginia Mayo, George Raft, George Macready (as the bomber), Anna (*Bedlam*) Lee (as his wife) and Margaret Lindsay.

She visited South Africa on a concert tour, winning great acclaim and South Africa's Medal of Freedom. Ilona then finally and fully retired in fashion worthy of a Hollywood star. As G. Richard Wilkinson wrote in his *Films in Review* profile:

> Miss Massey is still a beautiful woman and her present husband has provided an appropriate background for her. They live on an estate in the Washington, D.C., suburb of Bethesda, Maryland, they call "Happy Valley." She herself designed the exterior changes they made in the architecture of the house, which contains antiques, paintings and two dogs (a bellicose poodle and a peace-loving Great Dane). For weekends the Dawsons have a waterfront remnant of a 17th century land grant in Virginia known as "Chatterton." The bricks in its house were brought from England. They also have a villa in Majorca.

Ilona worked with the Reserve Officers Wives Club and the Daughters of the American Revolution and lived a very social life. She claimed to have no regrets about her retirement—"It's always nice to leave something at a certain point so it does not fizzle out," she told James Miller in his *Varulven* interview. Ilona revealed her personality and philosophy in a letter to Philip Castanza for his book *The Films of Jeanette MacDonald and Nelson Eddy*:

> Even now, when I have the opportunity, I see their films with nostalgia, for that era of loveliness has left us. I feel sorry for the now generation. They are void of illusion and the naked truth is

> sad. What can they look forward to? They have seen and tasted all. I am fortunate to have known Jeanette and Nelson… God be with them for eternity.

Ilona lived her final years in splendor, overlooking the Potomac River. In 1974, she became ill—cancer, reportedly—and General Dawson was influential enough to have her admitted to Bethesda Naval Hospital. It was there, following "a three-month illness," that she died on August 20, 1974.

In an irony, the actress who played foreign *femmes fatales* was buried at Arlington National Cemetery, beneath a standard military marker, bearing these words:

ILONA
MASSEY
JUNE 16 1910
AUGUST 20 1974
WIFE OF
MAJ. GEN
DONALD S.
DAWSON
USAF

In 1991, Gil Perkins, the 84-year-old Australian stunt man (whose credits include doubling Bruce Cabot in *King Kong*, Spencer Tracy as Hyde in 1941's *Dr. Jekyll and Mr. Hyde*, and playing 1957's *Teenage Monster*) told me about working on *Frankenstein Meets the Wolf Man*. Eddie Parker had doubled Lugosi as the Monster, but in the climax (or for at least a part of it), Parker switched to the Wolf Man makeup while Perkins donned the makeup and costume of the Frankenstein Monster.

"I remember I had to carry the Hungarian girl, Ilona Massey, who had practically nothing on," stated Perkins. As Perkins remembers, Ilona reported to the stage wearing only a see-through negligee and a pair of panties. And the gutsy, colorful Perkins, who had been awed by very little in his half-century of stunt work in over 1500 features and thousands of TV shows, added, with impressed tones:

"And I carried the real gal—I had the *real* Ilona Massey!"

The Films of Ilona Massey

1935

Knox und die Lustigen Vagabunden (Projektograph-Film, E. W. Elmo)

Der Himmel auf Erden (Projektograph-Film, E. W. Elmo)

1937

Rosalie (MGM, W. S. Van Dyke II)

1939

Balalaika (MGM, Reinhold Schunzel)

1941

New Wine (Gloria Pictures/United Artists, R. Schunzel)

International Lady (Edward Small/United Artists, Tim Whelan)

1942

Invisible Agent (Universal, Edwin L. Marin)

1943

Frankenstein Meets the Wolf Man (Universal, Roy William Neill)

1946

Holiday in Mexico (MGM, George Sidney)

1947

Northwest Outpost (Republic, Allan Dwan)

1948

The Plunderers (Republic, Joseph Kane)

1949

Love Happy (Artists Alliance/United Artists, David Miller)

1959

Jet Over the Atlantic (Inter-Continent, Byron Haskin)

SHORT SUBJECT

1942

Picture People No. 9 (RKO)

Ilona Massey does not appear in 1945's *Tokyo Rose* nor 1946's *The Gentleman Misbehaves*; historians have confused her with Osa Massen, who played in both. Nor was Ilona in 1957's *Sabu and the Magic Ring*; the leading lady in that film was Daria Massey.

Patricia Morison

She always had the exotic look of a sexy, angry, Shakespearean actress.

Patricia Morison had 39"-long auburn hair—the longest of any actress in Hollywood, and usually worn in a bun. She had fiery blue/gray eyes and the most sensual mouth of any lady in the movies. And there was a tinge of passion in her dramatics, which—spiked with this "vamp" look—made her a fascinating actress.

Perhaps inevitably, in 1940s Hollywood, she only truly had the chance to spark in "B" melodramas.

There was *Hitler's Madman* (MGM, 1943), a haunting, passionate movie, as much horror film as propaganda piece, with Patricia as the self-sacrificing village heroine who helps assassinate John Carradine's satanic Nazi.

There was *Calling Dr. Death* (1943), the first of Universal's notorious "Inner Sanctums," in which she was the madly jealous nurse who kills Lon Chaney's wife with a fire poker, and disfigures her face with acid.

And, perhaps most famously, there was *Dressed to Kill* (1946), Universal's final *Sherlock Holmes* film, with Patricia as foxy villainess Hilda Courtney—sparring with Basil Rathbone's Holmes, flirting with Nigel Bruce's Watson and slinking about London in furs and a chapeau that looks like a giant black toe.

Danger Woman ... Queen of the Amazons ... Tarzan and the Huntress...

Then came a show business miracle. On December 30, 1948, Patricia opened on Broadway in *Kiss Me Kate*. The lady who looked like a sexy Shakespearean actress was now playing one, singing the Cole Porter songs in her mezzo-soprano voice and delivering an explosive star performance.

For the past 50 years, Patricia has been a headliner of Broadway and civic light opera musicals, nightclubs and occasional TV appearances. Nevertheless, movie fans remember this survivor of Hollywood's Golden Age best for those horrors/thrillers—*Hitler's Madman*, *Calling Dr. Death* and *Dressed to Kill*—which offered only tantalizing glimpses of the full, dynamic talents of Patricia Morison.

Eileen Patricia Augusta Fraser Morison was born in New York City March 19, 1915, the only daughter of playwright/actor William R. Morison (who played in films under the name of Norman Rainey) and Selina Carson Morison (who worked in British Intelligence during World War I). "Pat" attended New York's P.S. #9 and Washington Irving High School; originally, she wished to become an artist, and won a scholarship to L'École des Beaux Arts in Paris. However, she also loved drama. She grew up a devoted Garbo fan, and after seeing Alfred Lunt and Lynn Fontanne star in *Strange Interlude*, she decided to join Manhattan's Neighborhood Playhouse. She also studied dancing and movement with Martha Graham.

"I wasn't going to be just another actress," she told Robert Kendall. "I vowed I'd become a *star*."

On November 23, 1933, Patricia made her Broadway debut at the Ambassador Theatre as Helen in *Growing Pains*, starring Junior Durkin and Johnny (*The Mad Monster*) Downs. She reportedly earned $10 per week; the play ran 28 performances.

***Chapter opener:* Patricia Morison with Vincent Price in "The Moor's Revenge," an episode of CBS-TV's *Have Gun Will Travel* (December 27, 1958).**

Patricia Morison, Basil Rathbone and Nigel Bruce take a ride on the boom between scenes of *Dressed to Kill*.

On December 26, 1935, *Victoria Regina* premiered at Broadway's Broadhurst Theatre, with Helen Hayes making theater history with her legendary title role performance. The play marked the Broadway debuts of Vincent Price, as Prince Albert, and British actor George Zucco, as Disraeli. Patricia, at the age of 20, had the task of serving as Helen Hayes' understudy. Miss Hayes eventually developed laryngitis, and Patricia looked forward to a glorious opportunity.

Instead, the play's producers closed the show for three days. Patricia was upbeat about it all, and later told columnist Herbert Cohn:

> *Victoria Regina* doesn't make me mad, because Helen Hayes was really the reason people came to see the show. It wouldn't have been fair to take an audience's money without giving the Hayes impersonation in return. Besides, I learned a lot from that job...

There would be some tough times for the aspiring star, and she supported herself as a dress designer. Then Patricia starred as Laura Rivers in *The Two Bouquets*, an English operetta that co-starred Alfred Drake and opened at Broadway's Windsor Theatre May 31, 1938. The *New York Times* praised the "uncommon skill" of her singing, and the "willowy elegance" of her acting. *The Two Bouquets* ran 55 performances, winning Patricia notice—and a contract with Paramount Studios, Hollywood.

Paramount was the headquarters of such major stars as Gary Cooper, Claudette Colbert, Bing Crosby, Bob Hope, Dorothy Lamour and Ray Milland. Patricia became part of Paramount's "Golden Circle," which boasted such newcomers as Robert Preston, Susan Hayward, and Richard Denning.

Of all the Hollywood studios, Paramount had the most sleek and sexy flair, and Patricia Morison showed promise of becoming a major star. With that 39"-long auburn hair ("which beats Dorothy Lamour by three inches," claimed her publicity) and those remarkable eyelashes that rivaled Garbo's, Patricia had the look of a sexy classical actress who might have scored as such Shakespearean vamps as Kate of *The Taming of the Shrew*, Cleopatra or even Lady Macbeth. She had a wonderful fashion sense and was especially striking in hats, which she wore with the flair of a buccaneer. She had a good figure, and her shapely legs inspired Paramount to lease her as a model for Townwear's "Stockings of Matchless Beauty." Her singing voice was far superior to most movie stars' talents. She had a pouty, sophisticated sex appeal—and, of course, she was a very fine actress.

Patricia's Hollywood debut: *Persons in Hiding*, a hit Paramount melodrama which previewed at Broadway's Criterion Theatre March 1, 1939. "She's BEAUTIFUL—but DANGEROUS—America's QUEEN OF GANGLAND!" blazed Patricia's PR for this Bonnie and Clyde–style thriller, of which *Variety* reported:

> J. Carrol Naish turns in a neat and believable performance as the small-time mobster who is steered into large operations by ambitious and notoriety-loving Patricia Morison. Latter is excellent as the scheming moll.

The *New York Times* praised Patricia as "an attractive newcomer," but the fire of her performance already had threatened to typecast her; as she told William Peper in a 1965 *New York World-Telegram* interview, "I was typed as a gun moll or a spy after that."

Paramount toyed with casting Patricia as Isobel, the girl Gary Cooper, Ray Milland and Robert Preston leave behind as they face Fort Zinderneuf and Brian Donlevy's horrific Sgt. Markoff in *Beau Geste* (1939). It might have been a major break for Patricia; instead, Paramount's very aggressive Susan Hayward snared the part in producer/director William A. Wellman's Foreign Legion epic.

Morison, new Paramount starlet, in a 1939 glamour pose.

As a consolation prize, Paramount tossed Patricia into a Bob Burns hillbilly farce called *I'm from Missouri* (1939). Then came the romantic lead in *The Magnificent Fraud*, an "adventure romance" which premiered at the Paramount Theatre in Times Square July 19, 1939, complete with a Bob Hope stage show. Akim Tamiroff (billed with Lon Chaney's old sobriquet, "Man of a Thousand Faces") gave a riotous performance in three roles; Robert Florey directed, and Patricia's co-stars included Lloyd Nolan and her *Victoria Regina* colleague George Zucco. The *New York Times* reported:

> In the item of Miss Morison alone the glamorizing agencies of Hollywood have prepared an extraordinary bargain... When the smoldering Miss Morison bursts into flame even at the kiss of Lloyd Nolan, boy! What will she do if they ever give her a role opposite Gable?

Audiences saw her in Paramount's *Untamed* (1940), a Technicolor remake of 1926's *Mantrap*, which had starred Clara Bow (and was based on the Sinclair Lewis novel). Her leading man was Ray Milland; the scenery-gnashing heavy was Akim Tamiroff. ("The thing we liked best about Mr. Tamiroff," noted the *New York Times*, "was his face after he had been frozen to death. That, in Technicolor, is something to see.") *Rangers of Fortune* (1940) was a Paramount Western with Fred MacMurray and Albert (*Dr. Cyclops*) Dekker. Paramount farmed out Patricia to 20th Century–Fox for

Romance of the Rio Grande, a Cisco Kid Western which starred Patricia as Rosita and was the Christmas 1940 attraction at Broadway's Palace Theatre. Cesar Romero, who played the Cisco Kid, often escorted "Pat" (as her friends called her) around Hollywood in those days; neither star ever married.

While Patricia acted in such 1941 Paramount products as *The Roundup* (with Richard Dix and Preston Foster) and *One Night in Lisbon* (as ex-wife of Fred MacMurray, with Madeleine Carroll in the major female role), she won the most press for a role she did *not* play. Paramount loaned her to Republic for a Gene Autry Western, *The Singing Hill*—and Patricia refused to report to the set.

"Like heaving a pie at the Duchess of Windsor," was how one reporter likened Patricia's refusing to work with the immensely popular Autry. Paramount contritely sent contractee Virginia Dale to Republic instead. Once again, Patricia was good-natured about it all: "Oh, I'll probably be suspended for a couple of weeks. And that will be that."

She was partially right—Paramount suspended her—but that wasn't that. "It would be easy to blame Paramount for ruining my career," Patricia told William Peper in 1965, "but it was partially my own fault. I didn't protest. I took what they gave me and assumed they knew best." She was too gracious; when she returned to the studio, Paramount treated her so badly that one might suspect the studio was vindictively destroying her career. Patricia's winning a lead in a Hollywood Bowl revival of *Rose Marie* in the summer of 1941 didn't seem to impress the studio brass, and in 1942, Patricia played in three Paramount mediocrities. *Beyond the Blue Horizon* was ridiculous Technicolor Tarzan-style escapism, starring Dorothy Lamour and Richard Denning in sarongs; the comic was a chimp, the villain was a rampaging elephant, and Patricia was wasted in what *Variety* called "only a bit part." *Night in New Orleans*, a comedy/mystery with Preston Foster and Albert Dekker, cast the sleek and sophisticated Miss Morison as a Gracie Allen type. *Are Husbands Necessary?* was a weak farce, starring Ray Milland and Betty (*Of Mice and Men*) Field.

Actually, what Patricia did on screen in 1942 wasn't as interesting as what she *didn't* do. She had won the part of Janet, sexy heroine of Dashiell Hammett's *The Glass Key*, and was set to co-star with popular Paramount stars Alan Ladd and Brian Donlevy. Patricia had reported for wardrobe fittings when, at the eleventh hour, Paramount's front office yanked her off the picture and replaced her with Veronica Lake (who had just clicked opposite Ladd in *This Gun for Hire*). The studio announced Patricia was set to play in *Wake Island*, but Barbara Britton got the only significant female role in that Oscar-nominated war epic. Paramount also claimed Patricia was set for Billy Wilder's *The Major and the Minor*, but Ginger Rogers, Diana Lynn and Rita Johnson nabbed the female leads. And she was announced to play the second female lead in United Artists' *I Married a Witch* with Fredric March and Veronica Lake—only to be replaced by her ambitious Paramount colleague, Susan Hayward.

It was the last straw for Patricia Morison at Paramount. As she recalled a climactic meeting with Paramount boss, Buddy De Sylva:

> He said I could stick around and play heavies. I said no! I over-ate my way out of the Paramount contract.

So Patricia, intentionally overweight, got her release—and braved freelancing. She also showed her bravery in another way, touring England and Ireland military bases in a U.S.O. show which also boasted Merle Oberon, Al Jolson, Frank McHugh and Allen Jenkins. "We were the first U.S.O. show from Hollywood to go to the E.T.O.," Patricia wrote me in 1995. She told Charles Higham in his Merle Oberon biography *Princess Merle* that the Germans had been tipped about the tour:

> We were flying very low because of German planes. It was clear that we were being tracked by the enemy shipping as well. Indeed, our whole trip was under constant surveillance and it's a miracle that we managed not to be shot down...

Higham wrote that Patricia "clearly was considered to be a first-class contact for use in Intelligence," and reported this tidbit in *Princess Merle*:

> An FBI agent who also worked at Universal Pictures asked Pat if she would seduce a prominent figure of the American government to find out if he was a Nazi agent. She declined the assignment.

Back in Hollywood after her tour, Patricia took the lead in Monogram's "ice spectacle" *Silver Skates* (1943), a musical which—absurdly—didn't even provide Patricia a chance to sing. She was excellent as Barby Taviton, a femme fatale in RKO's *The Fallen Sparrow* (1943), starring John Garfield, Maureen O'Hara and Walter Slezak.

There followed the films for which Patricia Morison is best-remembered today.

> *Hitler's Madman* is the story of Reinhard Heydrich, the most infamous of all brutal Gestapo executioners. He was assassinated by Czech patriots and in retaliation the Nazis on June 9th, 1942, completely destroyed the peaceful little village of Lidice. All male inhabitants were fiendishly executed en masse, the women were tortured and raped and packed off to vile concentration camps, together with the children. Thus was recorded one of the blackest criminal acts in the history of mankind! This internationally publicized chapter in Hitlerian bestiality gives showmen a rare chance to dramatize the horrifying atrocities of the Nazi regime... Cash in on the currently big box-office business being done by horror pictures of all kinds!
>
> —W. R. Ferguson, Manager of Exploitation, in the *Hitler's Madman* pressbook (MGM, 1943)

"If P. T. Barnum had ever been swept by a wave of righteous indignation, the result might not have been greatly different from *Hitler's Madman*," reported the *New York Times* when the movie premiered at Broadway's Rialto Theatre on August 27, 1943. Indeed, this strange, passionate film plays like a horror movie—and was sold by MGM as such.

There's John Carradine as Heydrich, acting "the Hangman" like a sly, horrific vulture, gleefully presiding over sadistic episodes still shocking today. The Tyrolean

Patricia Morison (center), with melodrama regular Elizabeth Russell (far left) and an unidentified actress, faces the knife of John Carradine in *Hitler's Madman*, 1943.

village of "Lidice" looks like it might be nestled right over the mountain from Universal's famous *Frankenstein* back lot village. And the climax—in which the ghosts of the executed patriots rise from the flames and ashes of Lidice, imploring the living to avenge their deaths as a choir of angelic voices sings over the apocalyptic carnage—propels this curious film into the realm of the supernatural.

Hitler's Madman had a fascinating production history. Seymour Nebenzal (who had produced 1931's *M* with Peter Lorre) produced the film independently in the fall of 1942, under the title *The Hangman*, with PRC resources. Originally, Frances Farmer signed to star as Jarmila, a singing teacher in Lidice, who assists her lover (Alan Curtis) and father (Ralph Morgan) in assassinating Heydrich. However, the erratic Miss Farmer suffered one of her highly-publicized breakdowns, and Nebenzal canceled her contract. Patricia signed for *The Hangman* on October 27, 1942; according to *The Hollywood Reporter*, director Douglas Sirk began shooting the film the same week.

Although *Hitler's Madman* plays at times almost like an operetta, it captures the evil genius of Nazi madness with a fervent passion rarely glimpsed in the Hollywood of the 1940s. Carradine is superb; as Douglas Sirk told Jon Halliday in his book *Sirk on Sirk*:

> John Carradine *was* Heydrich ... a Shakespearean stage actor, with a reputation of going overboard. A lot of Nazis behaved like Shakespearean actors.

Naturally, Carradine is stage center in some of *Hitler's Madman* most sinister vignettes: lecherously inspecting a gaggle of village beauties—all to be sterilized and dispatched as prostitutes to the Russian Front (one girl cannot take the shame, and leaps to her death from a window) ... crashing a religious pastorale in his open car, slapping an ancient priest, provoking him by wiping his boots on sacred cloth, and sneering over the dead priest after an underling shoots him ... and a chilling death scene, lying in a giant, Gothic bed, begging for morphine and hissing "Shoot them!" as he curses the patriots who killed him.

The curse takes effect on poor Jarmila. Of course, top-billed Patricia is a bit too glamorous for a Bohemian village singing teacher; yet she plays the role with a wonderfully effective sadness and sense of grim purpose. The assassination episode is truly exciting: Patricia rides her bicycle across the forest road, attracting Heydrich's lecherous eye. As he leers at her from his open car, Curtis blasts his machine gun, Morgan tosses his grenades and the car crashes over a hill.

Very moving is Patricia's own death scene; she and Curtis escape into the forest and mountains, tracked by Nazis—who fatally wound the heroine. Curtis takes the dying woman into a forest hut, where she dies in his arms ("You're crying!" she exclaims; "No, I'm not," lies Curtis). She dies weeping; her lover buries her in the mountains. In Lidice, the horrible Nazi revenge begins. And as the film ends, the martyrs rise from the fiery destruction (Patricia curiously not among them) and beg the audience to avenge their deaths.

The fate of this movie was almost as strange as the film itself: Nebenzal and his Angelus Productions (who lacked distribution power for the film) offered the picture to a major studio, and the biggest major of them all—MGM—bought it for $288,000. According to MGM records, the studio began eight days of retakes on March 4, 1943; one of them was the "Sterilization" scene, which added such MGM contractees as Frances Rafferty, Leatrice Joy Gilbert and Ava Gardner as "Sacrificial Daughters of Lidice." The final negative cost: $405,678.81. The final title: *Hitler's Madman*.

In 1997, Patricia told interviewer Jack Gourlay:

> I enjoyed doing *Hitler's Madman*, because the people who made it were European refugees from Hitler, including the great German film director Douglas Sirk. They were all so nice and sweet and wonderful to work with... I really didn't get a chance to see John Carradine that much. I blew up his car in a scene in the mountains, but didn't have much contact with him. I always thought Carradine was a very interesting man, one of the mavericks in our business. Really a classical actor in the truest sense of the word; he even *lived* that way, in a grand, grand manner.

MGM classified its releases by the following codes: "AA," "A," "B" and "C." *Hitler's Madman* was considered a "C" product upon its August 27, 1943, release, complete with a wild exploitation campaign ("HANG HITLER IN EFFIGY! DISPLAY A

VICTIM IN A COFFIN!"). "Sensational!" was the film's slogan; the film's 24-sheet poster showed a sketch of Patricia, in a slit-up-the-leg dress, sprawled and cowering under a giant whip. The manager of the Luna Theatre of Battle Creek, Iowa, reported to *Box Office*:

> Did not expect to do anything on this one and imagine my surprise when they came in droves, thereby giving one of the best grosses in years on a Thurs., Fri., Sat., Sun. Younger folks came to the show expecting to see something rather risqué and sensational and they were not disappointed. Older patrons came for the same reason… Summing it up, *Hitler's Madman* turned out to be one of the top sleepers of the year in this locality…

Inevitably, the accent on horror worked against *Hitler's Madman*; many critics refused to take it seriously; also, Fritz Lang's *Hangmen Also Die!* (United Artists, 1943, starring Brian Donlevy as the assassin) had beaten *Hitler's Madman* into theaters. On October 7, 1943, MGM withdrew *Hitler's Madman* from release, and the film suffered a net loss of $95,000 (approximately the amount MGM had paid for the retakes).

However, in recent years, this forlorn little movie, with its sentiment and horror, has made a comeback with movie historians and fans. In 1992, as the world press remembered Lidice on the 50th anniversary of its tragic fate, the TNT cable TV station offered its own late night tribute: at 3:05 A.M. on June 11, the station telecast *Hitler's Madman*—complete with Carradine's Nazi villainy and Patricia Morison's heartbreaking heroine.

Calling Dr. Death (1943) was the first of Universal's "Inner Sanctum" horror films—a bizarre parade of "B" potboilers, all hell-bent on presenting Lon Chaney as handsome, brilliant, and desired by some of the loveliest ladies in Hollywood. Patricia Morison was the first actress to play mad passion for Chaney; such beauties as Evelyn Ankers (q.v.), Anne Gwynne (q.v.), Lois Collier, Jean Parker, Brenda Joyce and Tala Birell all would follow in her high-heeled footsteps.

Calling Dr. Death has a few advantages: Chaney seems to be trying hard, Reginald LeBorg directs with panache and J. Carrol Naish is excellent as a Javert-like detective. However, Patricia truly snares the honors as Stella Madden, Chaney's lovesick nurse (a role originally fashioned for Gale Sondergaard, who was supposed to co-star with Chaney in all the "Inner Sanctum" films, but ultimately played in none of them). Patricia's Stella reveals in a climactic hypnotic spell that she murdered Chaney's wicked wife (Ramsay Ames) with a fire poker—then destroyed her face with acid. Certainly it's one of the most grim and shocking crimes in the Universal horror canon.

"Patricia Morison makes a neat appearance as the suspected doctor's nurse," wrote John McManus in his *PM* review, "but the Doc himself (Lon Chaney) never fully emerges from a sorry subliminal fog."

Patricia was a guest on the A&E *Biography* show devoted to Lon Chaney, Jr. (10/25/95), and spoke very highly of her *Calling Dr. Death* co-star:

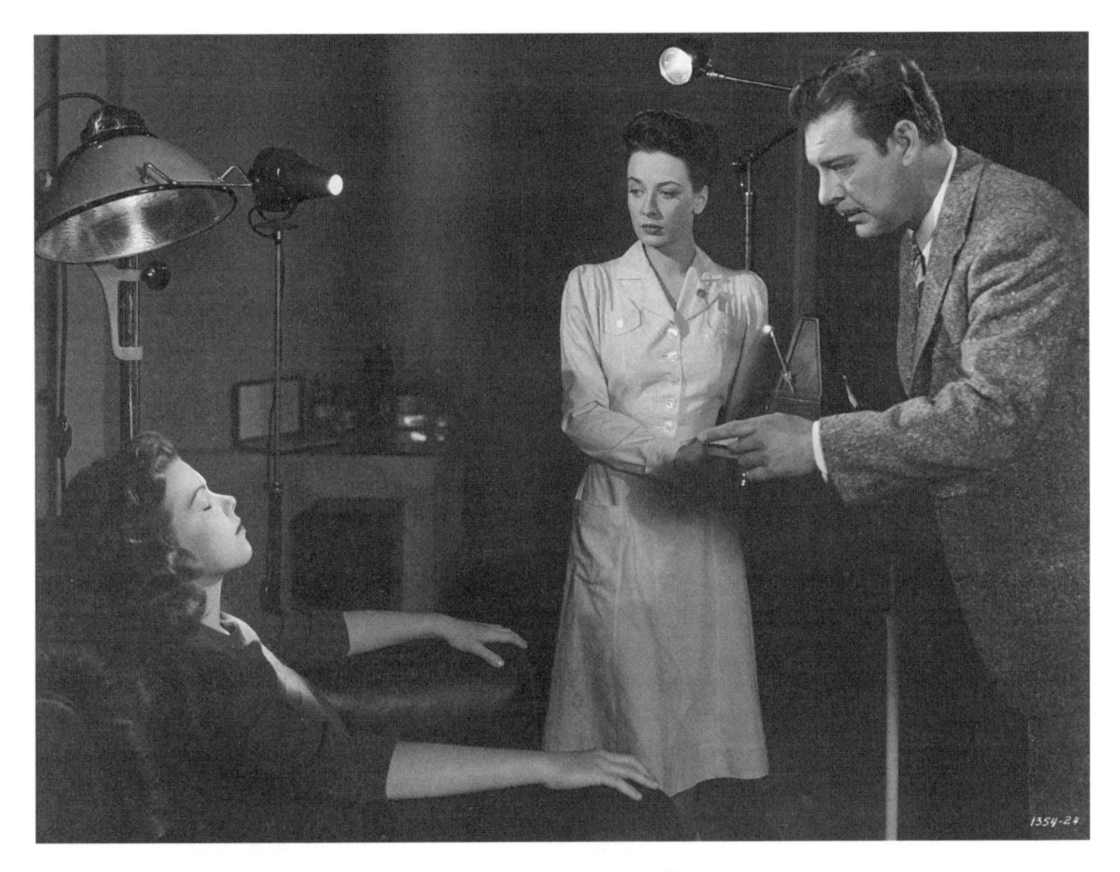

Patricia Morison (center) with Lon Chaney, Jr., and Mary Hale in *Calling Dr. Death*, 1943.

> I thought he was a very shy man—very vulnerable... He was a wonderful actor. He never forgot a line... I remember when the film was over, and we had the "wrap," he came over and it astonished me; he put his arm around me and said, "Thank you so much, it was lovely working with you," and I was very touched... He had his own magic. I thought he was a charming actor.

Calling Dr. Death played many engagements as a support feature for *The Lodger*, 20th Century–Fox's magnificent melodrama starring Laird Cregar as Jack the Ripper. It's curious to imagine Patricia in *The Lodger* in the role her friend Merle Oberon played: Kitty Langley, the London dance hall star who barely escapes the Ripper's knife. Patricia certainly had the beauty, the legs and the style to have played the can-can star; she could even have sung the songs (Miss Oberon was dubbed).

The limited opportunities continued, though Patricia made the most of them. She was beautiful in a virtual cameo as Napoleon's Empress Eugenie in 20th Century–Fox's *The Song of Bernadette* (1943), for which Jennifer Jones won an Oscar; showed a comedy flair as Edwina, a glamour girl in MGM's Spencer Tracy/ Katharine Hepburn vehicle *Without Love* (1945); and supported Deanna Durbin in Universal's *Lady on a Train*, a mystery directed by Deanna's last husband, Charles David, in which Deanna sang such songs as "Silent Night" and "Give Me a Little Kiss, Will You, Huh?"

Leggy villainess: Morison as Hilda Courtney, foe of Sherlock Holmes, in *Dressed to Kill*, 1946. Her accomplices are Frederic Worlock (left) and Harry Cording.

Patricia tried the stage. In January of 1944, she appeared in a stage show at the State Theatre in New York; Jackie Gleason was emcee, and *Variety* reported Patricia's "slinky" appearance in a black gown with an off-center slit. On April 20, 1944, Patricia opened at Broadway's Adelphi Theatre as Marcia Mason Moore in *Allah Be Praised!*, a risqué musical comedy. She had replaced, during rehearsals, former Paramount colleague Shirley Ross; the show lasted 20 performances.

Patricia was at her most slinky in *Dressed to Kill*, the 1946 swan song of the Universal *Sherlock Holmes* series. She was master villainess Hilda Courtney, mistress of disguises, smoker of Egyptian cigarettes and diabolic vamp who supplies Universal's own final challenge for Basil Rathbone's Holmes and Nigel Bruce's Watson.

Julian Emery (Edmond Breon), aka "Stinky," is a wealthy collector of music boxes and old schoolmate of Nigel Bruce's Watson. He has just removed his toupee for the night when he receives a telephone call from Patricia's Hilda Courtney—who seductively invites herself up for a drink. Breon has his toupee back on by the time Patricia makes her entrance—drop-dead gorgeous in a full-length dress and a remarkable white stole. Of course, Mrs. Courtney's interest is not in this old codger, but in his music boxes—one of which contains stolen Bank of England plates. Patricia turns up her vamp act, Breon moves in for a kiss, and we see one of the most memorable

Morison in a publicity photo for *Dressed to Kill*, 1946.

death scenes in the Universal Holmes series: Hilda's accomplice (Harry Cording) tosses a knife into Breon's back. He falls, dragging the villainess' white stole with him; it runs over her shoulders and down her arms like a giant, plunging snake. As Michael Brunas wrote about *Dressed to Kill* in the book *Universal Horrors*:

> Most critics seemed more interested in griping about the inappropriateness of the title. One wonders where these critics were

> looking when the sleek, elegantly coiffured Patricia Morison dispassionately retracted her ermine from under the body of poor old Emery ... and then cold-bloodedly walked over him.

Thereafter, Patricia's Hilda Courtney is a deadly black widow of a villainess: performing a marvelous disguise bit as an old charwoman; making her way around London in the aforementioned sexy black dress, furs and big-toe hat (with partners-in-crime Frederic Worlock and Harry Cording); and sparring with Rathbone's Holmes:

> HILDA: So fearfully awkward having a dead body lying about, don't you agree, Mr. Holmes?
>
> HOLMES: Another dead body shouldn't weigh too heavily on your conscience, Mrs. Courtney!

In the course of *Dressed to Kill*, Patricia's Hilda almost kills Holmes as her henchmen handcuff him to a pipe on a garage ceiling, filling the area with exhaust smoke; she also tricks Bruce's Watson, flirting with him and planting a smoke bomb in 221-B Baker Street. However, Holmes and Watson foil her in the end, and she marches off, her head arrogantly held high—and still dressed to kill.

"A brilliant antagonist," salutes Rathbone's Holmes. "It's a pity her talents were so misdirected."

Released in June of 1946, *Dressed to Kill* did very little for Patricia Morison. Hollywood continued to misdirect her talents: the title role in Universal's *Danger Woman* (1946), Screen Guild's *Queen of the Amazons* (1947) and RKO's *Tarzan and the Huntress* (1947), with Johnny Weissmuller and Patricia playing the title roles.

Then came major news: Patricia played in 20th Century–Fox's *Kiss of Death* (1947), starring Victor Mature, Brian Donlevy and (as giggling gangster Tommy Udo) Richard Widmark. Patricia played Mature's first wife, who cannot take the misery of her husband's imprisonment, is raped by one of his hoodlum pals (Henry Brandon), and commits suicide. Early reports claimed she was so heartbreaking in the tragic role that an Academy Award nomination was very possible. Instead, the censors cut the rape scene, and the depiction of suicide; by the time *Kiss of Death* was released, her entire role (and Brandon's) had been totally cut.

She was a vamp (again) in MGM's *Song of the Thin Man* (1947) and Marian in Columbia's costumer *Prince of Thieves*, starring Jon Hall and based on the Alexander Dumas novel. Universal-International originally envisioned her as Dr. Sandra Mornay, Dracula's sexy ally in *Abbott and Costello Meet Frankenstein*, but Lenore Aubert (q.v.) played the role in that 1948 box office smash. She finally sang in *Sofia* (Film Classics, 1948), a poor espionage film with Gene Raymond and Sigrid Gurie, mostly shot in Mexico (where Patricia has loved vacationing over the years).

Patricia starred in an early TV series, *Cases of Eddie Drake*, co-starring Don Haggerty. She played Karen Gayle, a psychologist studying criminal behavior. The producer/director of *The Cases of Eddie Drake* was Herbert L. Strock; in 1996, he spoke with Tom Weaver about the show's origins, tiny budget, hysterical shooting schedule—and leading lady:

> It was the first television show ever put on film. We shot it in 35mm black-and-white and it was based on the radio program *The Cases of Eddie Ace* with George Raft. I made the pilot, I think, in 1946. My budget was $7500 per half-hour, and we shot the average of one episode a day.
>
> Pat was always on time, never gave anyone one second of trouble. I enjoyed working with her because you never had to do Take Two with her—she was always right on the money, she knew what she was doing. I'd never seen anyone so charming and so sweet. And she was a lady, a princess—very ladylike, very dainty. She always knew her dialogue, as Don Haggerty did. (I think we were paying them $55 a day.) Pat worked her butt off, she was really a trouper and she was a pleasure to work with.

The Cases of Eddie Drake originally aired in 1949, and was dropped after nine televised episodes.

Meanwhile, everything changed.

Patricia won the role of Lilli Vanessi, hellcat Shakespearean actress in Cole Porter's *Kiss Me Kate*. The showcase role allowed her to play Kate of *The Taming of the Shrew* within her performance, duet with Alfred Drake (her *The Two Bouquets* co-star of ten years before) on "Wunderbar," sing "So in Love," and deliver the show-stopping comedy song, "I Hate Men." *Kiss Me Kate* premiered December 30, 1948, at Broadway's New Century Theatre, and the *New York Times* reported:

> As a greasepaint hussy, Miss Morison is an agile and humorous actress who is not afraid of slapstick and who can sing enchantingly. She has captured perfectly the improvised tone of the comedy, and she plays it with spirit and drollery.

Patricia romped through 686 Broadway performances of *Kiss Me Kate*, never missing a show; Anne Jeffreys replaced her as Lilli in June of 1950.* Patricia sang at the Cocoanut Grove in Los Angeles, the Hollywood Bowl and the Paramount Theatre in New York; then, on March 8, 1951, Patricia recreated her Lilli Vanessi for a hit London run of *Kiss Me Kate* at the Coliseum. It was a triumph all over again. An ill King George VI watched a closed circuit TV presentation from Buckingham Palace; during the run, Patricia was a guest of honor at the Royal Variety Show at the Victoria Palace, and was presented to Queen Elizabeth and Princess Margaret.

It was now a whole new life and career. For over 40 years, Patricia Morison has been a busy musical comedy and civic light opera performer. There are many highlights in her résumé—including taking over the role of Anna (on February 22, 1954) in Broadway's *The King and I*, and subsequently touring in the Rodgers and Hammerstein classic for almost two years.

"Then Pat Morison came to the show," said the late Yul Brynner. "She was marvelous. I could do anything with her."

She has reprised *Kiss Me Kate* on TV's *Hallmark Hall of Fame* (NBC, 11/20/58)

**In MGM's 1953* Kiss Me Kate, *filmed in 3-D, Howard Keel and Kathryn Grayson starred.*

and in a 1965 stage revival at New York's City Center. She toured the civic light opera circuit in such shows as *The Sound of Music*, *Milk And Honey*, *Gigi*, *The Merry Widow*, *Do I Hear A Waltz?*, *Song Of Norway*, *Company* and *Kismet*, and co-starred with Janet Blair in a coast-to-coast tour in the late 1970s of the musical *Winner Take All.*

Patricia Morison was nominated in 1948 for the first Annual Emmy Award as "Most Outstanding TV Personality" (losing for Judy Splinters, Shirley Dinsdale's puppet); she has appeared over the years on such shows as *Robert Montgomery Presents* (the musical "Rio Rita," NBC, 11/13/50), *Airflyte Theatre* (CBS, 11/30/50), *Pulitzer Prize Playhouse* ("Light Up the Sky," ABC, 1/19/51), *Celanese Theatre* (ABC, 6/11/52), *Four Star Playhouse* (CBS, 5/21/53), *Video Theatre* (CBS, 11/19/53), *Screen Directors Playhouse* (NBC, 5/16/56) and *Schlitz Playhouse of Stars* (CBS, 10/12/56), as well as *The Milton Berle Show, The Colgate Comedy Hour, The Ed Sullivan Show, 77th Bengal Lancers, Matinee Theatre, Lux Video Theatre, Have Gun—Will Travel, U.S. Steel Hour* and *The Voice of Firestone*. Her old series *The Cases of Eddie Drake* began a TV run in syndication March 6, 1952. In 1971, she performed "Shall We Dance?" from *The King and I*, with Yul Brynner, on the Tony Awards 25th anniversary TV special.

As for the movies, she returned to the screen after her Broadway success in *Song Without End* (1960), as George Sand. Her only other film credit of the past decades has been a cameo (along with dozens of Hollywood "old-timers," including her *Hitler's Madman* co-star John Carradine) in the spoof *Won Ton Ton, the Dog Who Saved Hollywood* (1976); she was seen as a star at a premiere, with Guy Madison.

In 1987, Patricia performed the shows *Song of Norway* and *Aloha* in New Zealand. She later guest-starred on TV's *L.A. Law* and *Cheers*.

Patricia Morison lives in a Los Angeles apartment, where her late mother lived with her for many years. She has never married. Richard Lamparski profiled her in his eleventh series of *Whatever Became of...?*, which reported:

> The walls of her Los Angeles apartment are decorated with an ever-changing array of her oil paintings, which she sells. On the piano in her living room are signed photos of such luminaries as Cole Porter, Oscar Hammerstein II and Bishop Fulton J. Sheen.

On June 9, 1998, Patricia Morison enjoyed a new triumph. She appeared at New York City's Town Hall as one of the stars in a tribute to Cole Porter (who died in 1964) for the 107th anniversary of his birth. Patricia sang "So in Love" and (with David Staller) "Wunderbar" from *Kiss Me Kate*. The *New York Post* reported "the rapturous standing ovation" she received, the *New York Times* noted that she "brought down the house" and *Variety* called her the "highlight of the evening."

Patricia has had the satisfaction of becoming a star in spite of Hollywood. She has long outlived the studio system which nearly destroyed her. And she has even seen her most "notorious" B films—*Hitler's Madman*, *Calling Dr. Death* and *Dressed to Kill*—win her a new coterie of fans.

The Films of Patricia Morison

1939

Persons in Hiding (Paramount, Louis King)
I'm from Missouri (Paramount, Theodore Reed)
The Magnificent Fraud (Paramount, Robert Florey)

1940

Untamed (Paramount, George Archainbaud)
Rangers of Fortune (Paramount, Sam Wood)
Romance of the Rio Grande (20th Century–Fox, Herbert Leeds)

1941

The Roundup (Paramount, Lesley Selander)
One Night in Lisbon (Paramount, Edward H. Griffith)

1942

Beyond the Blue Horizon (Paramount, Alfred Santell)
Night in New Orleans (Paramount, William Clemens)
Are Husbands Necessary? (Paramount, Norman Taurog)

1943

Silver Skates (Monogram, Leslie Goodwins)
The Fallen Sparrow (RKO, Richard Wallace)
Hitler's Madman (Nebenzal/MGM, Douglas Sirk)
Calling Dr. Death (Universal, Reginald LeBorg)
The Song of Bernadette (20th Century–Fox, Henry King)

1944

Where Are Your Children? (Monogram, William Nigh)

1945

Without Love (MGM, Harold S. Bucquet)
Lady on a Train (Universal, Charles David)

1946

Dressed to Kill (Universal, Roy Wm. Neill)
Danger Woman (Universal, Lewis D. Collins)

1947

Queen of the Amazons (Screen Guild, Edward Finney)
Tarzan and the Huntress (RKO, Kurt Neumann)
Kiss of Death (20th Century–Fox, Henry Hathaway) (footage deleted)
Song of the Thin Man (MGM, Eddie Buzzell)
Prince of Thieves (Columbia, Howard Bretherton)

1948

Walls of Jericho (20th Century–Fox, John Stahl)
The Return of Wildfire (Screen Guild, Ray Taylor)
Sofia (Film Classics, John Reinhart)

1960

Song Without End (Columbia, George Cukor and Charles Vidor)

1976

Won Ton Ton, the Dog Who Saved Hollywood (Paramount, Michael Winner)

SHORT SUBJECTS

1940

Chinese Garden Festival (Republic)

1941

Stars at Play (Republic)

Acquanetta

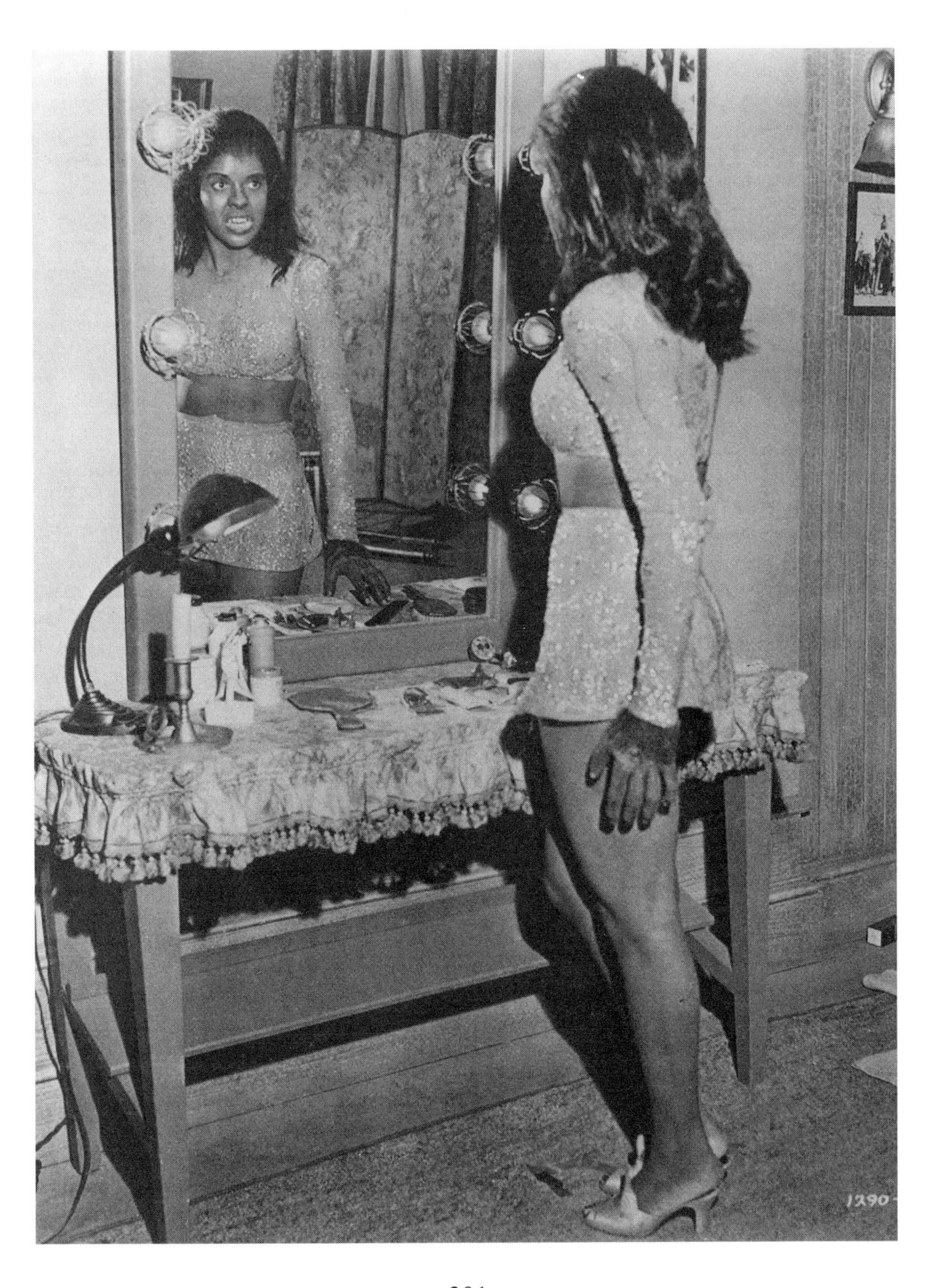

Take a tall, dark, beautiful brunette, whose parents (according to the lady) were an Arapaho Indian mother and a son-of-British-royalty father.

Place her in New York City, where she becomes one of the town's top-paid models.

Send this Cinderella to 1942 Hollywood, where she conquers the night club scene, and wins contract serenades from MGM and Universal.

Grab the Universal offer, and herald her as sexy rival to Maria Montez, the studio's Queen of Costume Spectacle.

Then cast her as an ape woman.

Thus spins the saga of Acquanetta—Universal's own Paula Dupree, "shockingly savage Gorilla Girl" of *Captive Wild Woman* (1943) and *Jungle Woman* (1944). Poor Paula—the unfortunate hybrid of crazed sex hormones, John Carradine's sinister surgery on a gorilla, and Jack P. Pierce's hair, fangs and putty—was Universal's only female monster since Elsa Lanchester's *Bride of Frankenstein*. She became the most tawdry member of Universal's Horror Mythology—hairy, sexpot little sister to Frankenstein's Monster, Count Dracula, the Wolf Man, the Invisible Man, the Mummy, the Phantom of the Opera...

She also was the least respected. Something about this busty, leggy ape woman gave off a perfume of the unsavory. Perhaps it was the ingredient of those wild female hormones Carradine discussed—a script device that makes one wonder if one or more of the five (male) writers who concocted *Captive Wild Woman* was battling with an edgy wife while contributing to this erotic little yarn. Perhaps it's the fact that sexual jealousy causes Paula's shape-changing back into Cheela the gorilla (just as it had caused the beast flesh of Kathleen "Panther Woman" Burke to come "creeping back" in Paramount's 1933 *Island of Lost Souls*). Or maybe it's the unfortunate fact that Paula turns black before turning ape—a touch that caused at least one major critic to blast the wartime series as "Nazi propaganda."

At any rate, any and all such hang-ups are lost on the role's creator—Acquanetta. If "living well is the best revenge," Acquanetta (her real name) is wreaking wrath on the Universal overlords who cast her as Paula, on the executives who sexually harassed her, on the '40s critics who had a picnic picking apart her acting, and on the historians of today who mock her as the thespic soul mate to Rondo Hatton. Forty-five years after the steam bath drowning of Maria Montez (whose jealousy damaged Acquanetta's career at Universal), decades after the disappearance of Vicky Lane (who replaced her in the third Paula the Ape Woman howler, 1945's *The Jungle Captive*), the very beautiful, wealthy and happy Acquanetta lives in Arizona—proud of her family, confident in her spiritual beliefs and serene in her memories of Hollywood.

"I've had, and am still having, a wonderful life," she proclaims.

> Poor Paula, she never even met Abbott and Costello. But she left behind her, if not an interesting body of work, an interesting body.
> —Denis Gifford, *A Pictorial History of the Horror Movies* (1973)

***Chapter opener:* Acquanetta regards her reflection as Paula the Ape Woman in *Captive Wild Woman*, 1943.**

"I'm 72 years old!" proudly proclaimed the tall woman with jet-black hair, a flashy, almost blinding smile, a knockout figure, beautiful Indian jewelry and a book of her own poetry to a room of fans at the 1992 FANEX Convention of horror/fantasy/science fiction fans in Baltimore. There were several cross-armed skeptics in the crowd, who would later accuse the lady (not to her face) of being guilty of everything from wearing a wig, to reading bad poetry, to wildly romanticizing her life.

The assemblage listened to her story of her birth on an Indian reservation near Cheyenne, Wyoming, on July 21 (probably) 1920. Whatever "vibes" of cynicism she might have sensed, Acquanetta narrated it all the same way she had in a telephone interview with me a few days before—with total sincerity, and considerable drama:

> My real name is Burnu Acquanetta—it means "Burning Fire, Deep Water." My mother was Arapaho, and my father was part Cherokee. Actually, my father had an interesting background: my father's father was the illegitimate son of the King of England and a French Jewess. His mother, the grandmother, was part Cherokee. My dad was born here, in the Carolinas—they were sent here to America, kind of "hush-hush"—there was no documentation, but later, we all knew. My dad had five or six different wives—I have half-sisters and brothers that I don't even know, and some I do know. When I was grown, and living in New York, I got a letter from a couple of beautiful Indian girls—in fact, they sent their pictures—and said they were my sisters. We have never met to this day.
>
> I was given away to a family in Norristown, Pennsylvania, when I was only a few years old. They had the name of Davenport, and the foster parents gave me the name of Mildred, which I used all through school—and which doesn't suit me at all, at all, at *all*! But before he left me there, my father sat me down and told me my background, and how my mother had died, and my real name—which, years later, I would take.
>
> So, as I grew up, I always felt as if I was among, but not of. I had very few friends, and was kind of a loner.

At the age of 15, and with $50 (or so the legend goes), Burnu Acquanetta fled provincial Norristown for the lights of New York City. She became a waitress. Then, one day on Fifth Avenue:

> It was very curious. I was standing looking in a window, and a photographer saw my reflection. He spun me around and said, "Are you a model?" Well, I had modeled for Wonder Bread (with a few other little girls!)—just by accident. But I said, "Yes!" He said, "Who are you with?" I looked at him kind of curiously and he mentioned two names I didn't know—John Powers and Harry Conover. I looked at him with a blank expression, and he pulled out his card, wrote on it, handed it to me—and sent me up to see Harry Conover.

Thus began a career that soon established Burnu Acquanetta as one of Manhattan's most expensive models—first for Conover, later for John Powers. The Cinderella story seemed complete; from Mildred Davenport of Norristown, Pennsylvania, Burnu Acquanetta was on the covers of *Vogue* and *Bazaar*, and was squired around New York by Aly Khan and Orson Welles. For a time, Howard Johnson proposed to her every day. She was a darling of the columnists, especially Walter Winchell; since Indians weren't "fashionable" in 1942, he dubbed her the "Venezuelan Volcano." Acquanetta felt obliged to go along with the ruse—despite the handicap that she spoke no Spanish. She insisted on speaking English to the suspecting reporters, claiming, "I want so much to speak English well that this is the best way to learn it." As Richard Lamparski noted in his Acquanetta profile in his seventh *Whatever Became of...?* book, "The press ate it up."

Then came Hollywood. Actually, says Acquanetta, she was en route to Rio, having been offered a job by "a couple of chaps" whose family owned the Copacabana; "I was a natural dancer and performer, so they offered me a job at the Copa."

> So we were on our way to Rio, and stopped at the Beverly Hills Hotel. They were very, very wealthy, they knew the crowd in Hollywood, and we went to the Mocambo—*the* big nightclub on Sunset Boulevard in those days. Well, the first night we arrived, there sat Louis B. Mayer, and Walter Wanger (who was getting ready to do *Arabian Nights* with Maria Montez), and all the reporters and people from the various studios. I was getting all the attention, and the next day I made all the columns...

Charles Feldman took notice. One of the legendary agents of Hollywood, he squired Acquanetta to MGM—where Garbo and Shearer were retiring, where Greer Garson was enjoying an Oscar-winning triumph as *Mrs. Miniver*—for a screen test.

> It was so crazy! I had long hair, and they pulled my hair up, and put a wig on me that was brown, curly, almost Shirley Temple-ish. And I didn't talk! They just had me stand and turn around and walk and that kind of thing. Well, I don't know what Charlie Feldman told them at Metro, but we got in his limousine and went to Universal Studios. There I met Dan Kelley, head of casting, and Charlie Feldman told him, "You know, we just came from Metro. They did a little test of her, and when they see it, they'll probably sign her." Dan Kelley said, "We don't need a test. Let's make a deal right now." And by golly, if Charlie Feldman didn't pull out some papers, and said, "Sign here, dear." So I obediently signed, and he said, "You're now a movie actress. You're under contract to Universal Studios." And that's the way I became an actress at Universal. I didn't even know what I was signing! Two weeks later, I was in a movie!

Come the summer of '42, Acquanetta was a new asset of Universal—where the top attractions were Deanna Durbin, Abbott and Costello, and, of course, the "Screen's Master Character Creator," Lon Chaney, Jr.

There was immediate trouble.

One of Universal's top stars of the day was Maria Montez. Her personal "M.M.F." campaign ("Make Montez Famous") included making entrances with the proclamation, "I am La Montez," and dropping such press-delighting *bon mots* as "Thank God I don't need to wear a brassiere." Producer Walter Wanger had offered Maria the starring role of Scheherazade in Universal's first Technicolor feature, *Arabian Nights*, which would be Universal's big Christmas attraction of 1942. According to Acquanetta:

> Maria Montez had already been signed for *Arabian Nights*. They tried to get her to give it up and let me star in it. Walter Wanger, Dan Kelley, all the brass—they said of me, "*She* is our Scheherazade." See, Maria Montez—they made her up beautifully, but she didn't have good features. I have *great* features!

Maria kept her starring role, and Acquanetta received the part of Ishya, one of the "Harem Queens." Even this did not sit well with "La Montez":

> When Maria was called in to be told I was to be in her film—oh! While I was still living in the Beverly Hills Hotel, I was invited to a Hollywood party at a private house one night, and I did not know it was her home. After I was there for ten or fifteen minutes, Maria came into the room where I was, and saw me—and she just threw a fit! And I left the party. She was very jealous of me—I wasn't jealous of her. I never had anyone treat me the way she did. And she never really became my friend.

Naturally, the feud tickled the press. As Louella Parsons wrote, "Maria was very cute when she told me her supposed rival in *Arabian Nights* was just a 'bit player' although she admitted that Acquanetta was not one of those 'hatchet-faced Indians'! Well, I always say a good glamour-girl feud never hurt anybody."

Produced by Walter Wanger ("one of the worst wolves in Hollywood!" says Acquanetta), directed by John Rawlins, *Arabian Nights* primarily showcased Jon Hall, Sabu and, of course, Maria Montez. Indeed, at a private showing for the Universal executives, Maria stood up after one of her own lush closeups, ordered the projectionist to stop the film and demanded of the assemblage, "Isn't that the most beautiful woman you have ever laid eyes on?" Yet Universal also provided quite a publicity bonanza for Acquanetta. Posters for *Arabian Nights*, while affording major space to the stars, tantalized:

And these bewitching Harem Queens
Elyse Knox • Acquanetta • Carmen D'Antonio

Universal dispatched Acquanetta to New York City for six weeks of interviews and personal appearances to promote *Arabian Nights*, well in advance of its Christmas Day, 1942, opening at the Rivoli Theatre. And Universal welcomed her back to Hollywood in late October 1942 with *Rhythm of the Islands*, released in March of 1943.*

**In August of 1942, Universal had announced Acquanetta would star with Charles Boyer in a circus segment of* Flesh and Fantasy *(1943), but she didn't make the film.*

Jane Frazee was the actual femme lead, while Acquanetta played Luani. The director was Roy William Neill, who began this 60-minute tropical tale right after finishing with Lon Chaney and Bela Lugosi on *Frankenstein Meets the Wolf Man*.

Acquanetta's sarong was hardly off before Universal awarded her the role for which she would win Hollywood infamy: Paula Dupree, the *Captive Wild Woman*.

> And so, beyond these gates is buried the legend of a mortal, who went beyond the realm of human powers, and tampered with things no man should ever touch.
>
> —Turhan Bey, in (unbilled) voiceover at the end of *Captive Wild Woman* (1943)

Acquanetta was very aware of what was happening to her, and her career, almost instantly at Universal.

> Dan Kelley—he chose me for those fast, "B" pictures. In those days, a "B" picture wasn't a second-rate picture; it was a "bread & butter" picture—that's what "B & B" meant. Those big pictures they spent a million dollars on in those days—and that was a lot of money—they didn't really make much money. They were the prestige pictures. The "B & B" pictures were fast, they didn't put too much money into them—but they *made* money. And when they found out how hot I became, right away, they just put me in one after another.
>
> So Dan Kelley said to me, "You're a natural." And I was a natural actress. I must have been in some former life. I loved it, and I could play any role...

One role that was whetting the imaginations of Universal City was Paula the Ape Woman—soon to receive her baptism of fire as newest member of the Universal classic goblins.

While RKO's 1933 *King Kong* is, of course, Hollywood's most celebrated simian, the gorilla was one of the favorite habitués of movie melodrama—from jungle capers (MGM's 1932 *Tarzan the Ape Man*, in which Johnny Weissmuller battles that ape monster in the native pit) to Biblical spectacle (Paramount's 1932 *The Sign of the Cross*, in which De Mille has a gorilla menace a naked blonde martyr, bound to a Roman pillar) to slapstick comedy (MGM's 1938 *Swiss Miss*, with Laurel and Hardy cavorting with an ape on a swinging rope bridge over a deep chasm). The ape was at his hirsute best in horror—Chaney, Sr.'s rampaging gorilla of *The Unholy Three* (both 1925 and 1930), Lugosi's "lonely" Erik the Ape of Universal's 1932 *Murders in the Rue Morgue*, the gorilla with Phillip Terry's transplanted brain in Paramount's *The Monster and the Girl* (1941). Karloff had starred in Monogram's *The Ape* (1940), as a mad doctor who slays for science under cover of a gorilla suit; Universal had just sold *The Strange Case of Doctor Rx* (1942) on the brief cameo of a caged gorilla, restless for his own brain transplant. And at Republic, Emil Van Horn was bringing the gorilla to new dramatic heights as Satan, loving pet to evil Vultura (Lorna Gray) in the 1942 serial *Perils of Nyoka*—not only milking a dynamo death scene, but winning the distinction of being the second-best paid member of the cast!

Left to right behind bars: Lloyd Corrigan, Milburn Stone, Evelyn Ankers, Vince Barnett, Acquanetta and John Carradine in *Captive Wild Woman*, 1943.

Then, on October 19, 1942, *Film Daily* reviewed 20th Century–Fox's *Dr. Renault's Secret*, in which mad doctor George Zucco transformed a gorilla into an ape man—Noel, played with pathos by J. Carrol Naish.

A gorilla girl was inevitable.

Thus, Universal's *Captive Wild Woman*—a female counterpart to Naish's Noel. Universal had cause to be upset by Fox's *Dr. Renault's Secret* beating their film to the theaters; after all, the Ape Woman idea had ping-ponged at the studio since the summer of 1941, originally under the banner of George (*The Wolf Man*) Waggner. Now, in late 1942, the film was under the auspices of "B" maven Ben Pivar (who, as remembered by the late director Reginald LeBorg, was barely literate). Edward Dmytryk (who had helmed the Karloff Columbia *The Devil Commands*, 1941) would direct—and tests began for Paula the Ape Woman.

Yvonne de Carlo (22 years before *The Munsters*) was a top contender for the part; however, in the end, Universal announced its "Paula": Acquanetta. While one can imagine Maria Montez shrieking with glee that her "rival" was being cast as an Ape Woman, Acquanetta claims no regrets about the role:

> Oh! It was fun. Oh, yeah! I thought it was great to play a gorilla. That doesn't bother me. Even to this day, I'd put on a gorilla suit

> and go on stage! I think it's great to play characters ... those were challenging. You get into it, you know. And they're fun!

On Saturday, December 12, 1942, *Captive Wild Woman* began shooting at Universal City. Shooting ran through the Christmas holidays and into the New Year of 1943. *Captive Wild Woman* would become one of the great "guilty pleasures" of Universal aficionados.

First of all, there's John Carradine as mad Dr. Sigmund Walters, his very first starring horror role. In his slouch hat, black mustache and lean-and-hungry look, Carradine evokes a Wild West Shakespearean actor—especially as he leers his dialogue at reverted Paula: "They wouldn't know it was jungle instinct that urged you to kill a female that stood between you and a mate...!"

Acquanetta remembers:

> John was beautiful. You know, he was always acting—on stage and off! He was always playing a role—he loved it! In the street, he would walk in a peculiar way, with a cane, and this expression on his face... He *was* Carradine—and he wanted people to know it! So he was an *actor*—on and off. I've always felt he was an actor from his first incarnation!

There was also Evelyn Ankers (q.v.), Universal's Queen of the Horrors, as Beth Colman, our blonde heroine—awaking in her boudoir to see Ape Woman Paula leering over her, and, naturally, unleashing one of her wonderfully operatic screams:

> Evelyn and I were friendly... We didn't go out on double dates or so forth, but she was a nice person... Always very friendly and warm and just a lovely, delightful lady.

Paula the Ape Woman's packaging bears a little scrutiny. The brain came from Fay Helm (slain in the woods by Chaney's *The Wolf Man*), here as Carradine's noble nurse, who delivers the timeless lines: "And suppose your experiment is successful. What will you have? A human form with animal instincts!" Those tricky hormones came from Martha MacVicar (later Martha Vickers), who had just played a Chaney full moon victim in *Frankenstein Meets the Wolf Man*. Martha was soon to act Lauren Bacall's nymphomaniacal sister in *The Big Sleep* (and to become a real-life Mrs. Mickey Rooney), and here as Beth's sister Dorothy. The male who inspired Paula's lust, jealousy and transformation was little Milburn Stone—fated to become *Gunsmoke*'s Emmy-winning "Doc," cast here as lion tamer Fred Mason because of his resemblance to Clyde Beatty (whose footage from Universal's 1933 *The Big Cage* padded the proceedings)—and playing his seated scenes sitting on cushions next to the statuesque Evelyn. And as for "Cheela the Gorilla," she was played by a he—Ray "Crash" Corrigan* (1902–1976), who had just grunted in his famous gorilla suit at Universal in *The Strange Case of Doctor Rx*.

**Among Corrigan's many ape appearances:* The Ape *(1940);* The Monster and the Ape *(1945 serial).*

Keeping the melodrama rolling with a three-ring circus style was Edward Dmytryk, directing with the confidence of a man who would helm RKO's *Hitler's Children* (1943) and *Murder My Sweet* (1945), survive the blacklist, and go on to *The Caine Mutiny* (Columbia, 1954), *Raintree County* (MGM, 1957) and *A Walk on the Wild Side* (Columbia, 1962).

> Edward Dmytryk? What a nice man. I think he was single at the time, and he tried to date me. I was dating Barry Nelson, who was on contract to MGM then, but Dmytryk was always asking me for dates. In fact, he would come by my home—and sometimes Barry would be there! But Eddie was just a big brother, with a lot of talent—a very nice gentleman.

Above all, however, there's Acquanetta as Paula—a mute performance played with a strange, quietly effective presence. The actress denies the rumors that a double played the ape woman scenes—"I did it all!" she attests—and remembers the challenge:

> Jack Pierce, of course, was the makeup man—very nice, very straight, no kidding around, just a very decent fellow. The makeup took a long time, too—sometimes it would take two hours to get the makeup done—the hair on the face and the fangs and all that.
>
> Of course, a lot of the reporters said, in the newspapers, "Oh! How can they do that—take a beautiful young woman and make her up into this ugly beast?" And I thought that was the charm of it. To be made up, and playing a role—that was great!
>
> Every day was Halloween!

There were problems. One day, the tight circus costume she wore, in the scene where Paul exerts her mysterious power over the lions and tigers, was too tight around the neck and too snug in the cummerbund—causing Acquanetta to pass out. And while that's obviously "Crash" Corrigan in his famous gorilla suit as Cheela, Acquanetta insists there was at one point a *real* male gorilla on the set—who wanted to get to know her:

> Once, we were working with this big gorilla, and I had the gorilla makeup on, and the gorilla went after me. Oh, yes. I mean, it wanted to embrace me! It thought I was another gorilla, I guess! The trainer had a big, heavy club—and he hit that animal. He struck him twice, and the gorilla cowered, like a human. And they put a chain around him. He could have crushed me. It was scary!

Did Universal have a real gorilla on hand for part of the shooting? Or had Ray "Crash" Corrigan perhaps freaked at the sight of that shapely ape woman, after all those years of working in his gorilla skins? (Edward Dmytryk, in a 1996 interview with Tom Weaver, denied that there ever was a real gorilla on the set.)

So Universal's *Captive Wild Woman* came to pass—sandwiched amidst *Frankenstein*

Meets the Wolf Man (which had wrapped November 11, 1942), *Son of Dracula* (which began shooting January 8, 1943) and the Technicolor *Phantom of the Opera* (which began January 21, 1943). The studio made big ballyhoo for Acquanetta: although she had played in *Arabian Nights* and *Rhythm of the Islands*, the credits read, "And Introducing Acquanetta"—while posters teased, "And Shockingly Savage Acquanetta as the Gorilla Girl."

On April 26, 1943, Universal previewed *Captive Wild Woman*—all 60 fur-flying minutes of it—for the press in a studio projection room. *Variety* noted:

> Universal injects a female werewolf into a circus melodrama in *Captive Wild Woman*, with resultant picture balancing the two elements for satisfactory element in the program houses... Acquanetta is introduced here, but her role is hardly an auspicious one for audience attention and she has little to do other than stand around and look bewildered...

The Hollywood Reporter, however, was more impressed:

> As long as there is a substantial market for screen thriller-dillers, the more robust the thrills, the better... John Carradine gives an exceptionally smooth performance of the mad doctor, and Acquanetta is the shapely realization of his creation. Her role is completely without dialogue, yet from the moment of her appearance she dominates proceedings...

Captive Wild Woman opened at New York's Rialto Theatre June 6, 1943. "The picture as a whole is in decidedly bad taste," announced the *New York Times*. Indeed, feminists of today inevitably swoon at the climax where reverted Paula, in full gorilla form, takes fatal bullets in her hairy rump while rescuing her man from the big cats. And the makeup transition from Paula to Ape Woman (which makes Paula black at its mid-point) understandably outrages the racially sensitive.

Yet it's really hard to get too sociologically concerned about a movie simply crafted as a crazy big-top shocker, and *Captive Wild Woman* has won its allegiances over the decades. Michael Brunas, John Brunas and Tom Weaver salute the movie in their book *Universal Horrors* as "the ultimate Saturday-afternoon-at-the-Bijou crowd-pleaser ... 60 minutes of chills, thrills and good old-fashioned B-movie entertainment." And, as for Acquanetta ... the lady has taken many a brickbat over the years for her performance as Paula. Perhaps Arthur Joseph Lundquist (in a retrospective on Universal's Ape Woman trilogy published in *Midnight Marquee* #33) put it most fairly when he described Acquanetta's *Captive Wild Woman* as "enraged cheesecake." But there's no doubt she gave the part a presence, a passion—and even a kinky sex appeal. "I *became* that," she says today of Paula the Ape Woman, with total sincerity.

Audiences agreed. Business for *Captive Wild Woman* was brisk—and a sequel definitely loomed on the horizon. It's retrospectively curious that, while Acquanetta was starring in *Captive Wild Woman* at Universal, Bela Lugosi was paying for Christmas presents via *The Ape Man*—released by Monogram in March of 1943, and featuring Emil Van Horn in his gorilla togs.

Meanwhile, Acquanetta was having some real-life melodramas in the Hollywood colony—some of which would fuel her desire to give up her career. There was the day she met the King of the Movies:

> I met Clark Gable at a golf course off of Wilshire Boulevard. He thought I was someone else; he came up, put his hands over my eyes and said, "Guess who?" I was so stunned—and he was surprised when I turned around! I said, "I'm Acquanetta"; he recognized me from my publicity, and he said, "Oh yes, you're our new starlet" ... he just stared at me. Then he reached over and took my hand with his two hands and said, "We will meet again."
>
> Well, about a week or ten days later, I got a call from the head of casting at Metro. He called me and he said Mr. Gable wanted to send his limousine for me. I said, "Tell him not to bother. First of all, I don't date anyone who can't ask me himself. And secondly, no one sends a limousine for me, because I don't have a date with Mr. Gable." Oh, yeah, that's the way I was. Absolutely!

There was also a memorable dinner party one night, in Coldwater Canyon:

> The dinner party—after every course, people were taking off one item of clothing. And I suspect some of them only had two or three items on! I chose not to remove even my gloves, right? So I left—and they let me walk out of the canyon. Oh, yes—nobody put me in a car and drove me out. I walked out of Coldwater Canyon!

And there was an overture from another studio, who hoped to woo Acquanetta away from Universal:

> Darryl Zanuck, at 20th Century–Fox. Oh, what a wolf he was! I tell you—he took me through a reception room into his private room; he turned, put his back to the door and locked it. I saw him. Then he went around and sat behind his desk. I talked to him—we discussed films, and all that—and then he made an approach. He started coming on to me, and started to *climb* over his desk—I hate to tell you what position and condition he was in!—*crawling* over this great big wide desk toward me!
>
> I said, "Mr. Zanuck, do let me out of here, or I will scream—and these walls will come rocking down!" And he said, "You'll never work at 20th Century–Fox." And I never did. But that's okay.

"'Horror Queen' of Screen Hurt" reported the August 27, 1943, *Los Angeles Times*. The accident took place on the set of Universal's *The Mummy's Ghost*, in which Acquanetta was to have played the juicy female lead of Amina, caught up in the black magic of Chaney's Kharis and Carradine's Egyptian high priest—and fated to transform into an ancient crone as the Mummy carried her climactically into a swamp.

Decades later, the film's resourceful director, Reginald LeBorg, claimed Acquanetta was so nervous that she fainted and hit her head—knocking herself unconscious. The actress remembers it all quite differently:

> The grips were on strike, so the studio had scabs working. They didn't realize they were supposed to use papier-mâché rocks—they brought in *real* rocks, and painted them white. Well, I was very realistic—I had a fainting scene, I was supposed to fall and hit my head on a rock. So I just collapsed—and the next thing I knew, I woke up at Cedars of Lebanon. It was a real rock. I could have been killed!

The finished film supports Acquanetta's version—the character does faint outside. The *Times* mentioned a possible brain concussion, while the *Los Angeles Examiner* reported she was unconscious "for more than 16 hours." Barry Nelson was reported to be an "everyday visitor" at her bedside while Universal, hell-bent on keeping *The Mummy's Ghost* on schedule, rushed Ramsay Ames into the role.

And then came *Jungle Woman*—first sequel to *Captive Wild Woman*. This 60-minute potboiler boasted a certain filmic significance: Acquanetta, "Paula the Ape Woman" of *Captive Wild Woman*, was co-starring with J. Carrol Naish—"Noel the Ape Man" of Fox's *Dr. Renault's Secret* (1942). And, as if Cupid smiled on this perhaps inevitable union of Hollywood Ape Girl and Ape Man, *Jungle Woman* began shooting at Universal on Valentine's Day, 1944.

There was a major problem. Although Naish was cast here as brilliant scientist Dr. Carl Fletcher, he still played the genius like Noel the Ape Man—a dopey, seemingly stoned performance that flummoxes fans of this great character actor.

Yet Naish's ditzy dramatics are just part of the shame of *Jungle Woman*, which placed Acquanetta back into the hair and fangs (but just barely) of Paula. What is it about this movie that makes even the most devout Universal fans cringe in embarrassment? Is it the claustrophobic coroner's courtroom set, where our principals (including Evelyn Ankers and Milburn Stone, reprising their now-wed roles from the 1943 film) intone their lines? The ennui of Miss Ankers, who acts as if she's the suffering model of a girdle commercial? The flashback-in-a-flashback of the circus acts? Director Reginald LeBorg's "Lewtonesque" rip-off of *Cat People*, as Acquanetta stalks Lois Collier in the woods (*à la* Simone Simon tracking Jane Randolph through Central Park)? The droning of Edward M. Hyans, Jr., as Willie, the scientist's feeble-minded houseboy, who makes one imagine he has a pin-up at home of Chaney in *Of Mice and Men*? Or, as many horror critics have piqued (as did the late LeBorg himself), is it Acquanetta—coping with dialogue?

Acquanetta was unhappy when the late Calvin T. Beck erred in his book *Scream Queens*, writing that she had no dialogue in *Jungle Woman* and opining that the studio felt she couldn't handle lines. However, she's losing no beauty sleep over the film's miserable reputation. For her, *Jungle Woman* was all worth it to work with LeBorg ("What a nice man!") and (especially) J. Carrol Naish. The Irish-American actor (1897–1973) was between Oscar-nominated performances for Columbia's *Sahara* (1943) and Paramount's *A Medal for Benny* (1945), and just two months away from

Acquanetta in a publicity shot for *Jungle Woman*, 1944.

playing Daniel, hunchbacked familiar to Karloff's mad doctor in Universal's *House of Frankenstein*:

> I have never known anyone that I have ever liked more without being in love with him. I liked Carrol, I liked his wife and his daughter—what a wonderful friend and man he was! No one has ever been kinder or more gentle, more caring , more sharing, more instructive—he was just a great pal, a great buddy. If he

"A great pal, a great buddy": Acquanetta with J. Carrol Naish in *Jungle Woman*, 1944.

> hadn't been married, I think I could have fallen in love with him! A great actor—he would give me little pointers, like a big brother…

In *Jungle Woman*, Naish's Dr. Fletcher is taking in the circus on the stormy night that Cheela/Paula is killed; he revives her, even buys the late Carradine's sanatorium to carry on his experiments—only to have Paula fall for the fiancé (Richard Davis) of his daughter (Lois Collier). In the melodrama, Naish kills the Ape Woman with a syringe; we get our one clear look at the Ape Woman makeup on the morgue slab, then these closing words of wisdom: "The evil man has wrought shall in the end destroy itself."

Jungle Woman sashayed into New York's Rialto Theatre July 14, 1944, following *The Mummy's Ghost*. John T. McManus, cerebral critic of the New York newspaper *PM*, was aghast:

> In *Mein Kampf*, Hitler calls the Negro a "half-born ape." *Jungle Woman* illustrates the point, changing a Hollywood glamour girl into an ape and vice versa with the Negro stage inserted right

> where Hitler says. Beyond its affinity with Hitler ideas, the film is an out-and-out steal on unsuspecting moviegoers, being mainly old footage from a last year's film called *Captive Wild Woman* with a few new inserts added. The 1943 version was challenged at the time of its production for its Nazi ideas, but Universal made it anyway. Apparently it is to be an annual outrage unless somebody passes a law against propounding Nazi race theories in America.

At FANEX 4 in 1990, *Jungle Woman* was the popular choice as Universal's worst horror movie. Perhaps even Universal agreed; while the studio released both *Captive Wild Woman* and the third film of the trilogy, *The Jungle Captive*, as part of its *Son of Shock!* TV package in 1958, it kept *Jungle Woman* hidden away in the closet for years.

Exactly one month after beginning *Jungle Woman*—March 14, 1944—Acquanetta started what would be her swan song at Universal: 1944's *Dead Man's Eyes*. This was the latest in Universal's "Inner Sanctum" mysteries, directed by LeBorg—and starring Lon Chaney.

> Lon Chaney was another wonderful man. He wasn't the kind of sharing, caring person that J. Carrol Naish was, but just a nice person. People say, "Did he get drunk?" I say, "I never saw him drunk. Ever." He was very professional—not as outgoing as Carrol, but I liked him, and he was very nice.

Dead Man's Eyes once again gave Acquanetta special billing, as "Tanya Czoraki"—a model who mistakenly mixes artist Chaney's eyewash with acid, with appropriately horrific results. Later she's found clubbed to death, and detective Thomas Gomez discovers the killer not to be Chaney, nor leading lady Jean Parker, but second male lead Paul Kelly (in a successful comeback after serving time in San Quentin for manslaughter).

Dead Man's Eyes opened at the Rialto on New York October 6, 1944 (the day after *The Hollywood Reporter* announced that Barry Nelson had "popped the question" to Acquanetta). Alton Cook, reviewing the picture in the *New York World-Telegram*, opined that Acquanetta probably would soon be back to playing a gorilla, and ended his critique thusly:

> A triumph for the makeup man would be dressing up an actor to look like the kind of person who would enjoy this picture. There would be a terrifying specter.

By the time *Dead Man's Eyes* braved the Rialto, Acquanetta was no longer a Universal star. On July 3, 1944, the *Examiner* noted that Acquanetta's contract with Universal would expire July 16, and she would move to Monogram and the mercies of "Jungle Sam" Katzman—at three times her "U" salary. "Katzman hopes to make Acquanetta the biggest femme property at Monogram," noted the story, "and is setting out to get a tailor-made script and story to launch her. Of course, she will still cater to the sarong clientele." Thus Universal City lost Acquanetta and a pregnant

Evelyn Ankers that summer of 1944, only months after losing Anne Gwynne (q.v.); it would be a different studio without them. Acquanetta recalls leaving Universal:

> When I told Dan Kelley I was leaving, he said, "You can't! You have a seven-year contract! You've got five years to go!" And I said, "Dan, I'm leaving." I blew him a kiss, turned, walked out of his office, got into my little Oldsmobile convertible, with two suitcases packed, and drove to Mexico City all by myself.

On August 31, 1944—a little over a month after Acquanetta officially had vacated the lot*—Universal began shooting *The Jungle Captive*, third and final installment of the Paula the Ape Woman trilogy. Otto Kruger was the mad scientist, while Universal tossed in real-life acromegalic Rondo Hatton as his assistant—and cast 18-year-old starlet Vicky Lane as Paula. *The Jungle Captive* finally weaseled into the Rialto July 6, 1945; the *New York Herald-Tribune* reported that the new Paula the Ape Woman "looks like an over-sized woodchuck with a hangover."

"It bombed," says Acquanetta of *The Jungle Captive*. It was the end of a series. Sic semper Paula.

It was also nearly the end of Acquanetta's career. The December 15, 1944, *Hollywood Reporter* announced she was "drying the ink on a contract" to star in *Queen of the Honky Tonks* for Monogram. However, she never made a movie there:

> My agent sold me to Monogram without my consent, really. He just threw a contract down and said, "Sign it." He had gotten approval of script, because by then, my pictures were making big money. They submitted various scripts to me; I read them; I didn't like them. So I was paid for a year, and then they didn't pick up my option—thank God.
>
> See, they were following the Universal script type thing—I didn't want to do those kinds of pictures any more. I really wanted to do a prestigious "A" film.

Nineteen forty-five found Acquanetta spending much time in Mexico, as one of President Roosevelt's "Goodwill Ambassadors." She was rumored to be engaged to various millionaires; she claims to have received many Mexican movie offers, but never learned Spanish fluently enough to accept them.

Instead, back in Hollywood, she did *Tarzan and the Leopard Woman* (1946) for RKO—complete with Johnny Weissmuller and a "Cheetah" the ape in "heat"—making Acquanetta's life miserable:

**A very different version of Acquanetta's departure from Universal came in Robert Nott's interview with screenwriter Ed Hartmann, published in* Filmfax *(#42). Hartmann claimed Universal discovered (or came to believe) that Acquanetta was part black: "Word was sent to all the producers that she had another four months to go on her contract. But while she was there, she was not to be in any scene where she is romantically linked with a white man… As soon as her contract was up, they dropped her… I told this story to an actress I knew who also knew Acquanetta, and she told me that her mother was black. She was at Acquanetta's house and Acquanetta introduced her mother as the cook to try to hide the fact." This story has at least one true fact in it: Acquanetta did* not *work in any films the last four months of her Universal contract.*

> Johnny Weissmuller ... he was great—just like a big kid. But you know, he was smart—and he was a good actor. Great swimmer. And nobody could yell that "Ooo-ooo-oo!" like him.
> They offered me the lead opposite him in the *Jungle Jim* series, but I turned those down. I just didn't want to do what I thought of as "B" pictures... I simply wanted to move out of that, and if Hollywood didn't offer it, then I was moving on.

She moved on. Acquanetta wed very wealthy Ludwig (Luciano) Baschuk in Mexico March 7, 1946, and they had a son, Sergio. In the spring of 1949, she attempted a comeback, testing for the role of the Indian girl in *Beyond the Forest*, which starred Bette Davis and Joseph Cotten under King Vidor's direction; she didn't get it. July of 1949 found her starring in the five-day Frontiers Day Celebration in Cheyenne, riding in the parade and presiding over the rodeo.

Things got ugly in 1949 and 1950, when Acquanetta, represented by ace L.A. lawyer S. S. Hahn, divorced Baschuk. He battled her demand for $2500-per-month alimony—by contending they had never actually married. A search of civil records in Cuernavaca showed no such marriage; Acquanetta insisted that a rabbi had performed the ceremony, reading in Hebrew under a red canopy, complete with the traditional breaking of wine glasses. In August of 1950, Acquanetta dismissed her suit, hoping to protect Sergio from Baschuk's attempts to get custody of him in Mexico.

On February 25, 1951, Acquanetta telephoned Louella Parsons from Palm Springs with news: She had been secretly married since August of 1950. The groom was Henry Clive, described by Louella as "one of America's foremost illustrators and painters"—and who had painted Acquanetta several times for covers of Hearst's *The American Weekly*. Clive was 69 years old and had been wed at least five times. Acquanetta explains:

> It was a marriage in name only—never consummated. He married me, he said, because he had been married, many times, to all these glamour women, and they had all left him. But he told me, "No one has ever cared for me or looked after me the way you have, and I want you to have my estate when I'm gone. To make sure, the only way you can have it is to marry me. You still have your life, you can do whatever you wish, you don't even have to live with me." So we were married—in name only. That was Henry.

Also in 1951, Acquanetta was back in the movies—as a "beautiful Indian maid" in *Lost Continent*, directed by Samuel Newfield, and starring Cesar Romero, Hillary Brooke and stop-motion dinosaurs. Early publicity claimed Clive would help his bride with her makeup. As Leonard Maltin kindly dismissed *Lost Continent* in his *TV Movies* guide, "Lavish production values are obviously lacking..." Acquanetta also worked in the films *Callaway Went Thataway* (MGM, 1951), *The Sword of Monte Cristo* (20th Century–Fox, 1951), and—her last feature for decades—*Take the High Ground* (MGM, 1953). Her roles were so small that *Film Daily* didn't include her in the cast lists of any of these films.

In March of 1952, the Clives separated. "This is simply a matter of clashing personalities," said Clive, "just like two Italian opera singers arguing over a dish of spaghetti." In May of 1952, they reconciled.

In the fall of 1952, Acquanetta suffered a deep tragedy when her five-year-old son Sergio died from cancer. The funeral took place November 5, 1952, at the Little Church of the Flowers at Forest Lawn Memorial Park, Glendale. She was reportedly "despondent" for months after Sergio's death; by year's end, she and Clive were back in divorce action.

In October of 1953, Acquanetta sued Muller Bros. Hollywood service station, claiming it had used her picture for an advertisement that "humiliated and disgraced" her. It was an newspaper ad for their paint jobs. "The ad said the paint put my war paint to shame," Acquanetta said. "That could only be a reference to my makeup. It was degrading and humiliating. " Defendants claimed she had authorized the picture; the judge dismissed her $50,000 suit.

In November 1955, a new law suit arose: Acquanetta sued to collect $4000 life insurance that the Manhattan Life Insurance company had refused to pay after the death of her son. Manhattan Life claimed Acquanetta had withheld information that the boy had a history of nephritis and anemia. Acquanetta won.

By this point, Acquanetta had wed Jack Ross, a wealthy Lincoln/Mercury car dealer in Arizona. She became a local TV celebrity, hosting movies and advertising her husband's dealership—as well as hosting radio shows and becoming very involved in community affairs. Her TV tenure in Arizona lasted for over 20 years. She became the mother of four sons, and enjoyed a lavish lifestyle, as described by Richard Lamparski: "On weekends she and her husband fly their own plane to San Diego, where they keep a yacht that will sleep 27."

In 1974, Acquanetta published her book of philosophical vignettes, *The Audible Silence*. It revealed a metaphysical side to the actress, which she discusses with conviction:

> I had an experience where I was projected back in time... It was like a waking dream, but it happened. The first time I ever came to Arizona, I felt like this was my home... It's the only place in the whole world where I've ever felt totally at peace, and as though this is where I belong. But I know why—because I had been here in a former life... I saw myself as someone else, I behaved as someone else, I looked at myself like in a mirror, and I was dark with long hair—I was an Indian living in Arizona in that place where I stood—a thousand years back. People may laugh, and that's okay—but I've had that experience, and I relived it in a waking dream.

Now divorced, Acquanetta has toyed with resuming her career, and acted in the direct-to-video release *Grizzly Adams—The Legend Never Dies* (1989). She has strong feelings about Hollywood, and her life:

> Had I stayed in Hollywood, I wouldn't have my beautiful family and my four children, and I wouldn't be in Arizona. You know

Acquanetta

> what? I wouldn't change one day of my life for all of Hollywood. I love my four children, and I'd do it again today—to the letter.

Acquanetta has attended Michael Fitzgerald's annual Universal Reunion in Los Angeles in recent years; in 1992, she joined actress Veronica Carlson, special effects master Jim Danforth and actor Russ Tamblyn as a guest of honor at FANEX 6 in

Russ Tamblyn, Veronica Carlson, Acquanetta, and special effects expert Jim Danforth at the FANEX Convention, 1992.

Baltimore—where it was this author's privilege to present her with a Special Achievement Prize at the Awards Ceremony.

During her FANEX appearance, Acquanetta enjoyed reading her poetry. And the depth of a woman most people knew only as Paula Dupree, Universal's hapless *Captive Wild Woman*, surprised a few as she recited her self-composed "Creed":

> I believe in the great Spirit ... it gives me hope and faith...
>
> I believe in Prayer ... it is the umbilical cord that ties man to his Creator and gives him strength...
>
> I believe in life continuance or immortality ... it defies death...
>
> I believe the purpose of life ... is to learn and to teach...
>
> I believe imagination is man's greatest gift ... with imagination man can conceive of any thing and all things ... without limitation...
>
> My Creed
> By Acquanetta

The Films of Acquanetta

1942

Arabian Nights (Universal, John Rawlins)

1943

Rhythm of the Islands (Universal, Roy William Neill)

Captive Wild Woman (Universal, Edward Dmytryk)

1944

Jungle Woman (Universal, Reginald LeBorg)

Dead Man's Eyes (Universal, Reginald LeBorg)

1946

Tarzan and the Leopard Woman (RKO, Kurt Neumann)

1951

The Sword of Monte Cristo (20th Century–Fox, Maurice Geraghty)

Lost Continent (Lippert, Samuel Newfield)

Callaway Went Thataway (MGM, Norman Panama and Melvin Frank)

1953

Take the High Ground (MGM, Richard Brooks)

Clips of Acquanetta from *Captive Wild Woman* appear in *Jungle Woman*; clips of Acquanetta from *Jungle Woman* appear in *The Jungle Captive* (Universal, 1945).

SUSANNA FOSTER

A subterranean lair, five cellars below the Paris Opera House. A masked figure dramatically plays the piano as a beautiful blonde soprano hauntingly sings "Lullaby of the Bells." With Pandora's curiosity, the lady furtively moves behind the mysterious figure, and pulls off the mask of the Phantom...

The Paris Opera House was actually Sound Stage 28 of Universal City. The masked Phantom was Claude Rains. And the daring heroine of Universal's lavish Technicolor, $1,750,000 1943 *Phantom of the Opera* was, of course, Susanna Foster.

For fans of *Phantom of the Opera*, Susanna Foster is still a star—yet as mysterious a figure as the Phantom she unmasked 50 years ago. The blonde actress/singer who could hit B-flat above high-C was a major find in Paramount's 1939 *The Great Victor Herbert*, blossomed into a major star via Universal's sumptuous, big box office *Phantom*—then retired from the screen in 1945. After touring in operettas, she soon disappeared.

"I want to do, what I want to do," said Susanna, who for years gave thumbs down to stage, film and concert offers, "and that has nothing to do with show business."

Today, however, half-a-century after she quit, Susanna Foster admits to an occasional temptation to sing and act again. She could do it, too—she's still blonde, and striking; in Hollywood in 1992, at a revival of *Phantom of the Opera*, she amazed an audience with her still-magnificent voice. Yet a life tinged with tragedy, and even recent poverty and illness, has bedeviled her ambition.

It has been a colorful life for the soprano whose beauty and voice sparked one of the greatest box office successes in Universal's 80-year history.

> THRILL TO...
> ROMANCE! In the shadow of sinister suspense!
> MUSIC! in spell-binding array!
> BEAUTY ... in magnificent Technicolor!
>
> —Publicity, *Phantom of the Opera*

December, 1981. Susanna Foster was to meet my wife and me in front of her hotel in Glendale, where she was sharing quarters with her son, his wife and their baby. As we drove down Colorado Boulevard that night, I could recognize her even a block-and-a-half away—tall, slender and blonde, dressed in a black pants-suit.

There was a class, a distinction about her, even as she stood alone on this oddly deserted Los Angeles boulevard. And there was absolutely no pretense about her as we introduced ourselves; the mystery soprano from *Phantom of the Opera* couldn't have been more delightfully down-to-earth and kind as we settled into a nearby restaurant for the interview.

She was born Suzanne DeLee Flanders Larson in Chicago on Saturday, December 6, 1924.

> I always had this ardor to sing, and an inordinate passion for music. I really thought when I looked in the mirror that I was

***Chapter opener:* Susanna Foster in a fashion pose, 1940s.**

> Jeanette MacDonald, whom I had seen with Nelson in *Naughty Marietta* 68 times (and then stopped counting). Actually, I was an ugly little thing—all eyes and nose. I looked like a Jewish war orphan.

The family moved to Minneapolis, where, in 1936, Susanna's mother took her backstage of the Palace Theatre after hearing a violinist beautifully play "Kiss Me Again." Susanna auditioned for Carl Johnson, who paid her $10 to sing "Ah! Sweet Mystery of Life" and the Waltz Song from *Romeo and Juliet* with his orchestra in a Palace weekend engagement. She became an instant local star and soon was singing on the radio and at Minneapolis and St. Paul conventions. Operatic star Mary McCormic predicted a glowing future for the 11-year-old soprano.

Meanwhile, in Hollywood, it was the era of the singing child star—and Metro-Goldwyn-Mayer was in mourning. The studio had dropped Deanna Durbin, who ensuingly saved Universal via 1936's *Three Smart Girls*. After Carl Johnson and Minneapolis critic Merle Potter sent a recording of Susanna's "Ah! Sweet Mystery of Life" to MGM producer William Koenig, Susanna was signed (sight unseen) to a Metro contract.

> In February 1937, my mother and I boarded the train for Hollywood. I was 5'7" tall, weighed 69 lbs., wore a tailored suit, a little derby hat, a blouse from the dime store, high heels and carried a Pomeranian Spitz dog. I was an anachronism! Well, we got off the train, and there was Ida Koverman, Louis Mayer's right-hand lady—looking at this *thing* the studio had just signed!

A limousine escorted Susanna and her mother directly to the Culver City MGM lot for an audience with "L.B." himself:

> There was a long carpet, and Louis B. Mayer sat at the end on a dais, like a god. As soon as I put down my dog, the Spitz did *everything* all over Mayer's carpet. It was *not* an auspicious beginning!
>
> There was an Oscar in his office, and I asked him what it was. "I got that for being the best-looking man in Hollywood," Mayer said. I replied, "Oh, don't give me such blarney! You got that for being the best *producer* in Hollywood." He laughed! I must say, Mayer was very nice to me—and he promptly sent me out to get clothes appropriate for a 12 year old!

MGM was the aristocracy of Hollywood studios, and Mayer soon sent Susanna on a tour of his kingdom.

> Jean Harlow looked adorable. She was the best-loved person on the MGM lot—not just sexy, but sweet and beautiful. They took me to meet Clark Gable, who was making *Parnell*, and that man treated me like I was the Queen of England. He took my hand, and I thought, "What a great gentleman!"

Susanna also visited the set of *The Firefly*, where she met her idol—Jeanette MacDonald:

> I still adore her, but I thought we would discuss music. Instead, she sat down and said, "Now, you imitate me." She cleared her throat and said, "Johnny Johnny Johnny Johnny Ooops Johnny." Well, the trick was that you had to clear your throat before you said it. I remember thinking, "Why is she treating me like a child? I'm 12 years old!"

The episode did nothing, however, to diminish Susanna's respect and love for Miss MacDonald, who continues to be (along with Deanna Durbin) one of her all-time favorite stars, and an inspiration to her.

The studio described Susanna as "having hair the same shade as Garbo." After a screen test (directed by George Sidney) in which she played a scene from *Anne of Green Gables*, MGM offered Susanna the lead in *National Velvet*. Susanna (whose family allowed her to manage her own career) couldn't see herself in the part finally played in MGM's 1944 release by Elizabeth Taylor, and turned it down because she couldn't sing in it. MGM—appalled by her action—dropped her in February of 1938.

> When MGM let me go, I went up to the office of producer Nicky Nayfack,* who was married to singer Lynne Carver. He said, "Kid, you can't sing. Go back to Minneapolis. You're through—you're finished!" I wanted to cry so badly, but I was determined I wouldn't. I marched down those stairs to my mother, who was waiting in the car. "Mom," I said, "I'm fired." Then *she* started to cry, and at that moment, I grew up—at 13 years old.

Difficult times were ahead. Susanna's father, who had been an executive in securities and had followed her to Los Angeles with her two sisters, couldn't find work. He and Susanna's mother separated; creditors took away the car and furniture. Meanwhile, Susanna studied voice with Gilda Marchetti (whose brother Milo became Susanna's agent). It was a stand-in-line audition at Paramount which led to Susanna singing "Kiss Me Again" for producer/director Andrew Stone—who awarded Susanna the role of Peggy in Paramount's musical extravaganza of 1939, *The Great Victor Herbert*.

> The stars, Allan Jones and Mary Martin, were both so supportive of me. For my scenes, Allan would stand behind the camera and sing to me and give it everything he had. I remember I had to cry a lot in the film, so they'd play my record of "Kiss Me Again," I'd think of my father walking up and down those hills trying to look for a job, and *that's* how I'd cry!

Paramount released *The Great Victor Herbert* in December 1939. At the gala Hollywood premiere, something happened which became a trademark of Susanna's

**Nayfack later produced MGM's* Forbidden Planet *(1956).*

films: The audience applauded her singing of "Kiss Me Again" (which she performed in her own interpretation, without any coaching) as if they were watching a live performance. Susanna missed the premiere (she was in Hollywood Presbyterian Hospital with bronchitis), and photographers invaded her hospital room to report her triumph. Susanna, however, remained characteristically unimpressed with herself.

> When I did see *The Great Victor Herbert*, and finally saw myself on the screen, all I could think was, "My God! I'm *not* Jeanette MacDonald!"

Overnight, 15-year-old Susanna was a Paramount star.

> Paramount was a lovely lot. I'd see Bing Crosby riding around on his bike and whistling, and Bob Hope, who was very friendly. Because of my age, I had to go to school on the lot from 9 to 12, and Richard Denning, Martha O'Driscoll, Barbara Britton and I formed a coterie, having lunch together every day.

Susanna has many memories of the Paramount stars:

> ALAN LADD: I sat in on the screen test Ladd made for *This Gun for Hire*. Sue Carol, who was Ladd's agent (she later married him), was there too, of course. I came out of the rushes and, not knowing Sue was romantically linked with Ladd, announced, "He *stinks*!" Sue Carol didn't care—she was too big a person—and later I came to appreciate Ladd; he was an "acquired taste."
>
> VERONICA LAKE: Veronica, like me, had been dropped by MGM. While at Paramount, we both went back to MGM in the same car to a big convention where Louis Mayer was speaking. I was going to sing. Well, Veronica was really enjoying it! "Oh, boy, I'm going to love this!" she said. "Here I am, a big star at Paramount, and I'm going back to let MGM know... We're going in there *together*, Susanna!" I didn't really care, personally. Anyway, I sang "Kiss Me Again" (again!) and a few other things, and brought the house down. Mayer got up and said, "Oh, what a wonderful voice!" (he didn't say anything about having let me go, of course!) and how he wished they could have me at MGM under contract. Meanwhile, Veronica was proudly punching me in the ribs!
>
> PAULETTE GODDARD: When Jean Harlow died [June 7, 1937], I was down in Palm Springs and Paulette was in the hotel room next to ours, the guest of some marquis. She would say to my mother, "Who is that little choir boy in there singing?" Always, for no reason, she went out of her way to say something nice to me. When we were on the Paramount lot, she'd walk past me and say, "Susanna! I heard you on *The Chase and Sanborn Hour* Sunday. You sang beautifully." She had no reason to be nice to me; I certainly was no marquis!

Meanwhile, Susanna reunited with Allan Jones and the erudite director Andrew Stone for 1941's *There's Magic in Music*, originally titled *The Hard-Boiled Canary*

("They changed it because they thought people would think it was about a heavyweight boxer who sang!" says Susanna). The film gave Susanna one of her best roles: Toodles La Verne, a burlesque chanteuse whom Jones rescues from a raid and takes to a musical camp. Susanna not only sang an operatic mixture of *Carmen* and *Faust* ("Ugh!" she recalls), but also gave impersonations of Bonnie Baker, Judy Canova and Marlene Dietrich. The *Hollywood Reporter* hailed Susanna's voice as "pure delight" and critiqued:

> This Foster lass has progressed in other directions than musically. In this picture, she shows that she can act. Likewise, she is developing into an extremely attractive young woman ... definitely on her way to becoming a star of real magnitude.

Susanna followed at Paramount with *Glamour Boy* (1941), with Jackie Cooper.

> He was an impressive person, strong and fun, and dating Bonita Granville at the time, who used to come on the set. During the filming, Jackie's mother died, and I went to the funeral, in pouring rain. I felt so for him—he was very broken-up—and he never knew I went to the funeral, or how I felt, as I was (for once) in a "shy" period.

Susanna, meanwhile, had earned a reputation at Paramount for being very candid and outspoken; *Movieland* magazine dubbed her Paramount's "Impulsive Rebel." The 16 year old simply had no patience with the blowhards and hangers-on who offered her unsolicited advice on everything from her career-planning to her singing.

"Listen," barked a veteran movie colony interviewer at Susanna one day at Paramount, "I'm old enough to be your father."

"I'll say," replied Susanna.

Paramount couldn't decide how to exploit Susanna properly. At age 17, she spent the entire last year of her contract doing nothing. In November of 1942, Susanna demanded and received a release from her contract, seriously considered giving up show business, and applied for work at Lockheed Aircraft.

Forty days later—with Myron Selznick as her agent—Susanna signed a Universal contract to star in *Phantom of the Opera*.

In 1925, Lon Chaney, Sr., had made Hollywood history on Universal's Sound Stage 28 as gloriously mad Erik; when Mary Philbin tore off his mask as he played his organ, Chaney's death's-head makeup, outraged vanity and that famous card—"Feast your eyes, glut your soul on my accursed ugliness!"—had created one of the timeless thrills of the movies. When Charles R. Rogers took over Universal in 1936, exiling the Laemmles and putting the monsters out to pasture on the back lot hills, even he considered a *Phantom* remake during his brief 1936 to 1938 reign.

Rogers made no *Phantom* but he was in office while plump, brunette soprano Deanna Durbin saved the new regime from bankruptcy via *Three Smart Girls* (1936) and *100 Men and a Girl* (1937). Indeed, one of the top Durbin fans was Susanna ("I thought *100 Men and a Girl* should have won an Academy Award—and Deanna should have won, too"). Deanna survived Rogers to become one of Universal's greatest stars, and come November 1941, Universal offered her what they believed was a top vehicle: a Technicolor remake of *Phantom of the Opera*, to be directed by Henry Koster (director of many of her Universal hits) and slated to star, as the Phantom, Broderick Crawford.

La Durbin would have none of it; she rejected the property. Koster walked with her; Arthur Lubin replaced him as director. Crawford went into the Army. Charles Laughton was considered for the role. Lon Chaney, Jr., claimed he was promised it; eventually Universal signed Claude Rains, who had won fame as Universal's *The Invisible Man* (1933) and had played Sir John Talbot in the studio's 1941 milestone *The Wolf Man*, to create what the *Phantom of the Opera* trailer heralded as "the year's most coveted role."

Nelson Eddy, free from MGM after his final teaming with Jeanette MacDonald (1942's *I Married an Angel*) signed on as the heroic opera star—and for top billing.

With Eddy for hero and Rains for Phantom, Universal still had no Christine. Susanna remembers:

> I used to go to the apartment of a *Hollywood Reporter* writer, Ed Westrate, once a week, and sing at the piano. One night he invited Arthur Lubin, who was going to direct *Phantom*. Arthur listened to me sing, and invited me down to his place in the desert, where I went with my teacher. Then I met Nelson Eddy at a party that W. S. Van Dyke gave, and then came the call from Universal to test for George Waggner, *Phantom*'s producer, and Edward Ward, who composed and arranged the music.
>
> Arthur, a great director who can really handle actors, directed my test, in which I sang "Last Rose of Summer" and "Ah! Sweet Mystery of Life." I didn't do any acting, though. Instead, Arthur had David Bruce do a spontaneous interview with me. Arthur knew I was naturally expressive, and thought Waggner could see more of my personality this way. It was an idea way ahead of its time.

It worked. Universal signed Susanna to star as Christine. On January 21, 1943, the three-strip Technicolor cameras began shooting *Phantom of the Opera*, based on Sound Stage 28—"The Phantom Stage"—originally built for the silent classic.

Susanna remembers *Phantom of the Opera* with great affection:

> There was a *class* on the set. All the people on the film were well-read and intelligent. Nelson was a gem; very erudite, jovial and full of harmony. On the last day, he gave everybody special presents; for me, a leather-bound, inscribed book of *The Indian Love Lyrics*; for Hal Mohr, our cameraman, a book of Aristophanes' plays, and so on. Hal was a rough-and ready guy, an intellectual, and he protected you and treated you like a lady (if you were one). Eddie Ward was my inspiration at Universal; I loved him, his bagful of melodies and those "12 fingers" which played the piano like an orchestra. Fritz Feld would play glorious Viennese songs on the set, Nelson would sing, I would sing; it was all great fun, and I think the class and fun really came across in the film.

Foster poses *à la* Dietrich at Paramount, early 1940s.

And, as for the Phantom himself, Susanna has nothing but praise:

> Ah, Claude Rains! He was English, and reserved, but you always felt in Rains there was an inner warmth. He had that devilish look, and that twinkle in his eye—I can see why he had six wives! You got this warmth from Rains when you acted with

> him. He was not just a good actor, but a great actor; can you ever forget Rains' animal cries after the acid is thrown in his face? Magnificent! In *Phantom* he just led the way and, thank God, I just followed.

There was exquisite attention to production values, music, hair styles, the Vera West costumes—and a great sensitivity to the Phantom's horrific makeup, designed by Universal's legendary Jack P. Pierce:

> This, of course, was wartime, and they were sensitive about how far they should go, because some of the boys in the war were scarred. There were many discussions, for although the soldiers received plastic surgery, the studio didn't want to upset families, girlfriends and so on. So, while the Phantom was a total mess in Chaney's version, our Phantom just had that acid scar on his cheek.

Indeed, Claude Rains was a kinder, gentler Phantom than Chaney's posing, rhapsodic mad genius (whose balletic movements were copied by Michael Crawford in his Tony Award–winning performance in the Andrew Lloyd Webber 1988 Broadway smash *The Phantom of the Opera*). Rains was not the kind of Phantom to strut gloriously down the Opera House staircase in the Masked Ball (as Chaney did in the color sequence in 1925); in fact, Rains, in his cape, mask and large Phantom hat, looks at times like a toddler all dressed up for Trick or Treat. Yet Rains creates his own wonderful pathos in the role as the aging Erique Claudin (how could Chaney, Jr., ever have hoped to convince anyone in this part?)—and masterfully lays the suggestion that he is, in fact, Christine's father. (*The Hollywood Reporter* noted that Rains' "accomplished acting" made "no other conclusion possible"; fans have debated it for years; Susanna remembers that Universal never could make up its mind throughout production, leaving it to the audience to decide).

After the famous unmasking scene (nicely mounted), there is the magnificent destruction of the Phantom's catacombs, and Christine escaping the cave-in with Eddy and Edgar Barrier (as the romantic police chief). Susanna remembers it vividly:

> We ran through the falling catacombs, and past the rats (real rats!), and they had doubles for Nelson and Edgar Barrier—but not for me! Believe me, Nelson and Edgar were afraid of nothing, but the studio was paying the salaries. Of course, the catacombs were just balsa, but that always struck me funny!

On August 12, 1943, Universal previewed *Phantom of the Opera*—all $1,750,000 of it—in Los Angeles. "LUBIN'S DIRECTION, WARD SCORE FINE; FOSTER, EDDY TOPS," headlined *The Hollywood Reporter*, which hailed the film as...

> ...a rare musical treat, an arrestingly beautiful spectacle in the magnificence of its Technicolor photography, or a handsomely performed psychological melodrama... Miss Foster so definitely bids for stardom that Universal was quick to put her under contract...

Foster as Christine, the beautiful soprano of Universal's 1943 *Phantom of the Opera*, with Claude Rains as the Phantom.

Phantom of the Opera proved a box office blockbuster, winning laurels for Eddy (it was his favorite film) and ensconced Rains as a major star of the horror genre. And it was a triumph for Susanna, who won wonderful reviews:

> *Variety*: ..a brilliant demonstration of voice and exciting personality, free from irritating mannerisms. The color cameras have a beautiful subject, and there is much talent to go with the allure.
>
> *Pacific Coast Musician*: [She] emerges as one of the most beautiful voices and delightful singers on the screen.

On the night of March 2, 1944, Susanna opened the 16th annual Academy Awards, singing "The Star-Spangled Banner" at Grauman's Chinese Theatre. There, Universal's *Phantom of the Opera* won two Oscars: Best Color Cinematography (Hal Mohr and W. Howard Greene) and Best Color Set Design (Alexander Golitzen and John B. Goodman) and Interior Decoration (R. A. Gausman and Ira Webb). There was glory for all as *Phantom of the Opera* became one of the greatest hits in Universal's history; Susanna suddenly reigned as one of Universal's most popular stars and potential moneymakers.

"I always think of Universal as *my* studio," says Susanna, and her stay there began very happily. Fan mail abounded, soldiers sent for "pinups," and everybody liked "The Universal Nightingale" who impulsively broke into song on the lot, played the piano and sang in her dressing room cottage, and regaled interviewers with her opinions on everything from sex in the movies to gasoline rationing. There was, however, immediate gossip after *Phantom of the Opera* of a hot, jealous feud between Susanna and Deanna Durbin. Susanna denies it.

> There's been talk that the studio signed me as a rival to Deanna, but I don't think Universal was thinking that far ahead when they signed me for *Phantom*. I'll say this for Deanna—she was elusive. I met her only once. It was early in the morning in Jack Pierce's office in makeup. She had no makeup on—she looked lovely—and I was thrilled to see her; after all, she was my second favorite, after Jeanette MacDonald. Well, she said, "How do you do?" and that was that. She was a bit condescending. I remember going through a sound stage, and she'd be talking to Joseph Cotten or whomever, and I wanted very much to say hello—but she'd just never look my way. I always felt that she didn't want to mix; she'd do her thing at the studio, not involve herself and go home.

Many people (including Gloria Jean) strongly believe that Deanna furtively nixed chances for Susanna in the front office. "If she did, it's news to me," says Susanna, who praises Durbin as "one of the best light comediennes and lovely voices the screen ever had."

Susanna quickly realized that creating major stars was *not* a Universal specialty.

> Universal was run like a team effort; there was no power figure in the front office, like Zanuck at Fox or Mayer at MGM. Universal had a big repertory company and they just didn't know what to do with it. For Maria Montez, for example, they should have built her as a Merle Oberon type; she proved she could do this in *Bowery to Broadway*. Instead, look what they gave her! How would you like to be *Cobra Woman*? Could anybody have excelled at that part? There was Turhan Bey, and I often think of how popular he was at the time. He looked Oriental (he was part Turkish), yet there was never any racial reaction to him from audiences, and he could play any part and be successful. There was Anne Gwynne, a lovely girl with beautiful legs and a real personality; Robert Paige, who should have been a big leading man; so many others.
>
> Myself included! They had a leading woman in me after *Phantom*, and most of what they gave me to do had no more to do with my *Phantom* role than the man in the moon.

The mystic, ethereal quality which Susanna so memorably displayed in *Phantom of the Opera* was lost on Universal—which decided, as Susanna puts it, to make "Donald O'Connor and me the Mickey Rooney and Judy Garland of Universal. I loved Donald as an artist, but I was taller than he was, and—well—it just didn't work out!"

In the summer of 1943, before *Phantom of the Opera* was released, Universal pushed Susanna into two back-to-back films with O'Connor. On June 17, 1943, Susanna completed *This Is the Life*, another "Durbin reject." It was based on the play *Angela Is 22* by Sinclair Lewis and *King Kong*'s own Fay Wray. The play had died in Chicago in 1939 before ever reaching Broadway. Susanna beautifully sang "With a Song in My Heart" and "L'amour, toujours, l'amour," in this film which Universal didn't release until the spring of 1944. *Top Man*, which "wrapped" August 4, 1943, found Susanna singing some of her favorite film music, including Herbert's "Romany Life" and Grever's "Jurame," while assisting O'Connor in the tried-and-true "putting on a show" formula. Released late in 1943, *Top Man* inspired the *Los Angeles Examiner* to note:

> Susanna Foster, who just skyrocketed to fame in *Phantom of the Opera*, is a pretty fancy dish to be high-schooling around in an O'Connor film. From Nelson Eddy to Donald is quite a thing, if you know what we mean…

Meanwhile, Susanna was very popular on radio. On September 13, 1943, she reprised (live) Christine on Cecil B. De Mille's *Lux Radio Theatre* version of *Phantom of the Opera* with Nelson Eddy and—as the Phantom—Basil Rathbone. She sang the very difficult "Nocturne" by Chopin, and remembers:

> During the radio rehearsal, after I sang it, Nelson lifted all 130 lbs. of me (at that time) in the air and onto his shoulder, yelling, "Hurray!" Rathbone was a great talker (almost as bad as I am!). He kept oxygen in his dressing room, believing it aided his voice in the broadcast. "Why do you need that?" I asked him. "You don't have to hit G above high C!"

Susanna's 1944 releases were a mixed bag. In *Follow the Boys*, she did a guest spot as one of the members of "The Hollywood Victory Committee"—i.e., Universal's contract roster, including (among many others) Evelyn Ankers (q.v.), Louise Allbritton (q.v.), Gale Sondergaard (q.v.) and Lon Chaney.

Bowery to Broadway was a Universal curio. Beer garden rivals Jack Oakie and Donald Cook steal each other's musical stars throughout the 1890s (and for decades beyond), setting the stage for musical turns from most of Universal's stars. Evelyn Ankers (looking very hefty, and in fact six months pregnant) oomphed a burlesque number called "Just Because You Made Those Goo-Goo Eyes at Me"; Donald O'Connor and Peggy Ryan performed "He Took Her for a Sleigh Ride in the Good Old Summertime"; Louise Allbritton played Lillian Russell, and sang "Under the Bamboo Tree"; and Maria Montez sang "Montevideo" (in Martha Tilton's dubbed voice). Susanna played Peggy Fleming, "The Girl with the $1,000,000 Legs," singing "There'll Always Be a Moon," accompanied at the piano by Turhan Bey.

It was Maria Montez, incidentally, who gave Susanna a lesson in studio negotiations during this busy time.

> Maria had such a show of tres sophistication, but really was the most naive, little girl type of person. Once, in hairdressing one morning, Maria, who I liked immensely, couldn't help herself from boasting, "I get $25,000 bonus on each picture I make!" I shouted "Really?!," got up with the curlers still in my hair, marched to the front office and demanded, "I want $25,000 more on each picture I make!" Well, I didn't get that much, but I did get $5000 more afterwards on every picture. They would have killed Maria if they knew she gave me the idea!

Bowery to Broadway opened at New York's Criterion Theatre November 29, 1944. John T. McManus, in his *PM* reviews, noted that the film included

> virtually every character on the Universal Pictures' contract list... The original plot even had a spot scheduled for Abbott and Costello but somebody, probably their agent, intervened. Boris Karloff didn't crash the picture either, but the trailer at the Criterion promises him very soon, with Susanna ($1,000,000 Legs) Foster, in a new Universal masterpiece featuring "mania, rising to flaming heights of terror."

That "Universal masterpiece" was *The Climax.*

The musical melodrama which rates as many horror fans' least favorite Universal thriller had a curious evolution. On September 23, 1943, Louella Parsons reported that Susanna, Claude Rains and Nelson Eddy, "the *Phantom of the Opera* trio," would reunite in "another operatic mystery opus at Universal"; George Waggner was producing (again), with Curt Siodmak working on an "adaptation and modernization" of the old stage play *The Climax* by Edward Locke (who would die while *The Climax* was in release). Rains went back to Warner Bros. for *Passage to Marseilles* and *Mr. Skeffington*; enter Boris Karloff. He was back in Hollywood after his *Arsenic and Old Lace* Broadway and national tour, and signed a two-picture, 12-week, $60,000 contract with Universal—the first $40,000 and eight weeks going to *The Climax*. Eddy bailed out and Turhan Bey (with whom Susanna had a serious romance, and still a friendship today) inherited the (now non-singing) hero role.

Susanna, as Angela, in the power of Karloff's mad hypnotist Dr. Hohner, had the distinction of being top-billed over Karloff (in his first color film). Her salary: $13,000, less than a third of Boris' recompense; Bey was set for $7000. *Phantom*'s Arthur Lubin was set to direct, but music-loving George Waggner replaced him. On February 1, 1944, *The Climax* began shooting, on a $742,250 budget—about one-half of the cost of *Phantom of the Opera*.

The result was not a happy affair. Susanna is one of the few actresses who was not charmed by Boris Karloff:

> I thought Karloff was cold. I'm sorry, but working with him was like working with a slab of ice!

Karloff, trying for a novel, low-key approach, looked tired and old—he might have been the father of the actor who starred as *The Body Snatcher* later that year. The

Ad for *The Climax*, 1944, ballyhooing Foster's *Phantom of the Opera* triumph.

picture was pockmarked by low comedy (e.g., Bey eating his program as Susanna sang), and Waggner directed with none of the competence he had shown on *The Wolf Man*. It all wrapped up (significantly) on April Fool's Day, 1944, at a final cost of $789,901.95 and six days over schedule. Karloff began work on *House of Frankenstein* three days later! Susanna looked beautiful in her period costumes, and sang "Now at Last" and "Someday I'll Know." *The Climax* opened at New York's Criterion Theatre

December 13, 1944 (two days before Karloff's *House of Frankenstein* premiered at the Rialto), and the *New York Post* reported:

> *The Climax* is chock full o' climaxes. It is also well-stocked with operatic sounding songs, each of which enables Miss Foster at some time or other to outdo a piccolo for sheer altitude... The color, the Foster voice and Karloff's peculiar nature get into the front center and stay there.

It was also during 1944 that Susanna refused to star in *San Diego, I Love You*; Louise Allbritton took the assignment. Meanwhile, George Waggner announced that he was preparing a musical version of *Joan of Arc* for Susanna, with music by Edward Ward. It never came to pass.

In 1945, Universal released *Frisco Sal*, produced by George Waggner, with script by Curt Siodmak. Susanna played the title role, co-starred with Turhan Bey and Alan Curtis. Susanna sang the ballad "Beloved" ("by beloved Eddie Ward") and, in chorus girl frills and tights, performed a dance hall number called "Good Little Bad Little Lady." "This is the first time the Foster figure has been revealed," noted *The Hollywood Reporter*. "It was worth waiting for." *Photoplay*, however, was less impressed: "Why are excellent performers involved in such stories?" (There was, incidentally, gossip on the lot that Deanna Durbin had scuttled the studio's plans to produce Susanna's *Frisco Sal* in Technicolor.)

Finally, there came Universal's 1945 *That Night with You*, which starred Susanna with Franchot Tone and Louise Allbritton. "Susanna Foster wades into her role with breathless enthusiasm," hailed *Time* of Susanna's flirtatious Penny, "bubbling and flaring as the script demands." The bubbling and flaring disguised a very exasperated actress:

> *That Night with You*—that's what did it, kid! Imagine—singing a female version of *The Barber of Seville*! And that makeup—my eyebrows all plucked out and penciled on, a toupee widow's peak on me, a lipstick mouth that went all over my face. I looked like a made-up doll!

Universal was nearing the end of an era. Contracts were expiring and the studio was soon to merge and become Universal-International. Susanna, weary of Hollywood, decided to vacate. She took $18,500 which Universal loaned her, and studied voice with some of the greatest singers and musicians in the world: Giannini of the Metropolitan in New York, Borgioli in London and Luigi Ricci of the Rome Opera. Their giant talent and great encouragement made it all the more difficult for Susanna to return to Universal-International, where she had been receiving no salary during her hiatus. Finally, in 1948, Susanna rejected U-I's *One Touch of Venus* with Ava Gardner and *The Countess of Monte Cristo* with Sonja Henie (Olga San Juan replaced her in both films), and retired from Hollywood.

"I sold my mink coat," says Susanna, "and came back East with $1500 to my name."

Today, Susanna has second thoughts about her decision.

> If I knew what I know now, I would have stuck it out here, and found the people and the vehicles. I'm not very practical, and I never really thought I was that good. Both RCA-Victor and Columbia wanted me to record for them, but I didn't think I was good enough. Nelson Eddy wanted me to go on a concert tour with him after *Phantom*, but I was scared; I didn't realize he would have protected and taken care of me. I'm sorry now. Also, in 1946, I was offered the chance to go on for Lily Pons at the Shrine in Los Angeles in *Lucia*—an overnight thing—but I had to refuse, because I didn't know the stage movements. That's when I knew my first teacher, while fine, was not enough.
>
> There were other factors, too, why I quit; I was terribly disillusioned with the movie business. For example, I could never believe Universal firing Eddie Ward, for his supposed drinking problem. There were some personal things that had hurt me a lot. And I wanted children badly—I couldn't wait to have kids.

It was this desire that led to her marriage to singer Wilbur Evans, whom she wed in Philadelphia October 23, 1948. The 42-year-old Evans was her leading man in *Naughty Marietta*, which had also starred Edward Everett Horton ("That angel!") for the L.A. Civic Light Opera in the summer of 1948.

"Wilbur Evans proposed to me six weeks after we met," says Susanna. "He wanted us to become the Lunt and Fontanne of the musical stage."

Indeed, they toured together in *The Merry Widow*, billed as "America's Singing Sweethearts"—which nauseated Susanna. It was while playing *The Desert Song* by night and rehearsing *Bittersweet* by day that Susanna lost her first pregnancy.

> I realized I didn't love my husband when he came to the hospital after the miscarriage—and all he could worry about was who he could get to go on for me in *The Desert Song*. I knew I had married him on the rebound, and was starved for affection, which he gave freely. But I discovered it was superficial.

Nevertheless, the Evanses did have two children: Michael David, born in Los Angeles December 20, 1950, and Philip Lamont, born September 4, 1952, in London, where Evans was playing Emile de Becque opposite Mary Martin in *South Pacific*. In 1955, Evans became director of the Valley Forge Music Fair, Pennsylvania, where Susanna starred in *Brigadoon* and *Show Boat*. They divorced, with unpleasant publicity, in 1956.

For years, Susanna lived on New York's upper West Side—sometimes seeing her co-star of *The Climax*, Boris Karloff, on the street during the many years he lived at the Dakota Apartment Building. She raised her two boys alone, working on Wall Street in the dividend department of Merrill, Lynch, Pierce, Fenner and Smith, and taking many jobs to support the boys ("I would have done anything—moral—for my sons").

"In the single interview she has given in a decade," wrote Richard Lamparski in his 1970 edition of *Whatever Became of...?*, "Susanna asked her radio audience the whereabouts of her ex-husband (knowledgeable listeners were to get in touch with her or her lawyer so they could serve him with papers), and for a part-time job."

"The Hollywood Victory Committee"—i.e., Universal's contract roster—in *Follow the Boys* (1944). In the front row, from left: Peter Coe, Susanna Foster, Gloria Jean, Alan Curtis, Maria Montez, Andy Devine, Louise Allbritton, Robert Paige, Evelyn Ankers. Second row: Donald O'Connor, Peggy Ryan, Nigel Bruce, Elyse Knox, Samuel S. Hinds, Thomas Gomez, Gale Sondergaard.

The boys grew up. Susanna, come the early 1980s, had moved back to Los Angeles. She entertained thoughts of resuming her career and found the encouragement and kindness of fans phenomenal:

> You don't know the people who have come out of nowhere, the friends I've made who are fans. It's just unbelievable. And they're so good to you—they'll do anything for you. It's incredible, and I'm so grateful...

Nevertheless, a year after we had met her, Susanna Foster made the *National Enquirer*: She was found living in a parked car in Hollywood. A family squabble had resulted in her literally being put out in the street. A fan took her in, but life was still precarious for her.

In the past decade, Susanna has survived illness—and tragedy. "My son Philip passed away in November of 1985," she told me. "He was an alcoholic, and he had been in the hospital so many times. The last time he just couldn't make it. There isn't

Susanna Foster in December 1981.

a day that goes by that my thoughts aren't with him. It's made me more religious than I was before, I think." Her other son, Michael, had been a successful car salesman before recently becoming a nurse; by Michael, Susanna has two grandchildren.

Andrew Lloyd Webber's *The Phantom of the Opera* was a Broadway smash in 1988, and Susanna felt the repercussions as fans enkindled new fascination for the Gaston Leroux tale. Michael Crawford, originator of the role in London and on Broadway (and whose flamboyant movements owed much to Chaney's 1925 Erik; "I wanted his passion," said Crawford), told James Brady of *Parade* magazine that one of his "thrills" while playing the show in Los Angeles was Susanna Foster coming backstage to meet him. Susanna, however, was not so impressed:

> I saw the stage show of *The Phantom of the Opera*—and I thought it was terrible! I thought Crawford was awful, and the only one I liked was the girl who played *me*! The rest of it was punk. And the music was so lousy. I couldn't find one melody in the whole show. Everyone tries to tell me there's a melody to "Music of the Night," but I can't find it!

Then came a surprise: Susanna returned to the screen for the first time since 1945. Producer/director Wade Williams decided to remake Edgar G. Ulmer's PRC *noir* classic *Detour*.

On a budget of $220,000, Williams engaged Lea Lavish to play super-bitch Vera (so viciously acted in the 1945 original by Ann Savage) and signed Tom Neal, Jr., for the role his father had played in the original. "I made the picture for fans of the original and fans of the '40s 'B' movies," said Williams. "The picture pays homage to old style '40s film production."

Williams had wanted Ann Savage to play the role of Evie, a roomer, but, as *The Big Reel* cryptically reported, "circumstances proved otherwise." So Williams signed Susanna:

> In *Detour*, I had just a small part—a roomer where the girl stays. It had some nice lines in it, which was good. We shot it in Kansas City, Missouri. I haven't seen it myself, but the filming I saw was very good. Wade Williams is a very nice guy, and I liked Tom Neal, Jr., very much—I thought he was a much better screen personality than his father. He did a good job, and the girl did too. But I just did it because it was a thousand dollars and I needed the money!

Detour won the Golden Palm Award for Outstanding Achievement in an Independent Feature at the Fort Lauderdale Film Festival, and had a "sneak preview" at the Film Forum in New York City on July 31, 1992.

Susanna Foster has only been to Universal City once since she returned to California in the early 1980s:

> You wouldn't even know Universal. Another place entirely. It's a big business. All those banks in the front—oh, God! So nauseating!

In late 1992, Susanna attended a Hollywood revival of the 1943 *Phantom of the Opera*, delighting the crowd by singing for them. In the audience, and paying eloquent tribute to her, was Turhan Bey.

Susanna still toys with the temptation to return to show business. A gall bladder attack and a mild heart attack have handicapped the comeback. "When you're old, you just become a mess," she says.

In 1984, George Waggner, Universal dynamo of the '40s and producer of *Phantom of the Opera*, died at the Motion Picture Country House. Strokes had robbed him of most of the memories he had of his prolific film career. Indeed, the only star he could remember from *Phantom of the Opera* was Susanna Foster. She visited her former producer not long before he died.

"I can still see you in *Phantom of the Opera*," said the sadly senile Waggner to Susanna, "singing and coming down those stairs."

Indeed, it's a lovely and indelible memory for all devotees of the grand moments in horror films.

The Films of Susanna Foster

1939

The Great Victor Herbert (Paramount, Andrew L. Stone)

1941

There's Magic in Music (*The Hard-Boiled Canary*) (Paramount, A. L. Stone)

Glamour Boy (Paramount, Ralph Murphy)

1943

Phantom of the Opera (Universal, Arthur Lubin)

Top Man (Universal, Charles Lamont)

1944

Follow the Boys (Universal—A. Edward Sutherland)

This Is the Life (Universal, Felix Feist)

The Climax (Universal, George Waggner)

Bowery to Broadway (Universal, Charles Lamont)

1945

Frisco Sal (Universal, G. Waggner)

That Night with You (Universal, William A. Seiter)

1992

Detour (Wade Williams/Filmworks Studio, Wade Williams)

Jean Brooks

First of all, there were her eyes.

Deep, beautiful mournful eyes ... what Joel E. Siegel, in his 1973 milestone book *Val Lewton: The Reality of Terror*, called "the haunted eyes of Jean Brooks."

The eyes were almost spiritual—yet there was a flicker of wickedness in them.

The face was lovely, like the angel of a cathedral stained-glass window—yet she was wearing a vampy, black Cleopatra wig.

And as *The Seventh Victim*, Val Lewton's morbid little masterpiece of 1943, wound its satanic way to a late 1960s late show climax, Jean Brooks' Jacqueline, traitor to a coven of Greenwich Village devil worshippers, ran in her very high heels through the dark alleyways, eluding her diabolic assassin, only to return to her flat (where she keeps a noose swinging at all times)—and hang herself. Roy Webb's finale music swelled, and Jean's disembodied voice quoted John Donne's Holy Sonnet:

> I run to death, and death meets me as fast,
> And all my pleasures are like Yesterday.

It was an unforgettable performance.

And it inspired an unforgettable nightmare. That night, as a very impressionable Catholic prep-schooler, I had a dream about *The Seventh Victim*, the devil worshippers, and especially that angel in the Cleopatra wig—a dream that caused me literally to wake up screaming.

Val Lewton would have been pleased. And so might have been Jean Brooks.

Whatever happened to Jean Brooks?

The query had become almost a cliché among film buffs, especially horror fans who cherished her "sensationalist" Jacqueline. Aside from *The Seventh Victim*, her best-known credit was also for Lewton: Kiki, the showgirl heroine of *The Leopard Man*, an attractive, kinetic performance, played in her own blonde hair and without any of Jacqueline's wanton aura.

Preceding it for Jean Brooks were engagements as a New York nightclub chanteuse, acting in Hollywood-made Spanish films (under the name Robina Duarte), a fling as a Universal starlet (under the name of Jeanne Kelly) and labors at Monogram and PRC.

Following her Lewton films were adventures with RKO's Falcon, a few "B" potboilers with roles of startlingly diminishing size, rumors of alcoholism and a sudden, mysterious departure from her studio.

Next—apparent oblivion.

No colleagues from Universal or RKO knew where she was. Even her ex-husband, Oscar-winning writer/director Richard Brooks (who later wed major movie star Jean Simmons), admitted late in his life that he'd had no idea of his ex-wife's whereabouts for decades, and didn't know if she were alive or dead. Jean Brooks seemed an enigma, as lost as *The Seventh Victim*'s Jacqueline before her sister Mary (Kim Hunter) located her in the sinister nooks of Val Lewton's backlot Greenwich Village.

***Chapter opener:* The pinup girl of Val Lewton's despairing, "Mr. Hyde" side: Jean Brooks as Jacqueline in *The Seventh Victim*, 1943.**

In this case, the credit for discovery must go to a cousin, a second cousin and a fan/film historian. The late Gloria White, Jean's first cousin, became interested in Jean Brooks while researching her own genealogy. Her daughter, Cecilia Maskell, became a dynamic Watson to her mom's Sherlock Holmes. And it was Doug McClelland, noted cinema author/historian and the #1 Jean Brooks fan, who attracted Gloria White's attention through film magazine tributes he wrote about Jean, and he generously put her family in touch with me.

And so the sad mystery of Jean Brooks was solved. We found no Cleopatra wig, no satanic cults, no noose hanging in a bleak apartment. But we did uncover some life and death facts and some sad, tragic twists in the life of a lady who deserved a kinder fate from Hollywood—and from life.

> When I was a child, I went to the movies to see Jean Brooks. I would say to my friends, "That's my cousin." And they would say, "Sure, sure!"
>
> —Gloria White, 1993

The actress who became known as Jean Brooks was born Ruby M. Kelly in Houston, Texas, on December 23, 1915 (if one believes the 1920 U.S. Census and Jean's second marriage certificate), or 1916 (if one believes her RKO publicity and death certificate). Her father, Horace, was in his 40s when Ruby (henceforth called Jean in this story) was born, as was her mother, Robina, who had been born in Costa Rica of Canadian and English parents. When Jean was born, there already were two teenage sons: Horace, who went to work for the Civil Service, and Ernest, who became a railroad accountant. (Another son, Allen, died of tetanus in 1912, at the age of seven.)

Jean's father died when she was a young girl, and Jean's mother took her child to Costa Rica to live on the coffee plantation of Ruby's grandfather. "Several of my relatives have told me," said Gloria White, Jean's cousin, "that when Robina lived in Costa Rica with Ruby, the house they lived in was haunted, and they would hear noises during the night."

By day, the haunted plantation was a happy place. As Mrs. White remembered:

> I've been told that Jean loved to go on rides in a cart pulled by an ox. She loved the country. Our first cousin, Edgar Villalobos, taught her how to ride horses. She was so beautiful and rode so well that all the local people would watch her. She was also a good dancer and would dance with her first cousin, Carol Jeffries Avlon, at the National Theatre and the local people would throw money at them.

As she matured, Jean apparently spent some time in the United States, with visits to Costa Rica. One visit from the teenage Jean presented a rather amusing tinge of "scandal," as Gloria White recalled:

> One time, Jean was arrested in Costa Rica! Remember how they used to have the women's bathing suits to the knee, covering

Little Ruby Kelly (aka Jean Brooks), many years before playing a devil worshipper in *The Seventh Victim*, here acts an angel in a childhood play. The girl on the moon is Jean's cousin, Carol Jeffries Avlon.

> practically the whole body? Well, Jean came from New York with a really gorgeous bathing suit, very modern, and she went swimming in the Pacific. And they were horrified by the modern bathing suit—and arrested her for indecent exposure! She knew that my father was chief of police over the whole country, so she called from jail and said, "Oh, my uncle, come and get me out of here! They say I shouldn't wear this kind of bathing suit in this country!" So my father just phoned and said, "Let her go." My father liked her very much.

On another occasion, the worldly cousin returned to South America with a lady friend who wanted to go on safari. Cecilia Maskell, Gloria White's daughter, says:

> A branch of our family moved to Panama. My mother's family especially tends to be very colorful, and they had a pet tiger. This tiger apparently was getting pretty big and unruly, with all the kids and everything, so they told Jean that they wished they could get rid of this tiger, but they didn't want to kill it. So Jean took the tiger back to the U.S. with her, and arranged for it to be donated to the zoo in San Francisco.

According to a 1942 RKO press release, Jean sailed with her mother to New

York City in 1934, with plans to attend college. Instead, she decided to go for a night club career. Mother was dismayed, but, according to RKO,

> Jean had made up her mind. It didn't matter to her that she had never had a singing lesson in her life... It occurred to her that a girl with golden-brown hair and blue-green eyes singing Spanish songs like a native should attract attention...

Result: Jean got a singing job at the Bali supper club, soon moving up to the Sert Room of the Waldorf Astoria. *Not* publicized by RKO, however, was the fact that Jean met a very celebrated (if sadly tarnished) Hollywood figure at this time who helped her entrance into the movies. His name was Erich von Stroheim.

The legendary auteur of *Greed* and *Foolish Wives* had fallen into a horrid professional and personal limbo by the mid–1930s. He was playing grotesque caricatures of himself (e.g., 1933's *The Lost Squadron*); he had witnessed his directorial "comeback," *Walking Down Broadway* (1933), butchered and largely reshot at Fox. His wife Valerie would suffer a terrible accident: catching fire during a beauty treatment at a Hollywood beauty salon. When a beautician tried to smother the flames on Valerie's face with the stole of a movie star, the star shrieked "Not *my* coat!" and haughtily pulled it back as Mrs. Von Stroheim suffered terrible facial burns. Their son Josef was seriously ill, with a paralysis. And now, "The Man You Love to Hate" met young, beautiful and ambitious Jean Brooks. "He was the one who helped Jean get into show business," says Gloria White. "It was rumored that she was romantically involved with Erich and even that he was her first husband, but I have no information confirming this."

Now employing the moniker of Jeanne Kelly (Gloria White says Jean had dropped her real name of Ruby Kelly because it sounded too much like Ruby Keeler), Jean entered the movies. Her first release was a curiosity called *Obeah*, released by Arcturus Pictures in February of 1935. Jean was the leading lady; her leading man was named Phillips H. Lord; the director and author was F. Herrick Herrick. The topic of this obscure opus: voodoo curses.

While the extent of von Stroheim's clout in securing Jean these roles is unknown, he probably was influential in her casting in *The Crime of Doctor Crespi*, a mad melodrama released by Republic Pictures (or, as von Stroheim called the studio, "Repulsive Pictures") late in 1935. Shot in eight days in September 1934 by producer/director/writer John H. Auer, the film was actually the product of Poverty Row's Liberty Films, and filmed at the Biograph Studios in the Bronx, where D. W. Griffith had ended his career directing 1931's *The Struggle*, with Zita (*The Mummy*) Johann. (Republic would release *The Crime of Doctor Crespi*, over a year after its completion, after purchasing the unreleased works of the sinking Liberty Films.)

Loosely based on Poe's *The Premature Burial*, *The Crime of Doctor Crespi* offered "Von" as glowering Dr. Crespi, chain-smoking, keeping a dwarf's skeleton in his office and burying alive his protégé who had eclipsed him in fame—and married Von's love. The "hero" of this curiosity, "Dr. Thomas," was *Dracula*'s fly-eater and *Frankenstein*'s hunchbacked dwarf, Dwight Frye, who digs up the buried-alive victim and inadvertently sets him loose on von Stroheim (who had beaten the daylights out of Frye earlier in the film when the latter vowed to reveal his monstrous crime).

Jean played Miss Gordon, a nurse at von Stroheim's hospital. It was a decent role, and allowed her to unleash an impressive scream when the formerly-buried-alive Dr. Ross creeps up behind her and ominously asks, "Where is Dr. Crespi?" She also got the final fade-out close-up as Frye asks her for a date. It's quite a sight—the former fly-eater from *Dracula* flirting with the future devil worshipper of *The Seventh Victim*:

> FRYE (smiling in close-up): "Uh—doing anything tonight?"
> JEAN (coyly): "Oh—Doc Thomas!"

Von Stroheim's personal opinion: "*The Crime of Doctor Crespi* was also the crime of Republic, the screenwriter, and the director!"

She landed a bit in RKO's *Frankie and Johnny* (1935), starring Helen Morgan and Chester Morris, and played in Paramount's Spanish release, *Tango-Bar* (1935).

Von Stroheim and his young protégé meanwhile parted company, and Jean found a new boyfriend in Al Woods, a New York stage producer. He cast her in the Broadway-bound melodrama *Name Your Poison*, starring Lenore Ulric. *Name Your Poison* premiered at the Shubert Theatre in Newark, New Jersey, on January 20, 1936, and the *New York Times* reported that Miss Ulric had "scored a hit" with the opening night crowd. Mysteriously, *Name Your Poison* never made it to Broadway.

Hollywood, 1938. Jean, reportedly accompanied by her mother, made a screen test for 20th Century–Fox, then headquarters of Loretta Young, Alice Faye and Sonja Henie. Darryl F. Zanuck, Fox mogul, passed. However, talent scout Ben Piazza saw Jean's test and signed her with a new studio, Major Productions, 1040 Las Palmas Avenue. Three weeks after Jean signed, Major Productions did (in Hollywood jargon) an "el foldo."

Jean's Spanish background came to the rescue: She tested at Paramount, where the studio was about to make a series of Spanish films with Tito Guizar. Publicity claimed she arrived at Paramount at two o'clock in the afternoon and departed at six that evening with a contract, "having demonstrated her acting, singing and Spanish-speaking ability." She starred with Guizar in four Spanish-language pictures during the latter part of 1938 and 1939. Jean's stage name for this career episode: Robina Duarte.

Post-Paramount, there were small roles at Columbia (*A Miracle on Main Street*, 1940) and PRC (*The Invisible Killer*, 1940). Then came a call from Universal, where Jean won the role of Eris Brooks in the 60-minute Johnny Mack Brown western *Son of Roaring Dan* (1940)—and a Universal Players contract.

It was poetically proper that the future Jacqueline of *The Seventh Victim* would pass a sojourn at the Hollywood home of Frankenstein's Monster, Count Dracula, the Mummy and the Wolf Man. The closest Jean came to melodrama, however, was in 1940's 12-chapter serial *Flash Gordon Conquers the Universe*, yet another galactic contest between Buster Crabbe's heroic Flash and Charles Middleton's unspeakable Ming the Merciless. The unbilled Jean had one fleeting moment of fame in Chapter 5, as Olga, oomphy space siren, looking stunning in a long black cape. She shoves our heroine, Dale Arden (Carol Hughes)—who slaps Jean's Olga right in the face. "She

Universal starlets (from left) Jean Brooks (then known as Jeanne Kelly), Anne Nagel and Kay Leslie laugh and splash it up at the Lakeside Country Club in North Hollywood, 1940. (Photofest)

struck me! She must be punished!" rants Jean as a guard intervenes—holding her back from what promised to be a whale of a catfight!

Jean's first feature lead was as Laura in *The Devil's Pipeline*, a Richard Arlen–Andy Devine South Seas potboiler, directed by Christy Cabanne, and which opened at New York City's Rialto Theatre in November 1940. *Variety* described Jean in one word: "Flat."

A more enjoyable showcase for Jean came via Universal's "super serial" for 1941, *Riders of Death Valley*. The stars were Dick Foran, Leo Carrillo and Buck Jones; the terrific heavies numbered Charles Bickford and future Frankenstein Monsters Lon Chaney, Jr., and Glenn Strange. Universal originally assigned the female lead of "Mary Morgan" to Nan (*Dracula's Daughter*, *Tower of London*, *The Invisible Man Returns*) Gray. Miss Gray absolutely refused the job, so Universal fired her—and gave the part to Jean. Judging by PR stills, Jean had a wonderful time, horseback riding all over the Universal lot, sharing ice cream with Buck Jones and playing the guitar with Dick Foran. Noah Beery, Jr., who played "Smokey" in *Riders of Death Valley*, told Cecilia Maskell that Jean was "a joy to work with."

Universal, however, hardly gave Jean a fitting star build-up. She can barely be glimpsed as a USO hostess in Abbott and Costello's 1941 mega-hit *Buck Privates*; joined Hugh "Woo-Woo" Herbert and Anne (*Black Friday, Man Made Monster*) Nagel (q.v.) in *Meet the Chump*; and played a new lead with Richard Arlen and Andy Devine in *A Dangerous Game*, a comedy-thriller set in an insane asylum and which, for no logical reason, later turned up in the original package of *Shock Theatre* in 1957. ("If there's such a thing as a class D picture," panned *Variety* of *A Dangerous Game*, "this is it.") Jean had a bit with Rudy Vallee, Helen Parrish and Lon Chaney, Jr., in the musical *Too Many Blondes*, and was back to the sagebrush in the Johnny Mack Brown western *Man from Montana* (which included the song "Bananas Make Me Tough").

And, as she shared Universal celebrity with such ladies as Deanna Durbin, Anne Gwynne (q.v.) and Evelyn Ankers (q.v.), Jean fell in love. In the spring of 1941, she met Richard Brooks, "radio writer and storyteller," destined to direct such films as *Blackboard Jungle* (1955) and win an Oscar for his screenplay for *Elmer Gantry* (1960, which he also directed). On the night of June 1, 1941, the 29-year-old Brooks wed Jean in the garden of the Encino ranch of Vic Dalton ("loan company executive and yachtsman"), where they had first met only two months before. It was Jean's second marriage (no concrete information has surfaced on her first). Jean left her apartment at the Lido in Hollywood and moved into Brooks' Malibu Beach home, delaying their honeymoon due to "respective professional engagements."

Universal rewarded Jean's delayed honeymoon by dropping her contract. Her final Universal feature release (again with Johnny Mack Brown): 1942's *Fighting Bill Fargo*.

Now using the name "Jean Brooks," she took work like Monogram's *Boot Hill Bandits* (1942), with Ray "Crash" Corrigan and Glenn Strange, and PRC's *Boss of Big Town* (1942), with John Litel. Then Jean paid a call on Ben Piazza, who had signed her to that three-week-long Major Productions contract. Piazza was now casting director for RKO—and Jean won a contract. It was at 780 Gower Street that Jean would play her most-memorable performances and become, in the words of Doug McClelland, "RKO's resident neurotic."

Jean's RKO debut was hardly auspicious: an unbilled bit at the tail end of *The Falcon Strikes Back* (1943). She's a vamp who screams, then seductively pleads (in Spanish) for Tom Conway's Falcon to assist her. She sashays away with him flirtatiously on her arm—THE END. It was the first of Jean's five Falcon films. The leading lady of *The Falcon Strikes Back* was Harriet Hilliard (of *Ozzie and Harriet* fame); also prominent were RKO contractees Jane Randolph (q.v.) ("Alice" of *Cat People* and *The Curse of the Cat People*) and Rita Corday (who would be memorable as the Widow in *The Body Snatcher*). Meanwhile, the creator of these horror films took notice of Jean Brooks...

His name was Val Lewton.

That there even still was an RKO was largely due to the burly, bear-like, brilliant Lewton. He had made show business history via *Cat People* (1942), a sleek, sexy little chiller that had saved RKO from bankruptcy in the wake of Orson Welles' *Citizen Kane* and *The Magnificent Ambersons*. *I Walked with a Zombie* (1943) was his second hit, and now came *The Leopard Man* (1943)—Lewton's third collaboration with

Richard Brooks, destined to become a noted writer and director, weds Jeanne Kelly in 1941. The couple divorced in 1944; Richard Brooks died in 1992 with no idea that his ex-wife had been dead for nearly 30 years.

director Jacques Tourneur, who had an uncanny visual skill for illuminating his sensitive producer's personal obsessions which frequently sparked his films.

Lewton presented the most dynamic women of horror. And he selected Jean Brooks to play the heroine, Kiki Walker, in *The Leopard Man*, based on the Cornell Woolrich story, "Black Alibi."

A striking portrait of Brooks (still using the professional name Jeanne Kelly) from Universal's *Fighting Bill Fargo*, 1942.

The Leopard Man is one of Lewton's most controversial films. He and Tourneur later disowned it. Joel Siegel, in *The Reality of Terror*, admires it, while finding it "little more than an exercise in sadistic voyeurism—three innocent women dying like trapped animals."

Murder #1: A poor teenage Mexican girl (Margaret Landry), afraid of the dark, is ordered out into the windy night by her mother to buy cornmeal. In a wonderfully frightening walk home, tumbleweed scares her, and a roaring train—and the leopard. She runs home. Her mother has locked her out. A horrible scream, leopard growls, and the mother sees blood seeping under the door…

Murder #2: A wealthy young Mexican romantic (Tula Parma) decides to meet her lover at her father's grave on her birthday. They miss each other. She gets locked in the cemetery. Wind, a full moon, rustling sounds in a tree, a scream…

Murder #3: A flamboyant Mexican dancer and golddigger (Margo) walks home through the night with money in her stocking from a wealthy admirer. Stripping off her stockings at home, she discovers she has lost the money. She goes back out into the night to search for it in an alley … a scream…

Jean Brooks was the heroine of *The Leopard Man*—Kiki Walker, a nightclub entertainer who (at the suggestion of promoter/boyfriend Dennis O'Keefe) makes an entrance one night with a leopard on a leash. (One wonders if Lewton fashioned this entrance as a nod to Jean, who had worked as a Spanish singer in New York niteries, as well as to Simone Simon, his *Cat People* star, who, as legend claimed, walked a leopard on a leash in Hollywood.) The leopard escapes—and Jean's Kiki and hero O'Keefe spend much of the rest of the film trying to snare the killer. Of course, only the first death is due to the leopard; the murderer of the other two women is demented museum curator Galbraith (James Bell), apprehended and killed in an eerie climax amidst a procession of hooded, hymn-chanting Palladists.

The Leopard Man premiered at New York City's Rialto Theatre on May 19, 1943. "The most horrifying thing about it," sniped the *New York Times*, "is that it actually gets on a screen." Even Lewton and Tourneur put the movie down; however, Danny Peary, in his excellent book *Guide for the Film Fanatic*, calls the movie "Essential

Making an entrance: Brooks with a feline friend in Val Lewton's *The Leopard Man*, 1943.

Lewton," and the film is gaining steadily and deservedly in its champions. One of *The Leopard Man*'s top assets is Jean as Kiki (although top female billing went to Margo as the castanet-clicking Clo-Clo). In a sense, all the leading characters of *The Leopard Man* are masked, like the killer. Jean's Kiki wears a mask of cynicism—when, in fact, she feels such deep guilt about the escaped leopard that she pays for the funeral of the Mexican girl, and later gives the rest of her money to the family of Clo-Clo. One also must admire Jean (and Dennis O'Keefe) for the sincerity they both bring to two bizarre love scenes: one in a cemetery, the other in front of a funeral parlor.

RKO liked Jean, awarding her the lead in the new Falcon flick, *The Falcon in Danger* (1943). Val Lewton liked her, too, and now cast her in the key role for which she would be best remembered.

> My personal favorite of my father's films is *The Seventh Victim*. I think it's the movie which is closest to his life—autobiographical, in a way. He and my mother had lived in Greenwich Village when they were first married, so he knew the Village very well. The Italian restaurant, for example, was based on a hangout called Barbettas, a favorite restaurant of his. And, as a reporter, he had done articles on the cosmetics industry, so he incorporated that into *The Seventh Victim* with the "La Sagesse" company.

> There's the romantic poet, who's a failure as a writer—I think that's how my father thought of himself. He seemed to revel in the fact that he was a "hack"—a Hollywood producer to whom people gave lurid titles, and he made up movies to fit them—but I think that, down deep, it hurt him that he never really was a literary figure.
>
> My father based the character of Jacqueline, I think, on his aunt, Nazimova, the famous actress, in the sense that she is dramatic and mysterious.
>
> And as for the religious aspect—as a reporter, my father used to go around and cover Stigmatas, the religious zealots who would start bleeding from the hands. He had all kinds of stories of how he had to go out and cover all these strange people.
>
> —Val Lewton, Jr., in an interview with the author (March 17, 1993)

I was a teenager at Baltimore's Loyola High School (a Jesuit institution) in the late 1960s when I first saw *The Seventh Victim* on a Baltimore late show. It disturbed me; something about Jean Brooks reminded me of a statue of an angel that stood in our chapel. That night I suffered a nightmare: dreaming that the *Seventh Victim* satanists had stolen the statue of the angel, blasphemously dressed it up in Cleopatra wig and sable coat and ankle-strap high heels, and brought her to life by some evil enchantment...

Voilà—Jean Brooks as Jacqueline.

I awoke very upset and with a yearning to go to confession.

The Seventh Victim is the most macabre, disturbing and haunting of Val Lewton's wonderful RKO shockers. It's a poetic battle between Lewton's "Jekyll" and "Hyde"—his familiar thematic war of Faith and Hope vs. Despair and Depression. When Dr. Judd (Tom Conway) and poet Jason Hoag (Erford Gage) rebuke the satanists, reciting the Lord's Prayer, it appears that Lewton's "Jekyll" is winning.

It's Jean Brooks' Jacqueline, however, who—come *The Seventh Victim*'s finale—becomes his Hyde in triumph.

Mark Robson (who died in 1978) recalled *The Seventh Victim* in an interview published in *The Celluloid Muse*, by Charles Higham and Joel Greenberg. He had made his directorial bow with *The Seventh Victim* ("at $200 per week") following work as editor of Lewton's *Cat People*, and touched on *The Seventh Victim*'s strange power:

> *The Seventh Victim* was a very low-budget film for those days; I think it cost about $100,000. I don't remember much about it now. I do remember however that it had a rather sinister quality, of something intangible but horribly real; it had an atmosphere. I think the actors and the director had to believe very strongly in the possibility of disaster: that something *was* there. We believed it ourselves. We talked ourselves into believing it. We had a kind of fidelity to that feeling...

DeWitt Bodeen (who died in 1988) had originally drafted a story taking place in Los Angeles—an orphaned girl marked as the seventh victim of a murderer must

Jean Brooks (left) and Kim Hunter in *The Seventh Victim*, 1943.

learn his identity. However, after Bodeen went to New York to research *The Curse of the Cat People*, Lewton tossed out the story, engaged Charles O'Neal (father of Ryan) to collaborate with Bodeen on a new version, and decided to base it in Greenwich Village—where Lewton had been very happy once upon a time as a newspaper man. And he communicated a strange mandate to Bodeen: "See if it's possible for you to go to a devil-worshipping society meeting."

RKO's New York office could work wonders in those days, and Bodeen attended a society of satanists under a pseudonym. As Bodeen told John Brosnan in *The Horror People*:

> And I must say that they were exactly like the devil worshippers in *Rosemary's Baby*. It was even in the same neighborhood on the West Side that they used in that film. It was during the war, and I would have hated to be Hitler with all the spells they were working against him. They were mostly old people and they were casting these spells while they knitted and crocheted. A bunch of tea-drinking old ladies and gentlemen sitting there muttering imprecations against Hitler. I made use of the experience in that the devil worshippers in *The Seventh Victim* were very ordinary people who had one basic flaw, an Achilles heel which has turned them against good and towards evil...

Kim Hunter, Jean Brooks and Tom Conway in a publicity portrait for *The Seventh Victim*, 1943.

Shooting of *The Seventh Victim* began May 5, 1943. It was a curious cast. Kim Hunter made her film debut as Mary Gibson, Jacqueline's boarding school sister—looking pleasingly plump (and a little like Deanna Durbin) in her snug overcoat and tam-o'-shanter hat. She was terrified in her film debut; over 40 years later, Miss Hunter told Michael Buckley in a 1986 *Films in Review* interview, "I was so frightened that I looked embalmed"—which perhaps added to the film's macabre quality. (For many years, Hunter has lived in Greenwich Village, very close to the theater represented in *The Seventh Victim*'s climax.)

Top billing went to Tom Conway as Dr. Louis Judd—the same role he had played in *Cat People* (in which he had been slain by Simone Simon's Cat Woman—was *The Seventh Victim* a "prequel" to the first Lewton saga?). Conway, the real-life brother of George Sanders (and known inside Hollywood as "the *nice* George Sanders"), possessed a velvety cynicism that made his climactic put-down of the satanists via prayer all the more powerful. Hugh Beaumont, future father of TV's *Leave It to Beaver*, seems (in retrospect) perfectly cast as Gregory Ward, Jacqueline's loving but almost aggravatingly adjusted lawyer husband, who indulged his morbid wife by helping her get her hangman's noose (telling Mary, "Your sister had a feeling about life—that it wasn't worth living unless one could end it... That rope made her happy..."); naturally, he falls in love with Mary. Then there's the village poet, Jason Hoag (Erford Gage), who fancies Cyrano and seems to be Val Lewton's own lampoon of his own hypersensitive self. (Lewton's widow Ruth told me, shortly before her death in 1994, of a time when the very young Lewton insisted on running out on the court during a basketball game and reciting Cyrano to the crowd. "They had to drag him off!" she laughed.)

Lewton chocked *The Seventh Victim* with wonderfully wicked moments. Following the death of the private investigator (Lou Lubin), stabbed with scissors as he and Mary explored the "La Sagesse" cosmetics factory in search of Jacqueline (its former owner), a terrified Mary rides the subway all night. Two men help a "drunk" onto the subway; his hat falls off—and we see the "drunk" is the dead investigator! (Lewton based this episode on a real-life experience.) There's also a shower scene for Kim Hunter which might have inspired Hitchcock in *Psycho*: As the shower-capped Mary sings in her shower, the squat shadow of satanist Mrs. Redi (Mary Newton) slowly fills the curtain, warning Mary to forsake her search for Jacqueline—Mrs. Redi wearing a hat which, in shadow, makes her resemble a looming, horned devil.

Jean Brooks, as the enigmatic Jacqueline, was the "hook" which connected it all. In one of Lewton's most hypnotic episodes, Nicholas Musuraca's camera slowly advances on Jean's Jacqueline—almost as if moving in for a passionate kiss—her eyes truly haunting as she recites a soliloquy in a world-weary voice:

> You know about the Palladists. You know who they are—what they are—I was one of them... I wasn't happy with them. I wanted to break away. It was miserable. I went to Louis for help. They felt that I'd betrayed them. They wanted me to die. Kill myself. They kept me locked up at La Sagesse. I was there such a long time... I was terrified. The darkness in the corners of the room. All those little noises. Then one night the door opened. A man came in—tiptoeing in. I had a scissors in my hand...

Also memorable is the scene in which the satanists loom over Jacqueline in their apartment, trying to force her to drink the poison that sits before her in a crystal goblet. The actress sits there, staring morbidly at the goblet, drumming one finger on the arm of her chair. "No, no, no," she recites, flatly. Three simple words ... yet in the Lewton atmosphere, and with the weird lighting focused on her, the haunting effect is unforgettable. This is a woman already in Hell, the Hell of her own misery and fear.

As the company "forced" itself to believe in the morbid spell of *The Seventh Victim*, as Mark Robson remembered, Jean had much to tap in her own life for sadness. As Jean reported to the RKO lot in Hollywood each morning, donning her Cleopatra wig and sable coat and ankle-strap high heels, that heartbroken look in her eyes was genuine: Her marriage to Richard Brooks had hit the rocks. On April Fool's Day, 1943, they had separated. Jean would wait until September of 1944, to file for divorce, claiming,

> For a period of two years immediately prior to the commencement of this action, defendant has continuously wrongfully inflicted mental suffering upon the plaintiff, without cause or provocation... It has become impossible for the parties hereto to

> live together as husband and wife on any terms essential to the achievement of the objectives of matrimony...

Also, Hollywood rumor claimed that Jean Brooks had another problem: alcohol. As Cecilia Maskell told me:

> From our research, it appears that Jean was an alcoholic. There's been a lot of alcoholism in our family, so it would have been an easy thing for her to fall into, and the diseases on her death certificate were alcohol-related. It sounds like she probably got worse and worse...

So, this sad, alcoholic actress played Jacqueline Gibson with an overwhelming sense of sadness and dread.

The Seventh Victim toys with the imagination like a cat with a mouse, inspiring all variety of weird speculation. Had Jacqueline ventured so deeply into satanism that she had officially become a witch—hence the very obvious wig? (Witches, after all, are supposed to be bald.) Are the emotional remarks of Isabel Jewell's Frances the beautician about Jacqueline ("Anybody who ever sees her never forgets her!") and her hysterics as she knocks the poison goblet from Jacqueline's hand ("The only times I was ever happy was when I was with you!") intended to suggest a lesbian relationship? Is the uncompromisingly mannish demeanor of Mary Newton's Mrs. Redi supposed to compound this sexual ambiguity? (And, for that matter, what are we to make of the longing glances of Eve March toward Miss Hunter when, as a teacher at the academy, she warns the heroine not to come back—"One must have courage to really live in the world"?) What about Evelyn Brent as the one-armed Natalie Cortez, who shuffles cards and plays the piano—are we to think she turned to satanism out of bitterness over her accident? (A study of the original script solves this riddle; "Life has betrayed us," says Natalie, speaking for the satanists. "We've found that there is no Heaven on Earth, so we must worship evil for evil's own sake.")

All these questions (and many more) might be dancing in our heads as *The Seventh Victim* heads for its climax. The devil worshippers release Jean's Jacqueline at midnight, only to send an assassin after her; there is a wonderfully eerie chase, Jean running in her high heels (just as Jane Randolph had done in *Cat People*), the scene stuffed with Lewton "bus" scare tactics, such as the sudden crashing of a garbage can lid knocked off by a dog, and a jarring burst of raucous laughter from actors leaving a theater. Jacqueline escapes to her hideaway apartment, and on the staircase, sees Mimi—a consumptive prostitute, played by Lewton favorite Elizabeth Russell (q.v.) (the original "Cat Woman" from *Cat People*).

> JACQUELINE: Who are you?
>
> MIMI: I'm Mimi. I'm dying... I've been quiet. Oh, ever so quiet. I hardly move and yet it keeps coming all the time, closer and closer. I rest and rest and yet still I am dying.
>
> JACQUELINE: And you don't want to die. I've always wanted to die. Always.

MIMI: I'm afraid. I'm tired of being afraid—of waiting.

JACQUELINE: Why wait?

MIMI: I'm not going to wait. I'm going out. I'm going to laugh and dance and do all the things I used to do.

JACQUELINE: And then?

MIMI: I don't know.

JACQUELINE (*enviously*): You will die.

Lewton's Jekyll vs. Hyde battle goes into a bloody final round. "Jekyll" seems to triumph as poet Jason and Dr. Judd repudiate the devil worshippers, reciting the Lord's Prayer. It's as if Val Lewton is scorning his own morbid hang-ups and obsessions. Also well-done is the final scene, as Mary and Gregory profess their love for each other—selflessly realizing they are never free to pursue it as long as Jacqueline needs their help.

However, come the finale, and "Hyde" wins in a fade-out that is horror/bleak/despair Val Lewton all the way. Mimi, all dolled-up, sashays out to the staircase for one final fling: suicide by sin. And she (and we) hear an ominous sound: a chair falling over in the room where Jacqueline keeps her noose...

I run to Death, and Death
meets me as fast, and all my
Pleasures are like Yesterday.

The Seventh Victim opened at New York's Rialto September 17, 1943. *Variety* nailed it as "totally unbelievable hocus-pocus," while the ever-appalled *New York Times* surmised that the blame might be the projectionist's—"maybe he did run it backward and upside down." The movie did not match the grosses of the previous Lewton works, yet—by the late 1940s—it had become one of the first of the "cult" films, especially in England. As Mark Robson remembered in *The Celluloid Muse*:

> That picture achieved some kind of notoriety in England after the war, as I discovered when John and Roy Boulting came out here about that time, wanting to meet the fellow who had directed it. They used to bicycle a print of *The Seventh Victim* around London, among them Carol Reed and Cavalcanti and people like that, thinking it an advanced, weird form of filmmaking.

So, in retrospect, *The Seventh Victim* presents Jean Brooks as Lewton's own exotic "Hyde," the pin-up girl of his despairing, faithless nature.

Tragically, while Lewton's "Jekyll" became increasingly prominent in later films such as *The Curse of the Cat People* and *Bedlam*, the situation did not run parallel in his own life. "I never knew anybody who was so desperately unhappy," the late DeWitt Bodeen told me of Val Lewton, "who lost all faith in himself." Lewton developed a stress that proved fatal, as he died of a heart attack in March of 1951, at the age of 46. His widow Ruth, aware of the demons that taunted her husband, believing that much of it came from his childhood, devoted her life to working with emotionally disturbed children, to try to spare them the torment that so plagued Lewton.

"Val's stress," Ruth Lewton told me in 1993, "was a wicked thing."

And, in *The Seventh Victim*, Jean Brooks personifies this "wicked thing" beautifully, tragically—and indelibly.

Jean was rewarded for *The Seventh Victim* with *The Falcon and the Co-Eds* (1943), one of the very best of the series—due in no small way to Jean's performance as Vicky. As Doug McClelland wrote in his Brooks tribute in *Film Fan Monthly*:

> *The Falcon and the Co-Eds*, if hardly *Maltese Falcon* and Mary Astor, provided Brooks' best Falcon exposure as the strict young fencing/drama teacher at an exclusive oceanside girls school. Appropriately attired in a brass-buttoned, militaristic-looking dark dress, she was a striking, commandingly attractive original...

Indeed, in the scene where Jean stands atop a Pacific cliff and smokes a cigarette, subtly flirting with Conway's Falcon, she appears a perfect *noir* leading lady. She also appears a top suspect for the Falcon, along with Rita Corday's hysteric psychic. However, the killer is revealed to be blonde Isabel Jewell, the fortune teller from *The Leopard Man* and Jean's satanist intimate from *The Seventh Victim*, who here takes a spectacular fall from a cliff into the Pacific.

Val Lewton starred Jean for the third time in *Youth Runs Wild* (1944), a juvenile delinquency film with a troubled production history. Jean played Mary, wife of a Purple Heart soldier, who creates a day nursery in her backyard to keep children out of trouble. RKO deeply hurt Lewton by severely editing the film—an entire subplot, in which a teenager (Dickie Moore) kills his abusive father (Arthur Shields) was cut. Nevertheless, John McManus, in his New York *PM* review, called *Youth Runs Wild* "about the best handling of juvenile delinquency that has yet come to the screen."

Starring in *Youth Runs Wild* was Glenn Vernon, who later played the tragic "Painted Boy" in Lewton's *Bedlam*. He has warm memories of Lewton—and of Jean Brooks. He recently told me:

> I miss Jean—I knew her very well. She was a great little actress. She was very devoted—she always believed in, "There are no small parts, there are just small actors." When you worked a scene with her, she wanted it to be perfection, or not do it at all. She was an actress who could play any kind of part—and a really great person...
>
> Jean had an alcohol problem. During shooting, however, you'd never know it. She was always on time—in fact, before time, and she'd be there for late hours, if you had them. Never a problem.
>
> We used to go to lunch together quite a bit on the RKO lot; after the "wrap" on *Youth Runs Wild*, Jean and I went over to the "Grotto" restaurant on Melrose Avenue, right around the corner from RKO, and we had dinner and a couple of drinks. But I

> didn't realize until long after I'd done that film with her that she had trouble with alcohol.
> I thought Jean was great.

For fans of Lewton's horror classics, *Youth Runs Wild* is a curio; besides Jean Brooks and Glenn Vernon, it offers Kent Smith (Oliver from *Cat People* and *The Curse of the Cat People*) as Mary's soldier spouse and Elizabeth Russell as an uncaring mother. Also, top-billed Bonita Granville is called "Toddy"—which will be evocative for all the horror fans who recall Karloff taunting Henry Daniell in Lewton's 1945 *The Body Snatcher*.

Jean Brooks seemed on the eve of major stardom. She had played everything from a cowgirl to a devil worshipper. The next obvious move was leading lady status and "A" pictures.

Sadly, it wasn't to be.

The handwriting was on the wall with *A Night of Adventure*, in which RKO cast Jean as Julie Arden, a drunken ex-model who becomes the corpse in question. Tom Conway was the star; Audrey Long got the top female billing and the chic wardrobe. Nineteen forty-four ended for Jean in *The Falcon in Hollywood*, with Jean as Roxana, a fashion designer whose former husband, an actor, is murdered on the eve of her marriage to a prominent director (Konstantin Shayne). This time, it was Veda Ann Borg who had the flashy female honors as a sassy cabbie.

What was happening?

By the end of 1944, Jean was officially divorced from Richard Brooks, who, after working at Universal on the scripts of the Maria Montez *White Savage* and *Cobra Woman*, had joined the Marines. An interlocutory decree of divorce came through September 13, 1944. In 1982, Doug McClelland wrote to Richard Brooks (who later wed movie star Jean Simmons, and who died in 1992) in hope of locating his ex-wife. Brooks' May 12, 1982 reply:

> I'd like to help locate Jeanne Kelly for you—but how?
> I last heard from her directly (by mail) while I was in the Marine Corps (at the time stationed in Quantico). After the war ended (1945), I tried to find her. No luck. We never had many friends before the war—and fewer later.
> Someone (don't remember now who it was) at RKO said she had returned to Texas. I have not heard from her or about her since.
> It would be comforting to think she had found someone more suitable to her needs than I. Loving women should never marry writers. Writers make lousy husbands. I think I know why—but that's too long and dreary a subject...

So there were few friends. Many of Jean's family, disapproving of her entry into show business, had turned their backs on her. And, by various reports, she was drinking.

If Jean sought solace in her career, there was little to be found. Her one 1945 film was RKO's *Two o'Clock Courage*, starring the ubiquitous Tom Conway—with Jean supporting as Barbara, a stage star mixed up in murder. The *New York World-Telegram* called this new Rialto attraction "a trifle of a mystery," and noted, "The customers have a chance to glance over Ann Rutherford, Bettejane [Jane] Greer and Jean Brooks along the way. At least, it's a change from looking at Conway." That suggested "glance-over" would reveal that Jean Brooks was noticeably gaining weight.

She was also losing control. Kirk Crivello, a Hollywood historian and collector, remembers a disastrous personal appearance:

> It was September 1945, and RKO sent a bunch of the studio contract players to San Francisco for the premiere of *First Yank Into Tokyo*. They came on "The Lark," the train which arrived in San Francisco at nine o'clock in the morning, traveling through the night from Los Angeles.
>
> The stars who came that morning were Tom Neal (the star of *First Yank Into Tokyo*), who brought his then-wife, Vicky Lane [who had just played the Ape Woman in Universal's *The Jungle Captive*]; Anne Jeffreys [who had just acted in RKO's *Genius at Work*, with Lionel Atwill and Bela Lugosi]; Bettejane (Jane) Greer; and Jean Brooks.
>
> Jean Brooks, sad to say, was smashed. It was terrible. She was very, very drunk; she must have been drinking all night on the train. And she looked heavy, and bloated—not attractive like she was in films like *The Seventh Victim*. And some of the people there were laughing at her. Anne Jeffreys and Jane Greer looked so embarrassed. It was really very sad.

The studio tossed Jean into one more Falcon film, *The Falcon's Alibi* (1946), with Tom Conway, Rita Corday, and Jane Greer; Jean played a ninth-billed Baroness. It would be her eighth and final film with Conway, who would turn up decades later as an alcoholic derelict in a Venice boarding house. He died in 1967.

Jean showed possibility of facing the same fate. More personal appearance work saw Jean passing out before the beholding eyes of the public. Word came back to RKO that Jean Brooks had become "a falling-down drunk," and the studio was angry.

Jean's professional kiss of death came via *The Bamboo Blonde* (1946), a comeback for Frances Langford after her overseas entertaining, and tradeshown in New York June 13, 1946. The plot concerned a B-29 bomber pilot (Russell Wade, "Fettes" from Lewton's 1945 *The Body Snatcher*) who names his superfortress bomber "The Bamboo Blonde" after comely Miss Langford; Jean was tenth-billed in the *Variety* credits as Marsha, catty crony of the pilot's bitchy socialite fiancée (Jane Greer). Jean had little to do but make arch faces; and, despite being wrapped in furs, wearing black gowns and (more than likely) coping with a very tight corset, she looked a bit plump. Even for a player who believed "There are no small parts, only small actresses," this assignment was a humiliation for a lady who, only three years before, was playing leads.

If RKO was unhappy with Jean, the feeling was mutual. Before they could fire her, she (according to her South American obituaries) tore up her RKO contract.

She played a small role in *Women in the Night*, which starred Tala Birell and Virginia Christine, (q.v.) and was released by Film Classics in January 1948. The *Film Daily Yearbook* didn't list Jean's name in the credits. Presumably, this was her last picture.

> Anyone know the whereabouts of Jean Brooks? Once married to director Richard Brooks, thus her name, she was aka Jeanne Kelly and under contract to both Universal and RKO in the 1940s… (Even Richard Brooks and several of the actress' former pals say they've lost all contact with her whereabouts.)
>
> —*The Hollywood Reporter*, August 7, 1990

It's sad to realize that, almost 27 years before the *Hollywood Reporter* ran this paragraph in the "Rambling Reporter" column, Jean Brooks had died.

In 1949, Jean's mother died in an accident in Houston. Jean returned to Texas for the funeral at Hollywood Cemetery in Houston. She was still single at the time.

Some time later, in the mid–1950s, Jean married Thomas H. Leddy, a printer for the *San Francisco Examiner*, who was over 20 years her senior. Jean also worked for the *Examiner* as a classified ad solicitor, for the last two years of her life. Cecilia Maskell says:

> Her husband was a Catholic and Jean was a Protestant. He had to work and work to convert her to Catholicism, and to convince her not to go to so many movies and parties and to go to church more. So finally, he was able to convert her, and Jean became very actively religious before she died.

It was, however, too late for Jean to save her health. According to her death certificate, she had been suffering from "nutritional inadequacy" for 15 years, likely due to her alcoholism. For the last five years of her life, Jean was ill with "Laennec's Cirrhosis."

In November of 1963, Jean entered Kaiser Hospital in Richmond, California. She fell into a hepatic coma, and at 6:35 P.M. on November 25, 1963—the day John F. Kennedy was buried—Jean Brooks Leddy died. The death certificate gave her age as 46.

The burial of Jean Brooks, which did not take place until September 10, 1964, might have intrigued Val Lewton (who died 12 years before she did). Like Val Lewton, like Jacqueline, Jean had her own obsessive fears. Cecilia Maskell tells the sad story:

> Apparently, Jean was scared to be buried. She had some sort of fear… She wished to be buried in Costa Rica, because she had fond memories of Puntarenas, the area by the ocean (where she was arrested for wearing the "modern" bathing suit), and where the sand is largely black, because of the volcano. Also, Jean knew that in Central America, when you buy a grave, it's above the ground; you can buy the tomb for 40 years, and everybody can be buried there—you can have 12 people in one grave.
>
> Well, my theory is that her husband (who actually was very fond of her, and never got over her death) felt he didn't want to spend the money to buy such a grave, and decided to send Jean's body down there and bury her at sea, because she was fond of the ocean.

> So that's what he did.
>
> Jean died about a year before she was buried, so she must have been on ice somewhere until her husband could get all the permits. They had a little service down there, then drove her by freeway to the ocean, took the casket on a yacht called the "Chorotega"; they put a black net around the casket, and tied an anchor to it, and then they drilled holes in the casket, and they dumped it in the ocean.
>
> The casket floated for ten minutes. And then it finally sank, and they put wreathes where it sank. Before the husband died in 1980, he asked that he be cremated and his ashes spread where our cousin was, out in the ocean. So his son, Jean's stepson, did that.

"DRAMATIC BURIAL AT SEA OF EX-ACTRESS RUBY KELLY; For Ten Minutes the Casket Floated in the Water" proclaimed the front page headlines of *Diario de Costa Rica* on September 11, 1964, giving Jean all the attention due a major Hollywood movie star. The newspaper ran several large photographs of Jean's 400-pound casket, with cross, being dropped into the ocean, dramatically described the spectacle of the floating coffin, and reported how Thomas Leddy cried inconsolably after the dramatic scene:

> For a long time Tom Leddy looked at the place where his wife was laid to rest. Of these events, the only thing that was left was the wreaths floating on the water.

Back in Hollywood, there was not a single obituary. For three decades, hardly a soul even knew that Jean Brooks had died.

"Her eyes," said Gloria White, of the cousin she knew only through the movies and her research. "She looks sad. Sad eyes."

It was those eyes that had scared me most in that nightmare of 25 years ago. In my dream, Jean's Jacqueline had stared at me, just as she had stared at the audience in that famous monologue in *The Seventh Victim*; I had moved slowly toward her, just as the camera had. And then, with a shriek, she suddenly pulled out the scissors (which Jacqueline had employed to kill the investigator) and plunged them into me.

That's what caused me to wake up screaming.

As I researched this story, I watched *The Seventh Victim* again (and again). I was curious to see if that closeup would chill me, just as it had so many years before.

Now, however, there was no fear. The eyes that had scared me so no longer upset me. They were, indeed, "sad eyes." There was no evil in them—just sadness, loneliness, despair. I felt no terror, but sorrow for a lonely lady who, like Val Lewton, and like all of us, had to deal with her own fears, disappointments and anxieties.

The angel in the Cleopatra wig no longer seemed so exotic, satanic. Rather, she seemed what Val Lewton probably had most wanted her to be ... lost, lovely and tragic.

And that night, there was no nightmare.

The Films of Jean Brooks

1935

Obeah (Arcturus Pictures, F. Herrick Herrick)
Frankie and Johnnie (RKO/Republic, John H. Auer)
Tango Bar (Spanish-Paramount, John Reinhardt)
The Crime of Doctor Crespi (Republic, J. Auer)

1939

Miracle on Main Street (Columbia, Steve Sekely)
Miracle on Main Street (Spanish-language version, Steven Sekely)
El otro soy yo (Paramount, Richard Harlan)
El trovador de la radio (Paramount, Richard Harlan)

1940

The Invisible Killer (PRC, Sherman Scott [Sam Newfield])
Son of Roaring Dan (Universal, Ford Beebe)
The Devil's Pipeline (Universal, Christy Cabanne)
Flash Gordon Conquers the Universe (Universal 12-chapter serial, F. Beebe and Ray Taylor)

1941

Buck Privates (Universal, Arthur Lubin)
Meet the Chump (Universal, Edward F. Cline)
A Dangerous Game (Universal, John Rawlins)
Too Many Blondes (Universal, Thornton Freeland)
Man from Montana (Univeral, Ray Taylor)
Riders of Death Valley (Universal 15-chapter serial, F. Beebe and R. Taylor)
The Green Hornet Strikes Again (Universal 15 chapter serial; F. Beebe and J. Rawlins)

1942

Fighting Bill Fargo (Universal, R. Taylor)
Klondike Fury (Monogram, William K. Howard)
Boot Hill Bandits (Monogram, S. Roy Luby)
Boss of Big Town (PRC, Arthur Dreifuss)

1943

The Falcon Strikes Back (RKO, Edward Dmytryk)
The Leopard Man (RKO, Jacques Tourneur)
The Falcon in Danger (RKO, William Clemens)
The Seventh Victim (RKO, Mark Robson)
The Falcon and the Co-Eds (RKO, W. Clemens)

1944

Youth Runs Wild (RKO, M. Robson)
A Night of Adventure (RKO, Gordon Douglas)
The Falcon in Hollywood (RKO, G. Douglas)

1945

Two o'Clock Courage (RKO, Anthony Mann)

1946

The Falcon's Alibi (RKO, Raymond McCarey)
The Bamboo Blonde (RKO, A. Mann)

1948

Women in the Night (Film Classics, William Rowland)

Louise Allbritton

The legend goes that, one day at Universal, early in 1943, the *Son of Dracula* company enjoyed an unforgettable practical joke.

Director Robert Siodmak set up the scene—the discovery of the body of Southern belle Katherine Caldwell, resting in the family crypt, actually under the spell of vampirism. Romantic lead Robert Paige, veteran character player Frank Craven and other actors rehearsed; the actress playing the vampire was already in her coffin, the lid closed.

"Action!" called Siodmak—and Paige grimly opened the coffin lid.

And there in the casket—wearing only her black wig and a sly grin—was *Son of Dracula*'s "vampire bride," Louise Allbritton.

Some versions claim Louise was wearing a flesh-tinted body stocking; a few claim that infamous "outtake" still lurks deep in Universal's vaults. A few cynics opine that, considering the rapid pace necessary to shoot *Son of Dracula*, there probably was no time for such a practical joke at all.

Yet it's a perfect anecdote to accompany a performance which—along with Ingrid Bergman of *Dr. Jekyll and Mr. Hyde*, Simone Simon (q.v.) of *Cat People*, Ilona Massey (q.v.) of *Frankenstein Meets the Wolf Man* and Linda Darnell of *Hangover Square*—is one of the most sexy performances of 1940s horror.

Trained in Shakespeare at the Pasadena Playhouse, noted for her "screwball," Carole Lombard–style performances in Universal comedies, the blonde, blue-eyed, five-foot, seven-and-a-half-inch Louise threw herself into the macabre spirit of *Son of Dracula* the same way she approached everything: from her pursuit of an acting career (in fiery defiance of her wealthy Texan father), to sports (breaking her nose three times), to being a Hollywood "playgirl" (her off-screen flirtation with one noted Hollywood "heavy" reportedly contributing to his self-destructive demise), to, finally, matrimony (to famed reporter Charles Collingwood, for whom she sublimated her career—and to whom she stayed married until her death in 1979).

She was sleek, energetic and sophisticated, both on screen and in life. And in the canon of Universal horror, Louise Allbritton achieved a wonderful, sex-reversal status: She played the woman who seduced Count Dracula.

Louise Allbritton was born in Oklahoma City July 3, 1920. The family moved to Wichita Falls, Texas; her mother, Caroline, died when Louise was a child, and Louise grew up waging affectionate war with her father, L. L. Allbritton, whom one Hollywood columnist later described as "a big shot Texan with a temper." In 1942, United Press Hollywood columnist Fred Othman described Louise thusly:

> She is the lady who helped her father run for mayor of Wichita Falls. She helped him with his speeches and gave him a lot of good advice. He lost.

Mr. Allbritton, who had eventually bought a 100,000-acre Texas ranch, hoped his daughter would pursue her early flair as a writer and cartoonist. After an English

***Chapter opener:* Publicity portrait of Allbritton for *Son of Dracula*, 1943.**

teacher got Louise hooked on acting by having her read aloud from the classics, Allbritton sent his daughter to the University of Oklahoma. She retaliated by taking every drama course the college offered, and—after two years—running away to California to join the famous Pasadena Playhouse.

When Louise arrived at Pasadena, she weighed 165 pounds. She energetically lost 40 lbs. via an apple diet, morning running and steambaths, and soon scored at the Playhouse in such plays as *The Comedy of Errors*, *Lost Horizon*, *Dinner at Eight*, *The Merchant of Venice* (as Portia) and *The Little Foxes*. When her father learned of her success, he slashed her allowance; as Doug McClelland reported in his *Screen Facts* profile of Louise, "Allbritton's landlady staked her—even to long-distance calls to Wichita Falls to sound off her defiance." Yet, as Louise later remembered of her relationship with her volatile dad:

> When things looked blackest, I always said to myself, "Listen, Louise. What's the worst thing that can happen? Only that you'll wind up back on a lovely ranch, very comfortably off."

But she wouldn't go back to the ranch; Louise aggressively campaigned for a movie offer. When she realized how tall she looked in casting offices while standing beside her 5'4" agent, Louise mandated that the agent wear "lifts" while she wore "flats." Finally, Columbia offered *Not a Ladies' Man* (1942), which offered a faint prophecy of Louise's horror-celebrity-to-come: The star was *King Kong*'s Fay Wray and the director was *The Raven*'s Lew Landers. She followed at Columbia with *Parachute Nurse* (1942), directed by Charles (*Abbott and Costello Meet Frankenstein*) Barton.

"I played the parachute, I think," quipped Louise afterwards.

Then Universal City made an offer. The try-out: *Danger in the Pacific*, a 60-minute potboiler in which Louise had the lead role of an aviatrix. The cast included Don Terry, Andy Devine, Leo Carrillo, Edgar Barrier and Turhan Bey; horror fans, however, will be most interested in the scene where Louise meets (and looms over) Dwight Frye, the erstwhile Renfield of *Dracula* and Fritz of *Frankenstein*, here reduced to the unbilled bit part of a hotel clerk. If stardom was on the horizon for Louise, who now won a Universal contract, it was long forsaken by Frye, who would die a year after *Danger in the Pacific*'s release.

Universal paired Louise and Patric Knowles as the romantic leads of Abbott and Costello's *Who Done It?* (1942), then cast the new contractee in *Pittsburgh* (1942), with Marlene Dietrich, John Wayne and Randolph Scott; it afforded her PR as the actress "successful in winning John Wayne away from the glamorous Dietrich." By the end of 1942, Louise Allbritton was a Hollywood star; Harriet Parsons, in her "Keyhole Portrait" column (11/29/42), introduced Louise to her readership:

> Off-screen she's Miss Perpetual Motion, a human dynamo, a young cyclone ... when she undertakes anything, whether it's losing five pounds or learning a new dive, she wants to do it all at once ... whatever is worth doing, she thinks, is worth doing hard ... which explains why she's broken her nose three times ... first time was at 13 during a scrimmage with the grade school football team ... second time was when she tried to do a perfect

Pasadena Playhouse boasted alumna Louise Allbritton in this *Theatre Arts* magazine advertisement from the early 1940s.

> jack-knife dive and hit the springboard instead of the water ... third (and final she hopes) break was the result of a little error in judgement while high-diving ... she ploughed into the side of the pool... "It's a wonder I don't look like Maxie Rosenbloom," she says ... but despite so much smacking around, the Allbritton pan is a very pleasant sight ... when she breezes across the lot, the boys whistle ... even though she's usually wearing blue jeans and pull-over sweater and travelling almost too fast for the naked eye to see ... on her way to the commissary the other day, she passed Abbott and Costello in high gear... Costello did a double take and cracked, "If Universal could find some way of tapping that girl for energy they could padlock the powerhouse for the duration."

Within a year at Universal, Louise Allbritton had become a marquee name. The studio's award was something Louise never expected.

> "I see you marrying a corpse! Living in a grave!"
>
> —Prophecy of "Madame Zimba" (Adeline deWalt Reynolds) to Katherine Caldwell (Louise Allbritton) in *Son of Dracula*

Like so many of the Universal horror films, *Son of Dracula* had its own peculiar genesis, and behind-the-scenes dynamics:

After European émigré Curt Siodmak attained a bit of clout at Universal, following his classic scripts for *The Wolf Man* and *Frankenstein Meets the Wolf Man*, he asked the front office a favor: "Please—give my brother Robert a job." Curt's older brother was a superbly stylish director, whose 1928 *Menschen am Sonntag* virtually started the careers of six people: directors Billy Wilder (who, according to Robert, his roommate at the time, worked "about an hour" on the screenplay), Edgar G. (*The Black Cat*) Ulmer, Fred Zinnemann, cinematographer Eugen Schufftan—and Curt and Robert Siodmak. Robert went on to films like *Sturme der Leidenschaft*, starring Emil Jannings and featuring one of Robert's pet themes: betrayal of a man by a woman. In fact, Robert was so adept at sexual tension in his films that Goebbels labeled him "a corruptor of the German family"—and he (and Curt) fled to Paris.

In France, Robert directed films like *La Crise est finie* (Curt worked on the screenplay) and *Pièges*, a tale of French police employing a girl who tricks an old man (Pierre Renoir) into proving he's the ripper who's been slaying prostitutes; the cast included Erich von Stroheim and (in a non-singing role) Maurice Chevalier! Curt, meanwhile, had gone to London, then Hollywood; Robert fled Paris the day before the German troops arrived. By the time Robert reached Hollywood, Curt—working at Paramount on *Aloma of the South Seas*—persuaded the studio to give his emigre brother a director's job.

It hadn't worked out. Robert made Paramount "Bs" like *West Point Widow* (1941) and *My Heart Belongs to Daddy* (1942); the studio also loaned him out to Fox and Republic; and after Robert (according to Curt) denounced the work as "Paramount shit," the studio fired him.

Once again, Curt had come to the rescue. Universal signed Robert and assigned him *Son of Dracula*, for which Curt had written the story. Jack Edmund Nolan, in his profile of Robert Siodmak in *Films in Review* (April 1969), quotes the director:

> The script was terrible—it had been knocked together in a few days. I told my wife I just couldn't do it, but she said, "Look! They've been making those films for 20 years and know exactly what to expect from a director. If you're a little bit better than the other directors, they'll take notice, and it will lead to better things."

So Robert accepted the job—and, as one of his first moves, took Curt off the picture.

Lon Chaney, meanwhile, had played the Wolf Man, the Frankenstein Monster and the Mummy; Universal probably figured the role of Dracula was the latest jewel in the crown of the actor they billed as "The Screen's Master Character Creator." But Lon wasn't so pleased; the role he really wanted was the *Phantom of the Opera*, so he could emulate and (in his dreams) "top" his father's classic 1925 performance. Universal awarded the Phantom role to Claude Rains in its Technicolor, $1,750,000 spectacular, which would start shooting less than two weeks after *Son of Dracula*'s start date. (Actually, the part Chaney wanted most of all was the real-life one of marine cook, and the 36-year-old alcoholic actor was trying very hard to get into the military throughout the shooting of *Son of Dracula*.)

Alan Curtis, then licking his wounds from his divorce from Ilona Massey, was assigned the romantic lead role in *Son of Dracula*—only to suffer a knee injury a week into the shooting. Universal replaced him with Robert Paige.

Finally, there was the casting of Katherine "Kay" Caldwell, the Louisiana belle whose morbid fascinations lead her to become the bride of Count Dracula (or of his son, depending on how one interprets the script). Eric Taylor, who wrote the screenplay dated December 23, 1942, might have had Louise in mind when he described Katherine:

Louise Allbritton and Lon Chaney, Jr., in *Son of Dracula*, 1943.

The girl is beautiful, tall, statuesque and appears rather eager as she peers off into the darkness…

Louise allowed Jack P. Pierce to crown her with a sultry black wig—which not only gave Louise a sinister, *femme fatale* look, but contrasted nicely with blonde Evelyn Ankers, who played Katherine's "better-adjusted" sister, Claire. Production began

Allbritton, with blonde pompadour, in a publicity portrait for *Good Morning, Judge*, 1943.

January 7, 1943. Robert Siodmak finalized shooting plans and, at a try-out director's salary of $150 per week, began shooting *Son of Dracula*.

From her first entrance in *Son of Dracula*—on the veranda of her plantation, "Dark Oaks," in the Louisiana bayous—Louise Allbritton makes a sexy, sinister impression. In her black wig and flowing, Vera West gown which looks like a shroud, she makes Katherine Caldwell a vampiric Scarlett O'Hara. In the course of this remarkably morbid film, Louise subtly dominates, playing Delilah to Chaney's porcine Count as Siodmak stages wonderful episodes:

• There is *Son of Dracula*'s (probably) most famous vignette, in which Louise stands on the shore of a bayou as Chaney's coffin rises from the swamps; a mist appears on the casket, and Chaney stands on this "punt," floating to his fiancée, whom he weds that night as lightning flickers, winds howl and thunder crashes outside the door of the justice of the peace.

• There's the sequence in which Frank (Robert Paige), Kay's childhood friend and fiancé, shows up at Dark Oaks and tries to shoot Dracula. The bullets pass through the vampire—and Dracula's bride falls gracefully to the floor. While no special effects were necessary for this scene, it's wonderfully effective.

• There's Dr. Brewster's call at Dark Oaks, after Frank insists he has killed Kay; the actor finds Katherine sitting up in a four-poster bed, clearly alive but frighteningly pale and sensually sinister as she insists they have no daytime visitors.

• Of course, Katherine's plan is a sly one: She has married Count Dracula, only to betray him. In the jail cell where Frank has been incarcerated, she outlines her evil plan: Frank is to destroy Dracula, and the two of them will be immortal. And when Kay's sister Claire announces plans to cremate her sister's body, Kay's plan becomes even more wicked: She wishes to destroy her own sister, as well as Frank Craven's Dr. Brewster and J. Edward Bromberg's Prof. Lazlo (a potato dumpling version of Prof. Van Helsing).

Of course, the climax of *Son of Dracula* is the most unusual feature. In Siodmak style, Chaney's Dracula meets a degrading fate, courtesy of the woman he loved: Paige sets fire to Chaney's lair in the drainage tunnel, and a bellowing Chaney—caught in the sun—plops into the muck, his skeletal hand jutting from the water with Universal's famous Dracula ring on its bony finger. Then Paige keeps his rendezvous with Kay, in the old attic playroom where they had spent time as children. As she sleeps, he places his ring on Kay's finger. And, in a surprisingly grim finale, beautifully scored by Hans J. Salter, the heroes arrive to find the attic in flames. Frank has cremated Kay, to free her soul from the curse of vampirism.

Son of Dracula plays as one of the most morbid horror films of '40s Universal. The episode in which Dracula, in bat form, chases Frank to the cemetery under a full moon, crawls upon the unconscious man's neck, then flees when the shadow of a graveyard cross falls upon him, is masterfully staged. Kay also visits Frank's jail cell, in bat form, and Siodmak has the camera linger as the bat almost sensually begins feeding on the sleeping man's throat. One of the top ironies is that Evelyn Ankers, who most fans would guess was on hand to dry Paige's tears and walk off with him in the finale, is nowhere in sight at the end.

Son of Dracula had its problems. Curt Siodmak has oft-told the story of Chaney, in a violent drunken mood, sneaking up behind the fastidious Robert Siodmak and smashing a vase over his bald head. Also, as Robert Paige remembered, Louise sometimes left the stage in tears and fled to her dressing room. While this might partly have been due to her discomfort in so atypical a role, Paige claimed it was primarily because she was so emotional an actress, so caught up in the Gothic romance, that she often just lost control.

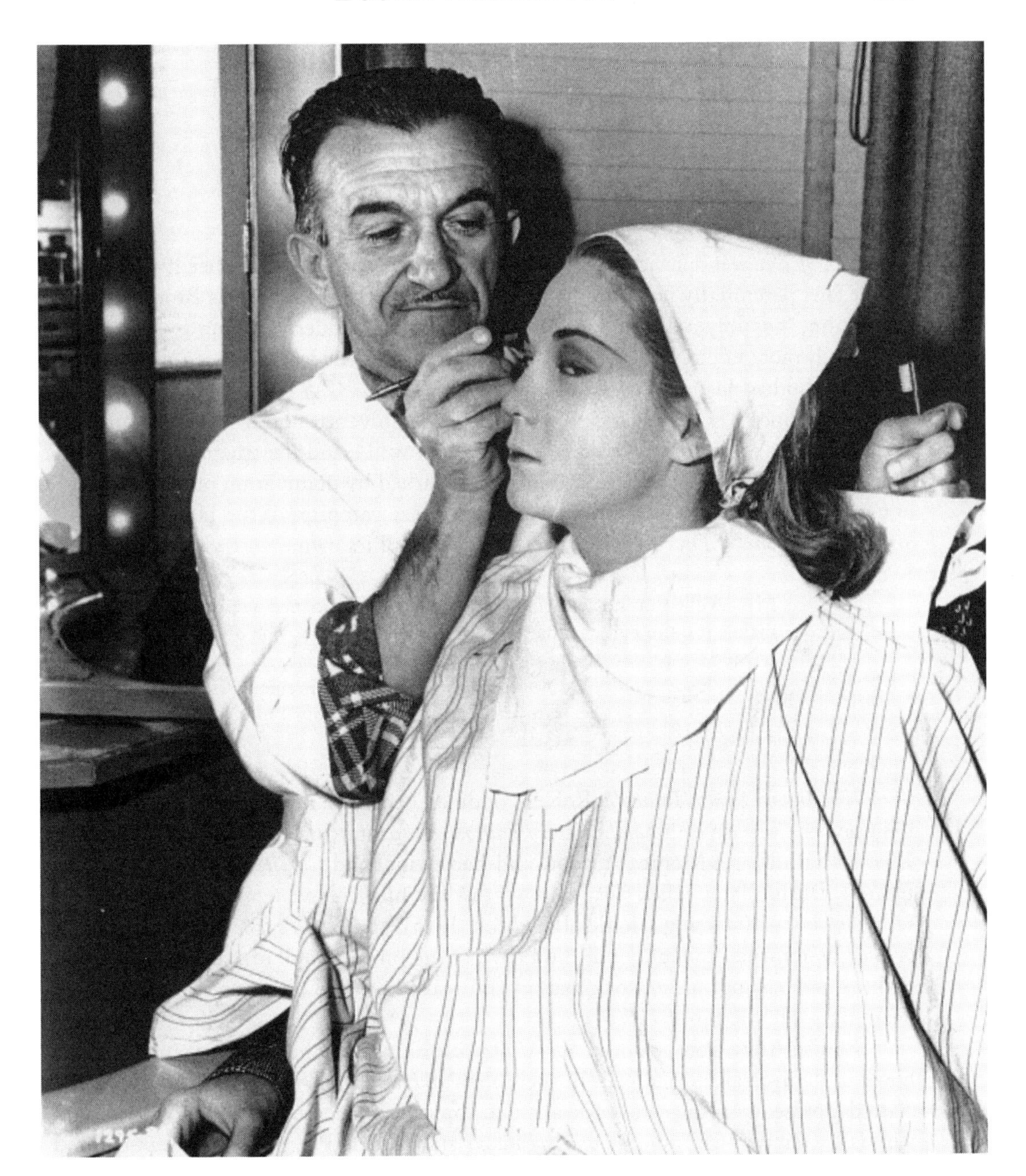

Jack Pierce prepares Allbritton for her black wig and succubus makeup for *Son of Dracula*, 1943.

Still, high spirits prevailed (as well as that famous gag with Louise naked, or in body-stocking, in the coffin). When shooting "wrapped" early in February of 1943, the cast principals signed Robert Siodmak's script:

> I can't wish all foreigners luck but I do for you. LON.
>
> With best wishes and appreciation for your swell direction!
> EVELYN ANKERS.

> To Robert—With thanx and all of the best. JOE BROMBERG.
>
> My dear Siodmak—With all your faults, I love you still—old song. With sincere good wishes, FRANK CRAVEN.
>
> Thanks, Bob, for everything. You gave me a lot, including a great deal of respect for your "touch." Best of luck and happiness! LOUISE ALLBRITTON.

Son of Dracula opened at New York's Rialto Theatre in November 1943. Many horror fans perennially lament Chaney's miscasting as Dracula (or, as Bromberg says in the film, "possibly a descendant of Count Dracula"); indeed, it's fun to imagine how much more effective *Son of Dracula* would be had the vampire been played by Lugosi (who had just completed *Frankenstein Meets the Wolf Man* at Universal) or John Carradine (who had just completed his first Universal horror movie, *Captive Wild Woman*). Yet Siodmak handles Chaney very well—and the true menace of *Son of Dracula* is Louise Allbritton. In a genre trademarked by domination of females, she out-vamps Dracula himself, foreshadowing the sexy vampires of the Hammer films and sparking *Son of Dracula* with an exotic charm all its own.

> Miss Allbritton not only checks in a slick performance but also makes it quite evident that she's on her way to being one of Hollywood's top comediennes if given the right material...
>
> —*New York Journal-American* review of Universal's *San Diego, I Love You* (11/10/44)

Thanks to *Son of Dracula*, Robert Siodmak became a major director at Universal; 1944 saw the release of his *noir* piece *Phantom Lady* (starring Ella Raines), *Cobra Woman* (with Maria Montez as good-and-bad twins) and *Christmas Holiday* (which Deanna Durbin later called her "only worthwhile film"). He later scored with Universal's *The Suspect* (starring Charles Laughton, 1945), and RKO's *The Spiral Staircase* (1946); he returned to Europe in the 1950s, living on the shore of Lake Maggiore in Switzerland, toying in the stock market and real estate and directing various European films. He died in 1971.

Louise Allbritton's work in *Son of Dracula* didn't earn her such rewards. She was, however, Universal's top farceur in such films as *Her Primitive Man* (1944), which starred Louise as "bring-'em-back-alive" anthropologist/lecturer Sheila Winthrop, who falls (temporarily) for *Son of Dracula* co-star Robert Paige's riotous, war-painted impersonation of a Lupari headhunter. *This Is the Life* (1944), starring Donald O'Connor and Susanna Foster (q.v.) (following her hit performance in *Phantom of the Opera*), found both O'Connor and Patric Knowles in love with Foster, and O'Connor delivering the incredible line, "We both have a yen for the same wren"; Louise was Harriet, whose "more mature allure" (as New York's *PM* put it) eventually captured Knowles. It was based on a play by Fay Wray and Sinclair Lewis, *Angela Is 22. San Diego, I Love You* (1944), directed by horror specialist Reginald LeBorg (*The Mummy's Ghost*, *Weird Woman*, et al.) gave Louise her favorite role: Virginia McCooley, beauty in a house full of eccentrics, who tries passionately to sell her father's collapsible life

Allbritton in Saks Fifth Avenue finery for a 1944 Universal publicity shot.

raft. As Doug McClelland wrote in a *Screen Facts* profile of Louise, "appearing in almost every scene, the star kept the picture afloat with her energetic, airy performance in a particularly Carole Lombardish role (pratfalls, black eyes, dunkings, etc.)." Also in 1944, Louise was a member of Universal's "Hollywood Victory Committee" (i.e., the virtual contract roster) in *Follow the Boys*, and was a very glamorous Lillian Russell, singing "Under the Bamboo Tree" in the studio's *Bowery to Broadway*.

Meanwhile, off-screen, Louise proved a dynamo in the gossip columns. Between late October of 1943 and early January of 1944, she was reported to be seriously romancing a major, a private and a lieutenant (with whom she reportedly almost eloped to Las Vegas). In February of 1944, she was touring the Mediterranean war zone in a U.S.O. show (headlined by George Raft until he was forced to come home with a sinus condition); Louise gained six pounds on G.I. food, and told the *Los Angeles Examiner* upon her return:

> It was the most unforgettable experience of my life. At Cassino, we were taken within a mile of the front to play for men who had been pulled out of battle for a few hours' rest. The American artillery was behind us and several times the noise of our 240-mm. guns stopped the show. But there was no time for the men to be moved further back for the show. They see movies under the same conditions—sitting in the rain, with gunfire drowning out the sound track.
>
> As soon as I have made one picture, I want to go again!

There was one area where Louise's high energy was, perhaps, misdirected. Laird Cregar's performance as *The Lodger* (20th Century-Fox, 1944) had everybody talking about the young actor's powerhouse Jack the Ripper performance; more sophisticated audiences gossiped about the effeminate touches that Cregar (quite well-known as a homosexual in Hollywood) gave the Ripper. Louise supposedly made a bet with her Hollywood playgirl friends that she could seduce Laird (who was a fellow Pasadena Playhouse alumnus) and "bring out the man" in him. According to mere gossip, she tried, and he responded—but without full success. It reputedly became one of the many private and professional woes that propelled Cregar to diet mercilessly during the fall 1944 shooting of *Hangover Square*, believing a weight loss would be a panacea for his many woes. Instead, he died December 9, 1944, following an abdominal operation, his heart fatally weakened by the diet regime; he was 31 years old. If true, in all fairness, Louise's worldly bet was just one of many agonies that brought on the self-destruction of this brilliant and tragically complex actor.

On September 11, 1944, Louise guest-starred on radio's *Globe Theatre* in "Phantom Lady," an adaptation of the *noir* thriller Robert Siodmak had directed for Universal, playing the role Ella Raines had portrayed in the film.

She played in two Universal 1945 comedy releases. *Men in Her Diary* cast her as Isabel Glenning, an insanely jealous wife who discovers the "dream romance" diary of her husband's (Jon Hall) scraggly secretary (Peggy Ryan). The *New York Herald-Tribune* critiqued, "Peggy Ryan plays the ugly duckling role as though she were dodging old eggs and cabbages; Jon Hall reaches a new high in 'phony' acting as the boss, and Louise Allbritton plays the boss's wife with her tongue halfway through her cheek." The supporting cast included Alan Mowbray, Virginia Grey, Ernest Truex and "Slapsie Maxie" Rosenbloom. *That Night with You* boasted Susanna Foster, Franchot Tone, David Bruce and Louise, the last as Sheila Morgan, a comic secretary.

Louise's only 1946 Universal release was *Tangier*, a Maria Montez espionage saga; George Waggner, who had made his mark at Universal as director/associate producer of *The Wolf Man* and producer of such classics as *The Ghost of Frankenstein*,

Frankenstein Meets the Wolf Man and *Phantom of the Opera*, ended his Universal sojourn as director of this film—which saw Louise and Preston Foster falling to their deaths in an amok elevator.

Louise's big news of 1946, however, was her marriage. On May 13, 1946, she married Charles Collingwood, the famed news commentator, at the Little Church Around the Corner in New York City. Louise had met Collingwood during her U.S.O. tour in North Africa; the adventurous radio correspondent had gone on to land at Utah Beach two hours after the D-Day invasion, travelling on through France and Germany to the fall of Berlin. The groom was 29, the bride 25. "I'm very, very happy," Louise told Louella Parsons.

After the marriage, Louise cut back on her career activity, and the 1940s saw her in only five more films; Universal's merger with International might have ended in bankruptcy but for *The Egg and I* (1947), the giant box office hit based on the Betty MacDonald best-seller, starring Fred MacMurray and Claudette Colbert, and introducing Marjorie Main and Percy Kilbride as Ma and Pa Kettle; Louise was delightful as the vampy neighbor, who tries to lure MacMurray with her "new machinery." *Sitting Pretty* (20th Century–Fox, 1948) gave moviegoers Clifton Webb, winning a best Actor Academy nomination as Mr. Belvedere; Louise played Maureen O'Hara's gossipy sister.*

Louise was back as "the other woman" in United Artist's *Don't Trust Your Husband* (1948), with Fred MacMurray and Madeliene Carroll as the leads; far down the cast list was an actress dumped by Universal just as Louise was joining the fold: Anne Nagel (q.v.). Louise was a Russian-speaking "red herring" in Columbia's FBI semi-documentary *Walk a Crooked Mile*, with Dennis O'Keefe and Louis Hayward, and stayed at Columbia for what would be her last film for 15 years: *The Doolins of Oklahoma* (1949), a Randolph Scott oater with Louise as Rose of Cimarron.

In 1946, Louise was an attraction of the radio show *Hollywood Jackpot*, and in the late 1940s, played summer stock in *Love from a Stranger*. Come 1949, she moved to Washington, D.C., with husband Collingwood, where he was the CBS capitol correspondent until 1952. He later headed CBS news offices in London and Paris, and he and Louise enjoyed a very social life in what Doug McClelland later described as "the best international circles."

However, "ham" was in Louise's blood, and she often grabbed chances to act. She toured stock and "the Caribbean circuit" in such plays as *The Philadelphia Story*, *There's Always Juliet*, *Affairs of State* and *A Roomful of Roses*. On May 27, 1952, she and Dana Andrews were guest stars on radio's *Cavalcade of America* in "Valley of the Swans." On November 6, 1952, she opened in New Haven in the pre–Broadway tryout of *Rise by Sin*, but it never made it to New York. She replaced the lead in Broadway's *The Seven Year Itch* during her vacation and, in 1955, starred on the NBC daily soap, *Concerning Miss Marlowe*.

"They've talked and talked about our having a husband-and-wife show," said Louise at this time, as Collingwood worked at CBS, "but I'm too stupid."

*The Egg and I *spawned Universal-International's Ma and Pa Kettle series for Marjorie Main (Oscar nominated for* The Egg and I*) and Percy Kilbride, while* Sitting Pretty *provided Webb with the Mr. Belvedere spin-offs.*

"And I'm a lousy actor," said Collingwood. In December 1955, Louise made her Broadway debut in *Third Person*, a play about homosexuality, starring Bradford Dillman. The play ran 84 performances, and the *New York Times* saluted Louise as "a handsome woman with a fine figure and winning manners." The same month that *Third Person* opened, the *New York Post* reported that a thief had "escaped with $5,000 to $8,000 worth of jewelry" (including Louise's platinum wedding ring) from the Collingwoods' three-floor apartment at 120 East 65th Street. Surprised by the housekeeper, the thief had left behind another $15,000 in jewelry and $10,000 worth of furs.

From 1957 to 1959, the Collingwoods lived in England, where Louise made her London stage debut in 1958 in *A Touch of the Sun*, with no less than Sir Michael Redgrave and Lady Diana Wynyard.

Louise wanted the role in *Breakfast at Tiffany's* that Patricia Neal nabbed; her swan song came in 1964, when TV director David E. Durston (who had known Louise at the Pasadena Playhouse) cast her in the juicy role of the wealthy widow of a famed humanitarian who blames herself for his accidental death and becomes an alcoholic recluse, in the mystery *Felicia*. Unfortunately, the film—her first in color—was never released.

Once again the Collingwoods returned to London, where they lived from 1964 to 1975. Before Charles and Louise returned to New York, Queen Elizabeth named Collingwood an honorary commander of the Most Excellent Order of the British Empire. Louise travelled the world with her husband of many honors, enjoying her reputation as one of New York's most popular hostesses, and living fully and elegantly.

On February 16, 1979, the 58-year-old Louise died of cancer at a hospital in Puerto Vallarta, Mexico, where she and Collingwood enjoyed a resort home. There was a memorial service at St. James Episcopal Church in New York City.

"Film fans remember Louise as the beautiful star of *Pittsburgh*, *Sitting Pretty* and *The Egg and I*," wrote columnist Liz Smith. "But some of us simply remember her as a great friend who will be sorely missed."

The star horror fans remember so vividly for *Son of Dracula* was cremated, and her husband of almost 33 years scattered her ashes near their home at Puerto Vallarta, Mexico.

The Films of Louise Allbritton

1942

Not a Ladies' Man (Columbia, Lew Landers)
Parachute Nurse (Columbia, Charles T. Barton)
Danger in the Pacific (Universal, Lewis D. Collins)
Who Done It? (Universal, Erle C. Kenton)
Pittsburgh (Universal, Lewis Seiler)

1943

It Comes Up Love (Universal, Charles Lamont)
Good Morning, Judge (Universal, Jean Yarbrough)
Fired Wife (Universal, C. Lamont)
Son of Dracula (Universal, Robert Siodmak)

1944

Her Primitive Man (Universal, C. Lamont)
Follow the Boys (Universal, Eddie Sutherland)
This Is the Life (Universal, Felix Feist)
San Diego, I Love You (Universal, Reginald LeBorg)
Bowery to Broadway (Universal, C. Lamont)

1945

Men in Her Diary (Universal, C. T. Barton)

That Night with You (Universal, William A. Seiter)

1946

Tangier (Universal, George Waggner)

1947

The Egg And I (Universal-International, Chester Erskine)

1948

Sitting Pretty (20th Century–Fox, Walter Lang)

Don't Trust Your Husband (United Artists, Lloyd Bacon)

Walk a Crooked Mile (Columbia, Gordon Douglas)

1949

The Doolins of Oklahoma (Columbia, G. Douglas)

1964

Felicia (Associated Producers, David E. Durston)

Elena Verdugo

April 20, 1944.

For weeks, *House of Frankenstein*, fated to be hawked by Universal as THE GREATEST SHOCK-SHOW THE SCREEN HAS EVER SEEN!, had been shooting under the working title of *The Devil's Brood.* Stage 17 was the haunted house of the lot, as Boris Karloff's mad Dr. Niemann, Lon Chaney's Wolf Man, J. Carrol Naish's hunchback and Glenn Strange's Frankenstein Monster all lurked within the sound stage shadows; John Carradine, in Dracula's cape and top hat, would join the "brood" the following week.

On this day, however, there came from the stage—singing. Karloff, Chaney, Naish and even Strange's Monster were all warbling a chorus of "Happy Birthday."

And beaming at the cake, in her black wig, gypsy garb and wonderful smile, was Elena Verdugo, who was playing Ilonka, the tragic gypsy girl—and who turned 19 that day.

In this three-ring circus of horror—Chaney's Wolf Man, Carradine's Dracula and Glenn Strange's Monster, with no less than Boris Karloff as ringmaster (complete with top hat!) and J. Carrol Naish as hunchbacked major domo—it was amazing that a leading lady could command any attention. Yet Elena Verdugo did so. As *House of Frankenstein*'s Esmeralda to Naish's hunchback, Elena gave a showcase performance—performing a gypsy dance, falling in love with the Wolf Man, flirting, crying, screaming and playing an operatic, *Romeo and Juliet*-style death scene in which she shoots Chaney's Larry Talbot with a silver bullet (that she made) and—fatally mauled in the bargain—crawls through the misty, Grimm Brothers forest to die with her head on his chest.

It's one of the best-remembered female performances of Universal horror—a portrayal that wonderfully captures the folklore of the lycanthrope. There was only one more Universal horror film for Elena Verdugo: the dreary "Inner Sanctum" *The Frozen Ghost.* Her later work ranged from Gene Autry's leading lady in *The Big Sombrero* to star in such TV series as *Meet Millie* and *Marcus Welby, M.D.*—always with a wonderful, trademark vivacity.

It's a vivacity which is very much a part of this lovely lady herself.

> Every time someone would write about me, they'd say, "Oh, Elena Verdugo—daughter of the Dons." And I think it, unfortunately or fortunately, typecast me. With that name, they don't call you up to do little American parts. They think you're a black-eyed, dark-haired senorita—and I'm blonde. So I put on my wig and tried to live up to what they thought "Spanish" to be—or "gypsy," or "native," or something.
>
> —Elena Verdugo

Elena Verdugo was born in Paso Robles, California, on April 20, 1925. Her ancestor was no less than Jose Maria Verdugo, who once owned the land on which Universal City (founded in 1915) still stands today:

***Chapter opener:* Elena Verdugo treats Lon Chaney, Jr., to a pedicure on the set of *House of Frankenstein*, 1944.**

> It's true. Much of North Hollywood, Studio City, Glendale, Burbank and Universal City was the original Spanish land grant, 36,000 acres, to Jose Maria Verdugo, a soldier in the Spanish army and my ancestor. He was a very dramatic individual; he would ride around on his horse and look at his land. He had his sisters and his brothers up in the Glendale mountains and hills, and they lived like Spanish Dons. I once got a laugh when I reminded an irritating director at Universal that he was standing on my property!
>
> My parents divorced when I was very young, so I never met those Verdugos—although they do "claim" me! They have Verdugo Days, and I've ridden in that parade, and it's wonderful to be part of that history.

Los Angeles had long since absorbed the Verdugo land grant by the time Elena was born. Hers was a show business family; "Almost all of my family were in some area of film or music locally," says Elena. At age five, she made her first movie, *Cavalier of the West* (1931):

> I remember that, in *Cavalier of the West*, I wasn't going to smile. The little dress I was wearing scratched me, because they had put little sparkles on it, and every time my arms brushed against it, it hurt. And the director gave me a dollar, which was put in my little dress, and said, "Won't you *please* smile?" Whether I did or not, I don't know!

Thereafter, Elena became a seasoned Spanish dancer: "I danced at every benefit, every California-type gathering... I danced at Los Angeles theaters for various Spanish shows, I danced at the Wilshire-Ebell, the Hollywood Bowl—I was dancing all the time." She also trained at the Ben Bard Drama School. Finally came the big break: a featured dancing spot in *Down Argentine Way*, a 1940 20th Century-Fox Technicolor musical starring Betty Grable, Don Ameche and Carmen Miranda:

> I remember going to Fox Studios—we had to park outside and traipse in, because we weren't anybody, and they didn't make it easy for you in those days. I went in with my mother, and aunt, who was the accompanist on the piano, and we forgot my dancing shoes—I was dancing in my regular shoes. But I started dancing, and all of a sudden, [dance choreographer] Nick Castle said, "Just a minute," and he called [associate producer] Harry Joe Brown and brought him down. He said, "Do you have another number?" and I had another one, so he was calling people to come in and see this girl dance. So I did *Down Argentine Way*—about 16 bars of dancing.
>
> It was very nice! I went on location with Betty Grable, and she was just wonderful—so darling. This was her first big picture at Fox, and she didn't know if she wanted to stay in movies or not. Then they called me back to do another scene in the picture, where I danced, and smiled...

It was one of the most dazzling smiles in Hollywood, and along with her dancing, it won Elena a Fox contract. On October 11, 1940, the *Los Angeles Examiner* reported:

> Hollywood has reached into the ranks of one of California's oldest families in its unending search for talent... Elena Verdugo, 15 ... appeared before Superior Judge Emmett H. Wilson for approval of her contract with 20th Century–Fox... Studio officials expect to groom her for feature dancing roles.

Elena sojourned at Fox. Many reference books list her as one of the Spanish dancers in 1941's Technicolor *Blood and Sand* (but she denies playing in it); she was cut out of *Belle Starr* (1941). Her favorite memory of the lot was the Fox school: "It was a great experience, because in that schoolroom I had Roddy McDowall as my buddy, and Linda Darnell, Anne Baxter, Joan Shawlee, Stanley Clements, June Haver ... we went to school every morning and then acted in the afternoon."

Elena enjoyed her first true flash of fame in 1942: She landed the juicy role of Ata, the native girl who lures George Sanders into sensual tropical bliss in Somerset Maugham's *The Moon and Sixpence*, to be released by United Artists. Directed and adapted by the ever-metaphysical Albert Lewin (who later performed the same tasks on MGM's 1945 *The Picture of Dorian Gray*), the film was considered the last word in sensual screen sophistication in 1942. Elena recalls that Gus Norin, Fox makeup man, suggested her to Ernest Westmore, makeup man for *The Moon and Sixpence*; "Now, there's your Ata," said Westmore to the producers after making her up and hiding her soft, brown/blonde hair under a black wig. Elena remembers George Sanders:

> I thought George Sanders was overwhelming. He knew that I was just a naive, dumb, virginal girl, and he sort of teased me. He'd say, "I go Verdugo!" There was this wig stand, and there was my black wig, all dressed, and one time Sanders had drawn a whole face in there, which was supposed to be my face. And I remember they were always looking for him—because he'd go off and fall asleep!
>
> Once, we were doing the wedding scene; I'm quite short, and he was very tall. I was just standing there as they set up the scene, and he wasn't saying anything, so I finally said, "Mr. Sanders, you're so tall! What is your heighth?" He said, "I beg your pardon?" And I said, "What is your heighth?" And Sanders said, "It is *height*, my dear, not *heighth*." So—you can imagine! I said, "Oooo! Okay! Thank you, sir!"

Elena's sensitive portrayal of Ata impressed everyone, including director Lewin (whom Elena remembers as "a little man, and a sensitive man"). On April 20, 1942, the company of *The Moon and Sixpence* presented her with a birthday cake, on which was written: "For the Passing of Sweet 16—From Those Who Have Seen the Birth of a Great Actress." ("I had them all snowed!" laughs Elena. "But it was a very special moment. In youth, one is so brave"). Released in fall of 1942, *The Moon and Sixpence* was a hit; *Time* magazine praised Elena and her "Mona Grable smile." Top stardom seemed assured.

George Sanders and Elena Verdugo in *The Moon and Sixpence*, 1942.

However, just before *The Moon and Sixpence* was released, Fox (which had loaned Elena to Lewin for the Ata role) dropped her from the studio. "I was upset," recalls Elena, "and asked, 'Well, could I just keep going to school here?'"

Instead, Elena won a new contract: the March 15, 1943, *Examiner* reported she had secured Superior Court approval of a contract that would reach $1500 per week in seven years at Paramount Studios.

> Cecil B. De Mille wanted me for *The Story of Dr. Wassell*—or so I *thought*. They held me at Paramount under contract for a year, and I tested with everybody—my God, all the men up for parts in the film—I didn't realize I wasn't the *only* one up for the part. Then De Mille asked me to play the second lead in the film. And my mother said, "No! You signed with Paramount to do the *lead* in *The Story of Dr. Wassell*!" I knew she was wrong, really wrong, but she was just so angry at C. B. De Mille! I used to think, "Where did she get all that gumption?" De Mille was a *God* around there at Paramount!
>
> De Mille himself said to me, "Honey, this is false pride." I thought he was right, but, you know, when you're 17, and you lived at home, you did whatever your mother told you to do—at least I did.

"Why didn't mother, or anyone else, protect me in this situation?" wonders Elena today. "And my agents, the Orsatti brothers—I never heard from them." Meanwhile, to get its money's worth out of Elena, Paramount stuck her in *Rainbow Island*, a Technicolor musical starring Dorothy Lamour and Eddie Bracken, eventually released in late 1944. The cast listed her eleventh in the billing as Moana, a native girl, below such featured players as Barry Sullivan, Olga San Juan and Adia Kuznetzoff (the Festival Singer from *Frankenstein Meets the Wolf Man*, who played the Executioner in *Rainbow Island*, performing "The Boogie-Woogie-Boogie Man" with Gil Lamb). Elena found herself in a sarong and—once again—a black wig.

> Oh, *Rainbow Island* was horrible! I did meet Dorothy Lamour, and she's wonderful, and Eddie Bracken, who years later indirectly helped me get *Meet Millie* on TV. But it was such a comedown, and I was so surprised to be there—here I was, after having done *The Moon and Sixpence*, just one of the little island girls in *Rainbow Island*. I had fun with the cast—but the film just about broke my heart.

Elena left Paramount—just as Universal was hunting for an actress and dancer to play the gypsy girl of *House of Frankenstein*. "Her name is Ilonka," noted the shooting script—"...gay, vivacious and pretty... Her dark eyes sparkle and flash as she dances with inherent, joyful abandon..."

"Well, there I was in a black wig again, wasn't I?" laughs Elena.

> Seems like a long time between flashes on Elena Verdugo, the beautiful Spanish blonde who played the native girl with George Sanders in *The Moon and Sixpence*. But this morning Elena pops up with her best break since that picture, the femme lead with Boris Karloff in *The Devil's Brood* at Universal. This is the super horror opus with a whole cast of bogey men, including Karloff, Lon Chaney, Jr., John Carradine and J. Carrol Naish...
>
> —*Los Angeles Examiner*, April 6, 1944

Boris Karloff, after a Broadway smash as nightmarish Jonathan Brewster in *Arsenic and Old Lace*, had led the national company on a 66-week tour. Come January of 1944, he was back on his Coldwater Canyon farm (replaced on the *Arsenic* tour by Bela Lugosi), and signing a new Universal contract—two films, $60,000 and 13 weeks.

The first eight weeks and $40,000: *The Climax*, a Technicolor turkey on the *Phantom of the Opera* set, with Susanna Foster (q.v.) and Turhan Bey. The last four weeks and $20,000: *The Devil's Brood*, a "monster rally" blueprinted to accommodate Karloff's availability and link his name once more with the Frankenstein legend.

Universal got the signatures of some of Hollywood's greatest villains on *The Devil's Brood* contracts: John Carradine ($3500 per week, two-week guarantee) as Dracula; J. Carrol Naish ($1750 per week, four weeks) as lovesick hunchback Daniel; Lionel Atwill as Inspector Arnz ($1750 for one week) and George Zucco as Prof. Bruno Lampini, proprietor of the Chamber of Horrors that Karloff pirates (one week, $1500). Lon Chaney, under Universal contract, was set for a flat $10,000 fee for his third Wolf Man appearance, while Anne Gwynne (q.v.) would receive a flat $3000 as the American bride seduced by Dracula. "Discovered' to play the Monster: Glenn Strange, veteran cowboy heavy, who signed for two weeks—at $250 per week.

For all of the monsters, the most bravura acting of the piece was expected of the gypsy girl, Ilonka—who had to perform everything from a gypsy dance to a death scene almost Shakespearean in its blood-and-thunder style.

Elena won the part. For all the flash of the role, Elena didn't consider *The Devil's Brood* a major career boost at the time:

> No, I don't think I was all that thrilled! I probably had wanted that other part so much, in what was supposed to be "a De Mille classic," that all of a sudden, in my childish mind, I thought, "A *horror* picture? Those things at Universal?" I mean, my judgment was very strange, you know—I was very young. And I was thinking, "What am I doing in one of *these* things?" That was the kind of film where everybody went, "Wooooo!"

Nevertheless, Elena signed to play Ilonka in *The Devil's Brood*—$250 per week with a three-week guarantee.

"They signed me—cheap!" she laughs today.

So Elena Verdugo joined this crazy carnival of a horror movie, for which Universal arranged a 30-day shooting schedule and a $354,000 budget. Erle C. Kenton began directing Tuesday, April 4, 1944. Karloff, J. Carrol Naish and Charles Wagenheim (as the guard Karloff chokes to get chalk) all arrived that morning on the set of *Green Hell*, James Whale's 1940 Inca ruins fiasco. On Friday, April 7, Elena officially began her first day of shooting on *The Devil's Brood*, at the back lot gypsy camp.

> When I first worked at Universal, you drove on this little lot, and all you saw were the hills, behind the stages, all full of flowers, and it was very pretty. There was a shoeshine stand at the walkway to the entrance, and the commissary had a screen door to it—a screen door!

The pleasingly plump Elena squeezed into the gypsy dress and tights and black heels of Ilonka—who, Universal decreed, could not be a blonde:

> As Ilonka, I used a brunette wig. In fact, I had to wear a wig in several pictures until I escaped those "gypsy" roles and played Lou Costello's girl in *Little Giant* [1946]. Sometimes dye was used instead of a wig. An industry joke was that I was Hollywood's only light-at-the-roots brunette! The lady who did my wig was Carmen Dirigo. She was so sweet to me ... just wonderful. We still correspond.

Meanwhile, censor Joseph I. Breen, studying the script, had cautioned the studio about "all scenes of strangling," Lampini's "choking cry and dying groan," horses being whipped, Ilonka being whipped, the "brutal details" of the Monster's climactic wrath—and:

Verdugo as Ilonka, the gypsy dancer in the 1944 film *House of Frankenstein*, which was shot under the title *The Devil's Brood*.

> Please exercise your usual good taste, in the scenes of Ilonka, to avoid any unacceptable movements in her dance.

Elena herself had a reservation or two about her dance; as a sensitive, maturing teenage girl, she was shy, self-conscious about working with so many distinguished actors, and insecure about playing a gypsy flirt:

> In dancing, and in Spanish dancing particularly, there's a lot of flirting that goes on; they flirt, and it used to embarrass me so much; I think back on playing Ilonka in *House of Frankenstein*—and I could have died! It was my first picture without my mother on the set all the time, and I was so shy—I wouldn't even go into the commissary by myself. I'd grab a couple of candy bars. But my dancing experience gave me the freedom to play a part like Ilonka; I just pretended I was dancing, I suppose.

By the first weekend of shooting, Elena had met top-billed Karloff and Chaney:

> Working with Boris Karloff, I had a keen awareness that I was working with a "great." He was a serious actor, but never unkind. I was aware that this was a wonderful man who was in his part—really *in* the part!
>
> Lon Chaney was a lovely, friendly man. I remember often sitting and chatting with him. I wasn't aware that he had any problem with alcohol, though once, when we were sitting on a little wagon together, outside the sound stage, where "the Wolf Man" was smoking, he might have had a beer hidden behind him. Maybe—I mean, I'd hate to be stuck as a Wolf Man! That's a heavy makeup and costume! And the San Fernando Valley gets hot!

Elena got a good taste of movie hours on Saturday, April 8, working from nine A.M. until midnight. That night, by a campfire by the old "Nagana Rocks" back lot site, she played the memorable scene on the wagon, where she flirts with Daniel.

"I watched you dance," says Naish's Daniel, shyly.

"Did you ... like me?" purrs Ilonka, with Elena giving the line a wonderfully sexy reading.

"You're pretty!"

"You're afraid of me, aren't you Daniel? ... If you weren't, you'd come up here, where I can see you better." Naish leaps up on the wagon—and Ilonka can't hide her shock when she sees, for the first time, that he's a hunchback. It's one of the best-played scenes in Universal horror films:

> I had met J. Carrol Naish on the set of my first picture, *Down Argentine Way*, when I was 15. He loved working. I simply loved him. Oh, God! What a gentle, sweet soul. He helped, he supported, he gave so much... He was an Irishman, you know—but he didn't look Irish, did he?

It's a salute to both Naish and Elena that they played the scene so well, so late that Saturday night, after over 12 hours on the job. There's evidence that Kenton had wanted to work even later, but cloudy and windy weather caused him to wrap things up at the witching hour.

On Tuesday, April 11, Elena performed the gypsy dance; the minute-and-a-half musical interlude was her own creation:

> I had to choreograph the Gypsy dance carefully myself. It was difficult, because at the last moment I learned that it was to be done on a slope that had not even been cleared of rocks! All kinds of rocks, and on a slope—everything a dancer hates, you know. When I see the film, I recognize the steps—they're all mine.

And so the adventure happily rolled along for Elena, her confidence nurtured by the kind and very professional cast. Glenn Strange joined the company nine A.M. on Wednesday, April 12:

Elena Verdugo and J. Carrol Naish provided most of the dramatic fireworks in *House of Frankenstein*, 1944.

> I'd see Glenn Strange in the makeup department every A.M. Glenn was dear, and Jack Pierce, his makeup man, was a genius. Jack had said to me, "'Lenny,' you want to see how I do all this makeup?" And I thought, "Sure!" So one time, in makeup, he showed me this array of masks, so I understood how he created all the fantasy.
>
> The "Frankenstein Monster" would come on the set, and everybody'd say, "How you doin', Glenn? How you doin'? Everyone loved Glenn—just loved him!

Erle C. Kenton proved to be patient and kind to the starlet; "He was adorable, so sweet," recalls Elena. The company shot exteriors all over Universal's picturesque back lot, and settled on the Niemann laboratory set on Universal's Stage 17. While Elena posed for gag photos with the Wolf Man—for instance, giving him a pedicure—her first real look at Chaney's lycanthrope had been far less casual:

> For the horror films at Universal, they used to have professional screamers on the sets. For the scene in which the Wolf Man attacked me—that was spooky! They called one of those screamers to our stage ... and I hadn't seen Lon in his makeup. Well, when the Wolf Man jumped out at me, I was so scared and

J. Carrol Naish, Elena Verdugo and Boris Karloff in *House of Frankenstein*, 1944.

> screamed so wildly that they canceled the professional screamer! They didn't need her! That was *my* scream—and I screamed bloody murder!

On April 20, 1944, Elena celebrated her nineteenth birthday—with the monsters. She arrived on the set at one P.M., and Karloff, Chaney, Naish, Strange and the company surprised her with a cake bearing the legend, "Happy Birthday, Elena—from the Devil's Brood." Chaney showed up for the party, even though he wasn't on call that day.

As lycanthrope legend dictated, Ilonka fell in love with the Wolf Man; she realizes he can only be killed by a silver bullet "fired by one who loves him enough to understand." Following a very emotional promise made to Chaney's Talbot in the garden ("I won't let you out of my sight!" she sobs), Elena's Ilonka keeps vigil that night of the full moon; Chaney changes (a terrific John P. Fulton special effect) and—as Hans J. Salter's music sends chills up the spine—he breaks through his French doors and Ilonka chases him into the forest. A scream ... a shot ... the Wolf Man is dead. Ilonka, dragging herself through the mist of the Process Stage forest, dies with her head resting on Talbot's chest.

Elena completed her work on *The Devil's Brood* on Monday, April 24, 1944, at 5:15 P.M. There was a long night ahead as the featured villagers and 45 extras chased Karloff's Niemann and Strange's Monster into the swamp with torches—the picture's climax, which Kenton finished shooting at three A.M. The film went on for two more weeks, as Carradine arrived for the Dracula episode; Karloff finished Saturday, April 29, right on his contractual deadline; the film wrapped at five P.M. on Monday, May 8, 1944, with Carradine, Anne Gwynne and Peter Coe on location at Sherwood Forest—exactly on its 30-day schedule.

As Elena says:

> All in all, I enjoyed making the picture very much. I was a still-growing teenage girl, and *all* of those fine actors were kind, considerate, and made me feel a part of everything.

In the seven months between completion and premiere, Universal changed the title of *The Devil's Brood* to *House of Frankenstein*. The movie opened at Hollywood's Hawaii Theatre December 22, 1944 (on a double-bill with *The Mummy's Curse*), just in time for Yuletide (as 1931's *Frankenstein* had been).

Elena recalls the Hawaii Theatre in Hollywood:

> I drove by the theatre, at the end of Hollywood Boulevard, and they had pictures all over the outside—pictures of the monsters, pictures of me in that gypsy costume, pictures all over the front, like a decoupage. The theatre was so adorned with all these huge photos! They really had gone all the way on it—a lot of hype and a splurge of publicity. It was elaborate showcasing!

"Oh, for heaven's sake, what's wrong with Universal, anyway?" wailed *Photoplay*—a lament typical of the film's critical reception. Yet *House of Frankenstein* is almost irresistible fun. Karloff's suave diabolics, Chaney's angst, Carradine's style, Naish's emotion—all put over this delirious entertainment with surprising class and never a dull moment.

Truly, one of the melodrama's outstanding features is Elena Verdugo's Ilonka. She's a complete departure from the classy soignée Frankenstein ladies of the '30s, and the statuesque Evelyn Ankers (q.v.) or the bounteous Ilona Massey (q.v.) of the '40's; this is a sexy teenager, a little temptress, heartbreakingly sympathetic—yet flirtatious enough to make one think her violent death is a nod to censors who frowned on those dance movements, coy eyes (and, of course, gypsy blood!).

"Vivacious Elena Verdugo acts up a storm as the ill-fated Ilonka," wrote John Brunas in *Universal Horrors*. It's a storm full of sex appeal, romance and tragedy, and *House of Frankenstein* is all the more colorful for it.

On June 19, 1944, Universal began shooting *The Frozen Ghost*, the studio's new "Inner Sanctum" Lon Chaney vehicle. Elena played Nina Coudreau, niece of a wax museum owner (Tala Birell), lovesick over hypnotist Chaney. "Just a little 'B' picture," says Elena of *The Frozen Ghost*; released in the summer of 1945 (on a double-bill with

Verdugo struts her stuff on a one-sheet poster for *The Frozen Ghost*, 1945.

The Jungle Captive), it was Evelyn Ankers' Universal swan song; Martin Kosleck picked the few available acting honors.

> On *The Frozen Ghost*, I remember conversation with Tala Birell. I thought she was charming! Very European, and wearing a black hat when we weren't working. I remember jitterbugging on the set with some young man, just to kill time!

As *House of Frankenstein* entered national release early in 1945, Elena was still coping with Hollywood celebrity and the pressures of being a teenager. She moved with her mother, aunt, uncle and cousins to "a beautiful ranch in the San Fernando Valley," but war time and gas rationing made her life very isolated, and the ranch had no phone. "I was lonely, I guess," says Elena, "and I found food as my fun—particularly sweets... I kept getting bigger and bigger and rounder." Universal had plans to put her on contract, but only if she battled her weight problem. Elena rebelled, but contract or no, Universal kept offering her parts—"I played more pictures for them than many of the studio's contract players."

Meanwhile, in 1945, Elena displayed her musical talents as she replaced Lina Romay in Xavier Cugat's orchestra. She recorded "Tico-Tico," which became a hit. And she had a chance to show off her own blonde hair and comic timing as Lou Costello's girlfriend in Universal's *Little Giant* (1946):

> Abbott and Costello were big gamblers—I mean, they'd gamble on who was the next person who was going to walk through a door! And for big hunks of money! They seemed to be having fun on *Little Giant*, but they were always gambling, playing cards, betting on something. That was their joy, that was how they entertained themselves—and they spent thousands every day!

It was on *Little Giant* that Elena met screenwriter Charles Marion (whose credits included Monogram's 1941 *Spooks Run Wild*, with Bela Lugosi and the East Side Kids). On March 24, 1946, 20-year-old Elena wed 31-year-old Marion at the Westwood Community Church. Jack Oakie was best man; Elena's cousin, Eleanor David, was matron of honor. "We were married on a Sunday," recalls Elena, "and I had to be back to work on Monday!"

Elena played in Universal's *Song of Scheherazade* (1947), escapism about Rimsky-Korsakov, starring Yvonne De Carlo, Brian Donlevy and Jean Pierre Aumont. ("Jean-Pierre had this whip—a heck of a long whip—and every time he'd try to crack it, he'd go 'Ooo!', and close his eyes and wince!").

Aside from *House of Frankenstein*, movie fans remember Elena best as Gene Autry's leading lady in *The Big Sombrero* (Columbia, 1949):

> Oh, I liked Gene Autry. I thought he had a kind of sexy quality about him—very cool and quiet, with a classiness about him. I remember once, Gene and his wife and Charlie and I were walking near Vine Street in Hollywood, and Gene said, "You know, I wouldn't have recorded 'Rudolph, The Red-Nosed Reindeer' if

> my wife hadn't insisted. She liked that song." We went different places to publicize the picture, and he was really very charming.

Elena also recalls Gene Autry's horse—who merrily and persistently broke wind as Elena waved good-bye to the cowboy star in *The Big Sombrero*'s finale.

Many potboilers followed for Elena, and she met some of Hollywood's legendary "B" moviemakers:

> Charlie went to work at Monogram, where everyone knew I was married to him. We were all friendly in those days, and they'd ask him if I'd do different movies there. And then I was pregnant, and I did four movies there because we had to build up for the baby coming. I was a villainess in *Sky Dragon* [1949], a Charlie Chan film, in which Roland Winters played Charlie Chan; he later played my boss on TV's *Meet Millie*, and we became very close friends. William Beaudine directed me at Monogram in *Tuna Clipper* [1949] and *Jet Job* [1952]; he had this waxed mustache and a twinkle in his eye, tall and lanky. He was fun, he was crazy, and he was "papa"—with a big family of children who all loved him.

In 1949, Elena and Charles Marion became proud parents of a son, Richard. That same year, Elena also visited Columbia, where she starred with Johnny Weissmuller in *The Lost Tribe*, produced by the infamous "Jungle Sam" Katzman:

> Sam was everything you'd expect in a caricature of a Hollywood producer—red-plaid pants, a cap, a cigar, a little stout, that funny little voice—and a wife with pink hair! "Bring it in cheap, bring it in cheap!"—he was really colorful and, I think, a nice fellow. He and his wife loved the track—they always had a box at the track.
>
> As for Johnny Weissmuller ... my mother had been private secretary for Johnny and Lupe Velez, to whom he had been married. So I had known Johnny when I was a child—this big, beautiful man, with his Deusenberg. And then I ended up being his leading lady! My mother (at my insistence) had called me "Helen" when I was a little girl, so when I came on the set, Johnny said, "Oh—little Helen!"

Elena acted with Johnny Sheffield ("Boy" from the *Tarzan* series) in Monogram's *The Lost Volcano* (1950); was Gene Autry's leading lady again in *Gene Autry and the Mounties* (1951); and worked for Sam Katzman again in two 1952 Technicolor Columbia releases: *Thief of Damascus* (her third film with Chaney), and *The Pathfinder*. A classy credit for Elena at this timer was *Cyrano de Bergerac* (1950), which won a Best Actor Oscar for Jose Ferrer; she had a lovely vignette as "The Orange Girl." "It's one of the nicest things I've ever done," says Elena, "if not the best. Something happened—it was just right."

Elena was a guest star on TV's *Dangerous Assignment*, and star Brian Donlevy offered her a regular spot in the series. However, Elena was going into her own TV show: in the title role of *Meet Millie*, a CBS sitcom which premiered October 25, 1952, and ran through February 28, 1956. As a New York City secretary secretly in love with her boss' son, Elena won a weekly following in the role Audrey Totter had created on radio—and became a top TV star:

> They wanted a sort of Judy Holliday, a combination of all blonde comediennes—and I'd never done anything in comedy except *Little Giant* with Abbott and Costello. I suggested my girlfriend Joan Shawlee for it. But I ended up playing Millie—and it was live television!
>
> Actually, if you ask for anecdotes about the show, my co-stars would have had the stories, because I'm the one who would go up in lines every once in a while. Florence Halop, who played my mother and was just great, used to say that she'd see that stare in my eye and know, "Oops! She's up!" Marvin Kaplan, my dear friend, was wonderful—he was great in that role of Alfred Prinzmetal, the poet.
>
> Again, I bless my dancing background, because I moved around those sets like I was choreographing a dance—I had high heels, and big skirts, and a lot of body action! It was very difficult, very nerve-wracking, but so rewarding—it was great fun to be the leading lady in a new business among top people.

With the TV fame came magazine covers and trips to New York; Elena also took over the role of Millie on the radio program. The frantic work schedule took its toll on Elena's marriage; she and Marion separated in 1954, and divorced in 1956.

> We had a big house in Brentwood with too much responsibility, and my mother was very ill, and we had the baby, and I was working on live television—and my husband and I just didn't make it through that crisis. We stayed friends—we were very devoted to our son, and we raised him with all the care and love that most people don't even get to do when they're still living in the same house together. I was really Charlie's best friend until the day he died—in fact, I found him after his heart attack, when he didn't answer the phone. We were devoted to our boy, and we were very close.

Elena's career for the next decade was a mixed bag: She had the title role in Republic's *Panama Sal* (1957), filmed in "Naturama"; starred in stock productions of *South Pacific* (as Nellie Forbush), *Oklahoma!* (as Ado Annie) and *Roman Candle*. She co-starred in several TV series: the Western *Redigo* (NBC, 9/24/63–12/31/63), as Gerry, assistant manager of the Gold Hotel; *The Phil Silvers Show* (CBS, 1963–1964); *Many Happy Returns* (CBS, 9/21/64–4/65), with Elena as Lynn Hall, staff member of Krockmeyer's Department Store, co-starring with John McGiver, Elinor Donahue and Jerome Cowan; and *Mona McCluskey* (NBC, 9/16/65–4/14/66), with Elena delightful as Alice, second banana to star Juliet Prowse.

Elena's career finale came at Universal City, where she played nurse Consuelo Lopez on ABC's *Marcus Welby, M.D.* The popular show premiered September 23,

1969, co-starring Elena as nurse to Robert Young's Welby and James Brolin's Dr. Steven Kiley, and running seven seasons.

> When they asked me to go and audition for *Welby*, they said, "There's a part of a Mexican-American, and if you have a black wig, take it." I said, "Oh, no! After having done *Millie* and all these things as a blonde comedienne, I'm back to the damn wig again?!" I was so mad! So I went in (with no wig!), and I couldn't get a parking place, and my agent wasn't there to meet me, and I went in and said, "What's going on around here?" God—the poor producer looked at me and said, "That's *just* the quality I want!" Consuelo was *not* a laid-back person!

So Elena joined *Marcus Welby, M.D.* As Consuelo, Elena had wigs at first, then slowly discarded them. Universal City, she discovered, was a very different place from the little studio which had given her a birthday cake on *House of Frankenstein*:

> I thought, "I'm coming back to the same lot where I did *House of Frankenstein*, but a whole different world." What a difference! During my early years at the studio, Universal was a small, close family. There was much USO activity, servicemen visited the lot—it was a happy place. Then I returned, after all those years—and discovered that Universal had become a factory. There were still some members of the crew who had been there in "the old days."

Elena had a continuing friendship with the show's star until his death in 1998:

> Robert Young was a very gracious man, but he ran a very tight ship. When we worked, we worked, and he was not a playful fellow. There were times when I'd think, "Come on, Bob, lighten up a little bit!" He was so intense, and as you can see, his work was very thorough.

Young (and Elena) were so convincing on *Marcus Welby, M.D.* that they were asked to speak at medical conventions! It was a very happy seven years:

> One thing I noticed was, I never walked out of the makeup department to go to my dressing room that a tram full of people on the Universal tour didn't come by. There I am, with all these curlers in my hair! And the tour guide would say, "There's Miss Verdugo, of *Marcus Welby*!" They came by every time I was walking out. I'd hide behind cars, so they wouldn't see me! But that should be my worst problem—I loved it all.

In 1972, during production of *Marcus Welby, M.D.*, Elena married Dr. Charles Rosewall, chief psychiatrist of the Los Angeles County Department of Mental Health. In 1979, while vacationing with her husband in London, the lady took time out from her vacation to answer a questionnaire I sent her regarding *House of Frankenstein* for my book *It's Alive!* Later, my wife and I met her and her husband at

Elena Verdugo and her husband, Dr. Charles Rosewall, in 1981.

a North Hollywood restaurant, and it was fun to see her enter and march back to greet us at our table, heads turning at this lovely whirlwind energy, still with her Ilonka twinkle and vivacity.

Today, Elena Verdugo is retired from acting, settled in a lovely locale over the Mexican border. "We overlook the ocean," she says, "and it's so exceptionally beautiful." Although no longer acting, she is very busy. She has served two terms as vice-president plus two terms as president of the Rosarito Red Cross, planning the annual Christmas Ball and raising money to finish their hospital. In August of 1994, she was guest of honor at the Memphis Film Festival; in July 1995, she joined *The Black Cat*'s Lucille Lund and *House of Dracula*'s Jane Adams (q.v.) as a guest of honor at the FANEX Convention in Baltimore.

Elena has two granddaughters; in 1995, 20-year-old Jessie was studying acting with the famed Uta Hagen in New York, while 11-year-old Maggie had the lead as Oliver Twist in her school play and was doing professional looping work at the studios.

Meanwhile, Elena still receives acting offers, as well as mail from many fans all over the world. Does she think she'll act again?

> Not particularly. Mexico is just far enough away from Hollywood that I don't think about it. Besides, I'm getting so much applause now as this "oldtimer," why go in and work? I'm getting all the applause I need!

House of Frankenstein remains a happy memory for Elena Verdugo—"I am delighted that there is so much action around the film," she told me in 1994. Indeed, in Universal lore, Evelyn Ankers, of *The Wolf Man*, was the lycanthrope's first and most famous love; Ilona Massey helped him find the infamous Frankenstein records in *Frankenstein Meets the Wolf Man*; Martha O'Driscoll, of *House of Dracula*, was the woman he embraced for the finale, after Universal cured his affliction. However, it's Elena Verdugo's Ilonka who seems most-linked to Larry Talbot; the leading lady he killed, and who in love killed him; the gypsy girl with the silver bullet—who loved him enough to understand.

The Films of Elena Verdugo

1931

Cavalier of the West (Artclass, John McCarthy)

1940

Down Argentine Way (20th Century–Fox, Irving Cummings)

1941

There's Magic in Music (Paramount, Andrew L. Stone)
Belle Starr (20th Century–Fox, I. Cummings)

1942

To the Shores of Tripoli (20th Century–Fox, Bruce Humberstone)
The Moon and Sixpence (United Artists, Albert Lewin)

1944

Rainbow Island (Paramount, Ralph Murphy)
House of Frankenstein (Universal, Erle C. Kenton)

1945

The Frozen Ghost (Universal, Harold Young)
Strange Voyage (Signal/Monogram, Irving Allen)

1946

Little Giant (Universal, William A. Seiter)

1947

Song of Scheherazade (Universal, Walter Reisch)

1949

The Big Sombrero (Columbia/Autry, Frank McDonald)
Tuna Clipper (Monogram, William Beaudine)
Sky Dragon (Monogram, Lesley Selander)
The Lost Tribe (Columbia, William Berke)

1950

The Lost Volcano (Monogram, Ford Beebe)
Snow Dog (Monogram, Frank McDonald)
Cyrano de Bergerac (United Artists/Kramer, Michael Gordon)

1951

Gene Autry and the Mounties (Columbia, John English)

1952

Jet Job (Monogram, William Beaudine)
Thief of Damascus (Columbia, Will Jason)
The Pathfinder (Columbia, Sidney Salkow)

1953

The Marksman (Allied Artists, Lewis D. Collins)

1957

Panama Sal (Republic, William Witney)

1965

Day of the Nightmare (Governor, John Bushelman)

1968

How Sweet It Is! (National General, Jerry Paris)

1969

Angel in My Pocket (Universal, Alan Rafkin)

1973

The Alpha Caper (TV Movie, Robert Michael Lewis)

1984

The Return of Marcus Welby M.D. (TV Movie)

Gale Sondergaard

She was Hollywood's Dragon Lady of the Screen.

And, if Shakespeare could have time-traveled to seek the perfect actress to portray his Lady Macbeth, the ultimate choice might well have been Gale Sondergaard.

Indeed, of all the ladies of Hollywood to embrace the evil and the sinister on movie screens, none achieved the fame, notoriety and wicked flair of this tall, sleek, deadly-attractive and superbly talented actress. From her Academy Award–winning bow as Faith in 1936's *Anthony Adverse*, to her infamous portrayal of the Eurasian woman who knives Bette Davis in the moonlight in 1940's *The Letter*, to the sinuous, arachnid-employing villainess of *The Spider Woman*, she was the cinema's most diabolical female. Gale took it all in stylish stride; as she said in an October 1974 *Coronet* interview with Michael B. Druxman:

> I guess that villains remain more dominant in the minds of an audience. They're usually more colorful than the hero and, from an acting standpoint, more fun to play.

Black-eyed, black-haired and (in the movies) usually black-hearted, Miss Sondergaard possessed a wonderfully theatrical aura, honed by years with New York's Theatre Guild; there was, too, a definite and striking sexuality about her, making her villainy all the more delectable—and dangerous. In actuality, she was one of Hollywood's most versatile actresses—her range extending far beyond villainy to such parts as Mme. Dreyfuss of *The Life of Emile Zola* and Lady Thiang of *Anna and the King of Siam* (for which she received her second Oscar nomination).

She was also one of Hollywood's legendary survivors. For in the late 1940s, Gale Sondergaard became the victim of a real-life monster—the Communist Witch Hunt—which sentenced her to a career limbo of 20 years. She would gallantly "strike back" too, acting into her 80s and playing an exciting and inspiring final act as an actress—and as a woman.

She was born Edith Holm Sondergaard in Litchfield, Minnesota, February 15, 1900. Her father, Hans T. Sondergaard, was a butter maker in a creamery, later teaching the cooperative movement at the University of Wisconsin; her mother, Kirstine (Holm) Sondergaard, taught music to her three daughters. "My parents were both progressive people learning much from Henrik Ibsen," said Miss Sondergaard, who later credited both her parents as strong influences on her controversial life:

> I came from a very progressive family. My folks were from Denmark, but they met and married here. My mother was a feminist from the start. She already threw off her binding corset. She was a Lucy Stoner, interested in keeping her own name and identity. Religion-wise, both my parents were free-thinkers. And we were brought up the same way, too.

One of Gale's early "dramatic" adventures was marching in suffragette parades with her mother.

***Chapter opener:* Gale Sondergaard reads to her children, Joan and Daniel.**

In high school, Miss Sondergaard realized her true ambition when assigned to read a passage from literature to the class. As she told Leonard Maltin in *The Real Stars*:

> I chose a very emotional scene from *Ivanhoe*, Rebecca's scene... I got up in front of the class, and I was reading, and enjoying myself, and suddenly a sort of sixth sense developed, and I saw the teacher in the back of the room, looking out the window, turning her back... I thought, I guess she doesn't like me. ... The teacher admitted that she turned her back because she was weeping, she was so moved...

At this teacher's urging, Miss Sondergaard's mother enrolled her in a drama school. Shortly thereafter, the girl was devastated at not winning the part of an ingenue in a play the school was producing. As the drama coach incisively told her at this time, "It's such a pity that you can't be an ordinary girl at an ordinary tea party. But you can't be—you have something much more interesting to offer."

She graduated from high school in 1917 and attended the University of Minnesota, studying music and dramatic arts and acting in stock on the Chautauqua circuit during the summers. She graduated from the University with a Bachelor of Arts degree in English and public speaking in 1921.

In 1922, "Gale" Sondergaard (she had chosen the professional name early in her stock days) married Neil O'Malley, a fellow University of Minnesota alumnus who had joined the Chautauqua circuit via his romantic interest in Gale. The marriage would last eight years.

Meanwhile, Gale Sondergaard joined the John Kellerd Shakespeare Touring Company, playing Jessica in *The Merchant of Venice* and Gertrude in *Hamlet*; made her New York City debut in November 1923, succeeding Isabella Leighton in *What's Your Wife Doing?*; did a 1922-1923 season of stock in Milwaukee; toured in *Seventh Heaven*, prophetically playing the wicked sister (a role she would reprise in Hollywood's 1937 version); and joined the Jessie Bonstelle Stock Company in Detroit, 1925–1927, playing Queen Gertrude to Melvyn Douglas' Hamlet during the second season.

Now the 27-year-old actress set her eyes on the famed Theatre Guild. As Ronald Bowers quoted Miss Sondergaard in a *Films in Review* profile (August/September 1978):

> One of the first things I did was to go see the Theatre Guild's production of O'Neil's *Strange Interlude* starring Lynn Fontanne. I thought she was absolutely marvelous, but I said, "That's my role!" I got hold of the script and studied the part of Nina Leeds. Glenn Anders asked me to audition with the Guild; I did a scene from *Strange Interlude* and they flipped. What I didn't know at the time was that Lynn wanted to leave and they wanted Judith Anderson to replace her; but Judith wasn't available and they were seriously thinking of giving me the role. Then Judith did come in, but because they knew I could do it, they gave me a three-year contract.

While on standby for the part of Nina, Sondergaard appeared (ironically) as the Witch in the Guild's production of *Faust*, which opened October 8, 1928, at the

Guild Theatre. Dudley Digges played Mephistopheles, Helen Chandler was Marguerite, and the play ran 48 performances. On November 19, 1928, Sondergaard followed at the Guild Theatre as Sarah Undershaft in Shaw's *Major Barbara*, which also starred Dudley Digges and ran 73 performances. In December 1928, Judith Anderson left *Strange Interlude*, and Sondergaard replaced her as Nina, playing the part for six months and securing a reputation on Broadway as a striking and gifted actress.

On October 7, 1929, Sondergaard was featured as "Marie's Sister" in the Guild's *Karl and Anna*, a drama of postwar Berlin starring Otto Kruger and Alice Brady, and with Claude Rains in the supporting cast; it lasted 49 performances. There followed *Red Rust*, a scathing look at Communism, which opened December 17, 1929, at the Martin Beck Theatre and ran 65 performances. Sondergaard played the gentle, pathetic Nina, a pitifully abused wife who won't kill herself because it's against the laws of the State (and is finally murdered by her brutal husband). The cast included Franchot Tone, Lee Strasberg and, in the role of the murdering husband, the play's director—Herbert J. Biberman.

Born March 4, 1900, in Philadelphia, a graduate of the University of Pennsylvania and Yale (where he earned a Master of Fine Arts), a former student at the Meyerhold and Stanislavsky theatres in Moscow, Biberman was the Guild's top experimental play director, and a man of great charm and brilliance. He had joined the Guild in 1928 as an assistant stage manager, and promptly scored as an actor (he had met Sondergaard in *Faust*, in which he played Altmeyer) and director. Biberman and Sondergaard fell in love, and after she secured a divorce from Neil O'Malley, they "secretly married" in Philadelphia in May 1930. They soon departed on a honeymoon tour of Mexico, Arizona and Oklahoma.

Biberman went on to direct such Guild plays as *Green Grow the Lilacs* (Guild Theatre, 1/26/31, 104 performances and which in 1943 metamorphosed into Rodgers and Hammerstein's *Oklahoma!*) and *Miracle at Verdun* (Martin Beck Theatre, 3/16/31, 48 performances), a truly avant-garde and horrifying play in which the ghastly dead of World War I crawled from their graves and invaded Paris and Berlin. (Biberman augmented the drama of this play by adding movie screens to the theatre and showing special filmed footage.) He also directed *The Man Who Reclaimed His Head* (Broadhurst Theatre, 9/8/32, 28 performances), starring Claude Rains and Jean Arthur, a Jean Bart revenge melodrama which Universal filmed in 1934, with Rains reprising his stage role opposite Joan Bennett and Lionel Atwill. Biberman also wrote and directed an ABC radio show, *Legend of America*, which starred his wife.

In May of 1931, Gale succeeded Eva Le Gallienne as Elsa in *Alison's House* at the Civic Repertory Theatre. On February 21, 1933, she opened in the Guild's *American Dream* (Guild Theatre, 39 performances), which also starred Douglass Montgomery and Claude Rains. The trilogy examined certain American families and their descendants of 1650, 1849 and 1933; Sondergaard played in the first and third act as (respectively) Lydia Kimball and Gail Pingree, described by the *New York Times* reviewer as "the most grasping and heartless of their womenfolk." In June 1933, the actress starred at the Westchester County Center in New York in *Iron Flowers*, directed by Biberman, an experimental play with dance and music interludes.

On November 6, 1933, Sondergaard was one of the three actress (Nazimova and Beatrice de Neergaard were the others) in *Doctor Monica*, which lasted only 16 performances at the Playhouse Theatre. Then, May 17, 1934, she opened at the Masque Theatre as Lorinda Channing, Machievellian villainess of the melodrama *Invitation to a Murder*. This wild thriller, which also starred Humphrey Bogart and Walter Abel, boasted (in the words of the *New York Times*) "enough horrors and villainies to make a Newgate turnkey go pale with anguish." Of the leading lady, the critic noted: "Gale Sondergaard played the female fiend like a cross between Lady Macbeth and Queen Elizabeth." *Invitation to a Murder* ran 52 performances.

Meanwhile, Herbert Biberman, on the strength of Maxwell Anderson's play *Valley Forge* (which Biberman co-directed with John Houseman), won a director contract with Columbia Pictures. "I considered myself an established Broadway leading lady at the moment," said Sondergaard of her husband's offer, "but when Herbert got the contract I said, 'I'm not going to stay in New York while you go to Hollywood.'" The Bibermans arrived in the movie colony and took a house high in the Hollywood Hills, under the old HOLLYWOODLAND sign, as Biberman made his movie directorial debut with Columbia's *One Way Ticket*, starring Lloyd Nolan.

Herbert Biberman's representative was the Hawks-Volck Agency, which handled such talents as directors Victor Fleming, Edmund Goulding, Howard Hawks and King Vidor, and such stars as Ronald Colman, Constance Bennett and Claude Rains. After Sondergaard had passed six relaxing months in Hollywood, Biberman's personal agent, William Shiffnen, told her, "Let me take you around. You're an actress." As the actress recalled her reaction:

> I said, "No, I don't belong in motion pictures." (I didn't think I was photogenic.) He said that Mervyn LeRoy was going to do *Anthony Adverse* and wanted an unknown face and would I at least come in and meet LeRoy. I walked in with silver-looped earrings and LeRoy decided then and there that I was Faith Paleologue.

Anthony Adverse was Warner Bros.' big picture for 1936. Fredric March had signed for the title role, Olivia de Havilland was set for the female lead of Angela, and Warners had recruited a wonderful supporting cast, including Claude Rains (as the evil Don Luis), Anita Louise, Edmund Gwenn, Louis Hayward and Donald Woods. There had been talk that Bette Davis was being considered for the part of the sly, sinuous housekeeper Faith, but it was a supporting role—although a very juicy one. In January 1936, *Anthony Adverse* began production at Warners' Burbank lot. "In the book, the woman was the mistress of Adverse," smiled Sondergaard years later, "but that wasn't allowed in those days. We got the idea across with merely a look."

"I believe Miss Sondergaard is a real find for pictures," proclaimed producer Hal Wallis. "She is so subtly convincing that Faith becomes one of the dominant characters of the whole story."

In the summer of 1936, *Anthony Adverse* had a gala premiere at the Carthay Circle Theatre. Warners erected a grandstand with 12,000 seats for the crowds to cheer the celebrities as they promenaded from their limousines to the theatre lobby. "Gale

Gale Sondergaard, Edmund Gwenn, and Fredric March in *Anthony Adverse*, 1936.

Sondergaard Walks Off with Plaudits," headlined a feature story in the *Los Angeles Examiner*, with critic Muriel Babcock writing of the actress, "She is so bad in a realistic fashion that she makes shivers run up and down your back..."

Anthony Adverse became one of the top moneymakers of 1936-1937, placed #8 on *Film Daily*'s "Ten Best" poll, and won a Best Picture Academy nomination (losing to MGM's *The Great Ziegfeld*). Nineteen thirty-six also saw a new Hollywood tradition born: the establishment of the Academy's Best Supporting Actor and Best Supporting Actress Plaque (which, a decade later, became statuettes *à la* "Oscar" himself). The first ladies to compete for this prize were Beulah Bondi for *The Gorgeous Hussy*, Alice Brady for *My Man Godfrey*, Bonita Granville for *These Three*, Maria Ouspenskaya for *Dodsworth* and Sondergaard for *Anthony Adverse*. Sondergaard was the winner, smiling broadly for the press with her male counterpart, Walter Brennan (who had won the first of his three plaques for *Come and Get It*).

So, with her first picture, Gale Sondergaard won not only an Academy Award, but an overnight (and lasting) reputation as Hollywood's greatest villainess. A strong, positive, very intelligent and decidedly un-neurotic lady, she gave little thought to vicious fan mail or hisses from the moviegoing public. And, with her ever-liberal attitudes, she never categorized her roles as "good" or "bad"; she recognized and

Walter Brennan (left) and Gale Sondergaard are the first winners of Best Supporting Oscars—he for *Come and Get It*, she for *Anthony Adverse*. Presenting the award: George Jessel. This is a posed shot; in truth the Best Supporting winners that year received only plaques, not statuettes.

played each role as an individual, relishing the chance the part gave her to work and create.

Now established in Hollywood, the Bibermans enjoyed their privacy, escaping the movie colony and driving 60 miles north to the beach town of Oxnard ("We have it almost all to ourselves," said Gale).

In the meantime, Gale had reported to Paramount for *Maid of Salem*, starring Claudette Colbert and Fred MacMurray and directed by Frank Lloyd. She played Martha Harding, a Salem villager caught up in the witch hunt bloodlust, who hysterically informs the town that suspected witch Colbert's mother had been burned in England—as a disciple of Satan. While *Anthony Adverse* had been a total, happy triumph for the actress, *Maid of Salem* introduced her to the more ruthless and heartbreaking side of moviemaking, when she went to the screening—and found her part largely butchered onto the cutting room floor. In the release print, her part lost most of its identity; Lloyd even sent her a letter of apology, promising, "We'll do better, next time." Gale learned why her part was so viciously cut, but would never divulge the reasons because, as she put it, "I don't want to hurt anyone." Her silence always inferred that the cuts were made to protect Miss Colbert's dominance of the picture, but the exact behind-the-scenes reasons haven't become public.

Gale played perhaps her most despicable villainess in 20th Century–Fox's 1937 *Seventh Heaven*, starring Simone Simon (q.v.) and James Stewart; the Academy Award winner played Nana, the evil, drunken, whip-lashing harpy who casts her sister Simon out into the streets. There followed, however, one of her best sympathetic parts: Mme. Dreyfuss, who pleads with Zola (Paul Muni) to save her innocent husband (Joseph Schildkraut) from Devil's Island in 1937's Oscar-winning Best Picture, Warners' *The Life of Emile Zola*. There was considerable worry at Warners when the studio discovered that the real-life Mme. Dreyfuss was still alive; however, so sympathetic was the script and so attractive was Gale's performance that the Dreyfuss estate allowed the internationally acclaimed film to be released with very minimal concerns and changes. It was Gale's favorite movie.

Nineteen thirty-eight found Gale under contract to MGM, where she played in two releases. *Lord Jeff* was a vehicle for Freddie Bartholomew, used by Gale to perpetuate crimes; *Dramatic School* starred Luise Rainer, then at her crest after consecutive Best Actress Oscars for *The Great Ziegfeld* and *The Good Earth*. In this very florid romancer, Luise is would-be actress Louise Mauban, inspired to embrace the stage after watching a performance by the huzzahed Mme. Charlot (Gale); years later, Miss Rainer finds herself studying acting at a school run by her failing, once-acclaimed idol. Gail was superb as Charlot, who lamented no longer being able to play Juliet and jealously resented the new generation of actresses whom she is training; the *New York Times* praised her "understanding and assurance" in the role. (Incidentally, after her success in *Anthony Adverse*, MGM had tested Sondergaard for the part of O-Lan in *The Good Earth*, the role for which Miss Rainer won her second Oscar.)

Gale might have been in one of Metro's greatest movies, as she originally was cast as the Wicked Witch of the West in the classic *The Wizard of Oz* (1939). While still at MGM, the actress had been recruited by Mervyn LeRoy to test for the part; as she told Michael Druxman in *Coronet*:

> The initial idea was for me to play a glamorous witch; however, shortly before filming began, Mervyn LeRoy came to me and said that the studio heads had changed their minds and wanted the role to have an "ugly" makeup. They felt, and probably rightfully so, that this new interpretation would be more frightening to children. I, of course, refused to do the part that way and Margaret Hamilton replaced me.

Gale professed nothing but admiration for Margaret Hamilton's Witch of the West, praising her performance as "a classic."

Gale began 1939 in Paramount's *Never Say Die*, a comedy starring Bob Hope and Martha Raye. She was Mrs. Marco, a multi-married fortune hunter and Olympic pistol champion, whose husbands all meet violent (and suspicious) ends. Sondergaard showed a wonderful flair for comedy, as she preys on millionaire Hope, telling the terrified comic of the demise of her most recent spouse:

> GALE: Poor Pierre ... he fell off the Matterhorn ... 13,669 feet! ... It was horrible. And when it happened, I wasn't a foot behind him.
>
> HOPE: Think of that. I bet you could have reached right out and touched him, eh, Mrs. Marco?
>
> GALE: Easily!

Never Say Die was the first of four pictures the actress made with Bob Hope, and she remembered of its shooting, "You'd come home absolutely hurting from laughing all day on the set." Her personal opinion of Hope, due to their political poles, was not so flattering.

In *Juarez*, Warners' 1939 extravaganza with Paul Muni, Bette Davis, Brian Aherne, Claude Rains, John Garfield et al., Gale was Empress Eugenie; she also appeared at Warners that year in the 21-minute historical short *The Sons of Liberty*, entitled "An Historic Episode in the Life of Haym Salomon." Claude Rains played the idealistic Jew who helped finance the American Revolution; she was his loving wife. Then, back at Paramount, she was "Miss Lu," a sinister-looking housekeeper in the Bob Hope/Paulette Goddard comedy *The Cat and the Canary*.

In 1940, Sondergaard joined Alan Mowbray as a larcenous duo on Paramount's *The Llano Kid*; was Tylette, the Cat, in the 20th Century–Fox Shirley Temple fantasy *The Blue Bird*; was Linda Darnell's wickedly flirtatious aunt in the Tyrone Power swashbuckler *The Mark of Zorro*; and, climactically, played Mrs. Hammond, the mysterious Eurasian wife in Warners' *The Letter*, the William Wyler–directed melodrama for which she is most vividly remembered. "I love that role," Sondergaard said, "but I'm still shocked today when people mention *The Letter* and say 'that evil role.' She was a noble woman!"

The Letter, of course, begins with that classic opening vignette of Bette Davis shooting (several times!) a lover who had spurned her—to wed Sondergaard's character. The actress had very strong feelings about her role:

> I went to wardrobe at Warners, to be fitted, before we were to begin, and they brought out all these cheap, horrible things of a second class whore... I looked at these things and I said, "Why would she look like that?... Is it because she's yellow? Because she's half-Chinese and not at all Caucasian?" So William Wyler, who is a marvelous director and a marvelous man in every way, said, "Well, let's think about it a little..." I came back the next day, and he said he hadn't slept all night; he'd thought about it, and he realized I was right. Why would we make her a lesser woman than the white woman...? So then we began to design some gorgeous fashions which gave her dignity—which made the picture so much more interesting.

The Letter—and the performances of Bette Davis and Sondergaard—are classics, and Bette Davis opined in the book *Mother Goddam*, "Gale Sondergaard's performance in *The Letter* ... was breathtakingly sinister. I was so lucky that she was cast in this part."

Bela Lugosi looks tickled to be between Gale Sondergaard (left) and Anne Gwynne on the set of *The Black Cat*, 1941.

On December 19, 1940, Gale returned to Broadway, starring in *Cue for Passion* at the Royale Theatre. George Coulouris and Doris Nolan co-starred; Otto Preminger directed; and Gale played Frances Chapman, acting, as the *New York Times* reported, "with blistering ferocity all the way through." The play lasted only 12 performances.

While in New York for the play, Sondergaard and Herbert Biberman began adoption proceedings, and became the very happy parents of a baby girl, Joan Kirstina. Later in the early '40s, the couple also adopted a son, Daniel Hans.

Then, back in Hollywood, Sondergaard became part of the crazy world of Universal Pictures, playing in over a dozen of that studio's escapist movies between 1941 and 1947. She first visited the lot for 1941's *The Black Cat*, a horror/comedy with Basil Rathbone, Broderick Crawford, Hugh "Woo Woo" Herbert, Bela Lugosi, Gladys Cooper, Anne Gwynne (q.v.) and an on-the-eve-of-stardom Alan Ladd. *The Black Cat* (which was neither relation to Poe's tale, nor Universal's exquisite 1934 Karloff/Lugosi classic) cast Gale as Abigail, sinister-looking housekeeper.

Gale's verdict on *The Black Cat*: "I hated doing that thing. It was beneath me."

Gale worked at various studios during the war years: at Paramount, she was a sultry Nazi agent in Bob Hope's 1942 *My Favorite Blonde*, which also featured Madeleine Carroll and George Zucco; at Columbia, she played a British agent who sacrifices her life to help George Sanders escape the Nazis in 1943's *Appointment in*

Berlin; and at PRC, Gale ran a gambling casino and flirted with John Carradine and Frank Fenton in the Edgar G. Ulmer oddity *Isle of Forgotten Sins* (1943).

It was at Universal City, however, where Gale was most active during the World War II years. *The Strange Death of Adolf Hitler* (1943) saw Gale strongly sympathetic as the wife of a man forced by the Gestapo to double Hitler; 1944's *Christmas Holiday*, a Deanna Durbin vehicle, cast Gale as murderer Gene Kelly's quiet mother. Universal, meanwhile, had fashioned the "Inner Sanctum" series as a showcase for Lon Chaney and Gale. However, the series premiere entry, *Calling Dr. Death* (1943), was rewritten for Patricia Morison (q.v.), and Gale appeared in none of the studio's subsequent "Inner Sanctum" movies.

However, Sondergaard's most notorious performance of the era was in Universal's Sherlock Holmes saga *The Spider Woman* (1944). As Adrea Spedding, who destroys her male victims with an African spider whose horrible bite causes the men to go insane and kill themselves, Gale found a role which not only made her a nightmarish movie villainess, but a charmingly "camp" figure as well. As Michael Brunas, John Brunas and Tom Weaver wrote in *Universal Horrors*:

> The highlight of *The Spider Woman* is the malignant presence of Gale Sondergaard in the title role. Described by Holmes as a "female Moriarty," the detective more than meets his match in the Dragon Lady of screen terror. Sondergaard is a delight, gloating and chewing up the scenery, her cold, fixed smile exuding poison with every frame.

In his famous tome *An Illustrated History of the Horror Film*, Carlos Clarens hailed Sondergaard in this part as "the one woman in pictures who could outwit Sherlock Holmes and out-act Basil Rathbone."

Offscreen during the war years, "the Dragon Lady of screen terror" worked exhaustively selling war bonds. In July 1942, the U.S. Treasury Department reported that Sondergaard, in the uniform of the Women's Ambulance and Defense Corps, "eclipsed the records made by most of the glamour girls" in her travels and speeches throughout the Middle West, East, New England and Middle Atlantic States. She also loved her time as a mother and caring for her daughter Joan and son Daniel.

The melodramas rolled on at Universal. Nineteen forty-four's *The Invisible Man's Revenge* had invisible Jon Hall haunting Gale and Lester Matthews because he thinks they tried to kill him to snare his riches; John Carradine was the mad Dr. Drury (with invisible dog), Alan Curtis was the hero, Leon Errol the comedy relief and Evelyn Ankers (q.v.) the heroine. Fifth in Universal's *Invisible Man* series, *Revenge* took 33 days to shoot, cost $314,790 and took in a world-wide gross of $765,700. Gale's fee as "contract talent" for this film: a "flat" $6000—compared to Hall's $20,000, Curtis' and Errol's $6000, Carradine's $3500 and Ankers' $2100.

Gypsy Wildcat (1944) was a Maria Montez/Jon Hall costumer, with Gale as Gypsy, the fortune telling wife of Leo Carrillo. Nineteen forty-four's *The Climax* was Universal's Technicolor "welcome home" to Boris Karloff, following the star's *Arsenic and Old Lace* Broadway/road tour triumph. This $789,901.96 rip-off of Universal's own 1943 *Phantom of the Opera* flanked Karloff with Susanna Foster (q.v.) and Turhan Bey, with Gale as

Title card for *The Spider Woman*, 1944.

Luise, housekeeper to the mad Karloff, from whom she saves the blonde, soprano Susanna. Gale's Universal fee was still a "flat" $6000, compared to Boris' $40,000, Foster's $13,000 and Bey's $7000. Gale's final 1944 release was Universal's *Enter Arsene Lupin*, in which she played the "affectionate and conniving" aunt of Ella Raines.

Certainly one of Gale's unhappiest experiences of movie making was *The Spider Woman Strikes Back*, originally designed by Universal as the first in a *Spider Woman* series for Gale. First, Universal called Gale back from a tour of eastern hospitals in late May 1945, to begin *The Spider Woman Strikes Back*—only to have it delayed, and not begin its shoot until October 1. Meanwhile, Gale's slinky Adrea Spedding role from the 1944 Sherlock Holmes melodrama somehow metamorphosed into Zenobia Dollard—a Nevada philanthropist who feigns blindness, feeds live spiders and human blood to huge, *Little Shop of Horrors*–style plants in her cellar laboratory, and poisons the local ranchers' cattle. Universal even tossed in Rondo Hatton, the studio's acromegaliac "Monster Without Makeup," as Gale's deaf-mute servant Mario, attempting (with romantic leads Brenda Joyce and Kirby Grant) to pad out this sad 59-minute movie, which its own director Arthur Lubin, called "a horrible picture."

"I almost had hysterics one time out of just hating it so," Gale remembered. There were many factors involved; as Gale related to David Del Valle, there was a strike going on at the time, and Gale had to cross picket lines at Universal to report for work on *The Spider Woman Strikes Back*—an action that pained this life-long liberal. Also, Gale had no idea at the time that Rondo Hatton was indeed suffering from acromegaly; she thought he was the recipient of Jack P. Pierce makeup. "If I had known the truth of his condition," she told Del Valle, "I would have gone over and talked to him more."

Still, when Universal released *The Spider Woman Strikes Back* in March of 1946, audiences saw Gale giving her best to the proceedings. As the Brunases and Weaver salute her in *Universal Horrors*:

> Gale keeps a pretty tight rein on her performance and only occasionally succumbs to some good old-fashioned camping. The mere sight of the exquisitely wicked Sondergaard dropping spider snacks into the gaping blossoms of the vampire plants, her face beaming with perverted joy, is enough to warm the cockles of a horror fan's heart.

Nevertheless, Gale was greatly relieved when Universal canceled plans for a *Spider Woman* series.

She enjoyed a vivid role as evil sorceress Attossa in Universal's *A Night in Paradise* (1946), a Merle Oberon/Turhan Bey costume epic; and got into the spirit of 1946's *The Time of Their Lives*, an Abbott and Costello vehicle, with Gale again as a housekeeper, to whom Binnie Barnes quips, "Didn't I see you in *Rebecca*?"

One of Sondergaard's most impressive performances was as the gentle Lady Thiang, "Number One Wife" in 20th Century–Fox's 1946 *Anna and the King of Siam*, which starred Rex Harrison and Irene Dunne. "That was one of my favorite roles," said the actress. "I just loved this woman ... such a noble, wise, far-seeing woman who accepted her fate." It stands as a testimony to the actress' versatility and earned Gale her second Academy nomination—as Best Supporting Actress of 1946. Her competition that year: Ethel Barrymore for *The Spiral Staircase*; Anne Baxter for *The Razor's Edge*; Lillian Gish for *Duel in the Sun* and Flora Robson for *Saratoga Trunk*. The winner: Anne Baxter.

As Sondergaard enjoyed the acclaim of an Oscar nomination, trouble was brewing—ominously. In 1947, a year in which Sondergaard played Maria Montez's guardian aunt in Universal's *Pirates of Monterey* and Dorothy Lamour's wicked aunt in Paramount's Bing Crosby/Bob Hope *Road to Rio*, a disastrous chapter in Hollywood history began—the Communist Witchhunt. The House of Representatives' Committee on Un-American Activities began a widely publicized investigation into "infiltration of subversive propaganda into motion pictures," and the publicity was ugly—and sensational. The House entertained a number of "friendly witnesses" from Hollywood, among them Robert Taylor, Gary Cooper, Louis B. Mayer, Jack L. Warner and Adolphe Menjou—who, in feverishly angry testimony, claimed that, in the case of a Communist takeover, he would move to Texas—where (in his opinion) the populace would shoot a Communist on sight.

However, there were also, infamously, *un*friendly witnesses, who became known as "The Hollywood Ten": Alvah Bessie, Lester Cole, Edward Dmytryk, Ring Lardner, Jr.,

John Howard Lawson, Albert Maltz, Samuel Ornitz, Adrian Scott, Dalton Trumbo—and Herbert J. Biberman.

During the happy, busy years that Sondergaard had been acting in Hollywood, Biberman had also been busy—not only as a director and writer but as a founder of the Directors Guild and Hollywood Anti-Nazi League, and a member of the Screen Writers Guild. "If a committee of Congress can label certain thinking un-American and can forcibly pry one's mind open to discover and punish the thinking," wrote Biberman in his book *Salt of the Earth*, "then it can also outlaw ideas it dislikes, through intimidation." The Hollywood Ten all refused to testify, hoping a contempt citation would enable them to take the Committee to court, secure a constitutional judgment and end the Committee's power.

It was a long, costly, emotional drama. Hollywood split into factions; John Wayne, Ward Bond and Charles Coburn headed the anti-Communist Motion Picture Alliance while such stars as Humphrey Bogart, Lauren Bacall and Danny Kaye visited Washington to charge the House with a violation of civil rights. A blacklist developed, and after Biberman's refusal to testify, Sondergaard—herself an outspoken champion of liberal causes—found herself on it. Her friend Mervyn LeRoy did what he could to help, casting her in the small part of Barbara Stanwyck's mother in MGM's 1949 *East Side West Side*. Sondergaard recalls her part as "a test to see what the industry's reaction would be."

It would be her last motion picture for 20 years.

The Hollywood Ten lost their case. In June 1950, they went to jail. Biberman received a six-month sentence at the Federal Correctional Institution in Texarkana, Texas, as his wife made speeches in his defense. And after Biberman's release from jail, on February 28, 1951, Sondergaard was subpoenaed to appear before the House of Un-American Activities in Washington—along with such celebrities as Larry Parks, Howard da Silva, John Garfield, Jose Ferrer, writer Waldo Salt, Abe Burrows and Anne Revere.

Larry Parks, who had starred in Columbia's *The Jolson Story* and *Jolson Sings Again*, admitted to being a member in 1944 and 1945 of an actors' "cell" of the Communist party because, as a young liberal, he was "for the underdog"; he had long since left the party, feeling it was "subversive." On March 21, 1951, Parks emotionally begged the Committee not to "make me crawl in the mud" and name his fellow Communists. But the pressure was brutal, and the broken actor finally surrendered under questioning:

> THE COMMITTEE: Who were the members of the Communist Party cell to which you were assigned?
>
> PARKS: Morris Carnovsky, Joe Bromberg, Sam Rosen, Anne Revere, Lee Cobb, Gale Sondergaard and Dorothy Tree.
>
> THE COMMITTEE: I asked you this morning about Karen Morley. Was Karen Morley a member of the Communist Party?
>
> PARKS: Yes.

Those "named" by Parks and other "informers" all reacted in their own ways to the trouble. J. Edward Bromberg, one of Hollywood's busiest character actors of the late 1930s and early 1940s, crumpled under the weight of the blacklist, despairing until he lost his health. In 1951, he took a stage job in England and was found dead in his hotel room, presumably of a heart attack (although there have been rumors of suicide); HUAC agents took note of the mourners at his funeral. Lee J. Cobb made peace with the Committee, but suffered a massive heart attack he blamed on harassment by the witch hunt.

However, Sondergaard and Howard da Silva became two of the most vociferous, uncompromising and gallant fighters against the HUAC investigation. "I cannot but be saddened and angered by this new offensive against the progressive conscience of Hollywood," said the actress, who, like da Silva, refused to answer questions, invoking the Fifth Amendment. She also appealed to the Screen Actors Guild to protect her and fellow artists from a blacklist; however, the Guild officially responded, "If any actor, by his own actions, has so offended American public opinion that he has made himself unsalable at the box office, the Screen Actors Guild cannot force any employer to hire him." Because of their refusal to talk, Sondergaard and da Silva (whom RKO fired from the production *Slaughter Trail*, reshooting his work with Brian Donlevy at a cost of $100,000) faced a possible maximum penalty of a $1000 fine and a year's imprisonment for contempt—and found themselves poison in the eyes of Hollywood producers.

"I was very happy those first years," Sondergaard said. "I devoted all my time to my two adopted children. I was always busy. I became Mommy Gale; no more governesses or nurses or housekeepers. It was hard on the children at times. There was the name-calling in school, but we had many, many friends and they played with the children of our friends who had been called up before the committee. So it almost became normal among that group of children to have had a father who had to go to jail."

Still, Sondergaard aggressively battled the witch hunt. On March 10, 1953, the actress, along with such players as da Silva and Anne Revere (herself an Oscar winner for 1945's *Mildred Pierce*) and a fleet of blacklisted writers and former studio employees, sued virtually all the major studios and executives of Hollywood for $51,750,000 in damages, with each plaintiff asking $1,250,000 for loss of "employment opportunity," plus $1,000,000 punitive damages. The suit dragged on for years, unsuccessfully, going through court appeal all the way into the early 1960s.

Meanwhile, blacklisted Biberman courageously formed his own Independent Productions Company and directed 1954's *Salt of the Earth*, a fictional account of the strike of Mexican-American zinc miners in New Mexico in 1951 to 1953. The producer was blacklistee Paul Jarrico, the writer was blacklistee Michael Wilson and one of the few professional actors in the film was blacklistee Will Geer. The controversial *Salt of the Earth* could find limited bookings, but did win the Best Film and Best Actress (Rosaura Revueltas) prizes at the International Film Festival in Czechoslovakia, and the Academie du Cinéma de Paris bestowed awards on Biberman, Wilson and Miss Revueltas. The success did little, however, to help the Bibermans. The *Los Angeles Examiner*, for one, was more interested in reporting that, on November 28, 1955, a burglar "slugged and robbed" the Biberman's 14-year-old daughter Joan at their home at 3259 Deronda Avenue, knocking the girl down and scooping $45 worth of costume jewelry from her dresser, than it was in reporting the director's uphill artistic achievement.

In the summer of 1956, Philadelphia's Playhouse in the Park engaged Sondergaard to play the Dowager Empress to Signe Hasso's *Anastasia*. The American Legion's Philadelphia County Council vehemently protested; meanwhile, the HUAC called her in again to question her about her Communist colleagues. On July 17, 1956, Sondergaard once again took the Fifth Amendment and said, "For the committee to recall me here at this specific time while I am deeply involved in a creative work, the first in five years, can only be construed as an act of harassment."

Except for touring in a one-woman show which she had prepared with her husband, *Woman: Her Emergence into Fuller Status as a Human Being in Relation to Her Mate*, featuring scenes from five plays (including Ibsen's *A Doll's House*), Gale Sondergaard wouldn't work for another nine years.

After years of staying solvent in California as a land developer, Biberman moved to West End Avenue in New York City in 1963, so to be near a black collaborator on a film project, *Slaves*, for which he fought to get financing. Nineteen sixty-five would be a tragic year for the Bibermans—their daughter Joan, age 25, died. Yet, ironically, it was also the year that Sondergaard at last began rebuilding her career. On October 20, 1965, the actress opened at the Gramercy Arts Theatre in *The Woman*, which ran seven performances; on January 18, 1967, she returned to the Gramercy Arts Theatre in *Kicking the Castle Down*, playing Mrs. Kane opposite Trish Van Devere. In September 1967, Sondergaard played in *The Visit* at the Tyrone Guthrie Theatre in her native Minnesota; her alma mater, the University of Minnesota, presented her with its "Outstanding Achievement Award."

In 1969, Biberman's *Slaves* premiered, finally co-produced by the Theatre Guild, where the Bibermans had met 40 years earlier (it was, significantly, the Guild's first film production) and the Walter Reade Organization. *Slaves* starred Stephen Boyd, Dionne Warwick and Ossie Davis, with Gale in the supporting role of the "New Orleans Lady." Critics blasted the film as old-fashioned. However, Vincent Canby of the *New York Times* welcomed Sondergaard back to the screen, hailing her as the "one, unequivocally pleasant thing about *Slaves*," noting her appearance "recalled many memorable appearances in earlier, happier times."

In August 1969, Sondergaard played Maria in *Uncle Vanya* at the L.A. Center Theatre. There followed work in a film curiosity called *Comeback*, which featured Miriam Hopkins, John Garfield, Jr., Minta Durfee Arbuckle (Fatty's ex-wife), Lester Matthews, Joe Besser and Sondergaard as devoted secretary to aging actress Hopkins; it was finally released in 1976 under the title *Hollywood Horror House*. However, the most noteworthy job came in the Christmas Day, 1969, episode of ABC's *It Takes a Thief*, starring Robert Wagner; it was Miss Sondergaard's first engagement in the "mainstream" of Hollywood studios for almost 20 years to a day, and she received a warm welcome—especially from the technicians.

Guest star parts followed on such shows as *Get Smart*, *The Bold Ones*, *Night Gallery* and *Medical Center*. In 1970, she became a regular on ABC's daytime soap opera *The Best of Everything*, which unfortunately expired after only about six months.

On June 30, 1971, Herbert Biberman died of bone cancer; he was 71. His marriage to Sondergaard had lasted over 40 years, and they had loved and sustained each other through many perilous times. The widow moved back to California, where she took a home at 1924 Lakeshore Avenue in Los Angeles. In 1973, she played Rebecca Nurse on the L.A. stage in *The Crucible*. Now the movie colony made a tentative move of hatchet-burying and invited her to sit among the 100 cinema celebrities on the dais at Paramount's celebration of the 100th birthday of its founder, Adolph Zukor. Bob Hope, a guest at the bash, called the party "a living wax museum," but Sondergaard enjoyed the evening.

It was on October 24, 1973, however, that Hollywood made its official repentance to a gallant survivor. Sondergaard was playing a supporting part in an effective ABC TV film, *The Cat Creature*, which starred Meredith Baxter Birney and featured John Carradine; the day after shooting "wrapped," the actress was called back for "some closeups." However, when Sondergaard arrived in makeup and costume on the set, Charlton Heston entered—and presented the delighted actress with an Academy gold statuette, to replace the plaque she had won for 1936's *Anthony Adverse*.

Thereafter, Sondergaard worked steadily: as the "Elk Woman" in United Artists' 1976 *The Return of a Man Called Horse*, a part the actress described as "very primitive and noble"; guest-starred on eight episodes of the ABC soap opera *Ryan's Hope*; played an old woman who refuses to be evicted from her country home in "Pleasantville," the 11/6/77 episode of PBS's *Visions*; and played herself in 1976's *Hollywood on Trial*, a documentary on the blacklist. She also worked on the stage. She toured 1977 summer stock in *The Royal Family* with Sandy Dennis, and played at New York's Roundabout Theatre in *John Gabriel Borkman*, once again essaying villainy so incisively that critic Clive Barnes described the actress as having "bile in her veins rather than blood."

Still youthfully excited by acting, keeping healthy by daily yoga and swimming, Sondergaard fascinated all those she met in her last years by her energy and joy of life. She cherished the opportunity to work again: "I get great pleasure out of working. I like to create. This is when I come alive." She once said: "I just look at the natural progress of history going on and, thank goodness, within my lifetime, it has gotten better. One of my deepest regrets is that Herbert isn't here today to see what is happening to me because it is really phenomenal."

The actress refused to surrender to the years and, in her late '70s, sidestepped a question about her age, saying, "I don't know about those things. They're only numbers. Sometimes there's a six, sometimes a seven. What does it matter? The important thing is to enjoy life. I'm happy that I've had a long life. I've enjoyed myself and I hope I will continue. The best tonic for me is to keep working as an actress. That's what keeps the juices flowing."

One of the most fascinating things about Gale Sondergaard was her apparent lack of bitterness about the blacklist and her long-standing exile from Hollywood. "I never felt bitter about what happened," she told Hollywood columnist Bob Thomas. "I felt that I had been a part of history, and that made me proud." In her later years, the actress had written her memoir, and was seeking a publisher. However, the manuscript was considered too bland because the actress refused to write about the temperament and idiosyncrasies of her colleagues. To the last, the woman who moviegoers loved to hate refused "to hurt anyone," and her autobiography remained upbeat—and unpublished.

Sondergaard continued a busy life, guesting on such shows as ABC's *The Fall Guy* (12/9/81) and maintaining high visibility in Hollywood. Finally, on August 14, 1985, Sondergaard died at the Motion Picture and Television Hospital in Woodland Hills, California. She was 85 years old.

"I've played a variety of roles, more, in fact, than anyone else I know," Gale Sondergaard proudly stated late in her life; it held for her real-life "roles" as well. Indeed, with her liberal views, and tendency to think about the motivations of the characters she played, Sondergaard had an unusual attitude toward her movie work—an attitude that probably was no surprise to those who knew this actress and lady:

> Most of those movies were fun to do. I don't consider that I really ever did anything that was "horrible." That's why when interviewers want to come and talk about horror films, I say, "I wasn't in any."

The Films of Gale Sondergaard

1936

Anthony Adverse (Warner Bros., Mervyn LeRoy)

1937

Maid of Salem (Paramount, Frank Lloyd)
Seventh Heaven (20th Century–Fox, Henry King)
The Life of Emile Zola (Warner Bros., William Dieterle)

1938

Lord Jeff (MGM, Sam Wood)
Dramatic School (MGM, Robert B. Sinclair)

1939

Never Say Die (Paramount, Elliott Nugent)
Juarez (Warner Bros., W. Dieterle)
The Cat and the Canary (Paramount, E. Nugent)
The Llano Kid (Paramount, Edward D. Venturini)

1940

The Blue Bird (20th Century–Fox, Walter Lang)
The Mark of Zorro (20th Century–Fox, Rouben Mamoulian)
The Letter (Warner Bros., William Wyler)

1941

The Black Cat (Universal, Albert S. Rogell)
Paris Calling (Universal, Edwin L. Marin)

1942

My Favorite Blonde (Paramount, Sidney Lanfield)
Enemy Agents Meet Ellery Queen (Columbia, James Hogan)

1943

A Night to Remember (Columbia, Richard Wallace)
Isle of Forgotten Sins (PRC, Edgar G. Ulmer)
Appointment in Berlin (Columbia, Alfred E. Green)
The Strange Death of Adolf Hitler (Universal, J. Hogan)

1944

Sherlock Holmes and the Spider Woman (Universal, Roy William Neill)
Follow the Boys (Universal, A. Edward Sutherland)
Christmas Holiday (Universal, Robert Siodmak)
The Invisible Man's Revenge (Universal, Ford Beebe)
Gypsy Wildcat (Universal, R. W. Neill)
The Climax (Universal, George Waggner)
Enter Arsene Lupin (Universal, F. Beebe)

1946

The Spider Woman Strikes Back (Universal, Arthur Lubin)
A Night in Paradise (Universal, A. Lubin)
Anna and the King of Siam (20th Century–Fox, John Cromwell)
The Time of Their Lives (Universal, Charles T. Barton)

1947

The Pirates of Monterey (Universal, Alfred Werker)

Road to Rio (Paramount, Norman Z. McLeod)

1949

East Side, West Side (MGM, Mervyn LeRoy)

1969

Slaves (Continental Distributing, Herbert J. Biberman)

1973

The Cat Creature (ABC-TV Movie, Curtis Harrington)

1976

Hollywood Horror House (*Comeback*) (Avco-Embassy, Donald Wolfe)

The Return of a Man Called Horse (United Artists, Irwin Kershner)

Hollywood on Trial (Lumiere, David Helpern, Jr.)

Pleasantville (TV Movie/Visions-KCET, Kenneth Locker and Vicki Polan)

1983

Echoes (Continental, Arthur Allan Seidelman)

SHORT SUBJECTS

1939

Sons of Liberty (Warner Bros., Michael Curtiz)

Virginia Christine

August 1944.

A swamp on Universal's back lot.

Suddenly, a hand rises out of the mud, reaching toward the rejuvenating sun. The quagmire quivers, and there arises a female mummy, with a face like the Sphinx, horrifically caked with muck, stretching, jerking and falling as she escapes her boggy grave. Feminine vanity prevails, and the distaff mummy makes for a pool to bathe away her full-length mudpack. Glamorously she emerges, in sexy black wig, clingy white nightgown and 1944 false eyelashes, as the oomphy reincarnation of Princess Ananka—stealing *The Mummy's Curse* from Lon Chaney's galumphing Mummy and giving one of the most dynamic performances of Universal's long-celebrated horror shows.

The actress: Virginia Christine.

A veteran of over 50 films, wife of super character player Fritz Feld for over 50 years, known to literally millions for over 20 years of commercials as "Mrs. Olson" of Folger Coffee fame, Virginia Christine—who died in 1996—enjoyed an incredibly rich career and life. One of her most memorable adventures (or *mis*adventures) was *The Mummy's Curse*, and she'd gently laugh as she remembered the role which has won her a special celebrity in the realm of fantasy films.

> Resurrected in Horror! Rising out of Death! Egypt's Ancient Lovers ... Live again in Evil ... to fulfill *The Mummy's Curse...*
>
> —from the preview trailer for *The Mummy's Curse*

Universal's classic *The Mummy* (1932) was more a macabre romance than a horror movie—a superb fantasy, with Karloff's 3700-year-old Im-Ho-Tep rising from his sarcophagus to seek his reincarnated "Anck-es-en-Amon," Zita Johann. Karl Freund's direction made it all seem a fantastic dream, and *The Mummy* survives as perhaps the most sublime of all of Universal's classic horror tales.

It's ironic, therefore, that the ensuing *Mummy* series was one of the most rowdy, silly, cheap and critically panned of Universal's horror series—the Mummy becoming the most raspberried of the studio's top hobgoblins.

First sequel: 1940's *The Mummy's Hand*, with cowboy star Tom Tyler playing "Kharis" (while actually suffering from arthritis); Peggy Moran (q.v.) made a cute heroine, Dick Foran and Wallace Ford were fun heroes and George Zucco stole the show as the evil high priest, whose yen for the supple Miss Moran brings on the climactic mayhem. Kharis absorbed a slew of bullets—then was barbecued in the temple (left over from James Whale's 1940 Universal *Green Hell*). The tab for this sequel: $84,000—and that was $4000 over budget!

Back Kharis came—now in the beefy form of Lon Chaney, Jr. ("The Screen's Master Character Creator"), in *The Mummy's Tomb* (1942). "The fire that sought to consume Kharis," rasped the palsied high priest Zucco, "only seared and twisted and

***Chapter opener:* Virginia Christine emerges from the swamp in *The Mummy's Curse*, 1944.**

After a bath, the formerly slime-covered Christine emerges as the sexy reincarnation of Princess Ananka.

maimed!" Young high priest Turhan Bey brought Chaney's Mummy on a revenge junket to New England, where Kharis shuffled on nights of the full moon, limping on his one good leg, strangling with his one good arm and rolling his one good eye before roasting once more in a New England mansion. Harold Young directed.

Come *The Mummy's Ghost* (1944), and Kharis was back once more, tended to by new Egyptian high priest John Carradine—dispatched by the ancient, still trembling Zucco to rendezvous in New England with Kharis for a new killing spree. Reginald LeBorg directed nimbly, with some nice touches—such as those sexy white streaks in the brunette hair of lush starlet Ramsay Ames, and which became more white whenever the Mummy came ambling by her path. In the finale, Chaney's Kharis knocked Carradine's lusty priest out of the elevated mining shack they shared, and a torch-bearing posse chased pudgy Kharis and his "Ananka" (nightgowned naturally, and aging quickly à la *Lost Horizon*) into the muck of a swamp.

Universal's *Mummy* series was great fun; for all the shortcomings, there was something wonderfully Halloween-ish about Kharis, loping about the countryside under a full moon, sipping those life-giving Tana leaves, performing that weird, shuffling dance to Hans J. Salter's moody, thundering musical strains. The series' leading ladies—Peggy Moran (q.v.), Elyse Knox and Ramsay Ames—made a striking

Looking smashing in a black wig, actress Virginia Christine reclines in *The Mummy's Curse*, 1944.

beauty parade. And it was fun to watch the eyes of Zucco, Bey and Carradine light up with the lust that invariably ran them afoul of the good graces of Amon-Ra.

Yet the films were cheap. All the *Mummy* sequels were shot in summer—like some annual Egypt-motif picnic on the Universal back lot. Chaney hated the makeup. In the San Fernando Valley heat, Lon had groused to reporters about the Jack P. Pierce makeup ("I itch and I can't scratch!") and opined that audiences who spent money to see Mummy movies were "nuts." And the critical notices seemed enough to kill off any self-respecting monster—such as these fourth estate reflections on *The Mummy's Ghost*:

> *New York World-Telegram*: The Mummy always has been the least impressive of movie monsters and he is doing nothing to enhance his reputation in his latest incarnation in *The Mummy's Ghost*... He is just repulsive without being picturesque or even particularly frightening... Let's hope that this time those Egyptians are satisfied and let their old mummy stay dead.

Yet less than a month after *The Mummy's Ghost* horrified the New York critics, defiant Universal began shooting the fourth Mummy sequel—*The Mummy's Curse*.

Chaney, of course, was back as Kharis; Dennis Moore and Kay Harding would play the love interest; Peter Coe was the high priest, and Martin Kosleck ("I am but flesh and blood!") inherited the lust as Coe's murderous acolyte. Leslie Goodwins would direct.

The flashy part, this time however, was not Kharis; it was a female mummy—Ananka. For the juicy role, Universal needed a starlet who was a fine enough actress to play a resurrected mummy, a woman beautiful enough to score as the "new" Ananka, and a trouper willing to be buried in a swamp.

A beautiful, talented trouper was just who Universal found.

Virginia Christine was born Virginia Kraft in Stanton, Iowa, on March 10, 1917 (some sources say 1920). Moving with her parents to Los Angeles when she was a teenager, Virginia attended UCLA, studied piano and voice, and landed the role of Irene Rich's daughter on the radio show *Dear John*. She also met actor Fritz Feld, the Reinhardt-trained character actor who would claim late-in-life to have played in over 400 films and TV shows—and who was instantly recognizable for his trademark "pop" sound he vocally delivered with such comic élan. They began over 50 years of marriage November 11, 1940; Feld was 40, Virginia 23.

Feld directed Virginia in an L.A. stage production as *Hedda Gabler* (1942), which won her praise—and a Warner Bros. contract. The striking blonde actress made her film debut in the 58-minute "B" *Truck Busters* (1943), then followed impressively in Warners' *Edge of Darkness* (1943), starring Errol Flynn. Virginia's role was a shy, pretty Norwegian housemaid with the prophetic name of Miss Olson.

Freelancing, Virginia worked at Universal in the 13-chapter western serial *Raiders of Ghost City* (1944), as femme fatale Trina Dessard, teaming wickedly with Lionel Atwill's gold-lusting villain.

"Lionel Atwill was a great ham, a poseur, and I mean that as a compliment," Virginia told me. "We got along very well—he was a delight."

Then Virginia signed for *The Mummy's Curse*—at the fee of $250 per week.

In 1986, relaxing at her ocean-view house in Brentwood, Virginia Christine remembered the melodrama:

> Before I could be okayed for the part, I had to go see Jack Pierce, the head of the makeup department, and he had to look at the contours of my face and see if he could make a mummy out of me. Jack was a big braggadocio—he did create all the Frankensteins, and was a master of the monster pictures—and he wanted the news to go around that he was about to do something new.
>
> So ... they saved that rejuvenation shot for the last day of shooting, so in case they killed me off, everything would be in the can! And Jack kept saying, all through the picture, "Virginia, don't you worry about your skin at all in the female mummy makeup. I'm using something different—just don't you worry."

Needless to say, with such warnings, Virginia *did* worry as *The Mummy's Curse* began shooting at Universal on Wednesday, July 26, 1944, on a $123,000 budget and a 12-day schedule. From his first review of the proposed script, Hollywood's almighty

Lon Chaney, Jr., director Leslie Goodwins and Virginia Christine relax in the summer heat during the shooting of *The Mummy's Curse*, 1944.

censor Joseph I. Breen had worried about the role of Ananka—as expressed in this letter of July 21, 1944 to Universal:

> Ananka, the Egyptian girl, is described in several places as rather lightly clothed in a nightgown. It will be absolutely essential to see that she is properly clothed in such a way as not to expose her body, and when the clothes are described as wet, they should not offensively outline her body.

Nevertheless, Virginia Christine's Ananka (in reincarnated form) was an eyeful. The "princess" makes her first glamorous entrance, in the woods, in clingy nightgown, black wig and unholy trance, weirdly crying "Kharis" and sounding (appropriately) like a lost cat in heat. Indeed, Virginia made the resurrected Ananka fascinating and remarkably sexy.

"I loved myself in that black wig," laughed blonde Virginia. "I thought I was smashing!"

However, if Virginia was smashing, Chaney was smashed. His Mummy had a thirst for more than Tana leaves. There were far worse ways to earn $8000 in 1944 than starring as the Mummy, yet Chaney hated the role; he fortified himself for the heat by retreating to his dressing room between scenes, opening his refrigerator and sprawling on the floor under the cool air. And there was plenty of liquid refreshment in the bungalow.

Virginia worked well with Chaney, although she found him "a big oaf—ham-fisted, not much sensitivity." However, there came the shot on the back lot where Lon's imbibing might have caused a terrible accident:

> Evelyn Ankers had played Lon Chaney's leading lady, and she was a big girl, a heavy girl. So Chaney had asked that they design a strap that went around his neck and around her waist to take some of the weight off his arms. One day on the back lot, we were doing this shot in which the Mummy was to carry me up to the old shrine, the monastery, up these steep, crooked, worn steps.
>
> They were hard enough to navigate if you were sober. And there I was, with this strap inherited from Evelyn Ankers attached to my waist, around Lon Chaney's neck, starting up these steps—and he is absolutely stoned. I always hate, when they're gone, to say bad things, but it was an actual fact—Chaney was just stoned. He was pretty much throughout the picture!
>
> We start up the steps, and he's *weaving*, going side-to-side on these uneven steps. Chaney was a big guy, and if he fell down those stone steps, with me *attached* to him, I hate to think what would have happened!
>
> Finally, the director, Leslie Goodwins, said, "Cut!" and they took Chaney out of the Mummy suit, and put the stand-in into it. So he carried me up—and I was enormously relieved!

The Mummy's Curse shot quickly—filming on such back lot sites as the jungle set from *Gung Ho!* (which became the exterior of the construction camp), the "Singapore Street" (which was used as the exterior of the Cajun cafe) and the hillside of Pollard Lake (with its exterior monastery steps from James Whale's 1940 *Green Hell*). The film came complete with a musical number ("Hey You," sung by "Tante Berthe," played by Ann Codee) and a few nice touches (when Tante fights the Mummy as he attacks Ananka in her boudoir, dust flies off the battling monster). Shooting unofficially "wrapped" on Thursday, August 10—two days over schedule. Yet Universal had left one very vital scene unshot...

It's uncanny how *Mummy* history repeated itself on the Universal lot. On the original *The Mummy* in 1932, Junior Laemmle and director Karl Freund had saved until the end the reincarnation episode (cut before release) of Zita Johann as a Christian martyr, fed to the lions, in case the actress was mauled (or worse) by the beasts.

Now, in 1944, Universal saved for the last day of *The Mummy's Curse* the scene in which Ananka rose from the swamp—and for which Virginia would have to wear the Jack P. Pierce mystery makeup and be buried alive in a back lot bog.

The scene was finally shot August 21, 1944. Virginia remembers well the scary eve of shooting:

> Well! By the time we came to the last day of shooting, I was a wreck, and my husband, Fritz Feld, called Jack Pierce at night,

> at home, and said, "Jack! *Please*! Tell me what it is you're going to do to Virginia tomorrow!"
>
> And Jack said, "Tell her not to worry. It's just a 'Denver mudpack.'"

In truth, Virginia *had* reason to worry. As *The Mummy's Curse* was shooting, Pierce had experimented with a makeup that was *very* severe. As a Universal memo of September 22, 1944 later confided:

> As originally planned, these scenes were actually to be made with trick photography. However, after we discovered that the makeup and conditions under which Miss Christine would have to work were apt to cause serious results to her features, this plan was abandoned…

So the studio decided to forsake Pierce's latest stroke of cosmetic genius—although what ultimately transpired was horrible enough. The actress never forgot Jack Pierce's lovingly painstaking application of the "Denver mudpack":

> I'll tell you how they did it. I was in the makeup chair, I think, at 4:30 in the morning. They took little patches of cotton, wet with witch hazel, put them on and lined them to fill in the youthful contours. Then Jack put on the "Denver mudpack," just a little bit at a time, then lined *that* with wrinkles, then blow-dried it—each little patch until I was an absolutely rigid mask. And we made a mistake in wardrobe. We had the arms bare—so we had to do the arms and the hands, too.
>
> Well, it took forever, and, of course, a very human thing happened—I had to go to the bathroom. Jack's wife was a body makeup lady, and she took me, like a child, to the bathroom, and pulled my panties down. Well, I have this sense of humor that's very close to the surface, but I couldn't laugh because the makeup would crack and they would have to start all over. It was just too ridiculous!

Fortified by a malted milk, Virginia, in full Mummy guise, was driven to the back lot. As Jack Pierce had hoped, word had spread about his new creation, and all of Universal (even Ingrid Bergman, who was on the lot that day, possibly to shoot a scene for Alfred Hitchcock's *Spellbound*) congregated to see the female mummy rise from its swampy grave:

> They took me out on the back lot, where the grave was dug, right in the soil—not clean, sifted sand! Then they covered me with burnt cork, then they sprayed it with water. Here, I'm lying in the earth with only my nostrils open for breathing—and I began to think of all the things that crawl in the earth…
>
> Then, at the last minute, they put the burnt cork (that looks like soil) over my face. I had to get up, and walk—into a stinking, slimy, infested pool, covered with algae, down two or three steps into the pond, and wade in up to my neck…

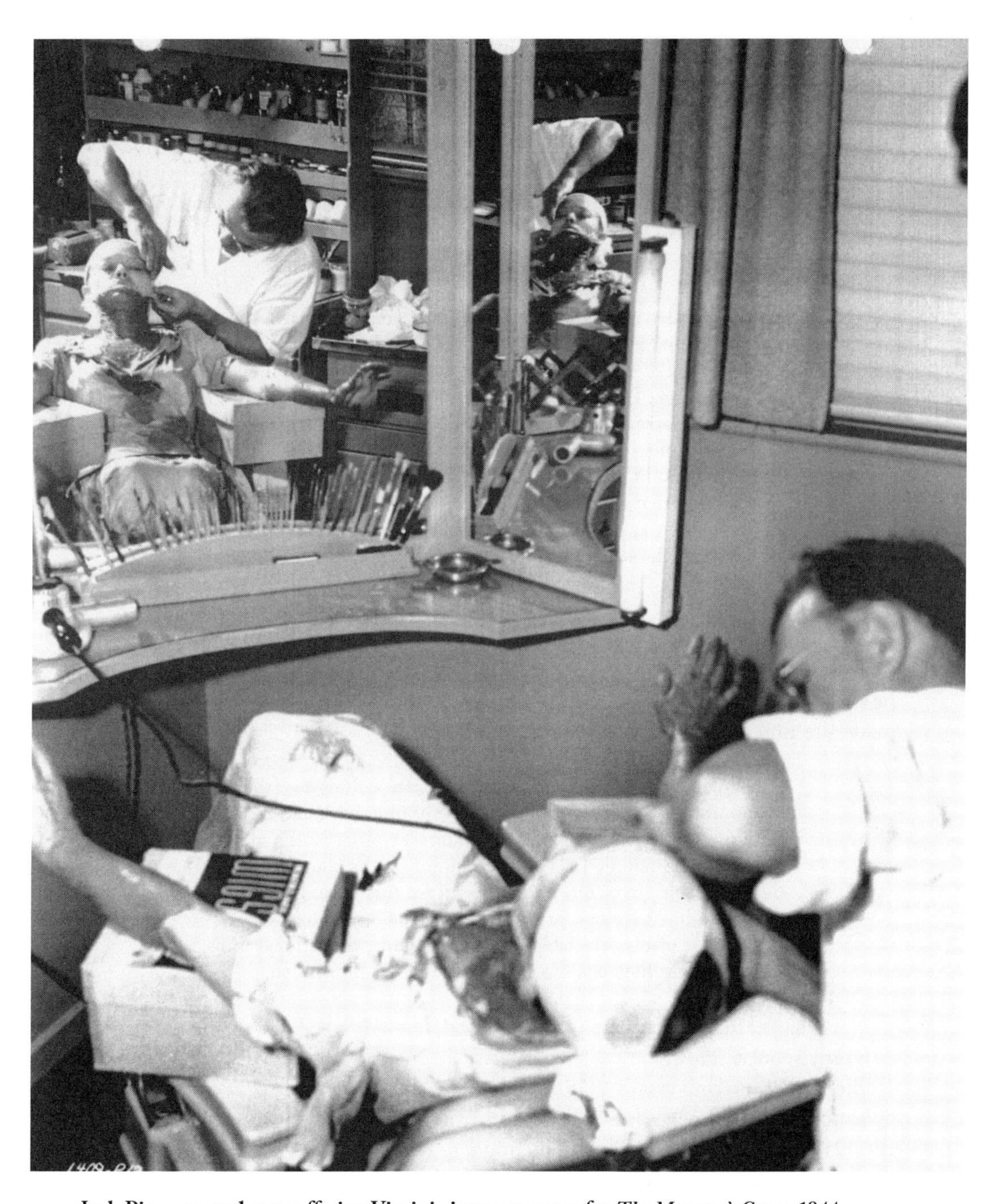

Jack Pierce turns long-suffering Virginia into a mummy for *The Mummy's Curse*, 1944.

Well, for the first time in my life, I was ready to scream, "No, I can't do it!" because it's *so* awful to look at! But then I thought, "You wanted to be an actress—let's go!"

Anyway, finally it was over, and then everybody was very helpful. The limousine was there, and they had a drink for me, and towels, and the whole bit.

The Mummy's Curse was finally finished. Universal tallied the final cost at $127,535.61—about $4500 over budget. Virginia's salary for two weeks and one day of work—$541.67! (She later collected an additional $250 for the time that elapsed between the "wrap" of the film and her callback for the resurrection episode.)

The first engagements for *The Mummy's Curse* came just before Christmas, 1944, when it opened in Hollywood on a double-bill with *House of Frankenstein*. On March 30, 1945, *The Mummy's Curse* braved New York City's Rialto Theatre as a headliner attraction. As *New York Post* critic Archer Winsten reported:

> A 13-headed dragon could be no more preposterous... There is, though, one bit of fancy which has its own charm. Out of the mud track of a passing bulldozer you see a hand and then an arm emerge. Lo! It's a female mummy, the onetime girl of Chaney, somewhat the worse for dirt after all those years. She staggers off to the nearest pool, and when she comes out, she'd remind you of anything but a mummy. You will be safe in assuming that there has never been a mummy half as well-built or a quarter as good-looking. Just for the record, her name is Virginia Christine. Lon Chaney pursues her, as who would not...

The movie shuffled into an unusually hot critical roasting. "Mummy Love," mocked the headline of the *New York Times* review ("It's time to tell that Mummy he's a bore," judged Bosley Crowther); John T. McManus, of New York's *PM*, almost made the film a national social and economic issue:

> While intrepid white men beat the bush looking for [the mummy], a Negro workman keeps running back and forth in mortal terror, reporting on the mummy's progress. Finally an abandoned temple falls on the mummy and a couple of other expendable characters and that's all for this time. Because the big studios have first priority on available ray film, there is a shortage of film available for independents, educational films, etc. This is how one big studio expends its film ration.

Perhaps Universal finally was chastened; *The Mummy's Curse* was the last of the Mummy sequels. He came back as "Klaris," in the form of famed horror stuntman Eddie Parker, in Universal's 1955 *Abbott and Costello Meet the Mummy*, then went away forever. Hammer Films of England would resurrect the Mummy character for the 1959 Christopher Lee/Peter Cushing *The Mummy*, which owed at least as much to the Universal sequels as it did to the 1932 original.

Whatever one thinks of Universal's late-lamented Mummy, there's no denying the intensity, poetry and passion with which Virginia Christine plays Ananka in *The Mummy's Curse*. Her fervent delivery of lines such as "Sometimes it seems as if I belong to a different world!"; her bloodcurdling scream; and (of course) that wonderfully horrific entrance—all make Virginia's Ananka one of the best, most striking, most originally played horror performances of the '40s. Returned to dead mummy form come the finale, after Chaney's mad old Mummy attacks the treacherous Martin

Kosleck and destroys part of the monastery, Virginia achieves a bit of the same romance and pathos that made Karloff's performance in the original *The Mummy* so beloved a classic.

Virginia returned to Universal for one more horror film—*House of Horrors* (1946), as a hooker whose back is snapped by Rondo ("The Creeper") Hatton. In her tight dress, beret and sexy grin, Virginia made a very spicy lady of the streets, sashaying through Universal's "Tenement Street" on the back lot—but the memory of the two-day job made her laugh.

"Jean Yarbrough wanted a cat to follow me down the street, so they put sardines or anchovies into the back of my high heel shoe!" Ironically, after Virginia suffered such an odiferous indignity, the cat was cut from the scene.

Virginia went on to appear in many exceptional films; for Stanley Kramer, she acted in such acclaimed movies as *The Men* (1950), *Cyrano de Bergerac* (1950), *High Noon* (1952), *Not as a Stranger* (1955), *Judgment at Nuremberg* (1961), and *Guess Who's Coming to Dinner* (1967)—very memorable in the last as the glamorous bigot whom Katharine Hepburn fires. She worked for everyone from Edgar G. Ulmer (PRC's *The Wife of Monte Cristo*, 1946), to Walt Disney (Buena Vista's *Johnny Tremain*, 1957), from the 1954 feature film of *Dragnet* (directed by Jack Webb himself) to both the 1946 and 1964 versions of *The Killers*. She played in the 1956 science fiction classic *Invasion of the Body Snatchers*, directed by Don Siegel ("an actor's director," said Virginia), and the infamous 1966 *Billy the Kid Versus Dracula* with John Carradine ("We had such a good time on that stupid Dracula picture!").

She also played in plenty of TV shows, including *Science Fiction Theatre*, *Thriller*, *The Twilight Zone*, *The Invaders*, *Tales of Wells Fargo* (a regular as "Widow Ovie" during the 1961 season), *Gunsmoke* and *Bonanza*. In a 1956 episode of *Adventures of Superman*, Virginia was the Lady in Black ("The producers had no money for anything, and I had to make my own hat with the veil!"). The climax of that show saw George Reeves' Man of Steel using his super breath to blow off Virginia's hat, veil and wig to reveal her true identity.

Virginia became most-recognized for her 20-plus year stint as "Mrs. Olson," the Swedish spokeswoman for Folger's Coffee. Her long-running identity with Mrs. Olson won her lush residuals, and a special honor in her hometown of Stanton, Iowa: the town water tower was made to resemble a giant coffee pot!

In 1985, after she had ceased to be the Folger's character, Virginia told the *Los Angeles Times*:

> As Mrs. Olson, I had a wardrobe of aprons the likes of which I'd never seen. She started out as a nice cleaning lady, but thankfully over the years, and after hundreds of commercials, she came of age. She traded in her polyester J. C. Penney outfits for knit suits, and like Cinderella, Mrs. Olson was finally invited to parties, if not balls.

Virginia and Fritz Feld had two sons, Steven and Danny. They vacationed all over the world, and regularly judged the annual American College Theatre Festival (which, in 1975, gave the Felds the Award of Excellence for distinguished service).

Brentwood California, 1987: Virginia Christine and her husband Fritz Feld are visited by the author at their ocean-view home.

They became two of the most beloved people in Hollywood, serving jointly at one point as honorary mayors of Brentwood. When my wife Barbara and I visited them in 1987, they were kind, gracious and delightful; "Fritzie" played the piano, and they showed us a magnificent scrapbook covering their careers.

In 1993, Fritz Feld died at age 93. Virginia, who had suffered a stroke, battled back, but she continued to have heart problems. On July 24, 1996, she died in her sleep at the Brentwood house. She was 79 years old (some sources say 76). Her survivors included the two sons, two grandchildren and two nieces.

In so full a career and life, one might have imagined that Virginia Christine would have tired of the notoriety of *The Mummy's Curse*, and have wanted to forget its various indelicate memories. However, this charming, talented and remarkably kind lady always insisted that wasn't so.

"After all," Virginia would laugh of her now-classic mudbath, "that was one of my life experiences!"

The Films of Virginia Christine

1943

Truck Busters (Warner Bros., B. Reeves Eason)
Edge of Darkness (Warner Bros., Lewis Milestone)
Mission to Moscow (Warner Bros., Michael Curtiz)

1944

The Mummy's Curse (Universal, Leslie Goodwins)
The Old Texas Trail (Universal, Lewis D. Collins)

1945

Counter-Attack (Columbia, Zoltan Korda)
Phantom of the Plains (Republic, Lesley Selander)
Girls of the Big House (Republic, George Archainbaud)

1946

Idea Girl (Universal, Will Jason)
House of Horrors (Universal, Jean Yarbrough)
The Inner Circle (Republic, Phil Ford)
Murder Is My Business (PRC, Sam Newfield)
The Wife of Monte Cristo (PRC, Edgar G. Ulmer)
The Killers (Universal-International, Robert Siodmak)
The Mysterious Mr. Valentine (Republic, P. Ford)

1947

The Gangster (Allied Artists, Gordon Wiles)
The Invisible Wall (20th Century–Fox, Eugene Forde)

1948

Women in the Night (Film Classics, William Rowland)
Night Wind (20th Century–Fox, James Tinling)

1949

Cover Up (United Artists/Nasser, Alfred E. Green)
Special Agent (Paramount/Pine-Thomas, William C. Thomas)

1950

The Men (United Artists/Kramer, Fred Zinnemann)
Cyrano de Bergerac (United Artists/Kramer, Michael Gordon)

1952

High Noon (United Artists/Kramer, F. Zinnemann)
Never Wave at a WAC (RKO, Norman Z. McLeod)
The First Time (Columbia, Frank Tashlin)

1953

The Woman They Almost Lynched (Republic, Allan Dwan)

1954

Dragnet (Warner Bros., Jack Webb)

1955

The Cobweb (MGM, Vincente Minnelli)
Good Morning, Miss Dove (20th Century–Fox, Henry Koster)
Not as a Stranger (United Artists, Stanley Kramer)

1956

The Killer Is Loose (United Artists, Bud Boetticher)
Nightmare (United Artists, Maxwell Shane)
Invasion of the Body Snatchers (Allied Artists, Don Siegel)

1957

Three Brave Men (20th Century–Fox, Philip Dunne)
Johnny Tremain (Buena Vista, Robert Stevenson)
The Spirit of St. Louis (Warner Bros., Billy Wilder)
The Careless Years (United Artists, Arthur Hiller)

1960

Flaming Star (20th Century–Fox, D. Siegel)

1961

Judgment at Nuremberg (United Artists, S. Kramer)

1962

Incident in an Alley (United Artists, Edward L. Cahn)

1963

Cattle King (MGM, Tay Garnett)
Four for Texas (Warner Bros., Robert Aldrich)

1964

One Man's Way (United Artists, Denis Sanders)
The Killers (Universal, D. Siegel)

1965

A Rage to Live (United Artists, Walter Grauman)

1966

Billy the Kid vs. Dracula (Embassy, William Beaudine)

1967

In Enemy Country (Universal, Harry Keller)
Guess Who's Coming to Dinner? (Columbia, S. Kramer)

1969

Hail, Hero (National General, David Miller)

Miss Christine appeared in two serials:

1944

Raiders of Ghost City (Universal—13 chapters, Ray Taylor and Lewis D. Collins)

1946

The Scarlet Horseman (Universal—13 chapters, Ray Taylor and Lewis D. Collins)

She also acted in the ABC-TV movies *Daughter of the Mind* (1969) and *The Old Man Who Cried Wolf* (1970), both directed by Walter Grauman, and in the 1943 color Warner Bros. short subject *Women at War*, directed by Jean Negulesco.

Jane Adams

"DRACULA!
Frankenstein's MONSTER!
WOLF MAN!
MAD DOCTOR!
HUNCHBACK!"

It was the fall of 1945, and the Horror Circus once again had come to Universal City.

In the box office wake of *House of Frankenstein*, the studio was now hosting *House of Dracula*. Back from the first "Monster Rally" were Lon Chaney in the yak hair and fangs of the Wolf Man, John Carradine in the cape and top hat of Dracula, and Glenn Strange as the Frankenstein Monster.

In a commissary full of Deanna Durbin, Abbott and Costello, Maria Montez, Basil Rathbone, Nigel Bruce, et al., *House of Dracula* might have inspired its share of gossip. The fact that Chaney, long campaigning for romantic assignments, was actually to receive a "cure" for his lycanthropy, and end up with blonde leading lady Martha O'Driscoll ... that John Carradine, not long before *House of Dracula* began shooting, had been tossed into jail by his ex-wife for back alimony ... the fact that Onslow Stevens, playing the starring role of Dr. Franz Edelmann, was a real-life nudist (and that Carradine's new blonde actress-wife, Sonia, had once been Stevens' mistress)...that 60-year-old Lionel Atwill, back once again as an inspector in a Frankenstein movie, had just become during the filming (along with his 28-year-old wife) the parents of a baby boy.

But there was gossip, too, that a new starlet on the lot named Jane "Poni" Adams was in *House of Dracula*—as a hunchback. For many vain glamour girls, it seemed a fate worse than death in catty Hollywood circles.

In fact, Jane Adams was having a wonderful time: enjoying her tragic role, posing with the "actor's chair" she'd been presented on the set, observing the work of Carradine, Chaney and others, posing for PR shots with Glenn Strange's Monster, and fascinated by the fantasy, mechanics and fun of making a horror movie.

Indeed, for Jane Adams, *House of Dracula* "is probably my favorite film."

It's always seemed a cruel "come-on" that, in hawking *House of Dracula* ("Universal's Spectacular Sequel to *House of Frankenstein*!"), the studio promoted Jane Adams as one of the ghoulish attractions. For as Nina—the deformed, doomed nurse of miracle-working scientist Dr. Edelmann (Stevens)—this beautiful brunette actress gave her character such charm, sincerity, gentleness and dignity that this "Monster Rally" achieved an actual depth as a consequence. Jane played the self-sacrificing Nina with the pathos that was always a dynamic part of Universal's horror mythology, and her death scene—strangled by the mad, Jekyll/Hyde Edelmann, whom she had admired and loved so much—gives *House of Dracula* a true touch of tragedy.

Actually *House of Dracula* was just one of several credits of interest to horror fans: She was also the blind pianist loved by Rondo Hatton in *The Brute Man* (1946)

***Chapter opener:* Dr. Edelmann (Onslow Stevens) strangles his devoted nurse, Nina (Jane Adams), in the climax of *House of Dracula*, 1945.**

and leading lady of the Bowery Boys horror-comedy *Master Minds* (1949). And, in serials, she had the distinction of being the last lady ever menaced by Lionel Atwill in that actor's final screen work, Universal's *Lost City of the Jungle* (1946). She was Vicki Vale in Columbia's *Batman and Robin* (1949); and she even got into the horror act on TV—guesting on "The Ghost Wolf" episode of *Adventures of Superman*, in which the Man of Steel sought the trail of a werewolf.

Her real life has been far happier than her screen roles. In July of 1995, she celebrated 50 years of marriage to Major Gen. Thomas Turnage (whom she wed shortly before starting work on *House of Dracula*); today she lives in posh Rancho Mirage, California. A delightful, upbeat lady whom husband and friends call "B.J.," she vows she never was bitter about playing *House of Dracula*'s hunchbacked nurse; if there were ever any unpleasant memories of her movie-making career, she's long exorcised them, and radiates exuberant joy whenever she remembers her Hollywood days.

"I *loved* it!" says Jane Adams.

For years, Jane Adams was a "lost" player. If horror fans imagined an aging glamour girl, hiding from the notoriety of *House of Dracula*, nothing could be further from the truth. Petite, still brunette, "B.J." graciously and energetically greets my wife and me at her Rancho Mirage house, taking us on a tour of the home and showing the magnificent vista of mountains across the golf course. Her husband, a retired major general who has been a personal advisor to several presidents, is equally charming; they joke and laugh, and Jane (born Betty Jane Bierce) remembers her life with almost Pollyanna happiness:

> I was born in San Antonio, Texas, but we moved to California when I was two. When I was four years old (this probably sounds boastful, but I don't mean it to!), I was tested, and found to have the second highest I.Q. in the State of California. And then I went on to become a concert mistress of the Los Angeles all-city high school orchestra. All of which is to say that I had a background in the arts—and the big thing for me was attending the Pasadena Playhouse.

The famed Pasadena Playhouse was the legendary training ground of such talents as Robert Preston, Louise Allbritton (q.v.), Laird Cregar; it also hosted famous actors—e.g., John Carradine and his Shakespearean repertory company played *Hamlet*, *The Merchant of Venice* and *Othello* there in the fall of 1943 before opening in San Francisco. Jane turned down a full scholarship to study violin at Juilliard to attend Pasadena Playhouse, and remembers her training there:

> Oh, it was great! We had three stages—main stage, lab stage, and theater-in-the-round. We started in that school with Roman tragedies and went all the way up through modern drama. We did everything, read everything, had classes all day in fencing, costume design, history of the theatre—everything. So I had my theater arts degree from there.

Meanwhile, Jane landed small parts on radio—Cecil B. De Mille's *Lux Radio Theatre* and the *Whistler* series. Jane's beauty won her a job as a Harry Conover model in New York City; it was Conover who dubbed her "Poni" (Jane has never understood why!). In New York, she worked in experimental TV and was the "Dodge Girl" for a year. She recalls making "four or five magazine covers," as well as "a full-page picture for *Esquire* magazine."

Jane had made some promotional short films for Dr. Pepper in New York, and the company was so pleased they sent her to Hollywood to be hostess of their new radio game show, *Darts for Dough*. In the midst of this eventful career rise, there was a tragedy: Jane had married an Annapolis cadet, who was killed during his first World War II mission.

Meanwhile, producer Walter Wanger had seen Jane's *Esquire* shot, and invited her to Universal City to test for the lead—in *Salome, Where She Danced* (1945).

"Yvonne de Carlo got the part, but I did get a nice contract," says Jane of *Salome, Where She Danced*, Technicolor escapism which also featured Rod Cameron and David Bruce—and gave Jane her film debut as "one of the girls." The film later became rather an inside joke for most who labored in it as one of the worst movies ever made by Universal, but Jane is grateful to it.

> They had signed about five girls at that time, but they soon let all of them go except Yvonne and me. I really think the thing that enabled me to stay there was my four years at the Pasadena Playhouse; they knew that, thanks to my training, they could give me any script.

It was a happy summer of 1945 for Jane Adams, new Universal contractee, who found herself in the Universal commissary with such attractions as Deanna Durbin, Abbott and Costello, Maria Montez and Lon Chaney. She enjoyed the studio, the challenging work, the constant activity—and a new marriage to Lt. Tom Turnage:

> I *loved* it. I found everybody very congenial. It was an interesting time for me. I married my husband on Bastille Day, July 14, 1945—and two days later, he was sent overseas for 14 months. So it was good to be busy working until he came back.

Then came an offer from Universal which Jane could not refuse.

> THE SUPER-SHOCK SENSATION OF ALL TIME! ...All Together! ... All Terrific! ... Bringing ALL NEW THRILLS!
>
> —from poster for *House of Dracula*

Ever since the December 1944 New York and Los Angeles premieres of *House of Frankenstein*, it was inevitable that a sequel would follow. Come the week of September 17, 1945, and *House of Dracula* began shooting at Universal City.

It was a veritable reunion for many of the *House of Frankenstein* talents: Lon Chaney was back as the Wolf Man, John Carradine as Dracula, and Glenn Strange as

Jane "Poni" Adams gets her own on-the-set chair for *House of Dracula*. "In Hollywood that spells success," reported this publicity photo's original caption.

the Monster. Paul Malvern was again producer, Joe Gershenson executive producer, and Erle C. Kenton director; and the screenplay was by *House of Frankenstein*'s Edward T. Lowe, who used a "hook" for the film: All the monsters, seemingly, wanted a cure at the seaside castle of Dr. Franz Edelmann.

One would guess that the showy, star role of Dr. Edelmann was designed for Boris Karloff (who, in an interview he gave about this time, in conjunction with his RKO films *The Body Snatcher*, *Isle of the Dead* and *Bedlam*, inferred that he had rejected it). Onslow Stevens (1902–1977) took on the part. Also, while *House of Frankenstein* had offered its "Hunchback" in the homicidal form of J. Carrol Naish's Daniel, *House of Dracula* presented a novel variation: Nina, Edelmann's devoted, deformed nurse.

What caused Universal to cast Jane in this role?

> Really, I think it was my size! I'm only 5'3", and I think that's one reason I got into horror films, because I'm not the chorus girl type; rather short compared to the other girls who were under contract.

One might have expected Jane, as an erstwhile Conover model, to have resented playing a hunchback—but she insists it wasn't so:

> No, I *loved* to do character parts. I never thought of myself as a glamour girl—I wanted serious parts. At the Pasadena Playhouse, I had become familiar with the Stanislavski "method" of acting in serious drama. A horror film allowed you to become totally engrossed in what you were playing. Also, one of my husband's favorite movies was the original *Frankenstein*—and here I was, acting in a Frankenstein sequel at Universal Studios. So I loved that sort of thing.

The role of Nina truly was a showcase: In the course of *House of Dracula*, she aids Edelmann in his bone-softening experiments, assists Chaney in talking the doctor out of reviving the Frankenstein Monster, helps destroy Carradine's Dracula—and surrenders her chance to have her back repaired by Edelmann so he might operate on Chaney's Wolf Man. And, come the climax, she is killed by Edelmann as she hears his demonic self again reviving the Monster, and unleashing the film's mad, fiery finale.

Jane remembers the *House of Dracula* company's total sincerity on the job:

> Well, I was familiar with Onslow Stevens and John Carradine, who acted on the stage at the Pasadena Playhouse ... really fine actors. On *House of Dracula*, my memory is that they were *all* very serious actors, and they were sitting around, studying their scripts... It was all quite a serious thing—the script was heavy and serious.

Jack P. Pierce, who naturally worked on the makeups for Chaney, Strange and Carradine, supervised Jane's "hunchback" prosthesis:

> The makeup was uncomfortable (for the Wolf Man and Monster, particularly), and my cast weighed a lot—14 pounds, as I remember. It was made of plaster of Paris, before they used plastics...

Jane admits to feeling a tinge of vanity about her hunchback job, revealing, "I tried to look my best from the neck up." Today, she wonders if it was a good idea—"because it looked a little strange to have this great big thing on my back, and false eyelashes and everything on!"

Still, there was lots of fun: Candids abound, showing Jane (usually in costume, but without "hump") hugging the Frankenstein Monster, sharing a candy bar with Martha O'Driscoll, laughing with Erle C. Kenton and happily receiving a star's chair with her name (or, actually, her nickname "Poni") on it. Jane had fun with "Monster" Glenn Strange:

> Oh yes! He was a *very* nice man. *Everybody* was on that set. Martha O'Driscoll was very nice, very helpful to me, because I didn't really know anything about movie-making, having trained in stage technique at the Playhouse.

This 1945 *House of Dracula* title card, put Adams in the company of the screen's greatest goblins.

> So, all in all, I just had a very rich experience. It was a great set, and a great studio.

There was a milestone for one member of the company. Lionel Atwill became a father on Sunday night, October 14, 1945, right in the midst of *House of Dracula*'s shooting, as his 28-year-old wife Polly gave birth to their son, Lionel Anthony Atwill, at Cedars of Lebanon Hospital. Yet Atwill appears in none of the camaraderie candids taken on the *House of Dracula* set, nor does Jane recall any celebration on the set. Was Atwill embarrassed by being a 60-year-old father? Or was he aloof because he already knew he was fatally ill with bronchial cancer, which would kill him six months later?

One of the curiosities of *House of Dracula* is Jane's death scene. Just as Elena Verdugo's Ilonka dies in *House of Frankenstein*, presumably because she's a gypsy flirt, Jane's Nina also dies undeservedly in *House of Dracula*—presumably because there was no room for a pretty hunchback in 1945 Hollywood. The death scene, too, is almost comically brutal: In the laboratory, as Chaney, Martha O'Driscoll and Atwill look on, the mad Edelmann strangles Nina—then tosses her sadistically to the floor, where she rolls backwards, feet-in-the-air, tumbling into the hole that leads to the cave.

"A double did that," says Jane.

A 1946 Universal pinup of Jane Adams.

Universal completed *House of Dracula* October 25, 1945; the studio previewed the film for the press November 28. *Variety* recognized the movie as Universal's "horror special" for 1945; "Jane Adams makes a very nice thing of the hunchback nurse role entrusted to her," noted the critic. *House of Dracula* premiered at New York City's Rialto Theatre Friday, December 21, 1945; surely it assisted Universal in enjoying a $4.6 million profit for fiscal 1946.

Before *House of Dracula*'s release—on November 30, 1945—Universal completed *The Brute Man*, which starred real-life acromegaly victim Rondo Hatton as "The Creeper," with Jane as Helen Paige, a blind pianist with whom the Creeper falls in love. Distastefully based on the unfortunate Hatton's real life (his character is portrayed as a pre-acromegaly football star, which Hatton was before being gassed in World War I), *The Brute Man* (Universal's shortest horror film, at 58 minutes) remains vivid in Jane's memory:

> That was both an interesting and challenging experience. The progressive state of Rondo's disease made it very difficult for him to remember his script and always be responsive—but, overall, he did a good job. It's unfortunate that he died soon after we made *The Brute Man*.

Hatton died February 2, 1946; Universal sold off *The Brute Man* to PRC, which released it October 1, 1946.

Jane got a good taste of the madness of serial-shooting with *Lost City of the Jungle*, the 143rd of the 144 serials Universal produced between 1914 and 1946. The stars: Russell Hayden ("Lucky" of the Hopalong Cassidy films) as Rod Stanton, United Peace Foundation trouble shooter; Jane as Marjorie, the heroine; Keye Luke as Rod's sidekick, Tal Shen; and Lionel Atwill as Sir Eric Hazarias, who terrorizes Pendrang, "isolated jungle basin in the Himalayas," in his quest to find Meteorium 245 (the only known antidote to the atomic bomb) and to conquer the world. Jane was the only contract player in the serial (budgeted at $258,750)—receiving a flat fee of $1500.

Adams gone glamorous for a guest spot on Brian Donlevy's 1952 television series *Dangerous Assignment*.

The shooting began Monday, January 14, 1946, under veteran serial directors Ray Taylor and Lewis Collins—and proved chaotic. The company ran all over the Universal back lot, shooting on the jungle set, at the lake, the old *Green Hell* set, the *Nagana* rocks set, madly trying to match shots with old stock footage from Columbia's *Lost Horizon* (1937), G. W. Pabst's *White Hell of Pitz Palu* (1929) and Universal's own

Maria Montez vehicle, *White Savage* (1943). On Friday, January 18, Ray Taylor became ill; the next day, Jane herself was out sick. John Eldredge (as the heroine's father, Dr. Elmore) was out sick Wednesday, January 23, and remained out for the rest of the week.

A truly sad case was, however, that of Lionel Atwill. Playing Sir Eric Hazarias, the English-born actor, in his Panama hat, natty white suit, spats, loud tie and monocle, looked like a Himalayan pimp—but in fact was dying from bronchial cancer. He gallantly reported on time every day to Universal, even as his colleagues fell ill, until February 4, 1946; that morning, he shot a native prince (Clarence Lung) in the back; that evening, he played his death scene (being blown to bits as his plane exploded in an atomic blast). It was the last scene he would ever play; that night, Atwill left Universal, never to return. The actor died at his Pacific Palisades house on the night of April 22, 1946.

Meanwhile, *Lost City of the Jungle* had to proceed. Universal engaged a new actor, John Mylong, as Malborn ("the power in back of Sir Eric"); for scenes in which Atwill's character had to appear, the studio hired George Sorel to double Atwill, usually shot from the back, or with his Panama hat pulled down over his face. Occasionally an old Atwill close-up or old line of dialogue was spliced in to aid the sad illusion. The serial ran a full week over schedule, finally wrapping at 7:15, Saturday night, February 16, 1946.

Amazingly, for all the mayhem, Jane Adams remembers nothing of the real-life perils of *Lost City of the Jungle*. "I just loved it," she says. Nevertheless, she and Russell Hayden both look rather somber throughout the 13 chapters; little wonder.

Universal kept Jane busy (farming her out to *Lux Radio Theatre* to do the commercials—all part of her Universal salary); she ended her contract as Lotus in *A Night in Paradise* (1946), a Technicolor musical based on Aesop's Fables, starring Merle Oberon as Princess Delarai and Turhan Bey (who flirted with Jane on the set) as Aesop; and in various Westerns ("I knew how to ride"). As Jane told film historian Michael Fitzgerald:

> I enjoyed the Westerns—the California hills locations. I enjoyed seeing the caravans that would be filled with props, extras and all. I enjoyed seeing the sets come alive. Of course, I had to be there two hours earlier than the men—one hour for hair, one hour for makeup. We were mainly outdoors all day—in the sun and the heat. We worked hard. Sometimes we'd have dinner—then go to the studio and work on a sound stage in the evening!

In 1949, Jane turned up at Monogram, where her credits included *Master Minds*, a curio featuring the Bowery Boys vs. mad doctor Alan Napier and the giant "Atlas" (Jane's old Frankenstein Monster chum, Glenn Strange). Also in the cast: Skelton Knaggs, who had played *House of Dracula*'s village idiot, Steinmuhl. She also starred as Vicki Vale in Columbia's 1949 serial, *Batman and Robin*.

Jane played in both the Cisco Kid feature *The Girl from San Lorenzo* (United Artists, 1950) and the *Cisco Kid* TV pilot; she fondly remembers "Cisco," Duncan Renaldo ("a lovely man," she told Michael Fitzgerald), and "Pancho," Leo Carrillo ("a

Adams with her husband, retired major general Tom Turnage, at their home in Rancho Mirage, California, 1992.

clown!"). After several Monogram Westerns, Jane ended her film career at Republic with a bit part in *Street Bandits* (1951). She did some TV work, on episodes of *Dangerous Assignment* (1952, with Brian Donlevy) and *Adventures of Superman* (1952), in the episode "The Ghost Wolf." The plot found George Reeves, as Superman, tracking a possible werewolf in the Canadian wilds, only to find the evildoer is not supernatural at all.

Jane finally gave up her career as she followed her husband to various military posts and gave her considerable energy to being a mother. Major Gen. Turnage had a most distinguished military career, and later advised several presidents (his favorite: Ronald Reagan). In 1995, he joined his wife at FANEX 9 in Baltimore, where the guests included *House of Frankenstein*'s Elena Verdugo (q.v.) and *The Black Cat*'s Lucille Lund.

Asked by the FANEX audience about which male star she found most attractive, Jane responded that ever since marrying Tom Turnage (they had celebrated their 50th wedding anniversary eight days before), she'd never really taken note of another man. She clearly meant it.

So Jane Adams lives today in Rancho Mirage, California, on a golf course, with a magnificent vista of mountains behind her, happy, enjoying her children and grandchildren and content in her Hollywood memories.

Poor little Nina, of *House of Dracula*, would have envied her.

The Films of Jane Adams

1945

Salome, Where She Danced (Universal, Charles Lamont)

House of Dracula (Universal, Erle C. Kenton)

1946

Smooth as Silk (Universal, Charles T. Barton)

A Night in Paradise (Universal, Arthur Lubin)

The Runaround (Universal, C. Lamont)

The Brute Man (Universal-produced/PRC-released, Jean Yarbrough

Rustler's Roundup (Universal, Wallace Fox)

Gunman's Code (Universal, W. Fox)

Lost City of the Jungle (Universal serial—Ray Taylor and Lewis Collins)

1949

Gun Law Justice (Monogram, Lambert Hillyer)

Angels in Disguise (Monogram, J. Yarbrough)

Master Minds (Monogram, J. Yarbrough)

Batman and Robin (Columbia serial—Spencer Bennet)

1950

The Girl from San Lorenzo (United Artists/Krasne, Derwin Abrahams)

Law of the Panhandle (Monogram, L. Collins)

Outlaw Gold (Monogram, W. Fox)

1951

Street Bandits (Republic, R. G. Springsteen)

Anna Lee

She's the first great feminist heroine of Hollywood melodrama.

The movie is *Bedlam*, the legendary Val Lewton's climactic 1946 finale to his fabled horror series at RKO. The producer's longest, biggest-budgeted, most ambitious chiller boasted a dramatic spectacle: Boris Karloff's Master Sims, evil Apothecary General of St. Mary's of Bethlehem Asylum (aka Bedlam) vs. Anna Lee's lovely, dynamic crusader, Nell Bowen.

In a striking, revolutionary portrayal, Anna blossomed as Nell, growing from the vain, pampered actress of the opening to a brave, socially conscious heroine. While so many of her imperiled horror heroine colleagues screamed and fainted and cooed as the villain leered, Anna's Nell plays a wild, wicked tennis match of acting skills with Karloff—the two volleying flamboyant dialogue, filling the screen with sparks as Nell overwhelms her menace and brings on the reformation of Bedlam.

Little surprise that *Bedlam* is one of the favorite performances of Anna Lee, the beautiful British actress. In January of 1993, Anna celebrated a 65-year dramatic career by receiving her own "star" on Hollywood Boulevard's "Walk of Fame." Her amazing career has encompassed everything from British classics of the '30s like *King Solomon's Mines* (1937) to Hollywood stardom opposite such leading men as John Wayne, Ronald Colman and Paul Muni, to membership in John Ford's famous "stock company" of players, to her present role of Lila Quartermaine on ABC's long-running soap opera *General Hospital*. There was even an early melodrama with Karloff—Gaumont-British's *The Man Who Changed His Mind* (1936), with Boris as a gloriously crazy mad doctor and Anna as a pioneering lady scientist.

"I was very fortunate," says Anna today, blonde and lovely and gracious as she relaxes in her lovely house in West Hollywood. "I was working in Hollywood during what I still say are the Golden Years. They truly don't make films like that any more!"

> Hollywood was a different place altogether when I arrived in 1939. It was very glamorous and the stars looked like stars. I've never won an Academy Award. But I have been in two Academy Award–winning pictures, worked with marvelous stars, and ended up, happily, in soap operas.
>
> —Anna Lee, *USA Today*, November 30, 1992

Anna Lee was born Joan Boniface Winnifrith in the little village of Ightham, England, on January 2, 1913. "Joan is going to be an actress," said her father, the village rector, of the most high-spirited of his five children. She *did* want to act, desperately, and enrolled in the Central School of Speech Training and Dramatic Arts at the Royal Albert Hall in London—alma mater of Olivier, Gielgud and Richardson.

The "Anna" came from Tolstoy's *Anna Karenina*; the "Lee" came from General Robert E. Lee. And there soon came the first of over 50 movies—British Paramount's 1932 *Ebb Tide*, and one of her many fascinating stories:

***Chapter opener:* Anna Lee and Boris Karloff fill the screen with sparks of drama in Val Lewton's *Bedlam*, 1946.**

> Merle Oberon and I started in films together—in *Ebb Tide*, one of the "quota" pictures made in England practically on no budget at all. In those days, Merle called herself Queenie Thompson, and we were both cast as "extras" (in those days they called it "the crowd"); they picked the two of us to sit on a piano and swing our legs around—we were supposed to be prostitutes in this bar.
>
> I remember Merle was so beautiful in those days; it was before she had any surgery done on her face; she had wonderful almond eyes, and was just gorgeous. One evening I went out to my car to drive from Elstree back to London, and I saw this poor little waif, standing by the roadside, waiting for a bus. It was Merle! I said, "Would you like to have a ride with me back to London?"
>
> Merle said, "Oh, I'd *love* to!"
>
> We went off, and I asked, "Would you like to have supper with me and my mother at our apartment in London?"
>
> And Merle said, "Oh, I'd *love* to!"
>
> Then she said, "Do you have a bathtub? I'd *love* to take a bath, because where I live there's only a shower, and it's always very cold." So she came back and had a bath in my apartment.
>
> Well, what's so curious about this whole story is that, years later in Hollywood, after Queenie Thompson had become Merle Oberon, and built herself into a legend, I was looking through *House Beautiful* or one of those magazines, and there was about a seven-page spread on Merle Oberon in her lovely house in Mexico—with all those gorgeous bathrooms!

"I regret to tell the class that one of our most promising pupils has prostituted her art by playing in the cinema!" announced Elsie Fogarty, the head of Albert Hall, as she dragged Anna before her peers after the *Ebb Tide* adventure—and expelled her. Anna nevertheless acted with the London Repertory Company, and soon won a contract with Gaumont-British Studios. In Egypt, near the Sphinx, she made *The Camels Are Coming* (1934), and met director Robert Stevenson—whom she married. Anna was leading lady in 1936's *The Passing of the Third Floor Back*, starring the legendary Conrad Veidt. Anna remembers the great German star for his vanity ("He had mirrors all the way around, rather like Marlene Dietrich"), and his "great sense of humor." "Like all young girls," Anna told Tom Weaver of Veidt in his book *Science Fiction Stars and Horror Heroes*, "I was madly in love with him."

And, in 1936, there came Anna's first melodrama with Boris Karloff—*The Man Who Changed His Mind* (aka *The Man Who Lived Again*), directed by Robert Stevenson for Gaumont-British Pictures.

Fresh from Hollywood triumphs, Karloff found one of his most juicy roles in *The Man Who Lived Again* as Dr. Laurience—a chain-smoking mad doctor with a shock of wild gray hair, lunacy in his eye, a spooky old house, an eerie crippled assistant (Donald Calthrop), a pair of experimental monkeys—and the power to switch minds electronically. Anna scores too as Dr. Clare Wyatt, blonde and brilliant scientist; she naturally attracts Karloff's madman, who rants to her with both tragic love and a tinge of lechery:

Boris
KARLOFF
in
THE MAN WHO
LIVED AGAIN
with
ANNA LEE
JOHN LODER
FRANK CELLIER
LYNN HARDING
Directed by
ROBERT STEVENSON
A GB Production

> This new power—I can share it only with you, for you alone are worthy to receive it… I could take a new body, a young body, and keep my own brain! And you too! You won't always be young. When you grow old, I could give you a young body! Think of it! I offer you eternal *youth*! Eternal *loveliness*!

It's Anna who saves the day after Karloff switches minds with the leading lady's love interest (John Loder); she works the laboratory machinery, returns the minds (and, as delicately hinted in the film, the souls) to the rightful owners, and promises the dying, repentent Karloff to destroy his mad science.

> Boris—oh, a *dear* man! We both loved poetry, and apparently we both loved the same poems. We'd have a sort of "poetry jam." We'd say a poem—he'd say one line, and I'd say the second line, he'd say the third line—we'd go on until we ran out! I remember one, it was called "The Children's Hour"—I'd say:
>
> "Between the dark and the daylight,
> When the night is beginning to lower…"
>
> And then Boris would *boom* out,
>
> "Comes a pause in the day's occupations,
> That is known as the Children's Hour."
>
> We used to go on for hours and hours, with little poems that we remembered—ones I hoped he *hadn't* remembered, but he always did! A *lovely* man!

It was a happy shoot. Karloff wrote in his journal for March 2, 1936, about an evening he and his wife Dorothy spent at Anna's home:

> We went to dinner at the Robert Stevensons… Their home is so lovely that Dorothy honestly covets it. It is Queen Anne, sixteenth century, and right across the river from St. Paul's Cathedral. Sir Christopher Wren lived in it while St. Paul's (he was the architect) was being built. There's a Queen Anne staircase from the ground to the third floor.

Anna remembers Boris (one of the founders of the Hollywood Screen Actors Guild) being "horrified" that there was no union at the time for British film actors. "We worked on Saturdays, we'd work all night long—and there was no overtime. And Boris said, 'But my dear girl, you have to have a union!' Eventually we did get a union." And she remembers Boris with the chimpanzees:

> I know Boris was a lover of animals—but I doubt if he loved the chimpanzees on *The Man Who Lived Again*, because they were rather smelly. *Very* smelly, I know—I had the dressing room next door! And I remember suffering! Boris was very kind to the chimpanzees, but I don't think he was great friends with them, like he would have been to a dog or a horse. *Very* smelly!

***Opposite:* Lee and Karloff share this one-sheet poster for *The Man Who Lived Again*, 1936.**

As Karloff wrote in his journal: "I'm working in a scene with two chimpanzees, and though Dorothy (who adores animals of all kinds) insists they are 'darlings,' they don't help the air any."

"MR. KARLOFF HAUNTS THE RIALTO" headlined the *New York Times* review after *The Man Who Changed His Mind* (with the U.S. title *The Man Who Lived Again*) previewed at the Rialto Theatre the night of December 14, 1936. (The critic regretted that Karloff never tried out his mind-swapping experiment on Shirley Temple and Mae West.) It's arguably Karloff's finest mad doctor portrayal of all, and Anna's dynamic heroine gives prophecy of the performance she would give a decade later, also opposite Karloff, in *Bedlam*.

Anna starred with John Loder, Sir Cedric Hardwicke and Paul Robeson in *King Solomon's Mines* (1937)—"One of my favorite films," she says. While a second unit filmed in Africa, Anna never left the British sound stage. Still, there was always plenty of excitement at home:

> In *A Young Man's Fancy* [1939], I was shot from a cannon! Bob Stevenson wrote the film, and decided he wanted a new approach to boy-meets-girl. So I was fired from this cannon, and landed in the lap of the young lord with whom I'd have the romance.
>
> Originally, they said, "We don't think we should put you in the cannon; we'll try to fake it with somebody else." And I said, "No, I'd *like* to. The whole point is, I *want* to be shot out of the cannon!"
>
> So I was! We filmed it on a sound stage, and I landed in a net. The funny part was, in the opening shot, I was wearing these gorgeous, pure silk black tights. And what they hadn't realized was, when you're fired through the cannon, the friction inside the cannon will shred the silk—so I arrived in the net with practically no tights on at all! So they had to reshoot the scene with cotton ones—still black, but they didn't look as glamorous. They managed to bear the brunt as the cannon shot me and I went flying through the air!

In 1939, Robert Stevenson signed a contract with David O. Selznick, and Stevenson, Anna and their daughter Venetia all came to Hollywood. They took a bungalow at the Garden of Allah; on their first night in Hollywood, the couple joined Selznick, Clark Gable and Carole Lombard at a rough-cut showing of *Gone with the Wind*. Anna made her U.S. debut in Universal's *Seven Sinners* (1940), with Marlene Dietrich and John Wayne, then starred in RKO's *My Life with Caroline* (1941), with Ronald Colman.

Then came *How Green Was My Valley*, 20th Century–Fox's Best Picture Academy Award winner of 1941—directed by John Ford. Fearing the Irish-born Ford was prejudiced against British actresses, Anna made up a bogus Irish grandfather ("Thomas O'Connor")—and won the part of Bronwyn, the young widow:

> It was very strange—John Ford worked like telepathy. It was almost like he was giving you directions without you being

> aware of it. He would never talk a scene over with you; we usually talked about something else, and then he'd say, "Get working." But he would certainly give you all the encouragement in the world, and if he liked you, he would take one of his handkerchiefs and wind it around your wrist or stick it in your apron or something, which gave you confidence.

During the shooting, Anna endured a tragedy: The five-months' pregnant actress suffered a fall and miscarried one of her twins. Nevertheless, her work with John Ford became one of the great joys of her life:

> He was a wonderful man, and I was devoted to him and I did altogether eight pictures with him. Ford always told me *How Green Was My Valley* was his favorite picture—an intimate family picture...

On January 24, 1942, Anna gave birth to her daughter Caroline at St. Vincent's Hospital in Los Angeles. Meanwhile, she worked—collecting happy memories of most of her co-workers, such as Paul Muni on *Commandos Strike at Dawn* (1942), John Wayne on *Flying Tigers* (1942) and Brian Donlevy of *Hangmen Also Die!* (United Artists, 1943). There were exceptions—such as genius director Fritz Lang, who was producer/director of *Hangmen Also Die!*

> Lang was an absolute monster to me. He had wanted his girlfriend, Virginia Gilmore, to play the part of the Czech girl. The banks wouldn't pass her, but they passed me. So, he did everything he could to wear me down. I think the main thing was that he wanted to make me cry...
>
> He used to come on the set in his big Prussian boots and stamp on my feet. He'd make me play all my scenes barefoot—"You're too tall, you're too tall!"—so he'd make me take off my shoes, just so he could come and stamp on them!
>
> There was one scene, as I recall, where the girl is riding to the Gestapo in a carriage, and for some reason, she wants to get out and she pushed her hand through a window. When the time came to play the scene, the property department was all ready with gelatin glass. Fritz came and looked and said, "No, no, I want the *real* stuff—I want *real* glass!" The property man said, "Yes, but Mr. Lang, Miss Lee may hurt herself, may cut herself."
>
> And Fritz said, "Well, I want it *real*!"
>
> Well, the first time, I sort of "touched" my fist right through the glass, and I hardly got a scratch at all—the shot was perfect.
>
> And Fritz said, "We take it once more!"
>
> By that time, the crew was just absolutely *livid* with him, because I think they liked me, and they hated to see him do this. This time, when I pushed my hand through it, I really got a bad cut—my whole wrist was cut open. It could have been quite dangerous if I'd hit that main artery, but fortunately I didn't. But, at any rate, that was his little way of playing around with me.
>
> At that time, Lang was a sick man, obviously on drugs; a nurse

> used to come and give him injections, and he was taking pills. Many years later, five or six years before he died, Joan Bennett gave a party for him in Hollywood, and I went, and thought he was really a very tired old man—very nice and quiet and well-behaved!

Anna appeared in Universal's 1943 *Flesh and Fantasy*; she and Edward G. Robinson played a couple spooked by a fortuneteller's prediction of murder. Anna joined the U.S.O. and went to the Persian Gulf with the Jack Benny troupe. She somehow became lost and had to "hitchhike" her way back by plane from North Africa. Her entertainment stint overseas tallied 64,000 miles. (For the tour, Anna took along her green and silver gown from *Flesh and Fantasy* to wear for the troops. It was subsequently stolen!)

Anna's next film, *Summer Storm* (United Artists, 1944), in which she co-starred with George Sanders and Linda Darnell, was no picnic—this time due to her leading man:

> George Sanders—*not* my favorite man! He always managed to get his own way over things. It was very funny about that film—originally it was not called *Summer Storm*, but *Goodbye, My Love*. I had a wonderful scene at the end, with Sanders, when he comes out of the cafe, and he's drunk, and he's lurching across the street; finally he gets hit by a cab or horse or something, and he falls down, and is lying in the street. I rush over to him, take him in my arms, we have a lovely little scene together and, as he dies, I say the final line—"Good-bye, my love."
>
> Well, when he saw it, he was very angry, because *he* wanted to have the last word and didn't want *me* to get the last closeup!
>
> So he insisted they rewrite and reshoot the entire scene—without me—he lies there dying by himself, as I remember, and I wasn't even there! Also, he said he did *not* want the title *Good-bye, My Love*. So they had to find another title—they called it *Summer Storm*, which doesn't have very much to do with the picture at all.

In early 1944, Anna and Robert Stevenson divorced. He had directed the Hollywood films *Tom Brown's Schooldays* (RKO, 1940), *Back Street* (Universal, 1941), *Joan of Paris* (RKO, 1942), *Forever and a Day* (one of multiple directors, RKO, 1943; Anna played in it) and *Jane Eyre* (20th Century–Fox, 1944—he also co-scripted). At the time of the divorce, Stevenson was a captain in the Signal Corps.* On June 22, 1944, Anna wed Captain George S. Stafford, 24, who had piloted the plane in which Anna and other entertainers toured the Mediterranean. Anna's friend Alfred Hitchcock "gave away" the bride. On December 4, 1944, Anna joined Clark Gable, Lucille Ball and Douglass Dumbrille on the *Lady Esther Screen Guild Players* radio show of "China Seas."

**Stevenson later directed such Walt Disney box office hits as* Old Yeller *(1957),* The Absent-Minded Professor *(1960) and* Mary Poppins *(1964). He died in 1986.*

Anna's next picture joined *How Green Was My Valley* as one of her two favorite films—and won her a very special place in the cinema of melodrama.

> Nell Bowen is a product of her age; a beautiful girl, bold as a frigate, merry as a flag and with no more thought for right and wrong, or the problems of the future, than the parrot on her wrist. She would rather say a bright word than do a good deed...
>
> —from Val Lewton's shooting script for *Bedlam*

By the time *Bedlam* was produced, Anna Lee had become a good friend of Val Lewton:

> I think we met at a party down in Santa Monica, at the home of Berthold Viertel, the big German director for whom I had worked in England in *The Passing of the Third Floor Back.* They had a sort of soiree every Saturday night, and they'd invite certain people over—mostly writers—but Garbo used to come there! That was the only time I ever met Garbo. She sat herself down, and didn't say a word all the time! But it was wonderful to be in the same room with her! That was when I met Val.
>
> Then I became friendly with Ruth, his wife, and his children, and, of course, I'd heard about his aunt—Nazimova... I liked him enormously.

Lewton finalized plans for *Bedlam* in the wake of the great box office success of *The Body Snatcher*, which had starred Karloff, Bela Lugosi and Henry Daniell. Lewton was awarded a *Bedlam* budget of $350,000 (double what had been afforded his other RKO horrors) as Lewton prepared the script with his protégé director, Mark Robson. As Anna remembers:

> It was all Val—Val supervised every bit of it. He was very meticulous in everything, and did a lot of research on the Hogarth drawings. He had them all screened, and used as background for shots and everything.

Karloff, having starred for Lewton in *The Body Snatcher* and *Isle of the Dead*, had just signed a new RKO contract, and was set to play the evil Master Sims, Apothecary General of Bedlam, for a $30,000 fee. Lewton had promised the role of Nell Bowen to Anna*—but RKO originally had other ideas:

> Val had always told me he wanted me to do *Bedlam*, but I think whoever was in charge at RKO wanted an American to play it—even though it was a very English part. I think it was Jane Greer whom they wanted. But anyway, Val fought for me, and finally I did it. As far as I'm concerned, it was the best part I ever had—really a wonderful part...

**Lewton had originally announced Anna for his 1943* I Walked with a Zombie, *but Frances Dee ultimately played the lead.*

Bedlam began shooting July 18, 1945. We first see Anna Lee's Nell Bowen in a resplendent coach, wearing a beautiful gown, festooned with beauty marks and holding a pet cockatoo on her wrist. A vain actress, Nell is now the protégée of the obese Lord Mortimer (Billy House)—whose coach halts at the news that a man has fallen to his death, trying to escape from Bedlam…

The next day, in Lord Mortimer's boudoir, we see the corpulent Lord having his own beauty marks tended to, and see Nell—sporting a familiar-looking riding habit and cap:

> You see, we had that wonderful costume designer who designed all the clothes for *Gone with the Wind*—Walter Plunkett. As *Bedlam* was done on a budget, he did everything he could to cut the costs. Plunkett said, "Well, we must make you a lovely riding habit. How would you like green velvet?" I said, "That sounds wonderful," and he said, "I have just the thing! I have one of the dresses Vivien Leigh wore in *Gone with the Wind*—where she took down the curtains to make the dress. We had to make three or four of them. I'll just adapt one of those." So my riding habit was Vivien Leigh's from *Gone with the Wind*!

Into the boudoir, for an audience, comes the apothecary general of Bedlam, Master Sims—Boris Karloff. Looking like a dapper devil in his black wig, period finery and silver-topped cane (even if the breeches comically accentuate his bow legs), Karloff's Sims bows, makes faces, fawns—and strikes a wonderfully dramatic animosity with Anna's Nell Bowen.

"You have a tender heart," sneers Karloff to Miss Lee. "Most people laugh at my ugliness."

"It offends me sir," sniffs Miss Lee.

"To move so beautiful a lady in *any* way," vollies Karloff.

This is the true show of *Bedlam*—the fireworks that explode in the battle of wits between Karloff's Sims and Anna Lee's Nell. There almost seems a Beauty and the Beast-style sexual tension between the adversaries—and a wonderful chemistry between the two stars.

It has its comic moments. Back at Bedlam, Sims, having promised to present a play starring his "loonies" to appease Lord Mortimer, consults his rhyming dictionary, relaxing by removing his black wig and exposing his stubbly gray hair. Enter Nell Bowen for a surprise visit—and Karloff dives for his wig as Miss Lee rolls her eyes and looks away from the man's vanity!

"I have a curiosity to see the loonies in their cages," announces Nell—and Sims is all too happy to be her sinister tour guide…

The first glimpse inside the prison walls of *Bedlam* is a *tour de force* of Mark Robson's direction, Nicholas Musuraca's cinematography and Val Lewton's sensitivity. The camera retreats from Nell's slightly alarmed face, Karloff grinning like a gargoyle over her shoulder, taking in the giant room and its inmates—like cattle, just as history books describe the Bedlam of the 1700s. A man plays a violin with a book on his head for a hat; an inmate makes a cat's cradle with string ("to catch peacocks for the

Bedlam, 1946: Karloff pats the cheek of Joan Newton as Anna Lee (wearing a Vivien Leigh hand-me-down from _Gone with the Wind_) watches.

royal dinner," smirks Karloff); another sits sadly alone, in a dunce cap. A flicker of compassion begins to light Nell's' arrogantly lovely face.

"They're all so lonely," she marvels. "They're all in themselves and by themselves ... like separate dreams..."

Karloff, meanwhile is frightening in his soliloquy on his wards:

> They're animals. Some are dogs; these I beat. Some are pigs; those I let wallow in their own filth. Some are tigers; these I cage. Some, like this, are doves...

And he suggestively pats the cheek of "Dorothea the Dove" (Joan Newton), who stands mutely like a Catholic Madonna statue.

"That mad girl with her staring eyes!" exclaims Nell, making her exit—and smacking Sims across the face with her riding crop. *Bedlam*'s Quaker hero (Richard Fraser) is happy to see compassion for the tragic inmates, but Nell denies that compassion:

> My heart is a flint, sir. It may strike sparks, but they're not warm enough to burn. I have no time to make a show of loving kindness

Caught between smiling villains: Lee with Karloff and Billy House in *Bedlam*, 1946.

> before my fellow men. Not in this life. I have too much laughing to do.

She rides away on her horse. However, Quaker Hannay (and the audience) know that her liberal conscience is stirring...

The Vauxhall garden party. Karloff's Sims, full of poetry, flair and himself, presents his amusement for Lord Mortimer, Nell and his celebrated guests. The star of the "masque" is "Reason," played by the Gilded Boy (Glen Vernon). Karloff bullies the suffocating boy to gasp out his speech as the paint closes his pores—and he drops dead. Nell (Anna is wearing a beautiful hand-me-down gown from Hedy Lamarr) is aghast.

Cruel, decadent laughter. If the party scene has shocked the audience, it has inspired Nell Bowen—and Anna now throws herself into a performance that makes her the female crusader of Hollywood horror.

Nell demands Lord Mortimer reform Bedlam. When he refuses, she walks out; he retaliates by seizing her property. Nell and her old theatrical friend Varney (Skelton Knaggs, best-remembered as village idiot "Steinmuhl" in *House of Dracula*) take her pet cockatoo to the town square, where it regales the crowd with its couplet:

> Lord Mortimer is like a pig,
> His brain is small, his belly big.

"We can always make her my guest," suggests Sims, sinuously and ominously, to Mortimer.

Lord Mortimer tries to make peace with Nell, and has her to tea. But when Sims offers her money to vacation in Bath, Nell contemptuously makes a sandwich out of the bribe money and takes a bite out of it.

Sims persuades Lord Mortimer to sign a paper committing Nell to Bedlam. In a flowing black cloak, Nell arrives for her sanity hearing. Sims sits in on the board. The decision is a quick one: Nell Bowen is committed to Bedlam. The judges and Sims parade out of the hearing room as Nell cries and collapses.

And that night, during her first night in Bedlam, Karloff's Sims pays a call—with a coin.

"Here in Bedlam, my dear, we can't feed you bank notes. Try chewing on this!"

And the apothecary general shoves a coin in her mouth.

It was a grim picture, but Anna Lee cherishes her memories of *Bedlam*:

> The reunion with Boris Karloff was wonderful—we renewed our "poetry jams"!—and the atmosphere on the set was fun, because Boris had a great sense of humor, and he used to laugh about everything! When I had the bank note in the sandwich, Boris said, "Anna, you're not *really* going to eat that?" And I said, "Don't you think I could?" "*No, no*, you *wouldn't* do that!" said Boris. "Yes I will!" I said—and I did! I swallowed a piece of it! And I remember the scene where he pushed the coin into my mouth—Boris was giggling all the time!

And, of course, Val Lewton was an inspiration to the whole company:

> Val was a great workaholic. I don't think he ever stopped working on any project he was doing... He had a great imagination, and was very erudite in everything he did. But it never dawned on me, in those days, that Val was driving himself that way to death.

Camaraderie and high spirits dominated as *Bedlam* continued its shooting...

The name "Nell Bowen" echoes throughout Bedlam—a habit of the lunatics, who parrot the cry of Quaker Hannay in the streets as he searches for Nell. The Quaker sneaks into Bedlam, searching for Nell, a quest that provides a couple of famous Lewton shocks—as arms lunge out of bars to catch the Quaker, and, a moment later, when a hag suddenly appears against bars to cackle madly. He manages to find Nell; they are falling in love, and the pacifist surrenders to Nell's pleas to give her his trowel, in case she need defend herself.

Nell forms a friendship with the "people of the pillar"—mad lawyer Sidney Long (Ian Wolfe); alcoholic Oliver Todd (Jason Robards, Sr.), who refuses to speak; and gentle Dan the Dog (Robert Clarke, later the '50s star of such fare as *The Hideous Sun Demon*). They play paroli and provide a true warmth to the film. At length, Nell begins making reforms; she becomes, in the words of Ian Wolfe's lawyer, "an angel in this darkness." Of course, her triumph incenses Sims. In a superb dramatic scene, Karloff, unwigged, leering, hissing, sadistically cages up Nell with the violent "Tom the Tiger."

"Enter the cage," commands Sims. "Gently with a word. Conquer him with kindness!"

> I always loved the scene where Karloff says I wouldn't go into the cage with Tom the Tiger. He *dared* me to go in—and I tamed the tiger!

Indeed Nell does—with tenderness and compassion. But the villain does not surrender. Karloff's Sims appears again, all dressed up; the wig is back and he looks very rakish as he informs Nell she is to have a new hearing the next day—not before, however, he gives her "the treatment." We never learn just what the "treatment" is, but the expression alone is enough to send chills into the inmates—and they come to Nell's rescue. They overwhelm Sims as Nell escapes with Tom the Tiger. Our triumphant heroine takes one mocking look back at the trapped villain—then the Tiger pulls her up to the roof to safety. The scene is Lewton poetry: the Tiger, so long-imprisoned, is filled with wonder at the night sky and the stars—and he lets Nell dangle precariously from his arm until he refocuses his attention.

"In the closeups, we were six or seven feet off the ground—it wasn't all that high," says Miss Lee. "But the Tiger was very strong."

Meanwhile, the inmates attack Sims—stripping him of wig and dignity. A kangaroo court prosecutes, with Wolfe's Todd the star lawyer; a "judge" officiates, and an inmate named Solomon intones, "Split him in two!" Sims offers an eloquent defense:

> I was frightened ... of the great world... I've had to fawn and toady and make a mock of myself until all I could hear was the world laughing at me... I was afraid.

The inmates allow Sims to go free. They, after all, are merciful. But "the Dove" is not. As Sims retreats, the beautiful girl silently raises her arm. There is the long-missing trowel that Hannay had given to Nell—and the Dove sinks it into Sims' back.

À la Poe's "The Cask of Amontillado," the terrified inmates wall up Sims behind a fresh edifice of mortar and brick. And then—just before the final brick can be put into place—Sims' eyes open! It's too late; the brick goes into the wall, and Bedlam's apothecary general is entombed alive in his asylum.

A brief epilogue. Persuaded by the Quaker, Nell returns to Bedlam to tend to Sims. He cannot be found; but Hannay, seeing the freshly mortared wall, suspects. So does Nell—who convinces the Quaker not to tell, out of concern for the patients—and out of love for her.

Promised reforms for Bedlam. A triumphant heroine. A promised Age of Reason.

And the final horror classic from Val Lewton.

Bedlam was completed August 17, 1945. The atomic bombs had fallen, the War had ended, and the world seemed destined for an "Age of Reason" as well. On February 25, 1946, *Bedlam* won a special accolade: *Life* magazine showcased the film as its "Movie of the Week," hailing Lewton as "the virtuoso of B-film producers." On Good Friday, April 19, 1946, *Bedlam* premiered at New York City's Rialto Theatre, showplace of the RKO and Universal horror films of the war years. The *New York World-Telegram* hailed Lewton as "the custodian of one of the most restlessly roaming imaginations in Hollywood," the *New York Daily News* praised Karloff's Sims as "the personification of evil genius," and Anna Lee enjoyed a special critical victory:

> *New York Times*: Anna Lee gives a fine performance here, bringing a spark and compassion to her role as the crusading young girl, and even putting life into the eighteenth century rhetoric that frequently handicaps the script.
>
> *New York Herald-Tribune*: Anna Lee is particularly good as a careless and arrogant woman who discovers her conscience...
>
> *New York World-Telegram*: Anna Lee plays the principal role with spirit and zest, apparently not bothered by the flowery writing...

"Done realistically and with a sense of responsibility to its subject, *Bedlam* reaffirms the conviction that a problem drama can combine thoughtfulness with traditional entertainment elements," reported the *Los Angeles Daily News*.

Finally, there was one problem in the foreign market: England banned *Bedlam* outright in 1946—and as far as anyone knows, the film is still banned there today, over 50 years after the film's release and over 175 years after Reformation first made its way through the tragic walls of Bedlam.

For a time, Anna lived in Texas; in 1955, she gave birth to a son. Meanwhile, she kept happily working. In the five decades since *Bedlam*, she has played in over two dozen films, including John Ford's *Fort Apache* (1948), *The Last Hurrah* (1958), *Gideon of Scotland Yard* (1958), *The Horse Soldiers* (1959), *Two Rode Together* (1961), *The Man Who Shot Liberty Valance* (1962) and *Seven Women* (1964). In 1959's *Jet Over the Atlantic* and 1960's *The Big Night*, Anna appeared with her actress daughter, Venetia Stevenson. Anna was Lady Constance, a witch in the fantasy *Jack the Giant Killer* (1962), in which she suffered via a nasty raven and painful "witch" green and yellow contact lenses; Mrs. Bates in *What Ever Happened to Baby Jane?* (1962), in which her dressing room was right between those of the rival stars Bette Davis and Joan Crawford ("So I got all the vibes that came across!"). She turned up in 1967's *Our Man Flint* and, in musicals, supported Debbie Reynolds in *The Unsinkable Molly Brown* (1964) and Julie Andrews in *The Sound of Music* (1965). Anna's last film was *Star!* (1968).

For a time in the late 1960s, to support her three sons after her second marriage ended, Anna worked in a Beverly Hills silver shop as an expert on Georgian silver. In 1970, she wed author Robert Nathan (*Portrait of Jennie*). "While we had each other, life was perfect," she told *USA Today* of her late husband. "No, I'm not lonely ... the house is so full of him. And I still have my memories."

Anna Lee in her home in West Hollywood, 1991.

In 1978, Anna began her role as Lila Quartermaine in the popular ABC daytime soap opera *General Hospital.* She loves the role and the constant activity, and in 1991 told me:

> My leg is giving me a lot of trouble—I'm working in a wheelchair now. In the mid–1980s, I had spinal surgery, and something went wrong. I don't have use at all in my left leg. However, my right leg is fine, I can still drive my car, and I can still go to work! That's the main thing.
>
> There were really two careers for me. The first in England (one of my favorite films is *King Solomon's Mines*); then I came over here. My leading men—Ronald Colman, Paul Muni, John Wayne—they've all died. *General Hospital* has just signed me for another two years, so I'll be working in my 80s, and I intend to go on, because it's part of my life now. I'm really enjoying it.

In 1988, Anna took part in a special evening in honor of her old nemesis from *The Man Who Changed His Mind* and *Bedlam*:

> We had a special ceremony at the Academy here in Hollywood to honor Boris. He had died in 1969, but his wife was there, and Vincent Price, and Mae Clarke, who had done *Frankenstein*, and myself. We talked about all the various things we remembered about Boris. He was a very well-loved man.

Then, as 1993 began, Anna Lee had her own honor: She received the Hollywood accolade of having her own "star" on the Walk of Fame. Cesar Romero and Mel Torme were among the celebrities on hand as Anna was honored for her 65 years in show business.

A fire destroyed Anna's West Hollywood house in the mid–1990s, but she's still going strong. In 1995, she was a guest of the A&E cable channel's *Biography*, devoted to Karloff. And she continues on *General Hospital*, loving the activity and the craft she's practiced for almost 70 years.

"I was very lucky to have that lovely day," Anna Lee had recalled after her Hollywood Walk of Fame ceremony. Then, remembering the man who produced *Bedlam*, her friend who gave her what she considers her finest role in films, Anna became emotional.

"Val," she said, "would have been very proud."

The Films of Anna Lee

1932

Ebb Tide (Paramount, Arthur Rosson)
Say It with Music (British & Dominion Productions, Jack Raymond)

1933

Chelsea Life (Paramount, Sidney Morgan)
The King's Cup (British & Dominion, Herbert Wilcox, Robert J. Cullen, Alan Cobham, Donald Malardle)
Mannequin (RKO, George A. Cooper)
Mayfair Girl (Warner Bros., George King)
Yes, Mr. Brown (British & Dominion, Jack Buchanan)

The Bermondsey Kid (Warner Bros., Ralph Dawson)

1934

Faces (Paramount, Sidney Morgan)
Rolling in Money (Fox, Al Parker)
The Camels Are Coming (Gaumont-British)
Lucky Loser (Paramount, Reginald Denham)

1935

First a Girl (Gaumont-British, Victor Saville)
Heat Wave (Gaumont-British, Maurice Elvey)

1936

The Passing of the Third Floor Back (Gaumont-British, Berthold Veirtel)
The Man Who Lived Again (aka *The Man Who Changed His Mind*, *Dr. Maniac* and *The Brain Snatchers*) (Gaumont British, Robert Stevenson)

1937

You're in the Army Now (*O.H.M.S.*) (Gaumont-British, Raoul Walsh)
King Solomon's Mines (Gaumont-British, R. Stevenson)
Non-Stop New York (*Lisbon Clipper Mystery*) (Gaumont-British, Raoul Walsh)

1939

A Young Man's Fancy (Associated British Films, R. Stevenson)

1940

Return to Yesterday (Associated British Films, R. Stevenson)
The Secret Four (*The Four Just Men*) (Monogram, Walter Forde)
Seven Sinners (Universal, Tay Garnett)

1941

How Green Was My Valley (20th Century-Fox, John Ford)
My Life with Caroline (RKO, Lewis Milestone)

1942

Commandos Strike at Dawn (Columbia, John Farrow)
Flying Tigers (Republic, David Miller)

1943

Forever and a Day (RKO, Edmund Goulding, Sir Cedric Hardwicke, Frank Lloyd, Victor Saville, R. Stevenson and Herbert Wilcox)
Hangmen Also Die! (United Artists, Fritz Lang)
Flesh and Fantasy (Universal, Julien Duvivier)

1944

Summer Storm (United Artists, Douglas Sirk)

1946

Bedlam (RKO, Mark Robson)
G.I. War Brides (Republic, George Blair)

1947

High Conquest (Monogram, Irving Allen)
The Ghost and Mrs. Muir (20th Century–Fox, Joseph L. Mankiewicz)

1948

Fort Apache (RKO, J. Ford)
Best Man Wins (Columbia, John Sturges)

1949

Prison Warden (Columbia, Seymour Friedman)

1958

The Last Hurrah (Columbia, J. Ford)
Gideon of Scotland Yard (aka *Gideon's Day*) (Columbia, J. Ford)

1959

The Crimson Kimono (Columbia, Samuel Fuller)
The Horse Soldiers (United Artists, J. Ford)
This Earth Is Mine (Universal, Henry King)
Jet Over the Atlantic (Inter-Continent, Byron Haskin)

1960

The Big Night (Paramount, Sidney Salkow)

1961

Two Rode Together (Columbia, J. Ford)

1962

Jack the Giant Killer (United Artists/Edward Small, Nathan Juran)
The Man Who Shot Liberty Valance (Paramount, J. Ford)
What Ever Happened To Baby Jane? (Warner Bros., Robert Aldrich)

1963

The Prize (MGM, M. Robson)

1964

The Unsinkable Molly Brown (MGM, Charles Walters)
For Those Who Think Young (United Artists, Leslie Martinson)
Bearheart of the Great Northwest (Pathé-Alpha/Medallion)

1965

The Sound of Music (20th Century–Fox, Robert Wise)

1966

Picture Mommy Dead (Embassy, Bert I. Gordon)
Seven Women (MGM, J. Ford)

1967

In Like Flint (20th Century–Fox, Gordon Douglas)

1968

Star! (*Those Were the Happy Times*) (20th Century–Fox, Robert Wise)

Lenore Aubert

A dark, Florida cove. Bela Lugosi's Count Dracula stands tall in the night. At his feet sprawls Glenn Strange's ailing Frankenstein's Monster. And at Bela's side is a glamorous, Amazon-sized brunette, clad in a slinky black gown and wrapped in a mink stole.

"Nervous, my dear?" asks the Count.

"This is risky business," says Dr. Sandra Mornay—played by Lenore Aubert.

"Not as risky as those curious operations of yours, which so intrigued the European police," smirks Lugosi. "Restore the Monster for me, and you shall have anything you wish!"

The wicked plan is to revitalize the Monster to full power—with a new brain. "I don't want to repeat Frankenstein's mistake," says Dracula, "and revive a vicious, unmanageable brute. This time, the Monster must have no will of his own—no fiendish intellect to oppose its master."

"There, my dear Count, I believe I have exceeded your fondest wish," says Dr. Mornay, flirtatiously, so tall as to almost look at the Vampire King eye-to-eye. The new brain she has selected is "so simple, so pliable, that he will obey you like a trained dog."

The line got a huge laugh in the theaters—for audiences could guess who the unwilling brain donor would be in *Abbott and Costello Meet Frankenstein.*

Lenore Aubert won a place in Horror's Hall of Fame via her sexy Dr. Sandra of *Abbott and Costello Meet Frankenstein.* The showy role allowed her to receive a bite on the neck from Lugosi, transform into a vampire love slave, try to nibble on Lou Costello's neck, begin aborted brain surgery on the Monster—and play a great death scene as the Monster lifts her and throws the villainess through the castle skylight.

Horror fans who also enjoyed her as heroine of *The Catman of Paris* (Republic, 1946) and as the vamp of *Abbott and Costello Meet the Killer, Boris Karloff* (1949) might well wonder why this dark, statuesque beauty disappeared from films so mysteriously. Lenore Aubert's was yet another of those scuttled female careers; her refusal to play mistress to the omnipotent mogul who "discovered" her earned her a blackballing that sentenced her primarily to the limbo of costumers and melodramas.

Yet she was a wonderfully sultry presence, and her Dr. Sandra Mornay of *Abbott and Costello Meet Frankenstein* survives as one of Horror's most memorable femmes fatales.

> I'm not the gal to get excited about these refugee actresses with so many home-grown beauties on hand. But Lenore Aubert—just signed by Sam Goldwyn for the second femme lead with Bob Hope in *They Got Me Covered*—must have something to land such an important role for her movie debut. For one thing, Sam himself tells me that she has the most beautiful eyes since Vilma Banky...
>
> —Louella Parsons, July 11, 1942

***Chapter opener:* Lenore Aubert as musical star Fritzi Schiff in *I Wonder Who's Kissing Her Now*, 1947—her own favorite performance (Photofest).**

Lenore Aubert was born Eleanore Maria Leisner in Celje, Yugloslavia, on April 18, 1913 (although 1918 was given in publicity). Her father was a general in the Austro-Hungarian army, and he sent his daughter to convent schools in Vienna. Both parents tried to squash Lenore's lifelong dream of becoming an actress.

Lenore wed actor Julius Altman; as Hitler's Anschluss began, she and her Jewish husband fled to Paris, and then New York, where the tall, beautiful Lenore won work as a fashion model. A bus trip to Hollywood resulted in a stage role at the Bliss-Hayden Theatre, notice by a Goldwyn talent scout—and a contract with Samuel Goldwyn Productions.

Goldwyn was one of Hollywood's legendary moguls: bald, robust, famous for "the Goldwyn Touch" in such classics as *Dead End* (1937), *Wuthering Heights* (1939) and *The Little Foxes* (1941), and for his infamous malapropisms (i.e., "Everybody wants to bite the goose that laid the golden egg"; "We have all passed a lot of water since then," etc.). According to Richard Lamparski's *Whatever Became of...?* (eleventh series) profile of Lenore:

> When Lenore was signed to a contract with Samuel Goldwyn Pictures, she was led to believe that she would be introduced to the public as the new Hedy Lamarr. It was not until she lunched with the producer that she learned all his plans for her.
>
> Goldwyn also expected that she would be his mistress. She declined, pointing out that she took her marriage vows and her Roman Catholicism seriously. She was then told that, since he had to pay her, she would appear in movies. "But," he added, "you will never, ever be a star for me or anyone else."

Lenore made her Hollywood debut in Goldwyn's *They Got Me Covered* (1943), starring Bob Hope and Dorothy Lamour; Lenore played a Nazi "Mata Hari," and the supporting heavies included Otto Preminger and Eduardo Ciannelli. But it would be her only film for Goldwyn. He spitefully refused to sell her contract to MGM, finally selling her to RKO—"not for more money," said Lenore, "but because he hated Mr. Mayer and thought it less likely RKO could do anything with me. He couldn't bear the thought of being shown up. He was the great Goldwyn."

Goldwyn leaked his own version of the story, and Louella Parsons ran this nasty notice September 29, 1943:

> Chatter in Hollywood: Lenore Aubert, it is now revealed, is married and has been for two years to Julius Altman, former European businessman. She married him in Paris before she escaped to Lisbon, and subsequently to America. He is in Hollywood and they are living in an apartment here. Wonder if Sam Goldwyn knew of this marriage? All of us, including this writer, fell for the story that she was an unmarried girl alone in her troubles and having a tragic time.

Amidst this publicity, Lenore played Mounirah in RKO's *Action in Arabia* (1944), starring George Sanders and Virginia Bruce; "Lenore Aubert looks exotic but doesn't act it as a high-class Arab girl," reported the *New York Times*. She played

Gilda in RKO's slapstick comedy/mystery *Having Wonderful Crime* (1945), with Pat O'Brien, George Murphy, Carole Landis and George Zucco (as a magician who mysteriously disappears).

Lenore meanwhile tested for leading roles in *For Whom the Bell Tolls* (Paramount, 1943) and *Saratoga Trunk* (Warner Bros., 1945), losing both to Ingrid Bergman; she went after the role of George Sand in *A Song to Remember* (Columbia, 1945), but Merle Oberon landed that part, played in top hat; and Marlene Dietrich nabbed the role Lenore wanted in *Golden Earrings* (Paramount, 1947).

It seemed that Goldwyn's blackballing potency was as powerful as he had boasted as Lenore visited Hollywood's "Poverty Row" to find work. She found herself at lowly PRC as Haydee, *The Wife of Monte Cristo* (1946), yet another oddity in the oeuvre of director Edgar G. Ulmer. As the *New York Journal-American* noted, "Miss Lenore Aubert is truly an eyeful" in her fencing tights, flashing a rapier and swashbuckling with hero Martin Kosleck and villain John Loder. "As for Miss Aubert," wrote popular critic John T. McManus in his *PM* review, "she can fence in our backyard any time."

Lenore starred in her first horror film, *The Catman of Paris*, a Republic 1946 release; the Lesley Selander–directed 65-minute thriller offered the spectacle of the Catman (Robert J. Wilke, in "Catman" fangs, pointed ears and widow's peak, as well as top hat and evening clothes) chasing Lenore all over the French baroque mansion and grounds. "Oddly enough, it never occurs to anyone to yell, 'scat,'" sniped the *Hollywood Reporter*.

Lenore received some publicity she would have enjoyed avoiding, while shooting *The Other Love*; as the *Los Angeles Examiner* reported:

> BEVERLY HILLS, November 6—Playing a real-life hero, Actor Bob Stack rescued his leading lady, Lenore Aubert, from drowning on a swimming pool set of *The Other Love* here today.
>
> Rehearsing a scene, Stack pulled Miss Aubert into the pool, but the actress' foot caught in a submerged two-by-four used as a guide for underwater swimming. She lost consciousness and Stack swam her back to the bank.
>
> Miss Aubert was revived by artificial respiration and confined to bed by her physician.

Happier news came three days later, November 9, 1946, as both Lenore and her husband (then an L.A. manufacturer) became U.S. citizens.

The Other Love, released in 1947, featured Lenore in a cast of Barbara Stanwyck, David Niven and Richard Conte. Lenore won a showcase role in 20th Century–Fox's *I Wonder Who's Kissing Her Now* (1947); June Haver and Mark Stevens starred in this Technicolor 1890s musical about songwriter Joseph E. Howard, with Lenore singing and dancing as musical star Fritzi Scheff. *I Wonder Who's Kissing Her Now* would be Lenore's own favorite performance.

Lenore won the top female role in Columbia's *The Return of the Whistler* (1948). Meanwhile, the role by which most fans would remember her loomed ominously on the horizon.

JEEPERS! THE CREEPERS ARE AFTER BUD AND LOU!
—Promotional Copy for *Abbott and Costello Meet Frankenstein* (1948)

February 5, 1948: It was a milestone day at Universal-International Studios—*Abbott and Costello Meet Frankenstein* began shooting (under the original title *The Brain of Frankenstein*). On the "Int. Baggage Room" set on Stage 19 for this first day of shooting: Bud Abbott, Lou Costello, Frank Ferguson (as McDougal, owner of "McDougal's House of Horrors")—and Lenore Aubert as Dr. Sandra Mornay (a role for which Patricia Morison [q.v.], had been considered).

The February 2, 1948, production budget report set the price tag for production #1572 at $759,524—with the following contracts for the leading players:

> Bud Abbott and Lou Costello, as Chick and Wilbur: $105,000 (plus a percentage)
>
> Lon Chaney, in his fifth appearance as the Wolf Man: $2000 per week for five weeks: total, $10,000
>
> Bela Lugosi, back as Count Dracula for the first time since Universal's 1931 *Dracula*: $2000 per week for four weeks and one day: total, $8,333
>
> Glenn Strange, in his third appearance as Frankenstein's Monster: $750 per week for three weeks and four days: total, $2,750
>
> Lenore Aubert, as Dr. Sandra Mornay: $750 per week for five weeks and one day: total, $3875
>
> Jane Randolph, blonde heroine from Val Lewton's *Cat People* (1942) and *The Curse of the Cat People* (1944), as insurance investigator Joan Raymond: $350 per week for four weeks and two days: total, $1517

Universal gave Lenore the full glamour treatment for *Abbott and Costello Meet Frankenstein*: On the first day's shooting, she was in Bud Westmore's makeup salon at 6:45 for her nine o'clock set call. And when Bud Abbott left the set early that day, complaining of aching ribs, director Charlie Barton spent the remainder of the day shooting wardrobe tests of Lenore.

The filming of *Abbott and Costello Meet Frankenstein* would become legendary—a wild, crazy melee of on-the-set pie fights, practical jokes, blown takes and gleeful "terrorizing" of the lot (as when Lenore, in her mink stole, put a leash on Glenn Strange's Monster and walked him across the lot, accompanied by Bud, Lou and Chaney's Wolf Man). There were also (near the end of shooting) some truly frightening accidents. Dominating all, however, was a sense of wonderful professionalism. Director Charlie Barton (1902–1981) told me in a 1979 interview:

> Bela Lugosi? He was a hell of a good actor. He was very helpful to Lon, and to me, and to everybody. Particularly that wonderful, beautiful girl, Lenore Aubert. I remember in the scene where Lugosi told her, "Look into my eyes," how he tried to help her look as if she were really hypnotized. It was a hard

One of horror's great femmes fatales: Lenore as Dr. Sandra Mornay in *Abbott and Costello Meet Frankenstein* (1948), examining Glenn Strange's Frankenstein Monster as Bela Lugosi's Count Dracula watches.

> scene to do, and damn, he worked with her like a real pro. He was a lovely, lovely guy…

Lenore makes her entrance as Dr. Sandra Mornay in the opening baggage depot scene, vamping Costello's Wilbur. She immediately impresses with her stature (towering over Lou), her slightly sinister quality and very definite sex appeal:

> BUD: Frankly, I don't get it!
>
> LENORE: And, frankly, you never will!

We soon see her at the castle, as accomplice to the mad power plan of Lugosi's Dracula: She's a notorious European mad scientist—studying the Frankenstein "Records of Life and Death" so to give Glenn Strange's Monster a new brain. A highlight of the film is the showdown between her and Dracula, as she defies him, attempting to escape the "too risky" business of the brain transplant.

"I must warn you, my dear Sandra," says Lugosi, masterfully, "I am accustomed to having my orders obeyed—especially by women with a price on their head!"

Lenore Aubert, set to play the evil Dr. Sandra Mornay in *Abbott and Costello Meet Frankenstein* (1948), towers over director Charlie Barton and a clowning Lou Costello.

"My will is as strong as yours," says Lenore's Sandra.

"Look into my eyes," demands Lugosi. "Look ... deeper. Tell me what you see..."

She falls under the Count's power—and as Frank Skinner's wonderful score swells in evil triumph, Lenore smiles wickedly as Lugosi avails himself of her neck. (The terrific scene has one problem—we also see the action in a background mirror, in which, of course, Dracula should show no reflection!)

Thereafter, Sandra is a slave of Dracula, slinking about in spooky trance and trying to seduce Costello in the woods.

> LENORE: ...I want to be a part of you. I want to be in your blood... You're so full of life—so round, so firm...
>
> COSTELLO: So fully packed. And I want to stay that way!

Lou accidentally cuts himself; blood appears. Sandra is fascinated:

> LENORE: Don't you know what's going to happen now?
>
> LOU: I'll bite
>
> LENORE: Oh, no. *I* will!

Abbott and Chaney scare her off, but soon afterwards, under a full moon, Lenore's Dr. Mornay begins the operation that will place Lou's brain in the Monster's skull. The moon transforms the now-heroic Talbot into the Wolf Man—and unleashes one of the great comic chases in movie history as the cast runs madly about the castle. The Wolf Man finally clutches Dracula (in bat form) as both tumble from a castle balcony into the sea, and the Monster perishes on the flaming pier.

The mad finale took its toll on the company. On Monday, March 15, 1948, on the "Int. Laboratory" set on Stage 17, Strange's Monster was to throw Lenore's Sandra through the castle window for her richly deserved comeuppance. Actually, stunt girl Helen Thurston replaced Lenore in this scene; the crew attached wires to her, to swing her through the "candy glass." However, when Strange tossed Thurston through the window, the wires swung her back into the scene. Strange gallantly tried to catch her, fell—and fractured his ankle. A great trouper, Strange reported that evening for night shooting on the back lot pier at "Lubin Lake," working until 11 o'clock. However, his injury forced him to miss the next day's shooting.

So, as Barton and company did a retake of Dr. Mornay's death scene, Lon Chaney donned the Monster makeup and costume ("just as happy as he could be to do it," recalled Barton), and, late that afternoon, threw Helen Thurston once more through the candy glass skylight. Aware of the danger of the wire and breakaway glass, Thurston upped her stunt fee for the day from $55 to $300, and was justified in doing so: The candy glass got in her eyes, and Universal had to send her to the hospital. Meanwhile, Lenore finished the day with glamour shots and close-ups at her dressing table.

Lenore completed her work on *Abbott and Costello Meet Frankenstein* the next day, March 17. Glenn Strange returned to work on March 18, and Barton completed the film Saturday, March 20, 1948, working with Bud, Lou and the three monsters. The final scene shot (appropriately): Chaney's Wolf Man snaring Lugosi's Dracula on the balcony, and tumbling into the sea and rocks. Post-production shooting included Chaney's man-into-wolf transformation in the woods, Wolf Man hand transformations in the London hotel room (Joe Walls standing in for Chaney) and an added scene (shot April 9, 1948), with Jane Randolph, Frank Ferguson and Howard Negley, which introduced Jane's "Joan Raymond" as an insurance investigator.

Abbott and Costello Meet Frankenstein received several production bonuses: the magnificent musical score by Frank Skinner; handsome special effects (i.e., the bats Lou sees in Sandra's hypnotic eyes) by David Horesly and Jerome Ash; and the cartoon credit sequence, which features Bud and Lou (as skeletons!), the shadowy forms of the Wolf Man, Dracula and the Monster—and the shapely shade of Lenore's Sandra, who sashays across the screen and blinks her eyes at the crowd. *Abbott and Costello Meet Frankenstein*'s final cost: $792,270. Because of the film running over schedules, all the monsters and featured players received bonuses.

Abbott and Costello Meet Frankenstein previewed at Hollywood's Forum Theatre on Friday night, June 25, 1948. It became one of the top hits in Universal's history and remains the most famous performance of Lenore Aubert—a fact which made Lenore (according to Richard Lamparski) "both chagrined and amused." Lenore makes Dr. Sandra Mornay one of the most sly, sexy, sinister ladies of the genre, and

Aubert takes a stroll with Karloff during the shooting of *Abbott and Costello Meet the Killer, Boris Karloff*, 1949.

it's wonderful that *Abbott and Costello Meet Frankenstein*—recognized as the last classic of Horror's "Golden Age"—features so alluring a villainess.

Lenore starred in Screen Guild's *The Prairie* (1948), a James Fenimore Cooper covered wagon saga. Meanwhile, in the wake of *Abbott and Costello Meet Frankenstein*, Bud and Lou met a variety of Universal's goblins. The first was *Abbott and Costello Meet the Killers*—which eventually premiered as *Abbott and Costello Meet the Killer,*

Boris Karloff. The erratic entry paid Karloff $20,000; Lenore, as seductress Angela, signed for four weeks at $750 per week. Charlie Barton again directed; the cast had fun with Karloff, and Leonard Maltin in *TV Movies* describes it as a "pleasant blend of comedy and whodunit with bodies hanging in closets."

Lenore's Hollywood swan song: Columbia's *Barbary Pirate* (1949), directed by Lew Landers (*The Raven*, *The Return of the Vampire*). According to Lamparski's profile, Lenore's husband, frustrated that he'd had no success as an actor, insisted they move to New York City. As he became a millionaire garment businessman, the marriage failed; Lenore went to Europe, acting in Germany's *Falschmunzer am Werk* (1951) and France's *La Fille sur la route* (1952). Lenore came back to the United States in 1959, as wife of an American businessman, with a Manhattan penthouse and another home in Florida; the marriage lasted 15 years.

To those who knew her in Hollywood, Lenore Aubert had seemed to vanish. Charlie Barton told me in 1979 that he had attempted to contact her in New York, to no avail. Jim McPherson of the *Toronto Sun* finally tracked her down in 1987 for an interview, and rather cryptically wrote this warning—reprinted in *Whatever Became of...?*:

> She is delighted to know that she is still remembered by movie fans—but it's not possible for her to meet them or acknowledge letters.
>
> About four years ago, she suffered a stroke and, while there is no physical evidence whatsoever, it has seriously impaired her memory and her powers of concentration—even the simple business of signing a photograph is a major undertaking.

One fan who did meet her was Richard Bojarski, author of *The Films of Boris Karloff* and *The Films of Bela Lugosi*. He lunched with her; later, he met Lenore at her Upper East Side apartment in New York City, where she was living alone. "She seemed to have difficulty with her English," says Bojarski, "and to have little memory of details of *Abbott and Costello Meet Frankenstein*, other than to repeat that Lou Costello was 'a funny little man.'"

More recently came news that Lenore was in a nursing home somewhere on the East Coast. An overly aggressive collector tracked down the institution, managed to get inside, found Lenore and reportedly shoved a stack of *Abbott and Costello Meet Frankenstein* stills at her for her signature. The dazed, elderly woman began obediently signing before becoming increasingly agitated—eventually writing "Help" on one of the photos, and finally crying until authorities evicted the collector.

On a happier note: Chris Costello, Lou's daughter, told me that a copy of the MagicImage book on *Abbott and Costello Meet Frankenstein*, containing the shooting script, many stills and a production history (by this author), was sent to the former actress at the nursing home. Chris said that Lenore carried the book around with her for weeks—a happy reminder of her long-ago, and barely remembered, Hollywood celebrity.

Simone Peterson of New York City idolized Lenore Aubert:

> As a child I saw her in *Abbott and Costello Meet Frankenstein*. Here was this beautiful woman, and instead of being fascinated with romance, she was fascinated with evil and science. In a child's mind, this really made an impression—to the point that, as a child, I'd see women who looked like her, and actually ask what their names were, to see if maybe I'd run into her. My father used to think I was insane!

In May of 1985, Simone met Lenore at the Movie Star News Shop in New York. "There are very few people in this world who ever see their dreams come true and meet their idols," says Simone. "She looked just as beautiful as you'd imagine her to be if you imagined her aging. We developed a very beautiful and close relationship." Indeed, they became so close that Lenore went through her power of attorney and adopted Simone—"a sentimental ceremony," she says, as opposed to necessity, because I was already grown."

Simone shared with me special memories of Lenore and her career:

> Lenore's favorite movie was *I Wonder Who's Kissing Her Now*, in which she played musical performer Fritzi Scheff. Fritzi Scheff even wrote her a letter, thanking her for playing her so well and saying she couldn't have picked a better or more ideal person to have played her—a great compliment! And Lenore loved *The Prairie*, one of those "cult" movies that for some reason cannot be found.
>
> In Hollywood, Lenore had a few marriage proposals: from Jean-Pierre Aumont, Edward G. Robinson, Charles Boyer—she dated them all. But she was Catholic, and as she had told Samuel Goldwyn when he'd wanted her to be his mistress, "I'm a Catholic, I'm married and I promised to love honor and obey."
>
> Lenore was a very pro-American. When *They Got Me Covered* premiered at Radio City Music Hall, Bob Hope, Dorothy Lamour and Lenore were all selling war bonds in the lobby. And a man came up to Lenore and said, "I'll give you a thousand dollars for a war bond for a kiss." And Lenore did! He handed her a thousand dollars—and she gave him a kiss on the cheek!
>
> Incidentally, while filming *They Got Me Covered*, somebody asked Dorothy Lamour (she and Lenore looked alike) what she thought of Lenore Aubert. And Lamour said, "Well, she can walk—and she's got eyes!"
>
> As for *Abbott and Costello Meet Frankenstein*—Lenore was chagrined to know this was her best-remembered performance. But she said it was a lot of fun. Abbott and Costello were constantly clowning around. Once Lenore was sitting down with Bela Lugosi, and of course, he being Hungarian and she being Austrian, they were talking about life before the war and how wonderful Europe was. And Lou Costello, being the clowner that he was, built a fire underneath Lenore's chair—lit a fire under her, so to speak! She said Costello had a dog house on the set, and would run in and out of it, pretending to be a dog...
>
> Lenore said that Lon Chaney, Jr., used to go into the desert to

drink cactus juice because he was an alcoholic, and the cactus juice was a way to fight alcoholism. She said Chaney was a nice man, but also very cold and not one to mess with; he just really kept to his family, was very family-oriented. And as for Glenn Strange as the Monster, Lenore said he was a really nice person, and she loved the fact that one of his obituaries showed a picture of Strange as Frankenstein's Monster with Lugosi and Lenore hovering over him.

She loved doing *Abbott and Costello Meet the Killer, Boris Karloff*. Karloff was very nice and they exchanged certain stories because they were both European. She was very close with actress Victoria Horne on the set and she loved her costumes.

Lenore had two strokes which affected her mentally, not physically. She started to lose her memory, and reverted to speaking French and finally Austrian, until even people who spoke Austrian couldn't understand her Austrian. She was in a nursing home on Long Island which just treated her terribly, then went into the Actors Home in Englewood, New Jersey—which didn't treat her all that well either. She was very unhappy in both homes and wanted to live with me, but she required certain constant medical care. By the end, she was rather infantile—it was like seeing a grown baby. It was very, very sad.

She passed away in May of 1992. Her family wanted no obituaries.

Lenore Aubert would have liked to have been remembered as a dramatic actress. And she could have been, if given the opportunity.

The Films of Lenore Aubert

1943

They Got Me Covered (Goldwyn, David Butler)

1944

*Action in Arabia** (RKO, Leonide Moguy)

1945

Having Wonderful Crime (RKO, A. Edward Sutherland)

1946

The Wife of Monte Cristo (PRC, Edgar G. Ulmer)

The Catman of Paris (Republic, Lesley Selander)

1947

The Other Love (United Artists, Andre de Toth)

I Wonder Who's Kissing Her Now (20th Century–Fox, Lloyd Bacon)

1948

The Return of the Whistler (Columbia, D. Ross Lederman)

Abbott and Costello Meet Frankenstein (Universal-International, C. T. Barton)

The Prairie (Screen Guild, Frank Wisbar)

1949

Abbott and Costello Meet the Killer, Boris Karloff (Universal-International, Charles T. Barton)

Barbary Pirate (Columbia, Lew Landers)

1951

Falschmunzer am Werk (Germany)

1952

La Fille sur la route (France)

*The desert footage in *Action in Arabia* was shot by *King Kong's* Merian C. Cooper and Ernest B. Schoedsack, for a film that was never made.

APPENDIX: OUTSTANDING PERFORMANCES

Which were the outstanding female performances of 1940s Hollywood horror? The following individuals all kindly took the time to complete a poll for this book as to their personal choices:

Forrest J Ackerman (editor, *Famous Monsters of Filmland*)
John Antosiewicz (writer, collector)
Rick Atkins (author, *Let's Scare 'Em!*; collector)
Ed Bansak (author, *Fearing the Dark: The Val Lewton Legacy*)
Buddy Barnett (editor, *Cult Movies* magazine; proprietor, Cinema Collectors Shop, Hollywood)
Richard Bojarski (author, *The Films of Boris Karloff*, *The Films of Bela Lugosi*)
Ronald Borst (editor, *Graven Images*; proprietor, Hollywood Movie Posters)
John Brunas (co-author, *Universal Horrors*)
Michael Brunas (co-author, *Universal Horrors*)
John Cocchi (author, *Second Feature*; researcher)
Mike Copner (editor, *Cult Movies* magazine)
Jim Coughlin (author, "Forgotten Faces of Horror Films" column in *Midnight Marquee*; co-author with Greg Mank and Dwight Frye, *Dwight Frye's Last Laugh*)
Joe Dante (director, *The Howling*, *Gremlins*, *Matinee*, etc.)
Vince Di Leonardi (collector, music historian)
Michael Fitzgerald (author, *Universal Pictures*)
Alex Gordon (producer)
Richard Gordon (producer)
Charles Heard (collector; editor, *Countess Dracula*)
David J. Hogan (author, *Who's Who of the Horrors and Other Fantasy Films*; reviewer, *Filmfax* magazine)
Keith Hurd (collector, proprietor of Hurd's Outpost)
Roger Hurlburt (entertainment/features writer, Ft. Lauderdale *Sun Sentinel* newspaper)
Tom Johnson (author, *Censored Screams*; co-author, *The Films of Peter Cushing*)
Don Leifert (editor, *Movie Club* magazine; writer, *Filmfax*, *Video Times* magazines)
Jessie Lilley (publisher, *RetroVision* magazine)
Tim Lucas (publisher, editor, *Video Watchdog*)

Arthur Joseph Lundquist (actor; writer, *Midnight Marquee*)
Doug McClelland (author, *Forties Film Talk*, *Hollywood Talks Turkey*, *The Unkindest Cuts*, etc.)
Barbara Mank (author's colleague—and wife)
Greg Mank (author, *It's Alive*, *The Hollywood Hissables*, *Karloff and Lugosi*, *Hollywood Cauldron* and this book)
Joseph Marcello (musician; author of music section, MagicImage book on *The Wolf Man*)
Mark A. Miller (author, *Christopher Lee and Peter Cushing and Horror Cinema*)
Doug Norwine (collector, musician, author of upcoming book on Jack P. Pierce)
John E. Parnum (editor, *Cinemacabre*)
Gary Don Rhodes (author of *Lugosi: His Life in Films, on Stage, and in the Hearts of Horror Lovers*, head of the Bela Lugosi Society)
Farnham Scott (actor, collector, musician)
Bryan Senn (author of *Golden Horrors, Fantastic Cinema Subject Guide*)
Gord Shriver (collector, writer)
David J. Skal (author, *Hollywood Gothic*, *The Monster Show*, *"V" Is for Vampire*; co-author with Eli Savada, *Dark Carnival*)
Don G. Smith (author, *Lon Chaney, Jr.*)
Sally Stark (librarian, collector)
Gary J. Svehla (publisher, editor, MidMar Press and *Midnight Marquee* magazine; coordinator, FANEX conventions)
Susan Svehla (publisher, editor, MidMar Press and *Midnight Marquee* magazine; coordinator, FANEX conventions)
Anthony Timpone (editor, *Fangoria*)
Richard Valley (editor, *Scarlet Street* magazine)
Tom Weaver (author of a series of interview books featuring science fiction and horror personnel; consulting editor, *Fangoria*, *Starlog* magazines)
Scott Wilson (historian, author)
Nathalie Yafet (opera singer, collector, writer)

The results came back, often with lengthy and very definite opinions.

I. Best Performance by an Actress as a Horror Heroine

The Winner: Evelyn Ankers, *The Wolf Man*

It was an easy victory for Evelyn Ankers, who screamed so magnificently under Universal's full moon. Evelyn's adventures at Universal with Frankenstein's Monster, the Captive Wild Woman, the Mad Ghoul and the Invisible Man no doubt helped the very popular actress top the list.

There was spirited competition from Anna Lee, who, for a time in the poll, was winning for her crusading Nell Bowen of *Bedlam*.

II. BEST PERFORMANCE BY AN ACTRESS AS A HORROR "MONSTER" (OR HORROR CHARACTER)

The Winner: Simone Simon, *Cat People*

Simone Simon slunk her feline way to victory as the sexy, tragic Irena Dubrovna.

Second place: Louise Allbritton, who, in her black wig, flowing gowns and arch little smile, made vampirism seem sensually fun in *Son of Dracula*, and lured many votes.

III. BEST FEATURED/SUPPORTING PERFORMANCE BY AN ACTRESS IN A HORROR FILM

The Winner: Maria Ouspenskaya, *The Wolf Man*

As Maleva, the old gypsy who quavers, "The way you walked was thorny..." to lycanthropes Lugosi and Chaney, Maria Ouspenskaya triumphed in this contest. Like Zita Johann in *The Mummy* (who won the "Best Horror Heroine" race in the 1930s book), Madame Ouspenskaya's performance has a tinge of spirituality, and—once again—voters responded to it.

Angela Lansbury, fated for Broadway Tony awards and *Murder She Wrote* TV stardom, won the #2 spot for her heartbreaking Sybil Vane in *The Picture of Dorian Gray*—the only Oscar-nominated performance, incidentally, on the ballot.

Honorable mention: Elizabeth Russell, whose scary Barbara of *The Curse of the Cat People* clearly has many admirers; and Elena Verdugo, for her dancing gypsy Ilonka of *House of Frankenstein*.

IV. BEST PERFORMANCE BY AN ACTRESS AS A "VOLUPTUARY" IN A HORROR FILM

The Winner: Ingrid Bergman, *Dr. Jekyll and Mr. Hyde*

In the 1930s book, Miriam Hopkins was victorious as the doomed Ivy of 1931's *Dr. Jekyll and Mr. Hyde*. In the 1940s book, Ingrid Bergman easily won for the 1941 MGM version with Spencer Tracy.

Lenore Aubert of *Abbott and Costello Meet Frankenstein* and Linda Darnell of *Hangover Square* tied exactly for the #2 spot.

V. MOST BEAUTIFUL HORROR STAR OF THE 1940S

The Winner: Evelyn Ankers

It's a double win for Universal's beloved Queen of the Horrors; Evelyn won not only Best Horror Heroine, but Most Beautiful Horror Star. While it wasn't quite the landslide victory that Frances Drake (*Mad Love*, *The Invisible Ray*) enjoyed in the 1930s book, Evelyn had no really close competition in this category.

Also attracting lots of votes (and, in some cases, effusive comments on the ballots): Ilona Massey.

VI. Favorite All-Time Horror Film Female Performance of the 1940s

It's a tie! Evelyn Ankers of *The Wolf Man* and Simone Simon of *Cat People* topped the voting, with *The Wolf Man*'s Maria Ouspenskaya runner-up. Also cited by the voters: Ingrid Bergman, *Dr. Jekyll and Mr. Hyde*; Anna Lee, *Bedlam*; Anne Gwynne, *House of Frankenstein*; and Louise Allbritton, *Son of Dracula*.

INDEX